Socialism in the
Third World

edited by
Helen Desfosses
Jacques Levesque

Socialism in the
Third World

PRAEGER SPECIAL STUDIES IN INTERNATIONAL POLITICS AND GOVERNMENT

Praeger Publishers   New York   Washington   London

Library of Congress Cataloging in Publication Data
Main entry under title:

Socialism in the third world.

   (Praeger special studies in international politics and
government)
   Includes bibliographical references and index.
   1. Underdeveloped areas--Socialism--Addresses,
essays, lectures.   I. Desfosses, Helen.   II. Lévesque,
Jacques.
HX44.S5857   335'.009172'4   75-19774
ISBN 0-275-55560-7
ISBN 0-275-89460-6 student ed.

PRAEGER PUBLISHERS
111 Fourth Avenue, New York, N.Y. 10003, U.S.A.

Published in the United States of America in 1975
by Praeger Publishers, Inc.

Printed in the United States of America

The study of socialism in Third World countries presents the analyst with a dazzling profusion of terms, models, and programs. The common denominators appear to be few, as do the links with the more codified theories of Proudhon, Fourier, or Karl Marx. In fact, many commentators in both the communist states and the West have concluded, rather harshly, that a developing country is socialist only because it defines itself as socialist. Other commentators simply remark that in many of these states it is quite difficult to see the link between certain policies and the socialism with which the leaders claim kinship.

It is true that Third World socialism often represents no more than a vague desire for greater social justice, and often lacks practical significance. It must also be acknowledged that its theoretical underpinnings are sometimes meager. However, given that socialism is expected to provide an explanation of the past, a guide to the present, and a blueprint for the future, it is not surprising that its definitions may be vague and its theories diffuse. We must recognize that in the Third World context socialism represents a search for a development model and a response to anti-imperialist sentiments. Furthermore, it provides a framework for coping with the dualistic mood of transitional peoples and leaders, who both seek and fear industrialization. In this sense, socialism can be defined as the "natural ideology" of a transitional society.

This correlation between the mood and the expectations of a transitional society, on the one hand, and the tenets of socialism, on the other, can be listed as the primary reason for the adoption of socialism in twentieth-century Asia, Africa, and Latin America. In these countries today, as in the Europe of a century ago, socialism promises the achievements and benefits of capitalism and industrialization, but without the exploitation that is attributed to the capitalist class. Socialism offers the hope that the benefits of the industrial age can be controlled to their best interests by the representatives of the masses. Thus, socialism responds to the love-hate attitude of transitional peoples toward industrialism: it holds out the prospect of rapid progress toward the wonders associated with development, and it presents someone to blame for the painfulness of the process. (In the Third World, the colonialists can be substituted for the frequently non-existent capitalists as the source of the evils of social transformation.)

The anti-Western westernism that can be read into socialism—the fact that socialism, as Adam B. Ulam remarked, is "capitalism without the capitalists"—is also a great source of its appeal to Third World leaders. The nationalistic strivings toward independence and self-determination, toward economic and political developments, also involve a hatred of foreign domination and a desire to appropriate the technological and income levels associated with the West, without sacrificing the more humane values of the indigenous society. Socialism, with its Marxist emphasis on achieving capitalism without the profit motive, its Leninist emphasis on national liberation revolutions, and its Maoist stress on the revolutionary struggle between bourgeois and proletarian nations, satisfies the need of Third World countries to explain their backwardness and to fight continued oppression.

The concept that indigenous societies are socialist in their traditional form constitutes a third reason for the adoption of socialism by many Third World leaders. To some intellectuals in the new states, this "natural compatibility" between their traditional societies and socialist ideology revolves around the absence of classes. In contradistinction to the classic Marxist view that class struggle leading to the victory of the proletariat is essential to the building of socialism, Third World theorists often argue that their societies have already done away with the problem of class. They feel that socialism can be achieved without a proletariat, that it is a question of organizing the whole people as a political force.

A related proposition of Third World socialists—especially those in Africa—is that the traditional forms of African agriculture are communal, and that this age-old foundation can be used to construct a uniquely African kind of socialism, rather than simply a variant of the Marxist type. The necessary objective, they claim, is to concentrate on these communal traditions and thus collectivize agriculture on this traditional base.

In analyzing the programs of Third World socialist nations, it is difficult to distinguish between those common to all developing countries and those that might be peculiar to those on the socialist path. This is partly a result of the use of Marxist terminology even by antisocialist Third World intellectuals, and partly a result of the blurring of the distinction between socialist and capitalist, in the programs of developing states. Consider, for example, that the so-called Soviet model of development is said to include a single-party system, dominance of the party over the state, party control of the instruments of both persuasion and coercion, and the centrally directed mobilization of all human and material resources for the purpose of rapid economic development. Elements of this model can be found in regimes as diverse as those of Senegal and Argentina, Cuba and Iraq—in those countries that call themselves socialist as well as in those supposedly following the capitalist path.

Similarly, we note that the key elements of the Chinese model include stress on a united front and the central role of the Communist party; an emphasis on the army as a liberation force and on the necessity of armed struggle; and finally, a cultural revolution that would raise the level of popular will and consciousness to unified and revolutionary heights. Countries as diverse as Chad and Algeria have attempted a cultural revolution, and the army is the key political factor in states of all regions of the Third World. The Soviets and the Chinese Communists, however, developed their programs to respond to many needs: economic growth, political development, national integration, social change, and (relative) ideological orthodoxy. Today's Third World leaders view socialism in a much less comprehensive way. They are selective in their adoption of elements of Marxism, Leninism, or Maoism.

Several factors have contributed to this selectivity. First, there is the nationalistic determination of the leaders of the new states to avoid the substitution of a socialist set of influences and controls for the long-decried Western ones. Second, these leaders wish to join the ranks of the developed states as quickly as possible. Development, rather than the realization of an ideology, is the dominant goal, and development is often equated with economic growth. Third, there exists a commitment to preserving the national heritage, and to minimizing the disruptive aspects of modernization. These concerns have dictated efforts to develop distinctive national models of development. These models usually combine the antiprivate property emphasis of socialism, the respect for the middle class stressed by capitalism, and a sensitivity to the cultural, religious, and ethnic peculiarities of the Third World country.

Such attempts to synthesize ideology and national realities have created many problems for those Third World countries claiming to be socialist. While they have experienced many hardships, which seem to be endemic to developing countries, the effort to follow the socialist path has often meant distinctive approaches and distinctive difficulties. For example, efforts to blend communal traditions and agricultural collectivization have often hampered rural development. In attempting this amalgamation, socialists in the new nations are ignoring many of the classic tenets of Marxism-Leninism. Marx, for example, spoke of the "idiocy of rural life," its tendency to breed political conservatism and to insulate the peasant against the need to develop a new psychology appropriate to the modern world. Soviet theorists, propounding a view long held by Lenin, argue that the peasant's life has often been idealized by Third World socialists. They claim that the peasantry's communal tendencies have been exaggerated, that this sector is, in reality, just "a scattered, atomized mass of small commodity producers, illiterate and extremely backward politically." Soviet ideologues theorize that although the peasant in Africa, for example, has traditionally cooperated in consumption, he has cooperated only rarely in production. It is cooperation in production, of course, that would be required if communal agriculture were to become the basis for development.

Thus, efforts to build on the "traditional socialist values of the peasantry" can be said to represent a departure from the collectivization of agriculture urged by the Marxist-Leninist and Maoist brands of socialism. Furthermore, there are many development specialists in both East and West who question whether building on peasant socialism will solve the agricultural problems of most Third World countries, and provide them with the surplus that they need for industrial development. The change from cooperation in consumption to cooperation in production involves persuading the peasant to alter his entire sphere of agricultural activity. Communalizing this entire sphere would require a frontal attack on the very basis of traditional organization of the rights in land, of kinship groups, of interlineage relations, and of the system of mutual obligations.

The problems of industrialism have also plagued Third World socialist states. Socialism has instilled a concern with appropriating technological progress, industrialization, and urbanization while avoiding the drastic inequalities associated with the profit motive of capitalism. For the leaders of these states, the nationalization of industry, the tighter government control over the conomy, and the legislation for the protection of workers have become synonymous with socialism. However, in the popular mind, and to many leaders as well, the expectation is great that socialism also means that the hardships, privations and inequality associated with industrialization in the West can be avoided. Such expectations have helped to generate tremendous support for socialism in the Third World; however, they have also meant that, when the inevitable disappointments occur, the stage is set for coups, strikes, and other manifestations of political instability. In sum, while equating socialism with equality has helped Third World leaders to garner support, it has also helped to pave the way for mass disillusionment.

Socialism's emphasis on industrialization and on the historical inevitability of this process has also entailed an undue optimism regarding the industrial potential of Third World countries, the rapidity with which the resulting benefits would be extended to the countryside, and the rate of assimilation of the worker into the modern ethos. As a result, neither the _anomie_ of the workers nor the isolation of the peasant masses has been given sufficient attention.

Modernization has had uneven effects on Third World populations, but to every inhabitant it has brought a sense of the impermanence of his way of life, and a new set of expectations of the central political authority. Third World socialist regimes have developed a variety of programs with which to respond to, and at times subdue, this popular discontent with the effects and pace of change.

The purpose of this book is to provide a series of original essays on these different combinations and experiments. We have excluded such important countries as North Vietnam and the People's Republic of China, for both the cold war and the war in Vietnam have induced scholars to produce an impressive number of works on socialism in these nations. We have, however, included essays on Pakistan, Sri Lanka, Libya, Algeria, Syria, Iraq, Ghana, Mali, Tanzania, Chile, and Cuba. These countries have not been examined previously in a comparative perspective because of the great variety and disparity of their socialist programs. However, while there are difficulties inherent in such an endeavor, the diversity and the absence of a common definition of socialism may prove advantageous. These factors should enable the reader to appreciate more fully the extent to which socialism has met the needs, aspirations, and objectives of countries often lacking any apparent ideological affinity. The reader can, by studying the material for comparison that these essays afford, understand the similarities in these socialist experiments and why their particularities prevail.

To help the reader, the contributors were asked to focus their essays on certain key issues. First, to provide an awareness of the social and political context in which socialism can develop, the political culture of each country is described. Second, the main factors leading to the adoption of socialism are examined, including economic contingencies, social pressures, external influences, and leaders' motives. Then, the sub-type and specific characteristics of the form of socialism adopted are delineated.

The authors were further encouraged to analyze the strategy used to implement the socialist program: the political and social organizations used; the importance, if any, attached to ideology, and the methods used to diffuse this ideology; the extent to which the new regimes emphasized mass participation, and the ways in which they dealt with opposition to it. The authors were also asked to examine economic development programs, and the interaction between the socialist program and foreign policy. Finally, there are evaluations of the successes and failures of socialism in Third World countries.

It will become obvious to the reader that the contributors to this volume represent different methodological and ideological approaches. It is our belief that again diversity may prove advantageous. The evidence on many urgent questions is incomplete and/or contradictory. What is more, much that has been written on socialism in the Third World is based less on hard data than on intuition and surmise. The following essays seek to provide the pertinent evidence and to suggest alternative interpretations.

CONTENTS

PART III: NORTH AFRICA

LIST OF TABLES

LIST OF ABBREVIATIONS AND ACRONYMS

ASU	Arab Socialist Union
BP	British Petroleum (Corporation)
CDR	Committee for the Defense of the Revolution
CFA	Communaute Financiere Africaine
CFDT	Compagnie Francaise pour le Developpement des Fibres Textiles
CMB	Cocoa Marketing Board
CPP	Convention People's Party
CUTCH	Chilean Trade Union Convention
CWC	Ceylon Workers Congress
DC	district commissioner
DWC	Democratic Workers Congress
FLN	National Front of Liberation
GNP	gross national product
GNTC	Ghana National Trading Corporation
GRPSM	Groupement Rural de Production et de Secours Mutuel
IBRD	International Bank for Reconstruction and Development
ILO	International Labor Organization
IMF	International Monetary Fund
JUI	Jamiat-ul-Ulema-i-Islam
JVP	Janatha Vimukthi Peramuna
KDP	Kurdish Democratic Party
KNII	Kwame Nkrumah Ideological Institute
LSSP	Lanka Sama Samaja Party
MAP	Moslem Association Party
MEP	Mahjana Eksath Peramuna
MIR	Revolutionary Left movement
NAP	National Awami Party
NASSO	National Association of Socialist Students Organizations
NCDR	National Committee for the Defense of the Revolution
NDC	National Development Corporation
NLC	National Liberation Council (military-police government)
NLM	National Liberation movement
NRC	National Redemption Council
OAU	Organization of African Unity
OPEC	Organization of Petroleum Exporting Countries
PCP	Pakistan Communist Party
PP	Progress Party
PPP	Pakistan People's Party
PSP	People's Socialist Party
RC	regional commissioner
RCC	Revolutionary Command Council

RDA	Ruvuma Development Association
RWP	Revolutionary Workers' Party
SLFP	Sri Lanka Freedom Party
SMDR	Societe Mutuelle de Developpement Rural
TANU	Tanzania African National Union
TUC	Trades Union Congress
UGFC	United Ghana Farmers Council
UGCC	United Gold Coast Convention
UGTA	Union Generale de Travailleurs Algeriens
ULF	United Left Front
UNP	United National Party
VLSSP	(Former name of MEP above)
ZER	Zone d'Expansion Rurales

Socialism in the Third World

ALLENDE'S CHILE
W. Raymond Duncan

The emergence and decline of Salvadore Allende, Chile's first elected Marxist president, are far less surprising than his violent end in September 1973. The reasons behind this proposition are complex, but they involve the pursuance of his Socialist policies within Chile's weak economy and strong political system. Allende sought internal structural change, a breakaway from dependency on foreign economic interests, and new institutionalized power for Unidad Popular (Popular Unity), his coalition government.[1] These programs were initially successful, but they precipitated severe economic dislocations and political forces not legitimized either by existing or new institutions. The purpose of this chapter is to explore these interrelationships, showing the constraints faced by Allende in, paradoxically, a highly democratic and reform-oriented political system.

THE EMERGENCE OF ALLENDE'S
SOCIALIST PROGRAM

The election of a Marxist president in Chile is not strange in light of Chilean politics. First, his program was Socialist and sponsored by Marxist and non-Marxist parties. Left wing governments were not new in Chile, nor were leftist reform philosophies. In addition to the "Socialist Republic" (1931-32), the Popular Front (1938-41), and the election of Carlos Ibanez in 1952 with communist support Socialist and Communist parties had played substantive roles in coalition governments since 1938.[2] Chile's history also records the increased emphasis on state planning, albeit one stronger in philosophy than actual effective state control.[3] Indeed, the government that preceded Allende—the Eduardo Free administration (1964-70)—contained a heavy dose of socialist reforms as its nationalization of Chilean copper and extensive agrarian reform program suggests.[4] Many observers have noted that the differences between Allende and Frei were more of degree and speed than of kind. These aspects of Chilean history show that a reformist philosophy and experience with Marxist parties predate the election of Allende and were key aspects of Chilean political culture.

Second, Chile is noted for its democratic tradition. By this is meant a high degree of personal freedom, low military intervention, and peaceful transitions of political power through legitimate institutions. A willingness to accommodate, bargain, and compromise relative to new power contenders and political philosophies characterizes this country, a fact reflected in its sophisticated multiparty system extending back into history and from the far left to the far right.[5] Until the military overthrow of Allende in September 1973, most scholars ranked Chile extremely high in political democracy, meaning an open competitive political system, the articulation of several political orientations, and gradual acceptance of the ideas of those advocating more Socialist versions of change over the years.[6] The political culture, then, was amenable to Allende, who garnered the highest portion of the vote in 1970 (36.2 percent) and who already had made a try at the presidency in 1952, 1958, and 1964.

Third, the Chilean political culture strongly supports constitutional legality. Chile's record of presidential and congressional elections, and its adherence to constitutional procedures, is enviable by Latin American standards. The basic social groups in Chile—the upper classes, the middle sectors, and labor—were organized and in many ways opposed to each other by the 1930s, but all were committed to institutionalized legalism. The Constitution of 1833 remained in force for almost a century, replaced in 1925 by a new one. Allende of course pledged to move Chile from capitalism to socialism, but through the traditional legal route. When he failed to obtain the absolute majority of the direct popular vote required to become president in September 1970, he agreed to abide by a Statute of Democratic Guarantees. Among other things, this committed him to preserve the political system and to guarantee individual liberty.[7] It should be stressed that Allende's Unidad Popular had always pledged to guarantee the exercise of democratic rights within Chile's legal setting, but that the Statute of Democratic Guarantees helped produce the needed Christian Democratic votes in Congress for that body to approve him as president.[8] Allende's coming to power, in view of these three dimensions, was consistent with Chilean history, culture, and political dynamics, and thus not so surprising.

THE PATTERN OF DECLINE ONCE IN POWER

If history and political culture help account for Allende's victory in 1970, they also held the seeds of his decline. This is to be seen in what one political analyst terms the "boom-and-bust" cycle on popular support for a Chilean president, the erosion of a popular base during the last part of his six-year term after a strongly supported first period.[9] The three presidents preceding Allende experienced it, and as in a Greek tragedy, the same scenario began to plague the Socialist president early in his second year. The central cause of this pattern appears to be the inability of any president to hold down inflation and spur economic development while checked by the legislative obstructionism of an articulate and diversified Congress lacking consensus on what to do or how to do it.[10] The key aspects of Chilean political culture that made possible Allende's election thus became keys to his decline.

The rise of left-wing and centrist parties (Socialists, Communists, Chilean Democrats) indicates an evolving commitment to long-range, fundamental social and economic reform within the Chilean body politic. These parties had contributed to an enlarged public sector and growing social services. But Chile's economy had stagnated for years in inflation, a single-export system (copper), poor agricultural productivity, and little diversified capital formation. The economy, then, had been of central concern years before Allende assumed power; the ideas of state-directed industrialization, state participation in the industrial and social welfare of the republic, and a public policy to deal with development and the high cost of living were accepted features of the political culture by 1970. Consequently the inability of any president to solve the thorny issues of inflation and a lagging economy became the basis of waning support and transference of popularity to another hopeful candidate. In Allende's case, the years of unfilled solutions for economic and social ills made him determined to alter what he saw as structural and dependency causes for the growing inequalities between Chile's property owners and the lower sectors of society of which millions were living in extreme poverty.[11]

The democratic multiparty system made it extremely difficult for any president to deal effectively with Chile's economic and social problems. Its divergent bases of power impeded presidential authority, undermined a sustained consensus on reform methods, and set up the conditions that led to a decline in his popularity. The Conservative and Liberal parties of the right, for example, represented large landowners, industrialists, businessmen, professionals—the upper classes that held sufficient power to block legislation affecting any drastic alteration of their power base. Those seeking change in-

cluded the Communist and Socialist parties of the left, which represented workers, intellectuals, and peasants. The Christian Democrats—left of center—constituted Catholic members of the middle
sectors, intellectuals, professionals, and technicians, who also
sought major changes. More to the center were the Radicals, comprised of some people desiring sweeping changes and others more
identifying with Conservatives and Liberals. Given this divided representative system, which much resembled the French Third and Fourth
Republics, the traditional pattern of presidential rule favoring economic reforms resulted in bargaining and exchange of favors at the
cost of greatly modified legislation. Indeed, the amount of compromise between left, center (the Radicals), and right political leaders
over the years gave rise to what some observers term an "equilibrium"
or "stalemated" political system in which all groups bargain and compromise and no group threatens to destroy the interests of the other.[12]
This situation had been altered somewhat during the term of Eduardo
Frei (1964-70), as his agrarian and copper reforms indicated. But
the need for a president to compromise with a divided and obstruction-
ist legislature remained strong when Allende came to power, producing discontent among those who wished him to move more quickly.

Chile's politicized culture meant more than problems between
the left and right. A president typically faced falling-outs among his
own coalition and even within his own party once in office. Three
clear divisions emerged within Eduardo Frei's Christian Democratic
Party (PDC)[13] and leftist coalitions typically were marred by dis-
agreements between the Communists and Socialists, and within Allende's Socialist Party.[14] This highly politicized setting put teeth into
the Constitution that gave the legislature the power to block presidential initiatives.[15] Most presidents tried to form coalitions large
enough to support their legislation, but the divisions within their own
ranks only exacerbated their problems with the opposition. No president could be guaranteed lasting popularity under these conditions as
the latter part of a six-year term usually showed. Moreover, Chile's
politicized culture and the rules of the political game made it impossible for Allende to alter the old structure constitutionally, as he had
planned, in an effort to build a new institutionalized form of power
for his Unidad Popular.

The pattern of decline affecting former presidents shows in the
voting record during Allende's rule. He received 36.2 percent of the
presidential vote in 1970. The 1971 municipal elections produced
49.7 percent for Allende's supporters. Yet the March 1973 congressional elections, in a campaign marked by numerous demonstrations
and violence, gave 43.4 percent to Allende's groups, representing a
decline from 1971. More important, the opposition continued to control Congress and by 1972 had become increasingly opposed to Allen-

de's Marxist program, while the extreme left clamored for more
rapid implementation of the Unidad Popular program.

POLARIZED OPINION, PROTRACTED MILITANCY,
AND ALLENDE'S FALL

The forces leading to Allende's fall include an explosive interaction of Socialist policies and traditional Chilean politics and economics. Given Chile's highly politicized culture and structural economic difficulties, the net effects were polarized opinion and pro-
tracted militancy during 1972 and 1973 between Marxist and anti-
Marxist groups. These conflicting positions became so intense that,
for the first time in over 40 years and in a society long known for its
legalism and nonmilitary involvement, a coup d'etat and the death of
the president occurred on September 11, 1973. Indeed, for some
time before this coup, Allende himself had expressed his fears that
Chile was on the brink of civil war.

Behind polarized and militant Chile lay the deteriorating economic situation, not unfamiliar but extremely serious in light of Allende's Marxist program and the anti-Marxist opposition. The official consumer price index showed an inflation rate of 42 percent in the
12 months up to June 1972 (about the average annual rate during the
1960s). By September 1972 this rate had climbed to 114 percent,
moving even higher to 163 percent by December 1972, 183 percent
by March 1973, and 283 percent by June 1973.[16] This inflation, produced by large across-the-board wage increases and unenforced
price controls over the private sector (trying to meet the congressional support problem), prompted a run on consumer goods, short
food supplies, and widespread black-market activities. These difficulties—coupled with permanent lines at grocery stores, a 40 percent
drop in agricultural productivity, a 50 percent drop in industrial production, and a sharply rising external debt—lay behind mounting
strikes, demonstrations, and increased violence.

Economic dislocations sharply undermined Allende's attempts
to move Chile legally toward rapid and complete socialism against
the wishes of powerful center and right opposition. First, the economic tensions aggravated the political opposition in Congress between Marxists and non-Marxists, as seen in the shift to the right
by the Christian Democrat who helped to block Allende's program and
to impeach his ministers when possible.[17] Second, the economic
situation also escalated the determination of Marxists and anti-Marx-
ists to use extraconstitutional means to promote or resist the president's program, especially since the president and Congress seemed
so ineffective. Chile's famed political culture of compromise and

legal, institutionalized change became transformed by the summer of
1973 as illegal factory seizures and urban violence mounted, while
in the countryside the extremist Revolutionary Left Movement (MIR)
inspired illegal land occupations. The reaction of the court system to
these events underlined the breakdown in traditional, institutionalized
conflict-resolution. While judges ordered workers and peasants to
return illegally seized factories and land, the Interior Ministry refused to authorize police forces to execute the orders. The situation
was serious enough to pass a weapons control law in early 1973, severely punishing civilians caught with revolvers, pistols, machine
guns, ammunition, and explosives.[18]

The degree of polarization and commitment to use extraconstitutional means to promote or oppose Allende's program is captured
by the remarks expressed by government and opposition leaders during 1973. The extremist MIR announced in April 1973 that it would
continue its struggle against the rich until "all economic power" was
"in the hands of the workers," whether this suited the "reformist" in
the government or not.[19] Similarly, the Rightist National Party advocated "civil disobedience" toward an "illegitimate" government,
and the extreme right-wing Patria y Libertad (Fatherland and Freedom) Movement stated that the opportunities of action by the traditional parties were "exhausted" and that "direct action" was necessary.[20] Finally, in August 1973, the opposition presented a resolution to Congress declaring that Allende had violated the constitution,
thus labeling his government illegal and setting up the conditions for
a military coup.

Chile's politicized culture certainly promoted the whirlpool effects of drawing all sectors of the population into antagonistic Marxist and anti-Marxist positions throughout 1972 and 1973. Competing
newspaper, radio, and television stations aggravated tensions and
sharpened the polarized setting while demonstrations and strikes
brought the country to an impasse. For example, on the eve of the
military coup, a prolonged series of strikes involved 40,000 truck
owners (most of Chile's commerce moves by road), 90,000 doctors,
professionals, 140,000 shopkeepers and owners of small businesses,
and 100,000 women.[21] Thousands of urban squatters, landless
peasants, and industrial workers had been organized by the left to
demonstrate and to seize factories and land, but not always with Allende's blessing. Thus the upper, middle, and lower sectors of society were locked in polarized militancy, with the lower classes see-
ing hope in Allende's changes and the middle and upper sectors suffering a decline in their living standards and expectations.

ALLENDE'S MOTIVATIONS

Why did Allende adopt socialism as a political ideology? What were his hopes and expectations in moving toward a political career based on a socialist ideology, rather than pursuing the medical practice for which he was trained?

Family background is one key to Allende's later adoption of socialism. All his uncles and his father were Radical Party militants during a period of Chile's history when being Radical meant that one held "advanced" and frequently controversial views.[22] Allende's family, with its masonic beliefs, also engaged in religious and educational struggles where conflict between conservatives and nonconservatives could be violent. Moreover, Allende's grandfather opened the first lay school in Chile, which earned him the nickname of "Red Allende." Thus the independence and militancy of Chilean socialism, much greater than that of the Chilean Communists, fits well with Allende's own family history of militancy against conservative groups.

Allende became a medical doctor, another fact that attracted him to socialism with its frontal assault on the status quo. As a doctor, he was distressed with the debilitating health conditions, malnutrition, and poverty throughout much of Chile. He spoke often and vehemently about health care and nutrition, stressing that the bad diets of most Chilean infants produced a mild form of mental retardation and eventual listless adulthood.[23] Unsurprisingly, one of the publicized points in his campaign platform of 1969-70 was the goal of making available a pint of milk a day to all Chilean children, a promise largely kept during the early period of his administration.

Family background and medical training inclined Allende toward an activist, grass-roots, and militant role in politics at an early age. He entered medical school at the age of 18, at a time when the medical students were traditionally the most advanced, and began to read Marx, Lenin, and Trotsky. As Allende put it to Regis Debray during their conversations in early 1971,

> At that time [as a medical student], we lived in a very humble district, we practically lived with the people, most of us were from the provinces and those of us living in the same hostel used to meet at night for readings of Das Kapital, Lenin and also Trotsky.[24]

A short time later, at the age of 24, he went to prison for his support of the Socialist Republic set up by Colonel Marmaduke Grove in 1932. In short, Allende was a "man of action," who from an early age "worked with the masses." As he stated to Debray, "I am aware of being a grass-roots Chilean politician and very close to the people."[25]

These personal aspects of Allende's early life help explain his essentially nationalist position, which led him to join in the forming of the Socialist Party in 1933. Personal involvement in militant grass-roots politics undoubtedly inclined him to reject the existing Communist Party to help establish a new and independent party without international ties. So at the age of 25 he did exactly that, adding a Chilean orientation to Marxist-Leninism in the new Socialist Party. Advocating an independent and typically more militant position, it naturally caused problems of association with the more pro-Soviet Communist Party—a dominating feature of the Chilean-Communist Socialist Party relations after 1933. In helping to form the Socialist Party, Allende's hopes and expectations were to improve the living conditions of Chile's impoverished masses through organized political action. But he believed that the road to socialism must be constructed on the complete political and economic independence of the country.[26] This nationalist position became clear again in his inaugural address in the National Stadium (November 5, 1970) when he posed the question: "What will be the way, the path of action that Chile takes to conquer its underdevelopment?" In answering, he said, "Our road will be one marked out by our own experience."[27]

VARIANT OF SOCIALISM

Like other Third World leaders, Allende turned to socialism as an ideology of development.[28] He adopted it as a means to achieve economic and social progress along a path that was neither Western capitalist in form nor one of complete state ownership based upon political repression as in Soviet or Chinese communism. Allende's Marxist-Leninist leanings provided a plan of action adaptable to Chile's conditions and leading toward a future of development and independence. Here it should be remembered that Latin American Marxists became attracted to this ideology back in the 1920s and 1930s, when its more pure form was a principal alternate to capitalism. Even in these early days Allende began to modify it to fit Chile's needs just as later Third World leaders would modify Socialist ideology to fit their needs in Africa and Asia.

Allende sought a form of socialism based upon Marxist-Leninist principles but with its own unique "national" characteristics. It conformed in this sense to the Report of the Central Committee of the CPSU to the Twentieth Party Congress (February 1956), delivered by Nikita S. Khrushchev. This report, it will be recalled, acknowledged many roads to socialism, dependent upon the peculiar historical conditions prevailing in each country.[29] Without going into every detail of each aspect of Allende's program as outlined for the 1970 elections,

we can identify specific features of it as a Chilean national variant of
Marxism-Leninism.

First, as might be expected, the urban proletariat was a central basis of Allende's support. The Socialist Party traditionally appealed to organized labor, including copper miners, marine workers, and railroad workers. But it also appealed to the oppressed urban slum dwellers of the callampas and to rural migrants (inquilinos), campesinos (peasants associated with the large latifundias), and rotos.[30] Moreover, some white-collar workers, intellectuals, students, and professionals were attracted to Allende's socialism. Allende, in his campaign for the presidency in 1969-70, stressed that Chile was divided between the rich—a small group of the wealthy elite—and the poor, the latter comprising the majority of the people. Allende's socialism, therefore, was not based strictly upon organized labor, as in more orthodox Marxism, nor was it a social democratic party in the European sense.

Less emphasis on the vanguard role of the party is a second variant of Chilean socialism under Allende. He emphasized instead the formation of a People's Assembly, a single chamber in which the sovereign will of the people might be expressed, as the central organ of power.[31] This phase of the "Popular State," which Allende described as the overall process to democratize, mobilize, and increase mass participation at all levels, also included a state planning system, workers' committees, and regional and local organs of power. The party, in short, was to have far less than the central importance accorded it by Lenin. Indeed, to push the point, the historic difficulties of Allende's Socialist Party—more so than its Communist counterparts at home and abroad—included ideological and personalist fragmentation. Allende, one of the few men who had not generated excessive personalist frictions and who therefore was a welcome presidential candidate in 1970 and earlier, was certainly aware of Socialist Party problems.[32] Given its tendency to split over specific ideological positions and strategy, it does not seem unusual that he would give less emphasis to its vanguard role than other traditional Marxists.

State control of the economy, a third variant, naturally followed from Allende's Marxist-Leninist perceptions. He intended to bring the major sectors of the economy—copper, steel, saltpeter, agriculture, exports, and imports—under state control. In his remarks to Debray in early 1971 he observed, "Now then, if these things—affirming our national sovereignty, recovering our basic wealth and attacking monopolies—do not lead to socialism, I don't know what does."[33] But even with these changes, state control would be less total than elsewhere, for he envisaged a trisectoral economy, composed of nationalized industry, a mixed sector, and a private sector. He undoubtedly felt this type of economy was more consistent with Chile's pluralist culture, and one that was more likely to maximize his base of power.

A fourth variant is the pronounced emphasis on anti-imperialism, but essentially an independent anti-imperialism. Chile's Socialist Party historically had few ties with international communism, as Socialist Party friction with the Chilean Communist Party suggested time and again after 1933.[34] Allende's Socialist Party attacked imperialist foreign capital, as discussed below, but asserted almost as much independence in its relations with international communism. Between 1966 and 1968, for example, many Chilean Socialists identified with Fidel Castro's policies, at that time insisting on armed struggle as the only road to socialism. This position sharply contrasted with the peaceful parliamentary reform stressed by Chilean Communists, other traditional Latin American Communists, and the Soviet Union. By 1969-70 the situation had changed with Castro's return to a more moderate stance, also followed by the Chilean Socialists who by then needed the support of the Chilean Communists for the upcoming elections.

Class struggle, a fifth variant, coincided with Allende's Marxist-Leninist ideology, but it was of a specific Chilean variety. It excluded, for example, the automatic proletarian revolution implicit in Marx and the party-led revolution associated with Lenin's work. Allende's plans of reaching socialism excluded civil war and insisted upon conforming to Chile's democratic, pluralistic, and free society.[35] But a militant version of class struggle was nevertheless built into Allende's Socialist program, vividly expressed in his attack upon monopolism and his determination to pursue his program once in office. During the later period of his rule, particularly after Fidel Castro's visit in November-December 1971, Allende began to label his centrist and conservative opponents as "fascists," showing the growing intensity of his class struggle beliefs at a time when he was trying to contain his Socialist program within Chile's constitutional forms.

In understanding Allende's interpretation of class struggle, it is helpful to think of it as more militant in principle than the Chilean Communists, but not so militant as to exclude the positive benefits of cooperating with them or with other parties in the parliamentary system. Moreover, it was important, as Allende saw it once he became president, to abide by Chilean constitutionalism or risk deposition and total loss of power. Some of his difficulties after 1970 stemmed from his failure to assert class struggle fast enough—at least in eyes of many people in Allende's ranks. They therefore took matters into their own hands. This problem of presidents moderating their position to stay within constitutional norms, but losing support from those who wished to move more swiftly, had plagued other presidents it is true, but none with so disastrous results.

Allende's Variant Summarized

Allende's nationalist version of socialism entailed specific policies to break away from Chile's economic and social stagnation.
They comprised a strong anti-imperialist and antimonopolist position.
This meant in essence destroying old structural relations in the economy that produced Chile's traditional dependency on and domination by
external imperialism allied with sectors of the Chilean bourgeoisie.

In terms of anti-imperialism, Allende argued that Chile must
regain complete control of its natural resources (principally copper)
and her industries, many of which were dominated by outside powers.
This recovery would encourage investment and planning decisions with
direct emphasis on Chile's needs rather than on foreign priorities.
"Our basic, most vital principle," he told Debray in early 1971, "is
one of anti-imperialism, as a first step towards the making of structural changes."[36]

Antimonopolism meant an attack on Chile's large capitalists
who controlled much of the country's small economy. Those to be attacked included the large landowners (latifundistas) who dominated a
quasi-feudal system of underproduction in terms of Chile's agricultural needs, and the private banking and commercial interests. Allende, to sum it up, believed that

> oligarchy—the national bourgeoisie and the imperial-
> ists—controlled the copper, foreign commerce, the
> banks, the big industries, internal trade, the media
> —and that even the state-owned corporations were
> bent to their purposes. This economic power, which
> allowed these men to dominate the whole society,
> must be taken out of their hands, and put into the
> hands of the people.[37]

EFFECT OF SOCIALISM ON LEADER'S
STRATEGIES

Economic Development Policies

Allende's government pursued four key economic objectives
during his three years in power. These were (1) nationalization of
copper and other industries, (2) accelerating agrarian reform, (3)
nationalization of private banks, and (4) redistribution of income.[38]
By moving rapidly and successfully on these fronts, the government
hoped to forge a solid electoral and popular base to continue its poli-

cies of increased control over the economy. This in turn would allow it to stimulate a production system of higher employment and one more in conformity with the consumer needs of the majority of the population. Unfortunately, these economic programs were far less successful than Allende and his Unidad Popular coalition had hoped. Their breakdown enhanced Chile's political tensions, leading eventually to the military takeover in September 1973.

Space does not permit a discussion of each of these economic policies, but two merit special attention: the nationalization of copper and accelerated agrarian reform. They played especially critical roles in Allende's socialist program, sharply reflected the interaction of politics and economics, and unleashed forces that led to Allende's overthrow.

Both houses of Congress approved the government's bill nationalizing copper, and the state completed the takeover of copper mines during July 1971.[39] This was undoubtedly the easiest part of Allende's program to implement because the nationalization of the big copper mines in Chile was the culmination of a movement that had been gaining strength for some time.[40] But for a number of reasons, many of them associated with the politics of Allende's socialist strategy, nationalization did not yield high economic returns.

What happened with copper nationalization? The big copper mines actually declined in production during the first six months of 1973 due to several reasons. A 75-day strike at the El Teniente mine and a shorter sympathy strike at Chuquicamata did not help matters. Moreover, rivalries among the political appointees representing the six Unidad Popular parties created operational problems at the mines, especially the largest—Chuquicamata—as did lack of technical expertise among the political appointees who became section chiefs.[41] Political infighting among the workers, the loss of trained administrative and technical personnel under Allende's rule, and spare parts shortages also eroded productivity.[42] It should be stressed that once Allende came to power, the professional or supervisory payrolls at the mines were enlarged by many nontechnical personnel—sociologists, psychologists, and public relations personnel who engaged in political work for the Unidad Popular. This encouraged rivalries among themselves and tensions with the workers.[43] The politics of Socialist reform thus produced economic costs.

Land reform, a second swift expansion of a formerly popular movement, netted more costs than benefits during Allende's years as president. Long a bottleneck to Chilean development during the postwar period, the government hoped to reverse Chile's need to import food which consumed approximately a quarter of the country's foreign exchange holdings. Allende announced Unidad Popular's intention to expropriate all holding larger than 80 hectares, which added up to

3,800 estates over six years and the settlement of approximately 70,000 families on communal farms.[44] This policy, he foresaw, would increase production, break the back of the feudal system, and provide a stable base for Socialist mobilization, participation, and planning.

The results of these efforts were, like copper, fraught with political difficulties and negative economic outcomes. Food imports more than doubled between 1965 and 1972.[45] Wheat production fell from 1,360,000 tons in 1971 to below 700,000 in 1972, leading to importation of more than half the country's wheat at a cost of over $60 million.[46] The cost of food imports rose from $180 million in 1970 to $313 million in 1971 and to $400 million in 1972.[47] The decline in production and resulting cost of importing, according to a statement in August 1972 by Senor Luis Corvalan, Secretary-General of the Communist Party, was in part due to "petty corruption" and inefficiency in running the centralized state farms.[48]

A visit to the wheat farms outside Santiago in late 1971 tends to affirm Corvalan's observation. They were marked by visibly low wheat yields and untended, weedy fields. Associated difficulties included social tensions between the inquilinos (migrants) and the campesinos (local peasants). The former had been moved onto the state farms by the government whereas the latter were prior residents, and the intermixture did not produce coordinated, cooperative, and efficient working conditions. Other problems plagued the Allende government, as they had Frei's efforts at land reform. These were the lack of large numbers of trained personnel to instruct the new farm tenants in agriculture techniques, the absence of adequate funds to supply fertilizers, the shortage of modern machinery and transportation outlets, and the tenacity of traditional attitudes and values. Finally, it could be argued that much of the state farm activity during Allende's years was more political than economic, such as busing inquilinos and campesinos into Santiago for demonstrations, painting walls, and discussing political strategy.

Organization Building

Unlike the leaders of other Socialist-inspired governments, Allende did not succeed in major organizational changes within the Chilean political system. His failure is not surprising in that an opposition-dominated legislature would not likely approve major innovations favorable to the Socialist program; since Allende had opted to stay within the constitutional system, legislative approval was mandatory. Moreover, the government banked on economic successes to widen its base of popular electoral support, rather than massive alteration of political institutions.

The Popular Unity Program did call for the establishment of two basic organizations designed to strengthen socialist policies. The first proposed a single legislative chamber, called an Assembly of the People. It went to Congress in the form of a constitutional amendment in November 1972. The Congress, fearing an end to the two-chamber system, shelved it quickly. The second proposal called for a reorganization of the judicial system. Unidad Popular wanted to establish "neighborhood tribunals" to judge minor offenses. These tribunals, remarkably similar to counterparts in Fidel Castro's Cuba, were to be comprised of two locally elected officials coming from "labor or social institutions" and one government appointee. Needless to say, this local judicial system was open to political influence, and it raised so much protest that the government withdrew it in March 1973.

In terms of other organizations, Popular Unity Committees had been established during the presidential campaign. Some observers believed these might become a base of local power for Allende's government, much like the Committees for the Defense of the Revolution (CDR) in Cuba. But they faded away after September 1970, unlike those in Cuba where local control groups widened their power and Fidel's as well during the 1960s. As these organization plans indicate, they were far less comprehensive than Latin America's other socialist government—Cuba. They did not call for an end to parliamentary democracy. The Constitution was to remain intact. Political parties were not to be dissolved. The old military would not be replaced by a new one, and the population would not be tightly organized at the grass-roots level. There would not be, as in Cuba, women, youth, worker, factory, local, judicial, and other militant, pro-Revolution and pro-Socialist organizations tightly integrated with the single political party under the direction of a single lider maximo. Allende's organization plans were distinctly Chilean.

Many reasons can be cited for the failure of Allende's modest organizational plans, but two merit special attention. First, they were highly unlikely to succeed through constitutional means—Allende's choice—because most of the electorate was opposed to Marxism and to Unidad Popular. The growing merger of Christian Democrats with the right wing National Party (merger of Liberals and Conservatives) after Allende's election accentuated this fact. Second, Unidad Popular's overall program and its organizational proposals threatened the income base that Chile's interest groups were determined to defend without compromise in a period of eroding inflation. [49] Allende's socialist ideology simply was ineffective as a means to legitimize new organizations and procedures. His appeals to a new Chilean nationalism equally failed to capture widespread sympathy in the setting of a deteriorating economy and polarized political opinion.

The nature of Allende's own coalition did not help matters. Once in power, personalist rivalries, splits, and tensions set in. His support from Radical Party representatives weakened, rivalries among the political appointees of the six Unidad Popular parties occurred in the mines and in other bureaucratic positions, and relations between the Socialists and Communists were strained, particularly over the question of illegal factory and land seizures. It would be an understatement to say that Allende, like the presidents of France's Third and Fourth Republics—or like Francisco I. Madero in the early stages of Mexico's Revolution—did not have full control over the situation. Old organizations and old power contenders were left largely intact while trying to promote radical innovations. Without other countervailing forces such as charismatic leadership, popular ideology, or a powerful single party to unify and build a base of compliance and support, the result was loss of power.

Beyond these coalition difficulties lay a history of division within Allende's own Socialist Party. [50] Splitting tendencies erupted over doctrine, personalities, leadership, strategy, and affiliation with other parties. Allende's Party was not as unified as Chile's Communist Party and lacked the strong organizational discipline required to play a vanguard role in promoting change in other political institutions. When operating in the framework of Chile's already divided political system, we have a more complete composite for the failure of Allende to establish new organizations as a base of political support.

Expanding Political Participation

Unidad Popular, in sharp contrast to its organizational goals, was able to expand political participation as it had intended to do. Previously excluded groups, like the urban slum dwellers in the callampas, migrant workers (inquilinos), and segments of the rural population (especially the southern Mapuche Indians) were brought dramatically and swiftly into the political arena. They became highly active in the political process as Unidad Popular appealed to and used them for support in demonstrations, rallies, and marches.

The problem for Allende, however, was that the rate and type of participation rapidly began to get out of hand, exceeding the government's political capacity to control. In identifying with Allende's goals and hoping to achieve them more swiftly than through the congressional jungle, many of these pro-Allende people engaged in illegal factory and land seizures, and in violent combat with centrists and rightists, frequently encouraged by the violence-oriented MIR. This militant, often illegal form of political participation, contributed to the overall drift toward the brink of civil war.

Allende's programs also resulted in massive, polarized opposi-
tion-participation. This type of involvement was equally out of his
control and not amenable to containment within the constitutional political system. Violent demonstrations (like the brawls in downtown
Santiago and the women's (5, 000) march of the empty pots in December 1971), armed resistance, and bloodshed came from the center and
right opposition as well as from the left. In reference to this participation issue, Chile seems to be the classic case of too rapid mobilization and too much participation relative to the capacity of the existing
political order to channel and institutionalize it.[51] In such a setting,
the ultimate phase of the scenario is military intervention, for the
military must in the end defend the constitution and maintain political
stability.

The Use of Foreign Policy

The costs of Allende's socialist policies, measured in foreign
policy dimensions, outweighed the benefits. His attempt to break the
dependency on outside capital and to restructure the domestic economic
setting resulted in immediate serious friction with the United States
and delayed support from potential allies. Conflict with the United
States cannot be cited as the cause of Allende's downfall, but it weakened Chile's economic situation, which in turn politically weakened
Allende himself. Meanwhile, the possible inflow of economic resources (hard currency loans, massive technological supports, extensive long-range credits in exchange for Chilean copper at fixed prices)
from sympathetic Marxist countries was not immediately forthcoming.
Ironically, the previous Cuban Revolution (beginning in 1959) was a
prime factor in this situation. Cuba had cost the Soviet Union approximately $1 million a day for many years, putting Cuba into a $4 billion
debt to the Soviet Union during the period when Allende sought outside
help. The Soviets were not favorably disposed to underwrite Chile
with massive economic aid as soon as Allende was elected.

It would be difficult to argue that Allende brought about his own
downfall externally through his efforts to break dependency internally.
Washington did not cause his demise. It is true that Washington suspended further commercial credits once Allende nationalized the copper mines still jointly owned by Americans. Moreover, as the major
power in the World Bank and the International Monetary Fund it helped
to prevent additional multilateral aid to the Allende government.[52]
Finally, the multinational corporations whose mines had been nationalized blocked reception of Chile's copper exports in foreign countries
where they could employ certain power leverages. But it should be remembered that the Allende government's own economic management

was not particularly conducive to making it a high-risk country for
loans, and that in any case, other Western powers made loans available. Holland, Sweden, and Britain continued to offer aid that was
all the more remarkable in view of the domestic strikes (including
the long copper strike), a high budget deficit, low productivity of nationalized industries, and the highest rate of inflation in the world
during 1973, according to the International Monetary Fund. [53]

Allende's real political allies failed to come to his aid in the
massive way required to keep the ship afloat as the reserves inherited
fromthe Frei years rapidly slipped away. Neither his highly publicized
and poignant address to the United Nations in December 1972, outlin-
ing the external pressures against his government (such as the drying
up of credit from traditional private banks) nor his visits to Algeria,
the Soviet Union, and Cuba were able to alter the negative situation in
time to strengthen his domestic political position. Had he not been
overthrown, there was the outside chance that forthcoming socialist
help might have strengthened the regime's position at home. The Soviet Union—two years after Allende had been in power and long after
it was clear that his government needed economic help—agreed to make
available credits worth $335 million (of which $185 million were to be
in sterling or other hard currencies) for purchasing such equipment
as Comecon machine tools and electric motors, and for technical aid
and foodstuffs worth $30 million. Cuba also promised to make Chile
a gift of 40,000 tons of sugar. But these offers were late in coming.

ALLENDE'S FALL: CONCLUSIONS

Four major explanations help to account for Allende's fall
through the military coup d'etat of September 1973. They suggest the
underlying links between his political style, a weak economy, and a
highly democratic political system, which in the end produced polarized discontent, enormous economic dislocation, and eventual military takeover. Interestingly enough, these four explanations coincide
with recent writing on political development in the Third World that
anticipates specific outcomes under special conditions. They center
on Allende's failure (1) to build and maintain legitimate authority, (2)
to institutionalize his goals, (3) to keep the rate of mobilization and
participation within existing institutions or to provide new ones, and
(4) to coopt the military in a highly unstable economic, political, and
social setting.

The Legitimate Authority Problem

Of all the problems faced by Third World leaders (indeed of developed countries as well), the problem of building and maintaining legitimate authority is central to all the rest. [54] When a leader fails to secure legitimate authority, particularly vis-a-vis other power elites, he risks the loss of support and compliance, and thus his base of power. By legitimate is meant the acceptance of a leader's rule without his having to resort solely to the threat or use of physical power. A leader may of course emphasize physical force as the basis of his authority, but this is no guarantee of long-run rule; it also diverts scarce resources away from capital formation and economic development, and requires enormous skills in keeping potential power contenders happy.

Allende's policies in retrospect were not conducive to his maintenance of legitimate authority, although ironically enough that was precisely one of his prime goals. The Allende government issued warnings to extreme left- and right-wing extremists occupying factories, villages, and building sites that the law would be applied against them. The government also brought the military (traditional constitutionalists and presumably above party feuds) into key cabinet posts in 1972 and 1973 in an effort to cope more effectively with terrorist activities while preserving national unity. President Allende declared time and again during the last days of his rule that he hoped to prevent civil war through use of constitutional means. But throughout 1973 it was clear that his base of authority was eroding swiftly.

A number of indicators of declining authority can be cited. Many of his cabinet ministers were charged and impeached by Congress for infringing the Constitution. These charges were brought in connection with the copper strikes, extremist activities and closing down opposition radio and television stations. The right-wing National Party increasingly advocated "civil disobedience" toward an "illegitimate" government. The military became sharply divided over its course of action, contributing to ebbing authority. All opposition parties issued a joint declaration in July 1973 criticizing the government for failing to prevent the occupation of factories by workers and for the alleged distribution of arms to workers. [55] Further acts of violence continued, leading to resignations by military officers from the cabinet, and to a key resolution by the Chamber of Deputies in late August, which approved a motion of censure against the government for having violated the Constitution and the country's laws. Once the government was declared outside the law, the conditions were ripe for a military coup, particularly since the congressional motion of censure also appealed to the military to "reestablish the Constitution and the law."

Institutionalizing Goals

A second major problem for Third World leaders is institution-alizing their goals. This use of "institutionalizing" means moving be-yond the mere compliance and support with governmental programs into active support and dedicated participation.[56] If a leader's goals —socialist or nonsocialist—are to be executed as legitimate authori-tative sanctions, they need the commitment of masses of people both inside and outside the country's bureaucratic structure. This means breaking with traditional patterns of thought and creating new aspira-tions, attitudes, and values in terms of where the country is heading and why.

Allende's socialist program failed to produce institutionalized goals for a sufficiently large segment of the population to give him an expanded base of support after the 1970 presidential elections. The presidential elections produced a modest 36.2 percent support, not strong enough to do what he intended to do. Once he assumed office he was unable to convince other power contenders of the utility of social-ist reforms, with similar results where the middle sectors were con-cerned. To institutionalize his goals meant in effect a break with preexisting institutionalized interests (parties, corporate interest groups, commerce, banking, trucking, and potentially the military) powerful enough to oppose him.

To institutionalize is to build political power, but to do so re-quires political power (to influence and persuade). Allende simply did not have that kind of massive power in Chile's politically divided and historically "democratic" system. It could be argued here that a polity and society less developed than Chile's may be more amena-ble to the kind of Socialist innovations sought by Allende because the political power to change may be the more easily mobilized. This appears to be the case in Peru, where the military leads, rather than opposes, state-directed innovation. Tanzania is another case in point, as is Cuba, which on the eve of the revolution was not a politi-cally sophisticated country in the sense that it was little diversified and had little institutionalized political articulation.

The Rate of Mobilization

Samuel P. Huntington, a noted political development theorist, makes the case that a more rapid rate of mobilization and participation compared to institutionalizing change leads to political instability.[57] By "institutionalizing change" he refers to providing rational organiza-tions and procedures for conflict management, programmatic innova-tion, and the peaceful transition of political power from one set of political leaders to the next. Thus political parties, elections, and interest groups would provide the institutionalizing framework to absorb mobilized political participants, and there should be enough of the latter to meet the pressures of the former.

Chile, under Allende's socialist government, appears to be a classic case of excessive rates of mobilization and participation compared to the rate of institutionalizing. Once Allende came to power, enormous hopes and expectations were unleashed by his followers.[58] These were stimulated not only by Allende's announced program, but also by the government's efforts to mobilize support via demonstrations, newspapers, radio, and television. These efforts resulted in factory and land seizures, physical violence in urban and rural centers, and even attempts to infiltrate the armed forces as a means to build support for the government. The de facto institutional structure —sophisticated and diversified as it was—was unable to absorb the sheer volume of mobilized participation. Meanwhile, Allende's own efforts to provide new institutions (the single legislative chamber, local judicial tribunals) failed. Unlike Fidel Castro's Cuba where mobilization and new institution-building followed a parallel sequence of development, the rate of increased participation in Chile exceeded existing institutional capacity and therefore spilled over into violent, noninstitutionalized forms of behavior. Violence, to be sure, is a typical form of political expression in Latin America, and some authors see it as an institutionalized power factor. But the resort to violence is far less common in Chile's case, thus making its presence a contributing factor to middle and right-wing opposition and to the final military coup.

The Chilean Military

Most studies on Allende's Chile emphasize the key role played by the military, and for solid reasons. In a growing situation of polarized opinion, fragmented power, and declining authority for Allende, the military remained the one body of organized power sufficiently strong to end the state of civil unrest. When "legitimacy vacuums" occur in Latin America—and for that matter in Africa and Asia as well—the military traditionally steps in. Chile evolved precipitously close to a legitimacy vacuum in late August and early September 1973, making it under this circumstance not so much an exception to traditional Latin American civil-military relations.

The government, through a series of cabinet reshuffles, tried from late 1972 onward to stabilize the country by putting military officers into power. But as fate would have it, these moves only exacerbated a deteriorating situation. Cabinet participation by the military changed the traditional Chilean civil-military balance toward dramatically increased military involvement.

First, it brought the military into the maelstrom of political controversy. This involvement exposed it to criticism and harassment from the extreme right and left, and severely tarnished its image as being "above politics" and the ultimate repository of neutral constitutional patriotism. Besides that, it undoubtedly made the elite military leaders feel very uncomfortable in a political setting devoid of neat clear lines for decisions.[59] The congressional resolution of August 1973 brought extra pressure to bear upon an already perplexed military by warning the armed services that their continued support of Allende would damage their reputation. This led to the resignation of General Carlos Prats the next day from his position as Minister of Defense and as Commander-in-Chief of the Chilean Army.

Second, cabinet participation by military leaders also produced severe divisions within the armed services. Among other evidence, the resignation from the cabinet by General Cesar Ruiz in August 1973 is a case in point. Simultaneously resigning his command of the air force, he stated that as Minister of Transport, he could not be sure that other officers would carry out his orders. Thus the coup of September 1973, preceded by an earlier attempted coup, resulted in part from a growing fear among the military that continuation of Allende's rule threatened the very stability of the armed forces itself. This proposition coincides with another fascinating principle of political development theory. It states that the military in more advanced developing countries is likely to play a more conservative role than in lesser developed countries. Particularly as society moves toward mass participation, away from middle-class politics or the world of oligarchy, the military typically becomes guardian of the existing order against lower-class incursions.[60]

Summary

Allende's socialist reforms were well intended. One sympathizes easily with his goals, for who could oppose a Chilean "New Deal" for its impoverished and hopeless masses? A visit to rural Chile or to Santiago's callampas can be persuasive on this issue. Allende tried desperately to push ahead in directions already deemed acceptable by former governments, dating back even before Eduardo Frei (1964-70), and to do so in forms consistent with Chilean traditions. If one can generalize about the conditions examined above, his failure resulted from a too rapid change of pace, given his own base of power and existing political institutions. He overestimated not only his own power but also the potential influence of those he sought to

serve and the psychological readiness of the rest of Chile's corporate
interests to concede to Socialist change. His Socialist reforms,
rather than solving Chile's complex economic problems, rooted
deeply as they were within political society, created economic and
political strains too severe to be resolved by constitutional means.

A Postscript

This analysis of the Allende era centers primarily on the internal domestic setting leading to the violent military coup d'etat of September 11, 1973. Its central thesis is that Allende's fall resulted
primarily from conditions inside Chile, rather than being the product
of external pressures brought to bear by the United States. Internal
problems created largely by the implementation and effects of Allende's
program account essentially for his demise. These include the lack of
a clear majority for Unidad Popular, polarization of public opinion,
Allende's eroding base of support, his inability to control inflation,
excessive printing of money, lack of investments, bureaucratic difficulties in economic management, bypassing Congress on key measures, and an inability to control the illegal actions of Allende supporters. The obvious conclusion is not that socialism is ineffective or
inefficient, but that Allende's particular record was.

To conclude with a negative assessment of Allende's socialism
is not to deny the existence nor importance of official and private
economic policies emanating from the United States that made life
difficult for the Allende government. The evidence shows Washington's involvement in slowing down foreign aid grants to Chile in development bank loans, a decline of credit from American commercial
banks, the Kennecott Copper Company's embargo of Chilean copper in
France and other Western European countries, and Central Intelligence Agency activity in Chile between 1970 and 1973.[61] This evidence
has been, and continues to be, debated from a number of points of
view, including (1) whether U.S. policy was "coordinated" at the public and private level to bring down Allende, (2) the alleged "cutoff" of
U.S. aid, and (3) credit worthiness of the Allende government, (4)
the question of a U.S. "blockade" of aid, and (5) the rising debt of
Allende's government as evidence of continuing external loans despite
U.S. pressures to the contrary.[62]

No scholarly assessment of the Allende years can deny these issues and U.S. activities. Testimony by the Director of the Central
Intelligence Agency, William E. Colby, that the Nixon administration
authorized more than $8 million for covert activities in Chile between
1970-73, is a particularly seedy side of U.S. official policy during Allende's tenure in office.[63] But the question here is more than one of

U.S. motivations and efforts to make life difficult for Allende by strengthening those forces that opposed him. The essential question is one of significance and impact of those policies in destroying Allende's socialism. It is here that the record—on balance and given available information—suggests strongly that U.S. policies occurred under deteriorating conditions largely generated by separate forces inside Chile. While external pressures contributed to those conditions, they cannot be singled out as the sole cause for Allende's downfall. Such a single-factor analysis of these years simply does not fit the record, although it will be debated profusely in the years to come.

NOTES

1. For an incisive analysis of Allende's development strategy, see Robert L. Ayres, "Economic Stagnation and the Emergence of the Political Ideology of Chilean Underdevelopment," World Politics 24 (October 1972): 34-61. To end economic stagnation, Ayres correctly points out, Allende's government sought structural change (break the land tenure arrangements; industrial concentration; control of private banking), an end to dependency (excessive capital outflows to foreigners; investment decisions made by multinational corporations without consideration of Chile's needs), and a break in the political stalemate (no single force able to impose a development ideology on state apparatus). On Allende's specific program, see Richard Gott, ed., Chile's Road to Socialism (Baltimore: Penguin Books, Inc., 1973), chap. 1, "The Programme of Unidad Popular, December 1969." Also useful here is Richard E. Feinberg, The Triumph of Allende: Chile's Legal Revolution (New York: New American Library, 1972); Michael J. Francis, The Allende Victory: An Analysis of the 1970 Chilean Presidential Election (Tuscon: University of Arizona Press, 1973); and Regis Debray, The Chilean Revolution; Conversations with Allende (New York: Random House, 1971).

2. See Federico G. Gil, The Political System of Chile (Boston: Houghton Mifflin, 1966), pp. 56 ff; also Ernst Halperin, Nationalism and Communism in Chile (Cambridge: Massachusetts Institute of Technology Press, 1965), pp. 121-44. See also Francis, op. cit., pp. 11 ff.

3. Gil, op. cit., chap. 4, esp. pp. 194 ff.

4. On the reforms instituted by Eduardo Frei Montalva, as well as the obstacles to those reforms, see Arpad von Lazar and Luis Quiros Varela, "Chilean Christian Democracy: Lessons in the Politics of Reform Management," Inter-American Economic Affairs 21 (Spring 1968): 51-72; W. Raymond Duncan, "Chilean Christian Democracy," Current History 53 (November 1967): 263-69, 308-09; George

W. Grayson, "Chile's Christian Democratic Party: Power, Factions, and Ideology," Review of Politics 31 (April 1969): 147-71; Robert R. Kaufman, The Chilean Political Right and Agrarian Reform: Resistance and Moderation (Washington, D.C.: Institute for the Comparative Study of Political Systems, 1967); Richard R. Fagen and Wayne A. Cornelius, Jr., eds., Political Power in Latin America: Seven Confrontations (Englewood Cliffs, N.J.: Prentice-Hall, 1970), pt. 1. Also Michael J. Francis and Hernan Vera-Godoy, "Chile: Christian Democracy to Marxism, The Review of Politics 33 (July 1971): 323-41. Some of Frei's achievements are that he made Chile the majority stockholder in the large U.S. copper operations, brought 28,000 families into agricultural projects (which helped raise agricultural production from the 1.8 percent yearly average to 4.5 percent during his years), and diverted resources toward education, community organization, and housing.

5. The Chilean political party system is well covered by Gil, op. cit., chap. 6. See also Ronald H. McDonald, Party Systems and Elections in Latin America (Chicago: Markham Publishing Co., 1971), pp. 116-51.

6. Chile was ranked high in political development by quantitative studies before Allende's overthrow, and most scholars gave it a high rating in terms of political stability and the other criteria stated here. On quantitative studies see Martin C. Needler, "Political Development and Socioeconomic Development: The Case of Latin America," The American Political Science Review 62 (September 1968): 889-98; Ernest A. Duff and John F. McCamant, "Measuring Social and Political Requirements for System Stability in Latin America," The American Political Science Review 62 (December 1968): 1125-43. Chile's ranking, compared to a number of other Latin American countries, in terms of a number of "democratic" indicators as perceived by Latin American scholars in the United States is found in Russell H. Fitzgibbon and Kenneth J. Johnson, "Measurement of Latin American Political Change," The American Political Science Review 4 (September 1961): 515-26.

7. The Statute of Democratic Guarantees committed Allende to preserve (1) the political system and constitutional guarantees of individual liberty, (2) the de facto legal system, (3) the armed services from political interference, and (4) the sanctity of the educational system, trade unions, and social organizations. See Leon Goure and Jaime Suchlicki, "The Allende Regime: Actions and Reactions," Problems of Communism 20 (May-June 1971): 53. Allende clearly did not feel that these guarantees conflicted with his own plans to change Chile. He said as much to Debray in their talks in early 1971, pointing out that the Chilean Constitution could be changed within the Constitution, that he intended to stay within the domain of legality, and

that he was by no means a <u>caudillo</u> (strong man or "boss"). See Debray, op. cit., pp. 94, 97.

8. The Chilean Constitution provides that when no candidate
receives an absolute majority, Congress must determine between
the two top-ranking candidates 50 days after the popular election.
The Christian Democrats, the largest party in Chile despite declining
electoral percentages, were the key group in this decision. Allende's
agreement to abide by the Statute of Democratic Guarantees helped
swing Christian Democratic votes, and he was formally inaugurated
on November 3, 1970. See Paul E. Sigmund's incisive analysis of
Allende's coming to power and his first two years in office, "Chile:
Two Years of 'Popular Unity,'" <u>Problems of Communism</u> 21 (November-December 1972): 38-51.

9. Ibid., pp. 38-39.

10. On the nature of the balancing acts that Chilean presidents
must perform in dealing with reform issues in a divided Congress,
see Robert Kaufman, <u>The Politics of Land Reform in Chile</u> (Cambridge, Mass.: Harvard University Press, 1972). As Dudley Seers
puts it, political power in Chile is like a violin, "held by the left hand
but played by the right," in "Chile: Is the Road to Socialism Blocked?"
<u>The World Today</u> 28 (May 1972): p. 203.

11. James Petras devotes attention to the condition of Chile's
lower sectors in his book, <u>Politics and Social Forces in Chilean De-
velopment</u> (Berkeley: University of California Press, 1969). He indicates Chile's high infant mortality rate (125 out of every 1,000) due
largely to malnutrition, the larger percent of urban and rural workers
compared to middle and upper classes, which receive small percentages of the total national income, and the over 85 percent of working-
class children in the 1960s that still dropped out of school after the
sixth grade (27.5 percent did not finish more than one year of school).
But these people were well off compared to the masses living in urban
and rural slum areas.

12. Sigmund, op. cit., p. 39. Also, Maurice Zeitlin, "Deter-
minants of Political Democracy in Chile," in James Petras and Maurice Zeitlin, eds., <u>Latin America: Reform or Revolution?</u>" (Green-
wich, Conn.: Fawcett, 1968). See also Francis, op. cit., p. 12.

13. See Duncan, op. cit.

14. Halperin, op. cit.

15. Gil, op. cit., pp. 117-19. Given the strength of the opposition during Allende's tenure of office, the problem of legislative obstructionism became extremely acute for the President.

16. Laurence Whitehead, "Why Allende Fell," <u>The World Today</u>
29 (November 1973): 468. By August 1973 the inflation rate had
reached 323 percent, making an effective devaluation in less than
three years of 10,000 percent. See David Holden, "Allende and the
Myth Makers," <u>Encounter</u> 42 (January 1974): 19.

17. See Whitehead, op. cit., pp. 463-66.

18. Jonathan Kandell, "Allende's Undoing: A Middle Class Stung by Declining Fortunes," New York Times, September 15, 1973.

19. Keesings Contemporary Archives 19 (1973): 26039.

20. Ibid.

21. Jonathan Kandell, "The March Shock; Accelerating Crisis," New York Times, September 16, 1973.

22. Debray, op. cit., p. 66.

23. Francis, op. cit., p. 43.

24. Debray, op. cit., p. 64.

25. Ibid., p. 68.

26. Chile's Road to Socialism, op. cit., p. 49.

27. Ibid., p. 61.

28. On the popularity of the socialist ideology in developing countries, see Charles W. Anderson, Fred R. von der Mehden, and Crawford Young, Issues of Development (Englewood Cliffs, N.J.: Prentice-Hall, 1967), pt. 3. Also William Ebenstein, Today's Isms (Englewood Cliffs, N.J.: Prentice-Hall, 1973), pp. 253-58.

29. See "Some Fundamental Questions of Present Day International Development," Report of the Central Committee of the CPSU to the Twentieth Party Congress, February 1956, by Nikita S. Khrushchev, in Alvin Z. Rubenstein, ed., The Foreign Policy of the Soviet Union (New York: Random House, 1960), p. 296.

30. Callampas refers to the slum areas ringing Santiago; inquilinos to the rural sharecroppers and migrant workers; rotos to the "broken," "destroyed," "shattered," individuals of the lower classes in Chile.

31. Chile's Road to Socialism, op. cit., p. 34.

32. It should be noted here that Allende probably did not have enormous influence even within his own Socialist party, where Raul Ampuero, its Secretary-General, dominated the party machine. But he was skilled in not arousing lasting hatred in anyone, making him an attractive candidate on that ground. See Halperin, The Chilean Presidential Election of 1964 (Cambridge: Massachusetts Institute of Technology Press, 1964), p. 13. Allende's political history shows splits with his own Socialist party, not unusual by Chilean standards, but underlining why party vanguardism was not stressed by him in 1970.

33. Debray, op. cit., p. 85.

34. In addition to Halperin, op. cit., see Duncan, "Havana and the Chilean Communist Party," in Problemas del Comunismo (Spanish edition of Problems of Communism) 14 (July-August, 1967): 64-74, which explores Socialist identity with Castro's Cuba and consequent rifts with the Communists.

35. Chile's Road to Socialism, op. cit., p. 61.

36. Debray, op. cit., p. 85.

37. Feinberg, op. cit., p. 110.

38. To redistribute income meant shifting it to lower-class and lower-income working groups through wage increases, greater tax exemptions, and strict enforcement of price controls. The objective was to increase the purchasing power of these groups, which in turn would stimulate industrial production without having an inflationary impact. The upshot would be consumer prosperity and increased volume of sales for the producers, even though his traditional profit margin would have been reduced. Simultaneously the government planned to orient production away from superfluous and expensive articles appealing to the high-income groups and toward production of cheap high-quality goods for popular consumption. Chile's Road to Socialism, p. 41. See also Ivan Yanez (professor of international economics at the University of Chile, Santiago, during Allende's term), "Chile on the Road to Socialism," Interplay (March 1971): 5-9; Sigmund, op. cit., pp. 42-43.

39. Even though Allende was blocked in Congress on much of his legislation, increased control by the state over sectors of the economy was possible through use of existing legislation. See Sigmund, op. cit. Complete nationalization of copper did require new legislation, but this was the one area where he could muster support.

40. Norman Gall, "Copper is the Wage of Chile," American Universities Field Staff Report 19 (August 1972): 2.

41. Ibid., pp. 6-7.

42. Ibid. See also Thomas G. Sanders, "Urban Pressure, Natural Resource Constraints, and Income Redistribution in Chile," American Universities Field Staff Report 20 (December 1973): p. 9.

43. Gall, op. cit., p. 7.

44. To undertake these projects, he relied upon the Agrarian Reform Law passed in 1967.

45. Sanders, op. cit., p. 9.

46. Keesings Contemporary Archives 19 (1973): 25825.

47. Ibid.

48. Ibid. See also Dudley Seers, "Chile: Is the Road to Socialism Blocked?" The World Today 28 (May 1972): 205. See also Holden, op. cit.

49. See Sanders, op. cit., p. 7.

50. See Francis, op. cit.; Halperin, op. cit.; Gil, op. cit.; McDonald, op. cit.

51. See Samuel P. Huntington, Political Order in Changing Societies (New Haven, Conn.: Yale University Press, 1968), pp. 78-82, 220-24, discussing political stability in terms of levels of political institutionalization and political participation.

52. Allende's overthrow by the military led to an immediate increase in U.S. private loans to Chile. Within a month, for example,
the Manufacturers Hanover Trust Company announced a $24 million
loan to Chile. Indeed, the estimated total amount of private loans offered to Chile within the first month after Allende's fall amounted to
approximately $150 million. The U.S. government intervened during
Allende's years to prevent Chile from receiving credit from the Export-Import Bank for airplanes and loans from the Inter-American
Development Bank and the World Bank to promote petrochemical and
agricultural development. This action came in response to Allende's
nationalization of American-owned copper mines, which were not, by
U.S. investor's perceptions, justly compensated. See Jonathan Kandell, "Private U.S. Loan in Chile Up Sharply," New York Times,
November 12, 1973.

53. Holden, op. cit. See also Paul N. Rosenstein-Rodan, "Allende's Big Failing: Incompetence," New York Times, June 16, 1974.

54. See Norman H. Keehn, "Building Authority: A Return to
Fundamentals," World Politics 26 (April 1974): 331-52.

55. The background to this resolution included a May 1973 Resolution by Chile's Supreme Court to President Allende for failure to
make police available to carry out eviction orders for illegal property
seizures. Chilean Radio Broadcast, June 13, 1973.

56. For an especially good analysis of this problem, see Edward
Feit, "Pen, Sword, and People: Military Regimes in the Formation
of Political Institutions," World Politics 25 (January 1973): 251-73.

57. Huntington, op. cit., incl. chap. 1.

58. A complimentary political development thesis is suggested
by Martin Needler. It maintains that if participation increases
greatly, constitutional integrity (stable constitutional government)
will deteriorate unless the country's economy develops at the same
time to provide a higher level of welfare to match the higher level of
participation. Significantly, Allende was overthrown by the military,
ending constitutional government (political instability) precisely under
conditions of increased participation and declining economic conditions. It thus fits Needler's hypothesis, suggesting that Socialist innovations bring political decay rather than political development under
some conditions. See Needler, op. cit.

59. The Chilean Communist Party, for example, severely criticized the armed forces for their continual raids on union headquarters,
factories, and other leftist groups under the arms control law. Chilean Radio Broadcast, July 23, 1973. Similarly, the Chilean Trade
Union Confederation (CUTCH) protested vigorously against the military for raiding the CUTCH headquarters in Osorno (southern province)
—another case the military trying to enforce the gun control law.
Chilean Radio Broadcast, July 21, 1973. Meanwhile, attacks came

from the right, accusing the military of too close association with
the Allende socialist reforms. For other analysis of the role of the
military as the coup approached, see Whitehead, op. cit., pp. 471 ff.

60. See Huntington, op. cit., pp. 220 ff; also Martin Needler,
"Political Development and Military Intervention in Latin America,"
The American Political Science Review 60 (September 1966): 616-26.

61. See Multinational Corporations and United States Foreign
Policy, Hearings before the Subcommittee on Inter-American Affairs
of the Senate Committee on Foreign Relations (Washington, D.C.:
U.S. Government Printing Office, 1973). Also Paul E. Sigmund,
"The 'Invisible Blockade' and the Overthrow of Allende," Foreign Af-
fairs 52 (January 1974): 322-40.

62. On the various dimensions of this debate, see Elizabeth
Farnsworth, "More Than Admitted," Foreign Policy, Fall 1974, pp.
127-41; and Paul E. Sigmund, "Less Than Charged," Foreign Policy,
Fall 1974, pp. 142-56.

63. Seymour M. Hersh, "C.I.A. Chief Tells House of $8-Mil-
lion Campaign Against Allende in '70-'73," New York Times, September 8, 1974. Also Seymour M. Hersh, "C.I.A. is Linked to Strikes
in Chile That Beset Allende," New York Times, September 20, 1974.
It should be stressed that the Central Intelligence Agency, by using
the Chilean black market, was able to increase the basic buying power
of money spent on clandestine efforts between 1970 and 1973. Some
sources indicated the unofficial rate, so that the CIA total cash impact could have been of more than $40 million. Sources also reported
that the CIA was "not looking for a military takeover," and that the
agency began to curtail its clandestine commitments in Chile late in
the spring of 1973 when weekly reports of an impending military coup
were evident. Secretary of State Henry A. Kissinger testified before
the Senate Foreign Relations Committee on September 19, 1974 that
CIA operations were not intended to "destroy or subvert" the government of the late President Salvador Allende but to keep opposition political parties alive. Democrat and Chronicle (Rochester, N.Y.),
September 20, 1974.

2

**SOCIALISM
IN CUBA**
Jorge I. Dominguez

THE COMING OF SOCIALISM: TACTICS AND VALUES

The most distinctive feature of socialist ideology in Cuba is that it comes from the gut.

Fidel Castro, leader of the revolutionary group that emerged triumphant at the end of the 1950s, Prime Minister of the Revolutionary Government and First Secretary of the Communist Party of Cuba, had at best a passing acquaintance with the classics of Marxism-Leninism when he began his career as a revolutionary. Theodore Draper pointed out a decade ago that Castroism is the only tendency in world communism that came into the movement essentially from the outside. Unlike Maoism or Titoism, Castroism did not develop from within a communist movement and later on establish its separate identity. Castroism is not somebody else's "model" of politics—but Fidel's own.[1]

Castro had been a member of a noncommunist university "action group" in his youth, which at times clashed with members of the Communist Party.[2] He had been a congressional candidate of the Cuban People's Party, known as Ortodoxos. The party competed with the Communists and had put forth an explicit doctrinal repudiation of communism.[3] Castro's main programmatic statement prior to winning power was fully within the noncommunist, democratic-left ideological context of Cuban politics in the early 1950s.[4] This was the edited version of a speech given at a trial in his own defense responding to charges brought against him by the Batista government for attacking the Moncada military garrisons on July 26, 1953. The Cuban Communist Party had criticized Castro and his movement as "putschists" for the attempt to storm the Batista government out of power without prior mass mobilization. And as late as April 1958—only months away from Batista's fall on New Year's Eve, 1958—the Communist Party failed to endorse Castro's call for a revolutionary general strike.[5]

Socialism came to Cuba as a result of decisions taken by Fidel Castro and his comrades from their perception of the relevant Cuban historical and international experiences. They perceived that a radical revolution in Cuba (along with Guatemala, 1954, at least in Che Guevara's mind—he was there) would mean a break with the United States. The United States was thoroughly intertwined in the Cuban social system. The revolutionary leadership's perception was decisive that the role of the United States in Cuba's internal structure was inconsistent with any substantial transformation of the country. Fidel Castro and his close associates gradually shifted their internal and international programs simultaneously, beginning in the late winter or early spring of 1959, until a full swing toward socialism was acknowledged and accomplished after the U.S.-sponsored exile invasion failed on the beaches of the Bay of Pigs in April 1961. For example, the first significant departure from earlier programs was the announcement that elections would not be held in the short term, and that no bilateral aid would be sought from the United States or from international lending agencies. Both of these planks had been prominently and favorably discussed through March 1959; both were abandoned at approximately the same time, prior to Fidel Castro's unofficial trip to the United States in April 1959.[6]

U.S. policies toward Cuba in early 1959 were conciliatory.[7] The United States did not make an issue of the intervention by the Cuban government of the U.S.-owned Cuban Telephone Company. The U.S. Ambassador to Cuba, Philip Bonsal, was publicly praised by Castro for his understanding of the Cuban revolution and his helpful and conciliatory attitudes. The early U.S. responses to some of the revolutionary government's major laws (such as the May 1959 Land Reform Act) were couched in moderate terms and publicly recognized then by Cuban leaders as such.[8] But conciliatory policies could not make hard structural facts go away: the massive U.S. private investment in Cuba stood in the way of virtually any radical program that could have been implemented in Cuba. Cuba's march to socialism was not inevitable. Reform did not require socialism. Reformist leaders, though never dominant, did exist. But once the dominant leaders settled upon a radical revolution, the structure of the internal social system inalterably posed the problem of a clash with the United States. Ninety miles from the United States, in a lively cold-war setting, Cuba faced the likelihood of embracing the Soviet Union directly, as well as through the alliance of Fidel Castro's revolutionaries with the old and formerly hostile Cuban communist party (formally called the People's Socialist Party or PSP). The structure of the international system was perceived by the Cuban leadership in such a way that it yielded the same answer as their perception of the country's internal structure: a shift from a radical to a socialist revolution, and a shift toward the Soviet Union.

Structural arguments, however, are necessary but insufficient to explain the motivations for adopting socialism in 1959-61. The second decisive explanation flows from the perceptions of the leadership that the values they held so dear as a result of their armed struggle against Batista were compatible with some of the doctrinal strains of Marxism-Leninism. Fidel Castro could have uttered Marx's critique of Feuerbach, "Social life is essentially practical. All mysteries which mislead theory toward mysticism find their rational solution in human practice and in the comprehension of this practice (VIII)." "The philosophers have only interpreted the world, in various ways; the point however, is to change it (XI)." It is this strain in Marx—oriented toward practice, toward action, toward subjectivism —that appealed to Castro and his colleagues. The Marx of historical forces, * the Marx for whom revolution is the product of history more than the product of the willful acts of men—this Marx has not been emphasized.[9] By the same token, it is the Lenin of an elite vanguard who set for himself an apparently maximalist and unreachable role, and acted on it, that appeals to this leadership, not the author of Left Wing Communism: An Infantile Disorder.

The doctrinal strains in Marxism-Leninism that appealed to Castro and his colleagues, therefore, were activism, voluntarism or subjectivism, elitism, and maximalism.[10] While this may be a bit closer to the views of the current Chinese rather than Soviet leadership, it is far too vuluntaristic to give comfort to either. Castro and his cohorts, too, had emphasized practical activity rather than mystical theory in their struggle against Bastista. They were a handful of men (and a few women) pursuing a maximalist, apparently unreachable goal. They relied on will, and when that gave out, then there was more will, more will, until victory.

The alliance with the old Communist Party of Cuba (PSP) flows naturally from the decision to align Cuba with the Soviet Union. The old Communists would be helpful intermediaries. Moreover, they could supply necessary political organizational skills. But clearly they did not supply the core of socialist ideology, Cuban-style. When the old members of the Communist Party counseled restraint, the Fidelistas were emboldened; when they feared the wrath of the United States, the Fidelistas provoked it; when moderate goals were suggested, maximalist goals were pursued;[11] when the course of history seemed to suggest the Mexicanization or Bolivianization of the Cuban revolution, a small group of willful leaders changed that course. Socialism

---

*"It is not the consciousness of men that determines their existence, but, on the contrary, their social existence determines their consciouness." (Contribution to the Critique of Political Economy.)

in Cuba came from the gut—from the experience of revolutionary leaders against all odds, from their awareness of their country's historical structure, from their perception of the structure of the international system. It was also the result of elite decisions rather than
the triumph of a long evolving Communist mass movement; socialism
came into the movement from the outside.

RECEPTIVENESS TOWARD SOCIALISM: THE
UTILITY OF THE PAST

If the coming of socialism to Cuba exhibits some of the characteristics of an historical accident, the sinking of socialist roots into
Cuban soil is much less surprising though by no means inevitable.
The idea of government intervention in the economy and government
regulation of broad aspects of social and economic life was not new to
Cuba. The sugar industry, the mainstay of the Cuban economy, was
subject to very extensive government regulation covering output, labor
relations, marketing and distribution of profits. Security of land
tenure in the sugar industry was guaranteed. More generally, Cuba
had very extensive labor legislation whose effect was very strongly
felt in the industrial sector. Beginning in the late 1940s the Cuban
government developed new organizational arrangements to expand
credit and investment through fiscal and monetary stimuli. Even the
nationalization of private enterprise was not unknown: Batista had
nationalized the western railroads of Cuba, with compensation, and
prominent political parties (as well as Castro) were calling for the
nationalization of public utilities. The extensive regulation of all aspects of sugar production was but a step away from even more active
government intervention.[12]

Similarly, political participation in the Cuban republic prior to
the revolution had been very extensive. In the 1944 presidential elections, 80.7 percent of all eligible voters actually voted; in the 1948
presidential elections the figure was 79.5 percent. These were reasonably free, orderly, and competitive elections. Moreover, the
Cuban voting public was discriminant. When fraudulent elections
were held, such as the presidential elections of 1954 when Batista was
the only candidate, only 52.6 percent of the eligible voters voted.
The capacity for voting abstention, even when the government sought to
stimulate voting, suggests a far greater degree of political sophistica-
tion than one may expect in a more traditional society.

Other data support the view that Cubans were aware of, and informed about, politics. In a 1951 poll only 7 percent did not know how
to evaluate the government. In a 1949 poll, 93 percent knew that Sena-
tor Chibas (a prominent opposition leader) had been imprisoned tem-

porarily. In a 1950 poll as many as 47 percent were aware that the
national government had embarked on a new policy. In the context of
comparative public opinion research, these numbers are strikingly
high.[13]

Even in the rural areas, where one may expect that parochial
orientations would prevail, one finds an orientation toward collective
political participation that is unexpected in the light of literature that
suggests the opposite types of behavior in rural areas. In a survey
of 1,675 families in rural Las Villas Province (Central Cuba) in 1958,
80.5 percent of all respondents answered affirmatively that they "believe that the unity of all the neighbors could lead to some solutions
of local problems." The same research team surveyed 677 rural
schools inthe province. They found that almost 79 percent of them
had implemented legislation mandating parent-teacher associations.
More impressively, 40 percent of all the associations had had four
or more meetings during the school year. Almost all the schools
with such associations had some funds to operate (which they had
raised on their own); 16 percent of all the associations had $26 in pesos
or more—a not inconsiderable sum in 1958 rural Cuba.[14]

Therefore, the Cuban revolutionary government came to power
in a country where extensive government intervention in the social
system was an accepted fact. What was new was the extent to which
this would be expanded to encompass government ownership of virtually all the means of production.[15] Revolutionary politics and mobilization would occur in a country where the citizenry were highly
politicized, very much aware of the impact of government on their
lives, alert to the details of politics, willing to organize politically
for participation even in rural areas far from the capital city of
Havana, and willing to bear a political participatory burden for their
own goals. What was new was that the expansion and control of political
participation would become a top priority item for the government.
The new policies would take variety and competition out of participation. Political participation is too serious an enterprise to leave to
the participants alone.

In practice, then, socialism would not find unfertile soil in Cuba.
Once the revolutionary elite set upon the course of promoting socialism, the expansion of government intervention in the social system
and the expansion and control of political participation were not unpre-
cedented. There would be considerable conflict and opposition, but the
goals of revolutionary elite would resonate warmly enough in the country's traditional political behavior for the new course to find support
too.

THE CONSOLIDATION OF SOCIALISM

Cuban socialism has become popularly known for its unorthodox aspects, often to the detriment of emphasizing the broad commonalities between Cuba and other communist countries. In the following section we shall consider the most striking instances of unorthodoxy, but here our concern is mostly with commonalities.

The Cuban political system emphasizes the role of the founding charismatic leader.[16] There is nothing intrinsic about Marxist-Leninist doctrine that would foreordain the presence of a leader; there is much evidence to suggest that this is a doctrinal "impurity." However, if we take ideology to mean not simply a body of abstract ideas but rather the observed ideas and values of a political system that serve as a "road map" for future action, then the crucial role of the great leader is shared by the more autonomous communist revolutions in Russia, China, Yugoslavia, Vietnam, and Cuba. As such it is part of the set of ideas that guides these societies, especially in their early years of revolutionary rule.

Fidel Castro's power is unmatched in the Cuban political system. It has been argued elsewhere that "distance" from Fidel Castro is the decisive, though not the only, political resource for competition within the existing system. Thus "every crisis could be ended and settled upon Fidel Castro's personal intervention."[17] Yet the Cuban political system is no mere one-man rule. Castro's role can be compared to a laser beam device, which concentrates focused light waves and emits them in a narrow, intense beam. When he focuses on an issue, nothing stands in his way. But his scanning powers are limited. He has established his own priorities, and this shields many areas of the political system from the sweep of his power.

A second commonality between Cuba and other communist countries has been an emphasis on organization-building, under clear constraints, and on expanding and controlling political participation. The dominant stress of the literature on Cuba is that Cuba exhibits an anti-organizational bias—that the impact of Fidel Castro overwhelms organizational life, atrophies what there is, and prevents the development of new organizations.[18] There is no denying that there is a powerful case to be made that organizations in Cuba are not institutionalized. Organizations in Cuba are neither very stable nor much valued for their own sake. They have extremely limited autonomy from the political center, and what they have can be taken away. Their capacity to adapt on their own in the absence of directives from the political center is subject to serious question, and at times has been actively prevented by the political center itself. However, the relative absence of institutionalized organizations is not the same as the absence of organizations. A bias against excessive administrative bureaucra-

tization is not the same as a bias against political organizations. The
presence of "purges" of functionaries is certainly no evidence that
Cuba differs from other communist countries.

The evidence is, in fact, impressive that the Cuban political
leadership has been alert to the organizational stakes of politics
from the very beginning. It linked organization building with political
mobilization in the early years of the revolution. The leadership was
slow to establish a formal Communist Party; therein lies the chief
organizational difference between Cuba and other communist countries.
However, mass political organizations performed many of the political functions of the party in the early 1960s until the party was ready
to take over later in the 1960s; these mass organizations have continued to be important up to the present. The observed changes in
the structure and activities of the political organizations suggested
increasing institutionalization until about 1967; this process was seriously interrupted at about that time, to be resumed once again in
the early 1970s.

When the revolutionary government came to power in January
1959, the political parties were suspended pending national elections
(which have not been held). The leadership group around Fidel Castro
deemphasized the role of revolutionary organizations such as the
Twenty-Sixth of July Movement and the Revolutionary Directorate, because they were subject to influence by other leaders. This was not
the result of a disdain for the organizational stakes of politics, but
rather the opposite. The concern of the Castroite leadership for organizational power would be fully displayed as they strongly and successfully sought control of the Cuban Confederation of Labor and of
the University Students' Federation in the fall of 1959.[19] At the same
time they undermined or took over autonomous organizations of producers and professionals.

The Castroite leadership linked political mobilization to the
building of new political organizations through the expansion of controlled political participation. The paramilitary revolutionary militia
was established in the fall of 1959 at a time when the beginning of a
profound political split in Cuba could be ascertained. At the highpoint
of internal and international political confrontation from the second
half of 1960 through the first half of 1961, the revolutionary government established the Federation of Cuban Women to organize all women who supported it. It established the Committees for the Defense
of the Revolution as an internal spy network on a neighborhood, factory, farm, and shop basis. (This organization would experience
considerable goal and role differentiation, however, in the years
ahead.) They established a revolutionary youth organization, and a
small farmers' federation. Finally, the Integrated Revolutionary Organizations—linking the ghosts of the Twenty-Sixth of July Movement

and the Revolutionary Directorate with the old communist cadres—
was established as a party in embryo. [20]

Prior to the establishment of the party, the mass political organizations performed many of its political functions. They engaged
in large-scale political recruitment to support the revolution: an effort to aggregate and articulate support for the policies of the revolutionary government. They provided the symbolism of partisan struggle. They performed traditional partisan social services too. They
were a demonstration of the government's coercive capacity, and an
effective instrument to implement that capacity. They activated the
commitments of revolutionaries and deterred counterrevolutionaries.

However, the role of coordinating and controlling these organizations fell to Fidel Castro and other leaders until the party was
firmly established. Even now, the leadership can easily countermand
lower-level party decisions that pertain to these organizations. Thus
the preeminence of a few leaders and the relative absence of organizational institutionalization also mark Cuban politics. But it is difficult to argue that this is terribly different from other communist
countries, except that the sequence of party formation in Cuba is
clearly unorthodox.

By the end of 1961 the Committees for the Defense of the Revolution already had one million members; the farmers' federation, the
women's federation, and the militia each had about 200,000 members.
In the early 1970s, however, over half of the adult population belonged
to the Committees for the Defense of the Revolution, and just under
half of the women belonged to their federation. The labor and the
farmers' confederations grouped virtually the entire relevant universe. [21]

The organizational bases of politics in Cuba are impressive.
They have been an integral part of revolutionary mobilization and
control. Government in revolutionary Cuba cannot be explained without reference to them. The role and functions of these organizations
changed over time: their fortunes varied. The variation was such
that institutionalization—including autonomy to set and pursue an organization's own goals, and a capacity to adapt on its own—has not
been achieved. The party suffered a massive membership purge in
1962-63; [22] there have been a variety of examples where the scope of
party power and the domain of party membership have been severely
affected. The Committees for the Defense of the Revolution were
forced from the outside to redirect their goals; the labor unions were
virtually crippled in the late 1960s, and the university students' federation was temporarily forced to disband. [23] The setbacks to the
institutionalization of organizations have been partly redressed by the
mid 1970s, but it is too early to tell whether this has been done successfully. Institutionalization, intrinsically, can only be judged after
the passage of considerable time.

In sum, organizational politics—under clearly specified constraints—have been an integral part of the socialist ideology of the
revolutionary leadership. Once again the term ideology connotes
what the leadership has actually done, not merely flights of rhetorical
fancy. Although the sequence and process of party formation and
growth was admittedly different from other communist countries (for
example, the revolutionary socialist party appears after the revolutionary leadership is in power, because pre-1959 revolutionaries
were not notably revolutionary), mass political organizations have
been important from the outset and performed in lieu of a party until
it was successfully established. Political organizations are a decisive part of the Cuban political system; institutionalized organizations,
however, are not.

A third commonality between Cuba and other communist countries is that the state owns most of the means of production. However,
in this regard, Cuba may be considered supersocialist, because the
degree of etatisme seems to exceed other communist countries. By
the early 1960s virtually all Cuban industry, foreign trade, wholesale
internal trade, banking, education and health had been nationalized.
In 1963 the second agrarian reform act raised the government's ownership share of all land to 70 percent; its share of land actually under
cultivation was 57 percent. (The lands of the private small farmers
were of better quality and had more diversified production, because
they were less committed to sugar production than the state farms.)
In 1968 all small businesses, retail trade, artisan shops, and petty
service enterprises were nationalized.[24] Thus, except for a minority
of the agricultural sector, state ownership of the means of production,
distribution, and provision of services prevails in revolutionary Cuba.

A fourth commonality has been the use of ideology to induce and
facilitate the cultural and psychological transformation of the population, and an increase in national integration. The domestic uses of
foreign policy are also important in this regard. Moral man in Cuba
is judged according to political, ideological, and revolutionary standards. The criteria are public, not private; centrally determined,
not dispersed throughout religious groups or individual standards of
ethical conduct. The good citizen, the good revolutionary, must be a
moral man. Hard work, study, patriotism and defense of country,
participation in mass organizations, anti-imperialism, motivation by
nonmonetary inducements, an orientation toward collective activities,
an exemplary family life—these are the essential qualities.

Cuban men and women are expected to fly to the public assemblies. The scope of privacy that is ideologically legitimate has been
sharply reduced. Jose Yglesias, in a study of a Cuban country town
in the 1960s, noted that members of the Committees for the Defense
of the Revolution exhibited a "pushiness about people's lives: an in-

sistence that the open life—open to the view of one's neighbors—is the natural life of man."[25]

One's life is not totally one's own. In December 1964 the Minister of Labor, Augusto Martinez Sanchez, attempted suicide. A communique, issued by President Osvaldo Dorticos Torrado and Prime Minister Castro, stated:

> According to fundamental revolutionary principles, we think that this conduct is unjustifiable and improper for a revolutionary, and we believe that comrade Martinez Sanchez could not have been fully conscious when he engaged in such a deed, because every revolutionary knows that he does not have a right to deprive his cause of a life which does not belong to him, and which can only be legitimately sacrificed facing the enemy.[26]

In a study of themes in the Cuban press in the early 1960s, Richard Fagen found statistically significant correlations between criticism and defiance of the United States, on the one hand, and praise for the Cubans, on the other. "The revolution needs the enemy," said Fidel Castro in 1963. The enemy, internal and international,   . helped to establish the identity and the meaning of the revolution, to legitimize the leadership and its programs, to provide a spur to action and a rationale for participation, and to contribute to define new patterns of behavior.[27] Thus the domestic uses of foreign policy—the fear of the enemy—have been an integral part of the ideology that seeks to induce psychological and cultural transformation and to increase national integration amid the strains of modernization and conflict.

THE BURDEN OF SOCIALIST UTOPIA:
IMPLEMENTING THE FUTURE

Though Cuba exhibits broad commanlities with other communist countries some elements of unorthodoxy have been noted even in that context. One was the late and slow development of a revolutionary Communist Party of Cuba. Another was the very extensive collectivization of the economy. We shall turn now to economic development strategies and the conduct of foreign policy.

One striking characteristic of Cuban economic development policy, in contrast with that of other communist countries, has been the emphasis on agricultural production generally, and on sugar production specifically. The Cuban revolutionary government emphasized an accelerated industrialization policy from 1959 to 1963. For a vari-

ety of complex reasons, that policy failed. From June 1963 onward
the stress has been on sugar. As Castro said then, "it is the base of
our economy and our development," and "industry will be born from
agriculture." He deliberately ruled out the production of capital
goods, and the production of such items as automobiles or airplanes.
Instead, "we have to develop chemistry as it relates to sugar . . .
we are going to develop sugar derivatives . . . we will develop an industry which starts from agriculture and through the international division of labor."[28]

Thus industrialization was given secondary priority to agriculture. Even within agriculture, Cuba concentrated on what it had always done well: sugar production. This was climaxed with the effort
to produce 10 million tons of sugar in 1970. Although that goal was
not reached, the production of 8.5 million tons was, nevertheless,
the highest in the country's history. Yet there remains a peculiar
economic policy that, out of foreign exchange necessity, has emphasized monoculture, at least for the short run—a policy that Cuban radicals had always criticized before the revolution and that contrasts
with the efforts toward more diversification in most communist countries.

An equally striking difference with most other communist countries—certainly with the Soviet Union and the Eastern European countries, though somewhat less so with China—has been Cuba's stress on
moral or nonmaterial incentives to motivate labor. B. A. Evans has
summarized well the logic of the moral incentives position. A moral
incentives position stresses that consciousness is derived from the
social and economic environment. Men learn by doing. Consequently,
actual experience, decisively shaped by work, is crucial for attitude
formation. If unselfish attitudes are to be favored, they must be in-
culcated in the work place. "Moral incentives reward and encourage
unselfishness, whereas material incentives appeal to and encourage
selfish motives." Thus socialist man must be motivated through
moral incentives. In turn, a morally motivated man can shape the
environment and hasten the coming of communism in its purest form.
After prolonged debate, the decision was taken in the fall of 1966 to
implement a policy relying primarily on moral incentives. Castro argued that "we will never have socialist consciousness, and much less
communist consciousness, with the mentality of grocers . . . (or)
with dollar signs in the minds and in the hearts of the men and women
of the country."[29] Moral incentives would shorten Cuba's leap into
communism. The future would be at hand. People would work because
it was the "right" thing to do, not because they would make more money.

Reliance on moral incentives was matched by a policy of reducing material incentives. Material prizes for good performance were
discontinued for the 1966 sugar harvest. Bonuses for the overfulfill-

ment of work norms were eliminated in 1967. The Minister of Labor
indicated that "workers will be paid according to their skills and the
number of hours worked." The quality of one's work, which would be
shown by norm overfulfillment, would not be rewarded in cash. In
addition, overtime pay was abolished. Payment for the number of
hours worked included only the regular shift; anything extra was "voluntary." At the same time, mass mobilizations to induce voluntary
labor increased. [30]

Not all material incentives, of course, were discontinued.
Cuba's wage scale continued to award higher pay to those with higher
skills. The renunciation of overtime pay by workers was induced by
promising sickness and retirement benefits equal to 100 percent of
wages. The motivation to do voluntary work was not entirely pure:
those who did such work were much more likely to be eligible for promotion, prestige, and possible nomination for membership in the
Communist Party. In a society where goods were rationed, cash did
not have unlimited value. Instead, access to the levers of power has
become the prime channel for social mobility. To gain that access,
one has had to behave as a "moral revolutionary." In sum, the Cuban
shift was essentially away from cash incentives—but not from incentives such as sickness and retirement benefits or from preferred access to political channels for social mobility.

One reason moral incentives proved so appealing to Castro and
his associates is ideological. As we have indicated, the chief doctrinal strains in Cuba's version of socialism include the view that the
consciousness of men can shape their social existence. Willful men
can reach out to apparently unfeasible goals: voluntarism or subjectivism are linked to maximalist goals, and call for immediate action.
The belief in the perfectibility of mankind and in man's capacity to
triumph over objective obstacles is crucial for an understanding of the
position of the Cuban leadership in the late 1960s. Fidel Castro noted
on July 26, 1968:

> If we agreed that man is an incorrigible individual,
> that man can only make progress through egoism,
> through selfishness; . . . if we agreed that man is
> incapable of developing his conscience—then we
> would have to agree that the "brainy" economists
> were right, that the revolution would be headed for
> defeat and that it would be fighting the laws of eco-
> nomics. But the actual fact is that the history of
> this revolution has furnished us with many examples,
> repeated examples that those who were in error were
> those who did not believe in man, that those who
> made the mistake and failed were those who had no

> confidence in the people, who had no confidence in
> man's ability to attain and develop a revolutionary
> awareness. [31]

The Cuban government in the late 1960s was ready to prove that the brainy economists were wrong in the 1960s just as the brainy politicians and political analysts had been wrong in the 1950s. The Communists and many others in the 1950s had argued that Fidel Castro's subjectivist and maximalist approach to Batista's overthrow would not work; the brainy economists in the 1960s argued that the subjectivist and maximalist approach to production would not work. The ideological perspective was comparable; the facts proved different. Batista fell in the late 1950s against the political predictions—and the Cuban economy fell, too, in the 1960s, as the brainy economists predicted.

The 1970s opened in Cuba with a gradual retreat from the position which upheld the primacy of moral incentives, which was completed when the Thirteenth Labor Congress met in the fall of 1973. On July 26, 1968, Fidel Castro was full of praise for egalitarianism, and eager to take steps toward it. In November 1973, in the closing speech at the Labor Congress, he spoke about "egalitarian principle(s) we must correct." The year 1973 was a time to "correct the idealistic mistakes we had made." He noted that "all of us find the communist principles more to our liking, more attractive and more humane. But communism cannot be imposed on human society by decree." And so, "together with moral incentive we must also use material incentive." Voluntarism was more restrained, though still present:

> The Cuban revolution is the result of conscientious
> and fitting action in keeping with the laws of the his-
> tory of human society. Men do not and cannot make
> history in response to their whim. . . . But, at the
> same time, the revolutionary course of human soci-
> eties is not independent of the actions of men. It
> stagnates, retreats or advances to the extent that
> the revolutionary classes and their leaders adjust
> to the laws that govern their destiny. [32]

The retreat from moral toward material incentives in 1973 and 1974 was swift. The theses approved at the Labor Congress make this clear. "Each one must be remunerated according to the quantity and quality of his work." Bonuses for overfulfillment of work norms were reestablished; wage penalties were instituted for underfulfillment of the norms. Overtime pay was again made effective, along with payment for double shifts and docking for absenteeism. [33]

Because the value of cash was sharply restrained by extensive physical rationing of goods, preferential access to rationed goods was used as a further material stimulus. In 1973 about 100,000 television sets were given to the best workers through labor assemblies, on the basis of party and union recommendations. Refrigerators and, indeed, all electrical appliances were to be distributed through this preferential marketing system rather than sold on the open market. For those higher up in the social status system, there would be appropriate material incentives too. Medical doctors and labor union leaders would have preferential access to buy new cars, which the Cuban government, spending precious foreign exchange, would agree to import for their sake.[34] It would do little good to a medical doctor to be paid more for work overfulfillment or overtime if he could not make use of the cash; with a government commitment to import cars, and to give him preferential access, surplus cash acquires new meaning.

Cuba has not forgotten moral incentives. Workers are still exhorted to contribute unpaid labor on their own time; to volunteer to work in agriculture on the weekends, to participate in neighborhood projects, and to work harder not merely because it pays more money but because it is the right thing to do since it benefits society as a whole. But the noble experiment, repeating in economics what had been done in politics, has failed—and that failure has been acknowledged. One could tell that an era had come to an end when the official newspaper reported the following words by Fidel Castro: "If you want some good news, the comrades in the services sector have suggested a slight drop in the prices of alcoholic beverages [applause]."[35] This would have been shocking in the late 1960s when the bars were closed, and when price mechanisms were considered unworthy of a society building communism.

Cuba has differed from other communist countries in the conduct of its foreign policy too. Differences with China were the most severe, although the least ideological. The Sino-Cuban dispute began to turn for the worse in 1965, and peaked with a near-total break early in 1966. At heart it was a trade dispute, aggravated by the Chinese effort to court support within the Cuban armed forces for an anti-Soviet position. Sino-Cuban relations did not recover until the early 1970s.[36]

Differences with the Soviet Union were never so severe yet remained more important, because economically Cuba has always depended very heavily on the Soviet Union and the Eastern European countries aligned with it. The disputes with the Soviet Union on foreign policy matters fall into three categories: What should be the appropriate behavior of communists toward revolution and revolutionaries in Latin America? What should be the appropriate behavior of communist governments toward nonrevolutionary governments and

revolutionary movements? What should be the appropriate behavior
of developed communist countries toward less developed countries
generally, and toward Cuba in particular?

The Cuban position, articulated by Fidel Castro, held that the
duty of revolutionaries was to make revolution. "Let no one harbor
any illusions about seizing power by peaceful means in any country
of this continent." The fundamental way to make a revolution is
through armed struggle, "to which the other forms of struggle must
be subordinated." In the long run, the armed struggle is the only way
to revolution. The test for communists in Latin America, therefore,
was whether or not they acted as revolutionaries in support of armed
struggle. Communist parties, such as those in Venezuela and Bolivia,
which retreated from or failed to commit themselves to armed struggle were soundly condemned by the Cubans. And revolutionaries engaged in armed struggle, who may or may not have called themselves
Communists, were strongly supported by the Cubans.[37] A dispute obviously arose with the Soviet Union for two different reasons. The
Soviet Union and its allied Communist parties supported electoral and
other nonviolent methods as legitimate forms of behavior for Communist parties in Europe, Latin America, and elsewhere. And the Soviet Union was loyal to those Communist parties that returned that
loyalty—whether or not they were engaged in one form of struggle or
another. Echoes of Fidel Castro's relations with the Cuban Communists in the 1950s were clearly audible.

Cuba has also differed from the Soviet Union and the Eastern
European countries on the subject of relations with nonrevolutionary
Latin American governments. Castro noted in 1968 that "we have dis-
agreed with, been displeased at, and protested against the fact that
these same [communist] countries have been drawing closer economically, culturally and politically to the oligarchic governments of Latin
America, which are not merely reactionary governments and exploiters of their peoples, but also shameless accomplices in the economic
blockade of Cuba." And earlier Castro had cried out that "if interna-
tionalism exists, if solidarity is a word worthy of respect, the least
that we can expect of any State of the socialist camp is that it refrain
from giving any financial or technical aid to those regimes."[38]

The third area of dispute was closer to the kind of dispute Cuba
had with China. Castro complained that some socialist countries
showed "tendencies toward maintaining practices of trade with the underdeveloped world which are the same practices of trade which the
developed bourgeois capitalist world maintains." Pointedly he added
that "we cannot imagine sending a bill to anyone for arms which we
give him or sending a bill to anyone for technical aid or even reminding
him of it." Cuba "on many occasions" had been sold "very outdated
factories." Castro railed against the "eagerness to sell any old junk

. . . old, outdated junk to a country which is making a revolution and has to develop."[39]

This, too, has now changed. Cuba now recognizes that there are many methods that are legitimate for communist parties and revolutionaries other than armed struggle. Cuba has been denounced by its former partners in armed struggle for turning soft on real revolution. Cuba has been reestablishing diplomatic relations with any Latin American government that is willing to do so, civilian or military, regardless of that government's internal policies—a far cry from the 1967 view that "we will only establish diplomatic relations with revolutionary governments in these countries." Even when Fidel Castro has been confronted, especially in his visit to Chile, with the embarrassment of close or improving relations with very conservative governments, he has defended this new course. And he became an eloquent defender of the Soviet Union's relations with less developed countries at the Algiers meeting of nonaligned countries in 1973. He would later state that "we do not understand the strange thesis about two alleged imperialisms presented by some leaders who consider themselves to be part of the Third World."[40]

Cuba's views have changed on these issues for a variety of reasons. The paramount one is that the central goal of the Cuban leadership in the 1970s has become internal economic development. Material incentives and Soviet assistance are crucial to achieve this goal. Reluctantly and slowly, the unorthodox policies of Cuba's revolutionary government have been abandoned. As unorthodoxy fades into history, Cuba may be becoming more and more a communist country with but minor differences in ideology from other such countries. It still differs from other communist countries, of course, by level of modernization. But the ideological thrust that had made Cuba peculiar, perhaps unique, and certainly attractive to many non-Communists in many countries, is now rapidly becoming a feature of the past.

CONCLUSIONS

Socialist ideology in Cuba has come from the gut, from the experiences of a few people in insurgency and government, far more than from theoretical speculation. Cuba's version of socialist ideology has emphasized voluntaristic or subjectivist strains, the pursuit of maximalist or apparently unreachable goals, and activism under elitist leadership. Precisely because of the weight of recent experience, some of the more extreme features of this version of socialism have been toned down. Cuba's leadership still scorns brainy economists and reaches for the stars, but it is now more committed to building a material base to get there. Willful men can still shape the course of history, though they may not determine it.

Though the coming of socialism to Cuba was almost an historical accident, the sinking of roots was not. Cubans had been accustomed to widespread regulation of the economy by government, and to
widespread political participation. Through socialism they would get
far more government control over the economy, and far more government control over political participation. But these two crucial features of socialism in Cuba—the expansion and concentration of the
amount of power available to the government, and the growth and regulation of political participation—found some fertile ground in old
Cuba. There were profound differences in this regard between the
prerevolutionary and revolutionary political systems, but the elements
of continuity cannot be ignored.

While admitting that Cuba has acquired a reputation for being an
international heretic in the communist community, we have argued
here that Cuba has in fact always exhibited a number of significant
ideological commonalities with other communist countries. There
have been differences in degree and in timing, but no fundamental differences concerning the role of leadership, organizations, collectivization, and efforts toward transforming political culture to enable
citizens to cope with the ordeal of change.

In addition to the differences in degree and timing, there have
also been more fundamental differences that arose out of both ideology
and delayed modernization. The chief difference arising from the
latter is the predominance of agriculture in Cuba's present and future.
The former amounted to a Cuban effort to implement the future, to
bring about communism, and to skip the "transitional socialist period."
Cuba sought international autonomy in a still hostile world. The future, however, was not to be hurried. The implementation of a socialist utopia proved so much of a burden that the project was abandoned by the mid-1970s. It has become increasingly difficult, therefore, to find ideological differences between Cuba and the Soviet Union
—though Cuba certainly continues to differ from the more modernized
communist countries.

The prospects for Cuba then are orthodox socialism, international dependence, and further efforts toward modernization. It is
possible that Cuba's organizational infrastructure will gradually become institutionalized, but this requires more time for evaluation.
The revolution itself, however, appears quite permanent. Though
not all of the members of the revolutionary mass organizations have
in fact "voted with their feet" to show that they want the regime to
continue, undoubtedly many have intended to do precisely that.
Though there is still evidence of protest in Cuba, especially over
shortages of consumer goods and excessive mobilizations for more
and more work, [41] these protests are increasingly depoliticized.
Cubans want food and shelter now, regardless of the government's

ideology. Efforts by Cuban exiles to overthrow the government, or
by internal groups to revolt, have been decreasing steadily since the
mid-1960s, and by the mid-1970s have become the exception rather
than the rule.

Socialism in Cuba is thus likely to continue. The youthful guts
of yesterday are the aging guts of today (Fidel Castro was born in
1927). If the prognosis is for continuation, it is also for more dull-
ness. Socialism in Cuba may always have more flair than socialism
in Moscow, but the ideological convergence with the Soviet Union of
the first half of the 1970s is unmistakable. There may be new differences ahead between tropical and Siberian communism, but we will
have to learn what the Cuban leadership has learned—to let the future
come along in its own good time.

NOTES

1. Theodore Draper, Castroism: Theory and Practice (New
York: Praeger Publishers, 1965), p. 52 and passim.

2. Nelson Valdes and Rolando Bonachea, "Fidel Castro y la
Politica Estudiantil de 1947," Aportes 22 (October 1971).

3. Grupo de Propaganda Doctrinal Ortodoxa, Doctrina del Par-
tido Ortodoxo (Havana: P. Fernandez y Cia., 1951), pp. 3, 62.

4. Loree Wilkerson, Fidel Castro's Political Programs from
Reformism to Marxism-Leninism (Gainesville: University of Florida
Press, 1965).

5. Andres Suarez, Cuba: Castroism and Communism (Cambridge: Massachusetts Institute of Technology Press, 1967), pp. 11-
29.

6. For reports on U.S. private investments in Cuba, trends
through time and composition, see U.S. Bureau of Foreign Commerce,
Department of Commerce, Investment in Cuba (Washington, D.C.:
U.S. Government Printing Office, 1956), p. 10; Fulgencio Batista,
Piedras y Leyes (Mexico: Ediciones Botas, 1961), p. 415. For Castro's shift in connection with his trip to the United States, see among
others, Revolucion, April 3, 1959, p. 1; April 10, 1959, p. 2; April
17, 1959, p. 15.

7. For a contrary view, however, see Maurice Zeitlin and
Robert Scheer, Cuba: Tragedy of a Hemisphere (New York: Grove
Press, 1961); and William Appleman Williams, The United States,
Cuba and Castro (New York: Monthly Review Press, 1961).

8. Philip W. Bonsal, Cuba, Castro and the United States (Pittsburgh: University of Pittsburgh Press, 1971), pp. 42-48, 70-76;
Revolucion, March 6, 1959, p. 1.

9. From Lewis Feuer, ed., Marx and Engels (Garden City:
Doubleday Anchor Books, 1959), pp. 43, 245.

10. For another approach with a generally similar judgment, see Edward Gonzalez, Cuba under Castro: The Limits of Charisma (Boston: Houghton Mifflin, 1974), p. 83.

11. Suarez, op. cit., pp. 38-43, 55-63, 72-75; and Edward Gonzalez, "Castro's Revolution, Cuban Communist Appeals, and the Soviet Response," World Politics 21, no. 1 (October 1968).

12. Agustin Ravelo Narino, El Contrato de Arrendamiento de Finca Rustica en la Legislacion Cubana (Santiago, Cuba: Tipografia San Ramon, 1956); Eduardo Varona Martinez and Rafael Gonzalez Labrada, El Colono (Havana: Impresores Ucar, Garcia S.A., 1958); Oscar Seiglie y Llata, El Contrato de Arrendamiento de Finca Rustica, el Latifundio y la Legislacion Azucarera (Havana: Editorial Lex, 1953); Isidro Vilches Gonzalez, Derecho Cubano del Trabajo (Havana: Jesus Montero, 1948); Leopoldo Horrego Estuch, Legislacion Social de Cuba (Havana: Editorial Libreria Selecta, 1948); Efren Cordova Cordoves, "Problemas Actuales de la Intervencion del Estado en la Economia Laboral Cubana," Anuario de la Facultad de Ciencias Sociales y Derecho Publico (Havana: Universidad de la Habana, 1955-56); International Bank for Reconstruction and Development, Report on Cuba (Washington, D.C.: International Bank for Reconstruction and Development, 1951); and Cuban Economic Research Project, A Study on Cuba (Coral Gables, Fla.: University of Miami Press, 1965).

13. Enrique A. Baloyra, Political Leadership in the Cuban Republic, 1944-1958 (Gainesville: University of Florida, unpublished dissertation, 1971), pp. 125-27, 152.

14. Universidad Central "Marta Abreu" de las Villas, La Educacion Rural en las Villas (Havana: Impresores Ucar, Garcia S.A., 1959), pp. 123, 152.

15. For the early plan for moderate expansion of the government's economic role, see Regino Boti and Felipe Pazos, "Algunos Aspectos del Desarrollo Economico de Cuba," Revista Bimestre 75 (July-December 1958).

16. Two authors who disagree on many points but agree on this one are Suarez, op. cit., and Lee Lockwood, Castro's Cuba, Cuba's Fidel (New York: Macmillan Company, 1967).

17. Jorge I. Dominguez, "Sectoral Clashes in Cuban Politics and Development," Latin American Research Review 6, no. 3 (Fall 1971): 66.

18. See, for example, Ernst Halperin, "Foreword," in Suarez, op. cit.; and Gonzalez, op. cit., pp. 83, 147; but see however pp. 163-67, 179, 220-21 for an alternative view.

19. Revolucion, October 14, 1959, p. 1; October 17, 1959, p. 1; October 19, 1959, p. 2; November 23, 1959, p. 4.

20. For evidence on the foundation of mass organizations, see Revolucion, July 27, 1961; January 14, 1963, p. 4; August 24, 1964,

p. 5; Cesar Escalante, "Las Comites de Defensa de la Revolucion," Cuba Socialista 1 (September 1961); Adolfo Rivero, "La Union de Jovenes Comunistas de Cuba," ibid., no. 12 (August 1962); Antero Regalado, "Cinco Anos de Vida de la ANAP," ibid., no. 57 (May 1966).

21. Richard Fagen, The Transformation of Political Culture in Cuba (Stanford, Calif.: Stanford University Press, 1969), p. 77 and 69-103 passim on the Committees; Antonio Nunez Jimenez, "Revolucion Agraria en Cuba," INRA 2, no. 6 (June 1961); Peter S. H. Tang and Joan Maloney, The Chinese Communist Impact on Cuba (Chestnut Hill, Mass.: Research Institute on the Sino-Soviet Bloc, 1962), p. 26; and computations from Granma Weekly Review, January 10, 1971, p. 9; October 4, 1970, p. 2; February 28, 1971, p. 2; and August 29, 1971, p. 8.

22. See Fidel Castro's speech launching the purge in Revolucion, March 27, 1962; see also Joel Domenech, "Experiencias del Trabajo de Reestructuracion y Depuracion de las ORI de la Habana," Cuba Socialista 10 (June 1962).

23. Granma Weekly Review, May 11, 1969, p. 8 on the Committees; October 4, 1970, p. 2 on labor; December 17, 1967, p. 10 on the students.

24. On the remaining private sector in agriculture, "Notas Economicas: Nueva Luz sobre la Agricultura Privada," Cuba Socialista 40 (December 1964); for a flavor of the supercollectivist spirit expressed in the 1968 nationalizations, see Castro's speech launching the "revolutionary offensive" in Granma Weekly Review, March 24, 1968.

25. Jose Yglesias, In the Fist of the Revolution: Life in a Cuban Country Town (New York: Vintage Books, 1968), p. 307.

26. Revolucion, December 9, 1964, p. 1; see also, for example, Ernesto (Che) Guevara, "Man and Socialism in Cuba" in Bertram Silverman, ed., Man and Socialism in Cuba (New York: Atheneum, 1971), p. 352.

27. Richard Fagen, "The Cuban Revolution: Enemies and Friends," in David Finlay, Ole Holsti, and Richard Fagen, Enemies in Politics (Chicago: Rand McNally, 1967), pp. 184, 214-15, 225-30.

28. Dominguez, op. cit., pp. 67-69.

29. Bette A. Evans, The Moral Versus Material Incentives Controversy in Cuba (Pittsburgh: University of Pittsburgh, unpublished dissertation, 1973), pp. 94, 148. See also Robert M. Bernardo, The Theory of Moral Incentives in Cuba (Tuscaloosa, Ala.: University of Alabama Press, 1971).

30. Granma Weekly Review, July 16, 1967, p. 3.

31. Ibid., July 28, 1968, p. 4.

32. Ibid., November 25, 1973, p. 7, and August 5, 1973, pp. 2, 5.

33. Ibid., September 2, 1973, pp. 8-9.

34. Ibid., November 25, 1973, pp. 10-11.

35. Idem., p. 10.

36. Granma, January 3, 1966, p. 4; January 12, 1966, p. 4; and Granma Weekly Review, March 14, 1971, p. 1.

37. Two of the more important statements are Fidel Castro's attack on the Venezuelan Communist Party, Politica International 5, no. 17 (First Quarter, 1967): 249-78, and his closing speech before the Latin American Solidarity Organization on August 10, 1967, Granma Weekly Review, August 20, 1967, esp. pp. 3-5.

38. Granma Weekly Review, August 25, 1968, p. 4; and ibid., August 20, 1967, p. 5. See also July 31, 1966, p. 11.

39. Granma Weekly Review, August 25, 1968, pp. 2-3. For a stronger, earlier statement by Ernesto (Che) Guevara, Revolucion, December 15, 1964, p. 2.

40. Jorge I. Dominguez, "Taming the Cuban Shrew," Foreign Policy 10 (Spring 1973); Politica Internacional 5, no. 17 (First Quarter, 1967): 272; Granma Weekly Review, August 1, 1971, p. 6; December 19, 1971, p. 15; August 5, 1973, p. 4; September 16, 1973, p. 12.

41. For example, Verde Olivo 9, no. 12 (March 24, 1968): 5; Granma, September 8, 1970, p. 5.

PART

II

MIDDLE EAST

3

SOCIALISM
IN SYRIA
George Lenczowski

To speak of socialism in the Arab world is to move in an area
of many uncertainties. This is so because the political orientation and
practice described as Arab socialism by its adherents lacks the con-
ceptual clairty characteristic of such well-defined systems as democracy or communism, and also because one may see in it only a convenient term to mask or disguise other more fundamental phenomena.
Socialism as a slogan, and as a semantical symbol designed to
convey the idea of change from the traditional and capitalistic society
into a new and different one, has been espoused by several groups in
Syria. In addition to the Communist Party with its profession of a
specific brand of socialism, at least four other groups proclaimed a
socialist orientation: Akram Hourani's Arab Socialist Party; a broad
agglomeration known as the Nasserites; another pro-Cairo group, the
Socialists-Unionists; and the Baath Party. These groups had come
into being at different times beginning with the late 1940s; all of them
could be identified by the 1960s; and all were in evidence, after a
checkered history of development and partial suppression, in the
1970s.
Of the four non-Communist groups professing socialism, the
Baath stood out as the most prominent. Founded in 1947 as the Arab
Renaissance (ba'th) Party by two secondary schoolteachers, Michel
Aflaq, a Christian, and Salaheddin al-Bitar, a Sunni Moslem, it
merged in 1953 with Hourani's Arab Socialists to form the Arab Socialist Renaissance Party (hizb al-arabi al-ba'th al-ishtiraki).[1] With
the passage of time, it outdistanced its socialist and communist rivals
and emerged as the dominant revolutionary force in Syria. This success could be ascribed to a combination of ideology and manipulative
skills. Its ideology, of which more will be said later, comprised
three main themes that evoked positive response in major segments

of Syrian society: nationalism, unity, and socialism. Nationalism
was the credo of the day in the Third World in the days following
World War II, and Syria was no exception. It carried with it a dual
notion of anticolonialism—important for a freshly emancipated country—and state-building on the basis of national solidarity rather than
according to Islamic tradition. It conveyed the idea of both freedom
and modernity. Unity was the cherished ideal of progressive Arab
nationalists everywhere: instead of division into many smaller states,
the one large Arab nation stretching from the Gulf to the Atlantic
should have a unified political form as either a unitary or a federated
state. Division was believed to be the nefarious product of imperialism and of local vested interests of reactionary nature. Unity would
have the merit of doing away with both. And, finally, socialism was
a notion in which many discontented elements, particularly among the
intelligentsia, believed as a way that would assure the twin goals of
development and social justice. By espousing these three themes,
the Baath outmaneuvered other left-wing groups that either lacked or
did not emphasize enough one or more of the themes in question. On
the manipulative side, the Baath blazed the trail and won strong influence in the two sectors that proved strategic in Syrian politics: the
schools and the army. As teachers, the two Baath founders had an
obvious advantage of access to their would-be recruits in comparison
with their rivals. Of particular importance was the Baath penetration
of the Homs Military Academy.

THE PARTY HISTORY: A SUMMARY

Since its founding in 1947, the Baath strove consistently to rally
around itself the younger have-not elements in Syria and to preach a
radical change in economy as well as in international and inter-Arab
relations. In spite of insistence on its revolutionary character, the
Baath advocated, in its early stages, liberalism expressed by such
devices as a multiparty system, genuine parliamentarism, and the
freedoms usually associated with the notion of political democracy.
Its beginnings were not easy: in its first phase (1947-55) it had to
contend with two well-entrenched conventional parties of Syria, the
National Party (hizb al-watani) and the People's Party (hizb al-sha'b),
both of which were dominated by influential leaders who had initially
gained fame as fighters for independence from the French rule. During that same period, the party was confronted with an interlude of
conservatively inclined military rule under the successive leadership
of Husni Zaim, Sami Hinnawi, and Adib Shishakli. During the second phase (1955-61), the conventional party system in Syria suffered
considerable erosion and new, nonconventional forces began emerging.

These, in addition to the Baath itself, comprised the Moslem Brotherhood, the Communists, the Syrian National Social Party (SNSP—hizb
al-suri al qaumi al-ijtima'i), and the other socialist groups previously
referred to. Their common denominator was that all of them rejected
to a greater or lesser extent the legitimacy of the Syrian political
system and all preached the need for a new dispensation to be based
on entirely new foundations. Beyond that, profound differences divided
them: while the Communists advocated a class struggle mixed with
certain tactics designed to win followers in an ex-colonial nation, the
SNSP fought for a distinct Syrian identity to be realized through unity
of the Fertile Crescent, and the Moslem Brethren agitated for a revival of an Islamic theocratic state.

The nonconventional forces proved to be a formidable obstacle
to the Baath forward march and mid-1950s were the years of great
turbulence and intensive political struggles. In 1955-56 the Baath
formed a virtual alliance with the Nasserites and accepted an occasional cooperation of the Communists in their joint effort to discredit
the right-wing and pro-Western elements. A showdown with SNSP in
1956 resulted in the rout of the latter, while the left-wing coalitions
formed in various electoral contests produced local victories of the
Baath candidates as against their rivals. With a representation of
some 23 deputies in a 150-man parliament by 1956-67, the Baath began to wield influence out of proportion to its numbers. By that time
the party also secured a few cabinet posts, including that of the minister of foreign affairs. But its position was tenuous because many of
its successes were due, first, to the support of the Nasserites and
Communists, and second to the favorable international developments.
As for the latter, the years 1955 to 1957 witnessed aggravation in
both Arab-Israeli relations and Arab-Western relations. The Ban-
dung Conference, the Soviet-Egyptian arms deal of 1955, the Aswan
Dam crisis and the Suez War of 1956, and finally the Eisenhower Doctrine of 1957 provided an international environment in which militant
nationalists and left-wing radicals found tremendous new opportunities
to surge forward in internal politics of many Arab countries. While
this helped greatly the Baath, it also permitted the Communists to
make marked advances. By mid-1957, the Baath leadership found to
its alarm that its Communist allies waxed so much in strength as to
be able to seize power in Syria if no quick resistance was offered.
Symptomatic of this situation was the appointment of General Afif
Bizri, an avowed Communist, to the post of Army Chief-of-Staff.[2]

Under the circumstances, the Baath had only two alternatives:
to reverse its position and enter into a coalition with the right-wing
elements, or to appeal to Nasser to achieve union between Syria and
Egypt and thus save Syria from Communism while promoting the ideal
of Arab unity. It is this latter course that the party chose and in early

1958 union was proclaimed. Of course the Baath, being a minority
party in the parliament, could not have accomplished this feat unaided.
Other elements, moderate and conservative, joined it and so did the
army, already working in close cooperation with the party. This was
probably the last time the Baath strove in a parallel direction with
the Syrian bourgeoisie. And while Syria's merchants and landowners
did not particularly admire Nasser, they preferred him to an outright
Communist rule.

In thus bringing Syria to Nasser "on a silver platter," the Baath
had to accept some painful conditions: the state was to be unitary
rather than federal and Syria's parliamentary system together with
all the political parties was to be abolished. To the Baath, which in
the meantime had established branches in other Arab countries, this
meant that its central organization in Damascus had to disappear
while its dependent extremities were to be kept alive—a situation full
of paradox and with a potential for fraud and complications. By the
same token, the Baath could not hope to act as a collective "viceroy"
for Nasser in Syria; at the most its leaders as individuals were eligible to fill the positions of power by Nasser's appointment.

In thus effecting the union with Egypt, the Baath did contribute
to the curbing of the Communist danger in Syria, but its own hopes
for a strategic role in the union and—via Cairo—in Arab affairs in
general were dashed. In fact, after a brief period of "honeymoon"
with Nasser, most of the Baathist ministers in the union cabinet in
Cairo or in the executive council in Damascus resigned or were dismissed and Nasser continued to rule Syria through his own men he
trusted.

For various reasons, of which more will be said later, the
Syro-Egyptian union broke down in September 1961 and Syria reemerged as a separate country. Its preunion parliamentary system
was restored, but no firm center of power emerged. The conditions
bordered on chaos: on the one hand there was much recrimination
against the dictatorial ways and abuses of the Nasser period; on the
other, a generation of Syrian politicians brought up in the spirit of
worship for the idea of union (an Arab version of "motherhood") felt
a sense of guilt following the separation and tended to be apologetic
about it. Nor was the restoration of the parliamentary life perfect:
political parties ("a divisive force" according to Nasser's Pan-Arab
credo) hovered in the limbo of uncertainty as to their legality while
various ambitious army groups tended to interfere in the political
process. It was clearly a period of moral-political vacuum, of
timidity on the part of the democratic-liberal leaders, and of collective self-doubt.

The Baath, to its relief, did not have to pay the penalty for all
these developments, perhaps because of the resignation of its leaders

from government in the early period of the union. Thus the party as a whole could not be blamed for the abuses of the Nasser era and did not have to bear special responsibility for separation. Profiting from this relative immunity from criticism, the Baath took quick measures to revive its organization in both the civil and the military sector. By the early spring of 1963 it was ready for action and, in a coup executed with the aid of the army on March 8, it assumed power. The constitution and parliament were abolished, a Revolutionary Command Council was established under an army general, and the party's highest collective organs became the major if not exclusive source of power in the country.

With the coup of 1963, the Baath definitely transformed itself from the party of opposition to a party wielding authority in Syria. The period when it exercised power could be divided into three phases: the phase of moderate leadership, 1963-66, exercised largely by one of the party's founders, Bitar, and his close friends; the phase of militant left-wing leadership identified especially with the person of General Salah Jadid, 1966-70; and the third phase, beginning in November 1970, under the leadership of General Hafez al-Assad and characterized by a retreat from some of the most extreme positions of the preceding period.

The Baath era in Syria's life since 1963 was replete with major domestic and international developments: these included certain ·drastic economic transformations, the assertion of dictatorial control of the Baath over opposition forces, the accentuation of Syria's sovereignty as against union with Egypt, establishment of close links with the Soviet Bloc, and the occurrence of two wars with Israel, in 1967 and 1973.

The exercise of power transformed the Baath at least in one important respect: from a party professing a belief in the democratic process it changed into a party of definite authoritarian character, which, moreover, closely intermingled with the army to produce to all practical purposes a military dictatorship.

ORGANIZATION

Although originating in Syria, the Baath was conceived from the beginning as an all-Arab party in conformance with its view of the Arabs as a single nation. Consequently, the party formed branches in Jordan, Iraq, and Lebanon and smaller, often clandestine, groups in other countries. In principle, every Arab country was looked upon as a potential arena for party activity. In practice, certain revolutionary states with ideologies akin to that of the Baath were exempted, notably Egypt and Algeria. On the other hand, the patriarchal-style

monarchies of the Arabian Peninsula also proved an unpropitious
ground for the Baath, hence its adherents there were few and acting
in secrecy.

The Jordanian organization was the first major one outside Syria. It took part in the elections of 1956 within the framework of the
left-wing popular front and it saw two of its leaders assume cabinet
positions, one in charge of foreign affairs (Abdullah Rimawi). The
Iraqi branch suffered a degree of suppression under the Hashimite
monarchy but it was prominent enough at the time of the revolution in
1958 to earn a cabinet position for one of its leaders (Fuad Rikabi).
The Lebanese organization was smaller and limited in its potential
owing to the special nature of Lebanon's political system. But it was
important to the party because it operated in a free country and could
provide reserve cadres, communication facilities, and asylum from
persecution to those members in Syria, Iraq, and Jordan who for one
reason or another had to leave their native countries.

The spread of the party to countries outside Syria caused it to
adopt an organization consonant with this expansion. Thus in each
country there was a "regional" organization with a pyramidal form,
consisting of the cells at the bottom, with local and provincial units
above, and the central authority called the Regional Command (qiyadah al-qutriyah). (In the party vocabulary a region meant a country.)
The supreme authority above the regional organizations was called
the National Command (qiyadah al-qaumiyah). The "democratic"
principle was served by the presence of the national and regional
congresses called at somewhat irregular intervals.

The cell system at the bottom of the pyramid was dictated by
the needs of the early, semiclandestine phase. With the party's advent to power in 1963 such a need ceased to exist, yet the party did
not change its basic structure. It is interesting, however, to note
that the aura of secrecy clung to the party even though there was no
apparent justification for it. Thus when on March 8, 1963, following
their coup, the Baath and the military established the National Council of Revolutionary Command, neither the names of its members nor
their number were made public. This truly fantastic situation in the
annals of history, in which the people were not even informed about
the identity of their rulers, prevailed for two weeks until March 24,
when finally General Louai Atassi was revealed as the president of
the Council. More time was to pass until the names of other members
were disclosed.

For a long time, the most influential role in the National Command was played by the party's two founders, Aflaq and Bitar. Bitar,
more a man of action, was Syria's foreign minister just prior to the
merger with Egypt. Following the party's advent to power in 1963
he formed several cabinets as prime minister. Aflaq had held a cab-

inet position only once for a short time during Colonel Hinnawi's ephemeral rule in 1949. Subsequently he dedicated himself primarily to the education and indoctrination task and became the party's chief ideologist. During the period of their dominant influence in the party (until 1966), membership of the National (or Pan-Arab) Command and that of the Regional (Syrian) Command partly overlapped. By the mid-1960s the two memberships became clearly distinct (with an occasional exception) and on February 23, 1966, the rivalry between the National and the Regional Commands led to a "palace" coup by the latter, the dispersal of the National Command, and the eventual flight and sentencing in absentia of the party's two founders, Aflaq and Bitar. By that time (since February 8, 1963) the Baath was also in power in Iraq but the two branches were critical of each other and by 1966 were in a mutual state of open hostility. Because each tried to prove its legitimacy, both claimed recognition by the National Command. But the National Command recognized by the Iraqi organization (and including for some time the deposed leaders Aflaq and Bitar) was different from the National Command set up by the victorious regional Syrian leaders. In other words, by 1966 the inter-Arab Baath organization had lost its unity, and deep personal and political divisions separated its regional branches.

Of the two types of congresses, the national and the regional, it was the national that, at least until 1966, were more significant and more frequent. Of these, the Sixth National Congress held in Damascus in the fall of 1963 was particularly important inasmuch as it codified new rules and adopted a comprehensive new program with new ideological accents. It was only after the victory of the regional Syrian leadership in 1966 that the Syrian regional congresses came into prominence with their meaningful debates and resolutions.

IDEOLOGY AND PROGRAM

The party's ideology may be conceived as a configuration of concentric circles. The innermost circle contains the most generalized fundamental principles, which amount to no more than a symbolic slogan of "unity, freedom, and socialism" with some additional glossary for these terms. Further, larger circles contain more elaboration of "theoretical" concepts until, finally, the largest outer circle provides considerable detail for proposed policies and, therefore, may be regarded as a program derivative from ideology.

The Baath ideology was elaborated in a number of writings by its founder, Michel Aflaq, and other leaders,[3] as well as in various resolutions of the party congresses and manifestos issued by the national and regional commands. Of all these documents, three stand out as particularly important inasmuch as they represent collective thinking at certain strategic moments of the party's history: the constitution of the Baath adopted at its first official congress in 1947 the resolutions of the Sixth National Congress of October 1963 and the Phased Program adopted by the Syrian Regional Congress in March 1965 and made public in July of that year. These consecutive documents not only reveal an evolution in the ideology but also reflect the political changes in the party's status and position in Syria and the Arab world at large.

The party's constitution of 1947 proclaimed three "fundamental principles" defined as (1) unity and freedom of the Arab nation within the Arab homeland; (2) a belief in the special character of the Arab nation expressed in repeated awakenings, inventiveness, and vitality; and (3) a belief in a special mission of the Arab nation, namely promotion of humanitarianism, which, ipso facto, conveyed the idea of opposition to colonialism. [4]

The Baath Party in its mission to achieve these fundamental principles was described as universal Arab, nationalist, socialist, populist, and revolutionary.

The statement of fundamental principles was followed by a program embracing the domestic and foreign sectors. In the domestic sector, the constitution advocated a representative and constitutional system of government; respect for freedoms of speech and assembly within the limits of the Arab nationalist ideology; an affirmation that the national bond was the only legitimate one as against the denominational, tribal, or regional; that there should be equality before the law and a single legislative code (as opposed to the traditional Islamic-Ottoman plurality of legal orders).

In the economic sphere, the constitution stipulated the need for agrarian reform; nationalization of public utilities, natural resources, large-scale industries and transportation; associating the workers in the management of factories; acceptance of nonexploitative private ownership and inheritance; promotion of unions of workers and peasants; and uprooting of nomadism.

In the foreign sector, the program was very brief and generalized: promotion of peace and harmony among nations and abrogation of unequal treaties.

The constitution thus worded reflected the current reality in Syria: first, the Baath Party as a party of opposition with its insistence on representative government and freedoms; second, a search for basic group identity by rejection of other than national (Pan-Arab) ties; third, a reformist rather than a truly revolutionary nature of the party itself, with its avoidance of references to class struggle and its acceptance of the public and private sectors in economy; and fourth, the fresh postcolonial stage in the history of Syria and the neighboring

Arab countries, with the references to harmful treaties that were still binding some of these countries to the imperial powers. The word "socialism" was used sparingly and inconspicuously; in fact, it was not yet included in the party's formal title. It was an ideology and a program in which emphasis on all-Arab nationalist ties and destiny definitely overshadowed the notion of socialism.

THE SIXTH NATIONAL CONGRESS

After the Baath Party's merger with Hourani's Socialist Party and also following Nasser's revolution in Egypt, both the socialist and the radical accents in the party's ideology became more conspicuous. Following its assumption of power by a coup in both Syria and Iraq in 1963, the party was ready for a fundamental review and codification of its doctrinal foundations and practical program. Within some six months of its advent to power the party held its Sixth National (Pan-Arab) Congress in Damascus, October 5-23, 1963. By that time the party had become enriched by the experience of its initial struggle for power within the constitutional framework of the Syrian Republic, the union with Egypt and the trauma of its dissolution, and the first months of wielding power following the coups of February 8 and March 8, 1963, in Iraq and Syria respectively. These experiences found their reflection in the resolutions of the Congress. The resolutions, which contained detailed provisions absent from the original constitution, were divided into the following six sections, themselves indicative of considerable change in the party's outlook and status since 1947: (1) The Party; (2) Revolutionary Transformation; (3) Economy; (4) Political Structure; (5) Inter-Arab Relations; (6) International Policies.[5] The tenor of the resolutions reflected, first of all, the fact that the Baath had turned from a party of opposition into a ruling party that began to be beset by problems associated with the exercise of power. Moreover, because seizure of power was accomplished with the aid of the army, a new major issue of accommodating the military within the framework of ideology and practice had to be faced. Last but not least, the party had traveled a long road from its early moderation toward a pronounced radicalism, which unmistakably betrayed a strong infusion of Marxist thinking in both its concepts and its terminology.

The Party

It was, in fact, symptomatic of this new trend that the resolutions began with the central issue of the party and its role in the state

and society. The resolutions proclaimed the principle of collective
leadership, partly in response to the one--man authoritarianism of the
Nasserite type during the union (1958-61); it also advanced the principle of democratic centralism in a clear reflection of communist theory
and practice. Workers and peasants were declared to constitute not
only the base of the revolution but of the party as well—a provision
reminiscent of the frequent exhortations of the Soviet Communist Party
to broaden the party's base and reduce its bureaucratic character.
By the same token, an appeal was made to guard against the infiltration by opportunist elements, to prevent a relapse into a bourgeois
orientation, and to stress the members' responsibilities as against
privileges. The resolutions, furthermore, insisted on a distinction
between the party and the state and warned against individual interference of the members in the affairs of the state; it was the party itself,
declared the text, that "is the commander of power." It was clear
that a mere six months in power brought about enough corruption and
temptations to cause such strong admonitions. This first section
ended by referring to theory: the party was to be guided by two fundamental principles of scientism and revolution within the national framework.

Revolutionary Transformation

The aim, said the text, was a socialist transformation of society
on the "democratic basis" and with participation of popular masses.
The new, Marxist influence was reflected in the statement that the
bourgeois class was incapable of playing a positive economic role and
that it had become an ally of new imperialism. In the first stage, the
text proclaimed, the socialist revolution was to be accomplished by
the workers, peasants, revolutionary intellectuals both military and
civilian, and by the petty bourgeoisie. (No mention was made of the
second and further stages.) Reference to the "military intellectuals"
(as well as placing them before the civilians in the order of enumera-
tion) provided an eloquent clue to the party's need to share power with
the military.

Economy

The third section proclaimed the "democratic and workers' control of the means of production" thus reflecting perhaps Tito's brand
of communism. It also stressed the need for an agrarian revolution
with the aim of forming collective farms to be governed by the peasants.
And again indicative of the dilemmas of power, the text lamented the

"crying contradiction between the pomp and prodigality" of the state agencies and the standard of living of the popular masses. This section concluded with a vow to "liquidate" (again an expression borrowed from the Soviet vocabulary) the private sector in medicine.

Political Structure

The fourth section dealt, significantly, with three issues reflecting the party's new status of dominance. First, a newly created paramilitary organization called the National Guard was proclaimed to be the "citadel for the protection of the revolution." The Guard was to be developed and enlarged; at the same time the party was enjoined to act energetically against any error committed "by certain members" of the Guard. (The "errors" in question were well-known cases of illegal search and arrest, intimidation, beating, invading private vehicles and homes, looting, and rape. The National Guard, initially joined by idealistic students, soon turned into a haven for ordinary thugs and the "lumpenproletariat.") The second issue dealt with was that of the political freedoms. Now that the party found itself in power, the early demand contained in its 1947 Constitution for a truly democratic constitutional process had to be abandoned. Such bourgeois democratic freedoms were clearly a luxury the party could not now afford, considering that its advent to power was by means of a military coup. Hence the text proclaimed freedom of association for the popular masses and specifically mentioned "the workers', students', professional and women's organizations within the framework of the nationalist and socialist line." The third issue was that of the role of the army. The army was to undergo a doctrinary instruction and the text proclaimed the need of fusion of the "military and civil revolutionary vanguards."

Inter-Arab Relations

The fifth section began with the announcement that a decision about the unity of Syria and Iraq (both then ruled by the Baath) had been reached. Beyond this bilateral unity, a comprehensive Arab unity was to be achieved as an ultimate objective. Egypt was declared as the next (third) partner for such a unity on three conditions: acceptance of democracy, regional equality, and collective command. The word "command" rather than leadership again indicated the influence of military categories of thought on the framers of these resolutions.

Inter-Arab relations were not to be limited to the spread of
unity. A struggle was to be waged against the reactionary regimes
in the Arab world, with Morocco, Jordan, and the regimes of the
Arabian Peninsula singled out as targets. The text contained a specific call for the use of force against the Jordanian regime. In a
somewhat repetitious statement, the text stated that Nasser's regime
could be accepted into the union as "a simple associate, but not as a
base" because of its individualist and dictatorial nature. This chapter
was concluded with a call for the liberation of Palestine and for the
creation of a general progressive Arab front.

International Relations

International relations was the topic of the final (sixth) section.
The party was enjoined to observe the following principles and policies: alliance with liberation movements, nonalignment, special
friendship with the "socialist camp," solidarity with the Third World,
positive neutralism, and opposition to racial discrimination.

THE PHASED PROGRAM

The third major document in the party's ideological evolution
was the Phased Program proclaimed in July 1965 by the Baath Regional
Command in Syria. In contrast to the resolutions of 1963, the program was not a national but a regional (Syrian) product. It reflected
the growing power and influence of the Syrian leadership of the party
as against the all-Arab National Command and also the further accentuation of the radical trends. The title "Phased Program" was something of a puzzle because the document did not state clearly how many
and of what nature the specific phases were to be. On the contrary,
in its lengthy elaborations it left the reader guessing as to the priorities. Many of its provisions were inevitably repetitive of the 1963
resolutions and need not be reproduced here. Like its predecessor,
the program was divided into sections; these, however, were grouped
in a different sequence and were preceded by a lengthy ideological
preamble. A number of concepts earlier developed or adumbrated by
the party were now expressed with perhaps a greater precision and
force.[6]
In the paragraphs that follow we will limit our remarks only to
those specific points on which the Phased Program clearly introduced
new formulations as compared with the preceding documents. Thus,
while reasserting the slogan of "unity, freedom, and socialism," the
program declared them to be only the "remote" (ultimate) aims to be

attained when a "radical transformation in the structure of society" has taken place. Socialism was defined as assuring justice in the distribution of wealth and providing a rapid way to economic development. Freedom was to be realized by the "popular democracy," the latter to be established by a vanguard party and to differ, because of its reliance on popular masses, from the "bourgeois democracy and conventional institutions."

As for Arab unity, the program made it clear that unity was strongly linked with revolutionary change as a corollary. While diplomatic action (such as intergovernmental agreements) was useful in attaining unity, it should be accompanied by revolutionary action, with special attention to popular organizations. To achieve the necessary revolutionary transformation, the party required power both to work against the obstacles and to quell the conspiracies of the opposition. Moreover, the party had to have a "scientific" concept of reality.

The program elaborated extensively on the concept of "popular democracy," to be based on the productive masses of the people. Because the party represented the will of the people, it was the party that must govern. The existing phase was described as one calling for special sacrifices and efforts.

In the economic sphere, sacrifices and efforts meant rapid industrialization and increases in production, both involving state-diverted savings and a struggle against excessive consumption. The program advanced the principle of "total planned economy," full employment, and the establishment of a socialist agrarian sector in the form of both collective and state farms, the latter being an innovation over the earlier concepts. In turn, economy in general was to be divided into four sectors: public, cooperative, mixed, and private. The public sector, however, was to be enlarged and strengthened and was to assume the dominant position. The program specifically referred to the first Five-Year Plan (1961-65) as an instrument for the achievement of the economic goals.

In the sector of foreign relations, the old principles were reaffirmed, with this innovation—that collaboration with the "socialist" countries (countries of the Communist Bloc) was henceforth to be conducted not only on official but also on "popular levels" (meaning in practice mutual visits and joint discussions between delegations of the Baath, on the one hand, and of the Soviet and satellite Communist parties on the other).

To summarize briefly the ideological and policy evolution of the Baath, we may say that it was affected both by the conversion of the party from one of opposition within an imperfect conventional-parliamentary system to one wielding power in conjunction with the military and by international developments of that period. The party

began to look upon itself as the sole interpreter of the people's will
and assert the right to a monopoly of power. Democratic freedoms
strongly advocated in the early stages of the struggle against the bour-
geois-feudal ruling classes were now discarded in favor of the concept
of "popular democracy" with a contemptuous rejection of conventional
institutions, like freely elected parliament and the multiparty system.
The concept of the class struggle, although not officially defined as
such, emerged with greater emphasis as against the early formulations of national solidarity. Socialism in the economic sector was
reaffirmed with dedication to total planning, forced savings, austerity,
and rapid industrialization without reference to either the economic
or the sociopsychological costs of such a method. Arab unity remained
an objective, but its priority was subordinated to a higher priority of
revolution in the Arab world. Revolution was to be a prerequisite of
unity. In the foreign sector, the familiar slogan of neutralism and
nonalignment was reasserted, but clearly modified by insistence on
close cooperation with the socialist camp on both the government and
the party levels. Liberation of Palestine was increasingly stressed
within the framework of the liberation movements in the Third World.
The evils of imperialism, Zionism, and native reaction were reem-
phasized as mutually interlocking and presenting a deadly danger to
Arab freedom, unity, and welfare.

OVERLAPPING AREAS: IDEOLOGY, ORGANIZATION, POWER

In the evolution of the Baath Party from a modest opposition
group to a ruling status it is not possible at every step to delineate
clearly the ideological, organizational, and power spheres. These
are necessarily interwoven and their overlapping explains the intensity
of certain crises. Of these, three deserve special mention: connection with Nasserism, relationship with communism, and intraparty
struggles.

Nasserism

In principle, Nasser and the Baath had followed a similar ideological course. "Unity, freedom, socialism" of the Baath was echoed
with an occasional change of sequence in Egypt. Nasser rose against
the remnants of imperialism; he preached Arab unity and practiced
Arab revolution; and, beginning with 1961, he enacted a series of socialist decrees. Except for the lack of geographical contiguity, therefore, union of Egypt and Syria appeared to be a natural development.

However, similarities were more outward than real, and profound
differences separated the two societies. Except for a Copt minority,
Egypt was homogeneous; its passive agricultural population was accustomed to centralized authority; the government traditionally assumed
major economic functions in this typical "hydraulic" civilization; and
Nasser was able to maintain himself in power with the aid of the army,
security forces, and bureaucracy although he did not have a genuine
voluntary political organization to back him up.[7] On every one of
these counts Syria was different. It was heterogeneous, with its
Druze, Alawi, Christian, and Kurdish minorities; it comprised individualistic people suspicious of virtually any government; it had a
commercial tradition not as strong as that of Lebanon but stronger
than the Egyptian, hence less prone to entrust too much responsibility
to the government; and it had a Baath Party that, for all its errors
and imperfections, was a genuine and dynamic political movement
with a collective leadership long before it assumed power. Because
Egypt was a large country with considerable natural and human resources, with Nasser standing out as a dramatic, charismatic figure,
it was inevitable that the union of Syria and Egypt would give him a
dominant role. Thus any hope on the Syrian side for equality and
meaningful participation in the rule was soon dashed. Moreover,
Nasser took care to subject Syria's army to his control by manipulat-
ing appointments and transfers and infiltrating it with his intelligence
apparatus. Ultimately he lost Syria in 1961 as a result of the convergence of his economic and military policies. His nationalization measures of July 1961 heightened Syrian discontent. His subsequent attempt to disarm Syria's army triggered the separatist revolt. Officially, the Baath condemned the separation in statements issued post
facto. In reality it gained by it because without separation it would
have been doomed to inactivity and obscurity.

But when the party assumed power in March 1963 it felt obliged
to revive the issue of the union. This time, however, it was wiser
by experience and it engaged in hard bargaining in Cairo. The issues
between it and Nasser revolved around the themes of collective leadership, the role of a national front (which Nasser favored and which
the Baath accepted, provided the party would play a dominant role in
it), the political arrangements of the proposed federation as contrasted with the previous concept of the unitary state, and the very
identity of the party. Ultimately, neither the Baath nor Nasser
changed their minds on any of these issues to a significant degree.
The April federative agreement that was signed created a pretense
rather than a reality of unity and it was never implemented.

Moreover, Nasser developed a morbid obsession in blaming the
Baath as much as the Syrian bourgeoisie for the secession. Consequently, even while the negotiations were proceeding between him and

the Baath through the spring and summer of 1963, his partisans and
agents in Syria's army repeatedly made attempts to dislodge the party
from power. The most serious of those attempts was made in July of
that year. It failed and was followed by quick trials and executions of
its authors. In the subsequent months Nasser's hostility to the Baath
increased and new attempts at its overthrow were made under his auspices in 1964. This murderous game for survival intensified the already existing trend in the Baath toward the imposition of a variety of
dictatorial controls, and the regime became exceedingly security-conscious with attendant deterioration in the field of civic freedoms.

Communism

The second critical issue was that of the Baath's relationship to
Communism. The Baath had been conceived as a non-Communist but
socialist answer to Syria's socioeconomic problems. Such at least
was the approach of Michel Aflaq, a disenchanted ex-Communist. Despite the vagueness and imprecisions of the Baath ideology, several
major points separated it from Marxism: Arab socialism as preached
by the Baath (and by Nasser) was nationalist, not internationalist; it
did not actively oppose religion; it did not (at least initially) preach
class struggle; it advocated a much more humane pace of economic
development than did Marxism-Leninism under Stalin's aegis; and,
because of its nationalist quality, it refused to acknowledge Moscow
as a leader and guide to the Arab revolution.[8] On the local Syrian
(and Iraqi) scene, the relationship of the Baath to the Communists
fluctuated depending on the circumstances. In principle, the two parties were competing for the same alienated clientele, hence much mutual hostility was generated. On the other hand, there were occasions
when the entrenched bourgeoisie (in the pre-1958 period) was the target; under such circumstances the two parties cooperated tactically
without losing their identity. With the advent of the Syro-Egyptian
union and later, with the assumption of power by the Baath in 1963,
the Communists suffered various adversities and their Syrian leader,
Khaled Bakdash, went into semivoluntary exile to Moscow. But after
1966 the situation changed: with the emergence of the left-wing leadership of the Baath, Syria's foreign policy veered toward a close cooperation with the Soviet Union, primarily centered on the Soviet aid
in constructing the Euphrates Dam. This new turn had its reflection
in Syria's domestic policy: tolerance was restored to the Communist
Party, Bakdash was allowed to return, and individual Communists
(usually two in number) began to be included in the Syrian cabinets.
In the 1970s, despite a slight turn toward the right, the Baath nego-
tiated with the Communists and certain other "progressive" groups an

agreement to form a National Front, thereby legitimizing the Communist presence in the ruling coalition, though reserving for itself the position of primacy. [9]

This reconciliation with the Communist Party, taken against the background of the improved economic, military, and political relations with Moscow, was reflected, as mentioned earlier, in the Baath Party's ideological stance. Without clearly repudiating its main points of difference with Marxism-Leninism, the Baath absorbed a number of Marxist ideas. The concept of the vanguard party enjoying the monopoly or near-monopoly of power, the intimation of permanent class cleavage through its abjuring of the bourgeoisie, the concept of total planning, and so on were indicative of this doctrinal adaptation. Moreover, the Communist totalitarian model, with its emphasis on security, hostile encirclement, obsession with conspiracies, and a steady erosion of private spheres of autonomy, strongly influenced the actual practice of the Baath-controlled government.

The third crisis revolved around the intraparty struggles. Difficult to pin down to a single date or event, these struggles reached a particular intensity in 1963, 1966, and 1970. The outward form was that of quarrels between the Iraqi and Syrian Baath leaderships and between the Regional Command in Syria and the National Command. The essence of all was basically the same: the struggle between the left and the moderates in the party. In 1963 the radical wing in the party was represented primarily by the Iraqi Baathists under the leadership of Ali Saleh al-Saadi. It is this group, sometimes referred to as "Stalinist"—to convey the idea of its ruthless revolutionary determination—which greatly influenced the tenor of the resolutions of the Sixth Congress with its pro-Marxist platform. It was also the same group that tried to establish for itself a firm power base in Iraq through its control of the Iraqi National Guard. Excesses committed by this group and the Guard detachments in Iraq led, first, to an intervention of the Damascus-based National Command (represented by Aflaq) in the affairs of the Iraqi regional organization, and, second, to an overthrow of the Baath rule in Baghdad by Iraq's president, Colonel Abdul Salem Aref. The Baath rule in Iraq thus ended after merely nine months in power and was not restored until a new coup in July-August 1968. [10]

The dramatic Iraqi developments profoundly affected the course of events in Syria and the fate of the entire Pan-Arab Baath organization. A rift between the moderates grouped around the founders, Aflaq and Bitar, in the National Command and the radicals, mostly rallying around the Syrian Regional Command, was deepened. By 1965 the radicals exerted a powerful influence on the party in Syria and this explains further accentuation of the Marxist tendency in the Phased Program that we have discussed earlier.

After the winter season of intensified struggle between the two
wings of the party, on February 23, 1966, the radicals struck back
and executed a coup that brought them back to power. It was for the
first time that the party experienced actual use of force by one of its
wings against another. Hitherto such violent steps had been taken
only against the non-Baathist groups. From now on, the party's
leadership was in the hands of men strongly influenced by Marxism-
Leninism, willing to cooperate with the Soviet Bloc, emotionally hostile to the West, uncompromising toward Zionism and its American
backers, and endowed with a "guerrilla mentality." The party, moreover, was becoming increasingly security-conscious and military-
oriented. The chief of state and of the Regional Command was General Amin Hafez, with General Salah Jadid playing the role of the
eminence grise. Premier Yussuf Zuayyen and Foreign Minister Ibrahim Makhous were young physicians in their thirties who had previously
fought in the Algerian war of liberation. This group was vindictive
not only toward the traditional bourgeoisie but also toward the moderate wing of the party as evidenced by the earlier mentioned sentencing in absentia of Aflaq and Bitar.

THE CONTINUING MALASIE: THE
BAATH AND THE PEOPLE

The Phased Program of 1965 clearly indicated the party's hostility to the private sector of economy. It dovetailed with the radical
nationalization measures adopted in January of that year. The party
was aware of the opposition to these nationalizations not only by the
owners of enterprises directly affected but also by many other, often
less than privileged, elements in the society. This explains why the
party gave repeated assurances that a given series of nationalizations
was carried out for "the last time." Seizures of property were often
arbitrary, embracing not only major enterprises but also extending
to small family-operated factories and workshops. In some cases
the stock ownership was so widespread that it was the small shareholders with limited means who suffered most through the takeovers.
Absurdities in this confiscatory drive had reached such proportions
that on several occasions the government found it necessary to dena-
tionalize the seized properties. Clearly the state did not possess
enough qualified managerial elite to be able to replace the dispossessed
private entrepreneurs. Moreover, the state-appointed managers
were often recruited on the basis of their party loyalty or as a reward
for the military service, with adverse if not disastrous effects on the
efficiency and profitability of the enterprises.

The results were predictable: a massive flight of capital, a brain drain among the educated and entrepreneurial classes, and an equally massive emigration of ordinary workers in search of greater job opportunities and economic security. The 20 years between the mid-1950s and mid-1970s have caused the migration from Syria to Lebanon of about 200,000 Syrian laborers; when added to the number of Syrians already working in Lebanon, the total had reached by 1973-74 some 300,000 individuals, an eloquent testimony on the disenchantment with socialist promises by a substantial portion of Syria's working class.

Another result was the active resistance to the new economic order by Syria's petty bourgeoisie—the shopkeepers and artisans in the bazaars of Damascus, Aleppo, Homs, and Hama. These elements reached a point of desperation that led them to go on repeated strikes, particularly in 1965 and 1966. Their resistance, however, met with harsh military and police reprisals. Confiscation of shops, punitive seizure and destruction of merchandise, and arrests and sentences were needed to intimidate and subordinate this large stratum of the urban population.

The increasingly repressive measures that the party was obliged to apply to maintain itself in power necessarily strengthened its authoritarian tendency and led it ever closer to a totalitarian model. Under the Baath rule Syria became a thoroughly militarized state, with large numbers of soldiers and officers in uniform, very visible in the urban and rural sectors, with frequent road checks, sentries around public buildings and bridges, and similar activities. Although some of this military presence could be attributed to the endemic crisis in the relations with Israel, the distribution of the army units in Syria did not necessarily follow the strategic dictates of external defense and could often be attributed to internal political insecurities.

Militarization of Syria's daily scene brought forth a more fundamental problem of the real nature of the socialist regime: Was it an emanation of the party or of the army? It was clear that without the aid of the army the Baath could not have ascended to, and maintained itself in, power. But was the army a mere instrument of the party or was it a ruler itself, using the party as an ideological legitimizing device? Moreover, what was the effect of indoctrination of the army enjoined repeatedly in the party programs and the real meaning of the expression "ideological army?"

A tentative reply to these questions may perhaps be provided by a closer look at the heterogeneity of the Syrian society and its reflection in the composition of the army. The minority communities living in compact groups in the provinces of Syria were often equated with underdevelopment and underprivileged status. It is these communities that traditionally provided a disproportionately high percent-

age of officers and noncommissioned officers in the Syrian armed
forces, largely because the military service was for them the quickest
and surest way to status and economic security. These Alawi, Druze,
and sometimes Kurdish elements had no appreciation of the conventional democratic process, no attachment to capitalism and free enterprise, accepted authoritarianism (and even modified tribalism) as a
way of life, and nurtured a good deal of resentment and envy toward
the wealthier Sunni classes, which ruled Syria before union with Egypt
in 1958 and which returned to power between 1961 and 1963. Consequently, without fully absorbing the finer points of Arab socialist
ideology, these minority army officers saw in the Baath program a
way toward the advancement of their own group. Moreover, the party's
indifference to religion meant, in practical terms, that adherence to
a minority sect would not be regarded as an obstacle in the desired
upward mobility. This explains why, since the advent of the Baath
to power, minority officers—especially the Alawis—were conspicuous
in the top army, party, and government positions. Their dominant
presence in the revolutionary establishment helps also to explain the
fierce Sunni Moslem opposition to socialist economic laws decreed
since the party's advent to power. Violent resistance that occurred
on several occasions in 1963 and 1964-65 in Hama, Homs, and Damascus was often led by Sunni religious leaders. The bombardment of a
major mosque by General Amin Hafez' forces in the 1960s added to
the further embitterment in these intercommunal relations.[11]

This leads us to a broader and concluding section. Socialism
in Syria does not have a precise economic definition. It rather refers
to an uncertain economic system in which the public and private sectors are present in a state of uneasy coexistence, the former over-
staffed, politicized, inefficient, and often unprofitable, the latter fearful, lacking confidence, and stagnant. The distributive side of the socialist system is far from meeting the popular expectations of plenty
and equality. Despite various pious exhortations, the military and
the party functionaries have been leading privileged lives. The cleavage between the people and the ruling establishment has been widening rather than narrowing, as attested by the workers' migration to
Lebanon, the opposition of the petty bourgeoisie, and the resistance
of the religious leaders. As for the younger educated strata, these
have also tended to seek better opportunities abroad unless they were
accommodated in more lucrative positions within the ruling establishment.

Broadly speaking, in spite of its frequent emphasis on close
contact with the masses the party has failed to evoke genuine response
from the population. Its leadership is not natural, if by this word we
mean spontaneous trust, loyalty, and confidence in mature wisdom
of their leaders on the part of the people. On the contrary, the Baath

rule has been criticized for its arrogance, ignorance, and ruthless disregard for the deeply embedded human values. Pronounced militarization of Syria's political system added a further harsh dimension to the absence of a wide popular basis, and the regime has never dared to undergo a test of free and unfettered elections since its advent to power in 1963. Syria's government is not a pure military dictatorship because the party exists and cultivates an ideology. But the harsh realities of power wielding without the genuine support of the masses have caused the Baath-military coalition to become a hybrid structure, with substantial reliance on preemptive slogans and coercion.

This rather gloomy situation underwent a degree of modification with the advent of General Hafez al-Assad to power in November 1970. His main merit appeared to be a realization of the regime's growing isolation domestically, internationally, and on the Arab scale.[12] Because his ascent was also a result of a sui generis intraparty coup, he could not be expected to indulge excessively in the luxuries of political tolerance and liberalism. But at least his rule came to be viewed as one of greater prudence, restraint, and moderation in the domestic and foreign policies. It is a moot question whether these changes should be regarded as durable, considering the fact that Syria has not developed a firm institutional framework and that so much in her political process has continued to depend on the personal characteristics of the actual wielders of power.

NOTES

1. Michel Aflaq began his preaching and organizational activity as early as 1940. In 1943, following the formal achievement of independence by Syria, his movement expanded. But the first founding congress took place only in 1947, at which time the party's constitution was adopted.

2. For a political analysis of this period, see Patrick Seale, The Struggle for Syria: A Study of Post-War Arab Politics, 1945-1958 (New York: Oxford University Press, 1965); and Gordon H. Torrey, Syrian Politics and the Military, 1945-1958 (Columbus: Ohio State University Press, 1964).

3. Michel Aflaq's principal works are Fi Sabil al-Ba'th (Beirut: Dar al-Tali'ah, 1959); and Ma'arakat al-Masir al-Wahid (Beirut: Dar al-Adab, 1959). Salaheddin Bitar's chief contribution is al-Siyasah al-Arabiyyah Bayn al-Mabda wa al-Tatbiq (Beirut: Dar al-Tali'ah, 1960). Another basic book is by Munif al-Razzaz, Ma'alim al-Hayat al-Arabiyyah al-Jadidah (Beirut: Dar al-Ilm Li al-Malayin, 1960). For a comprehensive treatment of the Baath, see Kamel S. Abu Jaber,

The Arab Ba'th Socialist Party: History, Ideology, and Organization (Syracuse, N.Y.: Syracuse University Press, 1966).

4. Text in The Middle East Journal 13 (Spring 1959): 195-200.

5. Text in Communique du Sixieme Congres National du Parti Baas Arabe Socialiste (Damascus: Bureau des Documentations Syriennes et Arabes, 1963).

6. Text in Programme-Etapes du Pouvoir en Republique Arabe Syrienne, Rendu Public a Damas le 22 Juillet 1965 (Damascus: Office Arabe de Presse et de Documentation, 1965).

7. Nasser's only licensed political organization, the National Union, later reconstituted as the Arab Socialist Union, was formed by him from above after his advent to power. As a result, it was difficult to distinguish between the true loyalists and the mere opportunists among its members. The NU and ASU were repeatedly subjected to reorganizations and suspensions without much effect on the reality of power in Egypt.

8. For an illuminating discussion of the differences between communism and Arab socialism, see Muhammad Hasanayn Haykal, "Communism and Ourselves: Seven Differences Between Communism and Arab Socialism"; Fathi Ghanim, "Our Socialism in Relation to Capitalism and Communism"; Clovis Maqsud, "The Crisis of the Arab Left"; and Michel Aflaq, "The Philosophy of the Ba'th and Its Differences from Communism and National Socialism"; in Kemal H. Karpat, ed., Political and Social Thought in the Contemporary Middle East (New York: Praeger Publishers, 1968). A selection of various writings on radical Arab nationalism may also be found in George Lenczowski, ed., The Political Awakening in the Middle East (Englewood Cliffs, N.J.: Prentice-Hall, 1970).

9. For an analysis of the Communist-Baath relationship, see George Lenczowski, Soviet Advances in the Middle East (Washington, D.C.: American Enterprise Institute for Public Policy Research, 1972), pp. 101-23.

10. For intraparty developments in Iraq and their connection with Syria, see Majid Khadduri, Republican Iraq: A Study in Iraqi Politics since the Revolution of 1958 (New York: Oxford University Press, 1969), pp. 188-214.

11. For a comprehensive review of politics, resistance, and repression under the Baath military regime, see George M. Haddad, Revolutions and Military Rule in the Middle East. Vol. 2: The Arab States (New York: Robert Speller & Sons, 1971), chaps. 3 and 4.

12. For General Hafez al-Assad's view of past mistakes and new directions, see "Discours du President Hafez el-Assad, Secretaire General du Parti Baas Arabe Socialiste, President de la Republique Arabe Syrienne, a l'Occasion du 9^e Anniversaire de la Revolution du 8 Mars," Revue de la Presse Arabe 747, Supplement No. 414, Damascus, March 7-9, 1972

4

SOCIALISM
IN IRAQ
Tarek Y. Ismael

Socialist thought in Iraq dates back to the early 1900s, the first socialist group having been organized in the 1920s. Expanding contacts with the West introduced Western political concepts, including socialism, into Iraq, but socialist doctrines played only a minor role in the political and intellectual ferment that developed a counterpoint to increasing Western involvement in Iraq. With the post-World War I mandate over Iraq the British brought with them democratic ideals and the paraphernalia of parliamentary democracy, while a growing core of young Iraqi intellectuals educated in the West were more likely to bring home nationalist ideals than socialist ideology. By 1948 the fires of nationalism had engulfed the entire Middle East, including Iraq, while socialist thought was relegated to the domain of intellectualism.

Throughout the late 1950s and the decade of the 1960s increasing contacts with socialist countries, together with the disaffection of the Arab world for the West (particularly over the Palestine issue) facilitated the dissemination and popularization of socialist ideas in Iraq as an alternative to Western capitalist models, which came to be associated with exploitation (from without and within). Some of the basic themes of socialism, in fact, had been popularized and integrated into nationalist ideology. Thus when the Arab Socialist Renaissance (Baath) Party came to power by coup d'etat in 1968 (it had previously come to power in 1963 but had lasted only nine months), social justice was already a key concept of nationalism. But at its outset in 1968, the Baathist government of Iraq represented more of a strongly pan-Arab nationalist regime than a socialist one. It was the nationalist issues of Palestine, Israeli occupation of Arab territory, and Arab unity that had fueled the growth of the Baath Party and finally brought it to power in Iraq, not its socialist orientation. Nevertheless,

while nationalism has remained a principal foreign policy position of
the Iraqi Baathist government, socialism took increasing precedence
in internal policy. Socialism in Iraq has developed from a vague
Baathist notion of socialist theory to the key approach to the Iraqi
social milieu.

SOCIAL AND ECONOMIC MILIEU

The social milieu inherited by the Baathists in 1968 is best summarized by the social divisions that characterize Iraqi society. The
three principal cleavages are the rich-poor dichotomy, the Arab-
Kurdish split, and the Sunni-Shiite division.

By the time of the revolution of 1958 the social structure of Iraq
had assumed the classic Third World model: 90 percent of the population was illiterate and lived in extremely poor conditions; 3 percent of
the population controlled over 95 percent of the nation's wealth. The
economic milieu of Iraq until 1968 showed little change from this standard Third World pattern. Until 1958 most of the cultivatable land
was owned by a very small number of absentee landlords. There
were 2,480 landlords, who owned roughly 16 million dunums of arable
land or half of all land available for cultivation.[1] The landlord had
what amounted to absolute power over the peasantry working on his
land through the system of crop sharing, which was most often used.
The peasant would generally receive only the bare minimum necessary
to support life.

The dominance of the large landowners was not interfered with
by the central government, which saw the landlords as their principal power base. Following the revolution of 1958, one of the first
acts of the new government was the confiscation of the large estates.
They were redistributed among the peasantry. This produced a number of advantages for the government. The quantity and quality of
production were increased and the exodus to the cities slowed. In
spite of this, further progress was limited by the exhaustion of over-
used land, salt accumulation, and erosion as a result of deforestation
—all this conspiring to reduce production.

Nuri as Said, many times Prime Minister of Iraq and one of the
most powerful political figures prior to the 1958 revolution, recognized the need for development in Iraq and realized the opportunities
offered by the exploitation of the nation's vast oil reserves. He foresaw, however, that the oil would eventually cease flowing. In order
to safeguard against this eventuality he decided that the oil revenues
must be used to produce a self-sustaining rate of economic growth
that would be independent of oil production. This required progress
in both agricultural and industrial development, and Nuri as Said was
unable to make progress in either area.

The revolution of General Abdul Karim Kassem in 1958 was in
part a result of the inadequate economic measures of the previous
government. It was hoped that Kassem would make use of radical
methods and succeed where the monarchy had failed. Industry experienced but small growth and remained a minor factor; in 1959 under an agreement with the Soviet Union 11 factories were to be constructed, yet by the time of Kassem's ouster in 1962 only one was in
operation.[2] Only 79,666 persons were employed in manufacturing related industries by 1962.[3] In 1964 the government of Abdul Salem
Aref (who with the Baath had overthrown Kassem in 1963 and toppled
the Baath nine months later) nationalized all firms in which it owned
25 percent or more of the stock and formed a General Industrial Organization to manage them. This it was hoped would provide the necessary impetus for industrial growth, yet growth has been even less
impressive since 1962.

The production of oil is Iraq's chief source of foreign exchange.
The main producer of oil was formerly the Iraq Petroleum Company,
which was owned by a consortium of foreign firms. Since 1958 the
company has had to gradually surrender more and more of its revenue
to the government; it also lost much of its concession land for exploration under Law No. 80 of 1961. Continued disputes with Syria over
oil price and shipment of oil during the 1967 Arab-Israeli war caused
a severe drop in Iraqi oil production and may have contributed to the
revolution of 1968.

The failure of Iraq to achieve political stability as evidenced
by the frequent creation of "five-year plans" and the cycle of violent
coups have been the chief obstacles to the growth of Iraq's economy.
Furthermore, the continued use of oil revenue for armament rather
than capital expenditures as well as the failure to establish viable industrial and agricultural progress indicated Iraq was no closer in
1968 to a solution to the problem of economic growth independent of
oil than it was in 1958.

By 1968, then, little progress had been made by a decade of
military oligarchy in closing the rich-poor gap. The republican era
had witnessed the growth of a small middle class made up of technicians, professionals, and military officers, thus providing a measure
of upward mobility through education or the military bureaucracy.
But this growth contributed more to the frustration of rapidly rising
expectations, as the small middle class did not attain a power or
status commensurate with its ability, and the poverty-ridden masses
became keenly aware of the alternatives promised but not yet made
available.

The Arab-Kurdish ethnic split is another major division char-
acterizing the Iraqi social milieu. The Kurds, who are concentrated
in the mountainous areas of Iraq, number between 10 and 20 percent

of the Iraqi population. The government estimates their number at
800,000, while the Kurds claim a population of 1,500,000 for Iraqi
Kurdistan. In any event, the Kurds are a geographically and culturally homogeneous group quite distinct from the Arab majority. The
Kurds reside in the mountainous northeastern part of Iraq, maintaining their own language and customs. The cultural distinction is aggravated by the rich-poor split, for the Kurds are a very poor segment
of Iraqi society who have felt economically, culturally, and politically
dominated by the Arab majority, particularly with growing Pan-Arab
nationalist fervor of the post-World War II era. The Kurds, too,
have developed a sense of nationalism, taking up arms as early as
1927 in an attempt to carve out their own separate nation state. Under
the charismatic leadership of Mulla Mustafa Barzani, the call for
self-determination has erupted into intermittent violence throughout
the post-World War II era.

In the summer of 1958, after his successful coup against the
Hashimite regime, Premier Kassem invited the Kurds then exiled in
the Soviet Union to return to Iraq. Mulla Mustafa Barzani, head of
the Barzani tribe, did so with some hundreds of his followers, and
was welcomed by the government. For the next few years Kurds and
Arabs enjoyed relatively harmonious relations. In January 1960 the
Kurdish Democratic Party, with Mulla Barzani its nominal head,
was licensed by the government. The party newspaper Khebat was
published in Baghdad, and party activities were conducted above
ground.

In March 1961 Mulla Mustafa Barzani began to press for greater
autonomy for Kurdistan. This was opposed by Kassem. The situation
deteriorated and military engagements began in the summer. The
Kurdish Democratic Party (KDP) was driven underground and its leaders imprisoned. A major military campaign was initiated by the government in September 1961, at which time the Kurdish nationalists
controlled some 250 miles of territory.

Rivalries among Kurdish tribes and the lack of a strong central
authority weakened the Kurdish effort. However, Mulla Barzani defeated the government forces, as well as pro-Baghdad tribes, on several occasions, capturing weapons and other supplies. The KDP and
Barzani have been somewhat at odds in their approaches to Kurdish
nationalism, as Barzani acts more as a traditional tribal leader than
a modern politician, and by 1965 there was a clear breach between
Barzani and some of the KDP leadership who subsequently split to
form the Barate (Brotherhood) party under the leadership of Jalal
Talabani. This party, more moderate in its demands, calls for the
achievement of autonomy within the framework of the Iraqi Republic.

The Kurdish rebels have drawn the government into several
cease-fires, none conclusive. In January 1963 Kassem allowed hos-

tilities to lapse, and the Abdul Salem Aref government began negotiations after the coup of the 8th of February. Hostilities resumed on
June 9, 1963, with no decisive results, although the Kurdish dominance in the countryside was somewhat increased. In February 1964
another cease-fire was announced, but negotiations proved unproductive and hostilities were resumed in 1965. In June 1966, after the
failure of a spring offensive, Prime Minister Bazzaz offered the Kurds
a 12-point plan that amounted to a guarantee of local autonomy. The
plan provided for decentralized administration, use of Kurdish language
in Kurdish areas, general elections, proportional representation of
Kurds in National Assembly and in public service, Kurdish civil servants in Kurdish areas, a Kurdish political party and press, and re-
habilitation of the Kurdish guerrillas. [4] The army remained opposed
to concessions to the Kurds, however, and an agreement about the extent of Kurdish authority could not be reached. When the government
of Ahmed Hassan al-Bakir took control in 1968 they offered the Bazzaz
plan to the Kurds again, [5] but failed to provide the number of cabinet
posts the Kurds demanded and no reconciliation appeared possible. [6]

The final major social division characteristic of Iraq is the
Shiite-Sunni religious split. The antagonisms between these two Muslim sects are religious in nature, reinforced by differential access to
power, wealth, and authority, and by the geographic distribution of
the sects that parallel economic differences between them. The Sunni
sect numbers roughly half of Iraq's population, but this includes the
Kurdish population who are mostly members of the Sunni sect. Thus
the Arab-Sunni sect is actually a minority, but has dominated the
political life of Iraq since the Ottoman days. Prior to 1958, Shiite
Muslims were limited to 26 percent of the total cabinet postings (six)
and only once was one of their number appointed Prime Minister.
In addition to this, the Shiite population is concentrated in the south
of Iraq, a much poorer area economically than the oil-endowed north
and central sections of the nation. Thus religious differences between
the two sects have been aggravated by political and economic differences.

Since the 1958 revolution, attempts have been made by the successive republican regimes to bring the Shiites into the mainstream
of political life in Iraq and to extend economic development to the
south. However, the instability of the governments have limited economic efforts in the south, and the continuing importance of ascrip-
tive criteria posed barriers to full Shiite participation in the government. By 1968 the area was still bound to traditional modes of agricultural production and land tenure; most of the land remained in the
control of a few powerful sheikhs. In the meantime, the rising expectations of the masses for land reform and an improved standard of
living, fueled by the promises of successive nationalist regimes,

were frustrated and led to the growing popularity of radical movements, particularly communism.

BAATH SOCIALISM IN THEORY

Among the nationalist—noncommunist—Arab parties, the Baath
was the foremost in raising the banner of socialism. Baath notions
of socialism, however, have evolved from Utopian, undefined teachings whose hallmark was their opposition to Marxism and communism,
to Marxist-oriented formulations that borrow from the ideas of scientific socialism and assimilate them to nationalist ideas.

In Article 4 of the 1947 Constitution the Baath was defined as a
socialist party believing "that socialism is a necessity," and that
"socialism constitutes, in fact, the ideal social order."[7] As to the
means for the establishment of socialism, the Baath in its early pronouncements avoided the use of the term revolution and replaced it
with coup. Article 6 of the same Constitution, stipulated that "the
party of the Arab Baath is revolutionary. It believes that its main objectives for the realization of the renaissance of Arab nationalism or
for the establishment of socialism cannot be achieved except by means
of revolution and struggle."[8]

The Constitution does specify the economic plan of the party.
Article 26 described the Baath as a socialist party claiming that all
the economic resources of the Arab nation should be owned by Arabs
themselves. Article 27 declared that this economic wealth had been
distributed unjustly; hence, it should be redistributed equally among
the people. It followed in Article 28 that the exploitation of man by
man was condemned, for all citizens are equal. The state manipulation of the means of production was also approved by virtue of Article
29. The aforementioned article clearly stated that the state should
run cooperations of public interest, natural resources, factors of production, and the means of transportation.

Nevertheless, private property was not abolished, for Article
34 of the Constitution considered it a natural protected right, but limited it in Articles 30, 31, and 33. According to these articles, private landownership was limited to the ability of the owner to utilize
the land efficiently without the exploitation of others. The state would
supervise that and it would be carried out according to the general
economic plan. Entrepreneurship was limited to the economic standard of the rest of the population. Ownership of real estate was open
to all citizens, provided that they did not accumulate more than they
could directly utilize and did not use it to exploit others. Thus the
state would enforce the minimum ownership of real estate.

With respect to social classes, the Constitution in Article 42 considered the separation and differentiation among classes as "the consequence of a faulty social order." A more just and equitable social order, it was felt, would eradicate class differences.[9]

The Baathist call for socialism was, until recently, invariably accompanied by an emphasis by the party that its teachings contradict those of communism and that it would even be characterized as an anticommunist party. In its political statement, the Third National Conference, 1959, in a section entitled "Position of the Party on Communism" had the following to say:

> The party has since its founding clearly defined its ideological position on communism and revealed the latter's errors and dangers to the Arab liberation movement. We will continue our intellectual ideological struggle against communist revisionism, elaborate the difference between the theoretical and practical premises of Arab liberation which we advance, from those advanced by the communist movement and explain how the movement for Arab liberation surpasses the shortcomings and limitations of communism.[10]

Michel Aflaq had written earlier that communism was a product of the abstract eighteenth-century philosophy and that its practice in Russia seems to be the product of Russian spiritualism and scientific European thought. To him, communism had no semblance to any Arab intellectual traditions or to the past and present life of the Arabs.[11] The insistence of the Baath on differentiating its socialism from Marxist scientific socialism has led to the coining of the term "Arab socialism," implying that the Arab form is not a derivative of Marxism but an opposing and contradictory ideology.

Despite its outward criticism of Marxism, the Baath party was not content with its own brand of socialism. As early as 1960 the party circulated an internal memo that admitted to the general nature of the party's notions of socialism and to the lack, within party literature, of any specifications as to the means and stages for establishing a socialist order. This memo also criticized party doctrine for its vagueness on private property, means of production and the role of individuals, unions, popular institutions and the state in social organization and economic development.[12] The report submitted by the Baath national leadership to the Fourth National Conference (1960) presents another illustration of the dissatisfaction with the party's position on socialism. Lamenting the negligence in party writings of the subjects of socialism and democracy, the report observed the hesitancy of socialists to join party ranks.[13]

Deliberations of the Sixth National Conference (1963) significantly enhanced the Baath notion of socialism and subjected all past beliefs to critical reevaluation. In Certain Theoretical Considerations, the conference explained the adoption of the slogan "Arab socialism" as a negative and incomplete response to the challenge of local communism. It warned that such an attempt might lead to a nationalist chauvinism that rejects the universal, intellectual heritages of socialist thought. Arab socialism, the conference added, has remained, on the whole, partial and without any scientific content. Assessing the impact of the party's distorted image of socialism, the conference pointed to the dominance in the party organization of bourgeois elements and the prevalence of the petit-bourgeois mentality in party ranks. Middle-of-the-road practices govern party activities, the conference cautioned. A new conception of socialism was formulated by the Sixth National Conference, which also visualized the nature of the process of socialist transformation in the Arab world.

In the new formulation, socialism aims at the establishment of a new social order in which the objective economic, social, intellectual, and political conditions are established that free the individual from all forms of exploitation, subjugation, and stagnation and allow him to become a completely free human being. The new socialist order will eradicate material exploitation, deepen the democratic content of socialism, and give the citizen a socialist and scientific education that frees him from the yoke of the inherited and backward social customs and traditions. Meanwhile, the process of socialist transformation will necessitate public ownership of the means of production, completely abolish the need for the capitalist middleman, make the income of the individual dependent on his labor and abilities, mold the various social classes into one class, and finally eliminate the profit economy and replace it with one based on need. Automation, the role of the small bourgeoisie, state capitalism, the changes of bureaucratization, nationalization, landownership, socialist planning, and the functions of an organized popular, revolutionary vanguard were among the many issues on which the conference voiced its opinions.[14] This new conception of socialism, which the Sixth National Conference had approved, was soon to be attacked by both rightist and leftist elements within the Baath. The former discredited it as being extremist while the latter condemned it as being selective and not sufficiently radical.

In the area of actual policy, the Baath, after assuming power in Syria and Iraq in 1963, conducted a series of unplanned nationalizations and reforms. These augmented the measures adopted by Gamal Abdul-Nasser in Syria and Abdul-Karim Kassem in Iraq. The basic guidelines adopted by the Sixth National Conference, however, remain in need of elaboration into a concrete program. The two ruling Baath parties have yet to do that.

As for Iraq, great changes have occurred in various facets of
life since the Baath seized power. For years after that, a whole program was published whereby the stages of socialist development were
defined, and the shortcomings of the government institutions were
acknowledged.

BAATH SOCIALISM IN PRACTICE

Baath socialist ideology, then, could be summed up as opposition to class distinctions and a commitment to establish an equitable
social order. Thus, armed with an ideology vague enough to be highly
flexible in practice, and a nationalism position militant enough to counter the popular disillusionment following the decisive defeat in the
Arab-Israeli 1967 war, the Baath came to power in Iraq by military
coup d'etat on July 17, 1968. The internal problems they assumed
were indeed grave. A Kurdish rebellion in the north was in progress;
Shiite dissatisfaction in the south was polarized between a reactionary
traditional leadership and popular radical movements; and the general
disarray of the economy was compounded by the Syrian action in closing the pipeline that carried Iraq oil (from December 1966 to March
1967), seriously affecting Iraq's balance of payments.

On July 30, 1968, the Revolutionary Council stated that the best
way to achieve progress was through a revolutionary democratic regime. The regime announced it would carry on a policy of radical
agrarian reform and establishment of an oil policy through the National
Petroleum Company. On the first anniversary of the revolution, President Ahmed Hassan al-Bakir enunciated the following steps for completion of the socialization of Iraq: Strengthening the revolution by
elimination of competition and external interference in Iraq; formation of trade unions, new levels of military preparedness, plus the
use of a "people's militia"; increased economic progress through
scientific planning and conservation of natural resources; increasing
reform of the land usage, thus increasing cash flow to the peasantry;
equal opportunity and the strengthening of the individual through ideology; and finally, a solution to the Kurdish question.[15]

The party proceeded to implement the aforementioned policies
as quickly as possible. Political prisoners were freed and civil servants dismissed for political reasons under previous regimes were
reinstated. In industry, however, grave difficulties existed. Contrary to the practices of previous regimes, which generally abandoned
projects of the deposed governments, the Baath's first task it was decided would be the conclusion of the current Five-Year Plan (1964-
69) and other industrial projects begun long ago but never completed—
the glass factory of Ramadi and the textile factory in Hulla are exam-

ples. The percentage of completed projects during the first four years of the plan had been a lamentable 50 percent; by 1969 this figure increased to 86 percent. In this period an annual growth rate of 6.8 percent in the GNP was achieved.

The result of this was a new five-year plan to conclude in 1974 that called for a series of projects, the most important of which are here summarized: Use of modern technique in production; presence of a healthy equation of consumption; savings, and reinvestment; finding an equilibrium between the needs of the populace and those of industry; finding and persuading the investment of capital in important projects while seeking the skill, know-how and other essential resources from friendly governments.[16] In order to administer this program, the Baath wished to establish a center for economic planning and programming. They also, it appears, hoped to establish a master plan of coordinated economic and social development. Unlike the central planning found in many Western socialist economies, the Baath hoped to have a guiding authority at the center, but multicentrism for administration so that a form of regional autonomy would be achieved in the nation's economy. This is a basic difference between Baath socialism and European social democracy or Marxism. Total expenditure for the plan was calculated to be 1,144 million dinars[17]—the largest expenditure since the first Five-Year Plan.

The Baath did not plan to exclude private investment; in fact they encouraged it in such areas as the agricultural sector, transportation, services such as theaters, casinos, and restaurants. This is in keeping with the attitude of the party to private ownership as stated in their Constitution of 1948. Still, private investment was given clear guidelines in the agricultural sector to prevent a renewal of "exploitation." It was allowed to loan farmers money for machinery, to set up services for pest control, and to strengthen trade and transportation so as to assist the marketing of goods. In the industrial sphere the government attempted to give incentives to increase investment capital through a tax exemption on machinery and capital equipment. Also, an Industrial Bank was established to assist in financing very costly projects. These measures and the great increases in demand of Iraqi oil have dramatically increased the national wealth of Iraq. Whereas in 1969 the GNP stood at 896 million dinars, by 1972 it had reached 1,218 million dinars; estimates for 1974 are 2,550 million dinars, which would translate into a 185 percent increase in the GNP since the beginning of the last Five-Year Plan. Individual income has increased from 100 dinars per capita in 1969 to an estimated 236 dinars per capita at the end of 1974. In the agricultural sector growth averaging 15.5 percent per year was realized in the period 1969-72. Growth in this sector, however, continues to be hampered by a lack of adequate irrigation facilities and soil exhaustion.

In the industrial sector growth was also pronounced, the average increase for the period 1969-74 being 14 percent per year. The labor force employed in manufacturing has risen to 3.2 million by 1974, compared with only 2.5 million in 1969. The high prices Iraq receives for its petroleum products has done much to bring about this state of affairs. Western nations concerned with a balance-of-payments problem have been able to sell entire plants to the Iraqi government. Examples are an Italian company, which has contracted to build a tire and rubber plant for 11 million dinars, and a French company, which is proceeding with construction of an iron and steel complex, the first stage alone of which will cost 40.5 million dinars.

Agricultural reform was one of the chief pillars of the Baath's economic ideology and reform in this sector was speedily undertaken following their assumption of power. The Iraqi government is of the opinion that the most effective method for increasing production in the agricultural sector would be to collectivize and thereby pool the technical and material resources of the farmers, hopefully in this way to take over management of production themselves. The Baath hope that by pooling resources on certain collective farms they can turn them into showcases of development for the more conservative small farmers and encourage them to collectivize. This is being done because the party feels individual production will only continue to deteriorate, as the small farmer cannot hope to benefit from financial loans and increased mechanization. With this in mind the government has formulated a new plan for rural reform that is mainly concerned with the expansion of the collectivist system. New cooperative organizations would be established to coordinate all areas of agriculture, production, marketing, and transportation.[18]

In the 1974-75 investment programs, the Ministry of Agriculture and Agrarian Reform stressed coordination between the General Federation of Agricultural Societies and the General Federation of Agricultural Cooperatives in order to mobilize the forces of the peasants, direct them in carrying out programs, and coordinate agricultural and industrial output with the Ministries of Irrigation, Industry, and Economy. The ministry's plan concentrated on modern techniques for following a suitable agricultural cycle, for expanding mechanization, and for using improved seeds, chemical fertilizers, and other services.[19]

The new marketing system attempts to provide stable prices to both producer and consumer by paying a high price to the producer and subsidizing the price to the consumer through oil revenue. The question of land distribution is also associated with marketing procedures in that the larger a farm, the more profitable it invariably shows itself to be. The Minister of Agriculture stated that land for individual farmers would be confined to areas where large coopera-

tives would not work. The government had no plans to expropriate
the land of these small farmers; it merely hoped to encourage them
to form cooperatives.[20]

In the northern part of Iraq, however, the government has moved
to establish state farms. The government hopes to solve the nagging
problem of migration to the cities by making agriculture more profitable and at the same time more attractive through creation of what it
terms "ideal rural communities." By 1973 the policy of agrarian reform seemed to be proceeding but at a slow rate considering the number of people and amount of land involved. By February 1973 the Ministry of Agriculture reported only 56 collective farms in operation
and only 1,200 cooperative societies.[21] Resistance among traditionally
conservative farmers seems to be high indeed.

The 1976-80 plan announced in January 1975 allocated $10 bil-
lion for agricultural development. Hasan Fahnu Jum'a, Minister of
Agriculture and Agrarian Reform, revealed that the new plan will
concentrate on "expanding agriculture both vertically and horizontally
for certain products and regions in order to meet Iraq's demand for
foodstuffs and the requirements of the industrial and export sectors."[22]
The main features of the plan are:[23]

- Production of large quantities of foodstuffs, including rice,
  meat, fruits, and animal fodder.
- Implementation of irrigation and drainage systems for an area
  of 1,250,000 dunums of agricultural land.
- Leaching and cultivation of 1,250,000 dunums of reclaimed land.
- Surveying of 12,900,000 dunums of agricultural land.
- Building of 96 experimental stations for research and six soil
  labs, and training of 5,000 technicians.
- Raising the water storage capacity by 25 percent.
- Construction of 450 new agricultural cooperatives in the areas
  covered by the Agrarian Reform and 335 new cooperatives in the
  areas outside the Agrarian Reform.
- Increasing the areas of state farms to a million dunums.
- Raising total cultivatable land to 17 million dunums by 1980.

The Baath's main concern of course is to socialize the state
and improve the lot of the citizens. Since 1968 an intensive program
has been aimed at carrying out this program to increase the quantity
and quality of social services. According to government statistics,
expenditures on medical services has increased 40 percent since
1968. The ratio of doctors to population has improved from 1:4,200
to (1972) 1:3,200. Seventy percent of the population is now covered
by free health care services. The number of beds in hospitals also
increased from 12,300 beds in 1968 to 20,322 in 1973, an increase of

8,000 beds. The number of medical assistants increased by 57.8
percent by 1972.

In education the increases have not been as dramatic. Expenditures increased only 10 million dinars between 1967 and 1970. The
number of students at the elementary level have increased from
990,000 pupils in 1967 to 1,110,000 in 1970. The number of students
at university level increased from 30,000 in 1967 to 38,000 in 1970.
The students attending technical schools increased from 10,000 in
1967 to about 12,000 in 1972.

Before the Baath took over, 96 percent of the villages in Iraq
did not have clean drinking water supplied to homes. Hence, the Iraqi
government planned a huge project that will cost more than $80 mil-
lion to provide drinking water to most villages. However, this project will take many years before completion. For the near future, the
government has allocated 28 million dinars to be spent on similar
minor projects. These minor projects will cover 90 percent of the
needs of the cities and suburbs and only 5 percent of village needs.

The Iraqi government admits that its progress is fueled mainly
by Iraq's vast oil reserves and production. Before Law No. 80 of
1961, which deprived the oil companies of 90 percent of their concession areas, Iraq received very little indeed of the oil revenues generated by her diminishing natural resources. The Baath sought to change
this state of affairs and did so by means of their new platform at the
Sixth Party Congress. The companies were progressively nationalized by increasing the government's share steadily until by June 1,
1969 the process was complete. In spite of local ownership, distribution is still in the hands of the companies rather than the Iraqi National Oil Company, which now has all oil rights in Iraq. In light of
its nationalist bent it is hardly surprising that the foreign relations
of the Baath have taken on a decidedly anti-Western look.

The foreign relations of Iraq prior to 1968 were motivated
mainly by much anti-Zionist, anti-Western rhetoric but quite little
action. Once an Iraqi armored division was dispatched to aid Jordan
but did not arrive in time to be of any use. Relations with Western
nations in general deteriorated badly after 1967 as these were identified as supporters of the enemy—Israel.

Trade relations suffered even more following the nationalization
of the foreign-owned oil companies. Oil became the chief if not only
diplomatic tool the Iraqis had to exert influence on the Middle Eastern
situation. The Seventh Regional Conference of the Baath Party in
1968 placed emphasis on the importance of oil in the "Arab nationalist
battle." The conference further states that the previous laws and
agreements entered into by the previous government would be re-
examined to ensure they safeguarded "the people's interests." The
Iraqis nationalized the oil resources and proceeded to set an example

to the rest of the Arab world that they were capable of operating their own field and refining plants. In the October 1973 War, Iraq was the first Arab state to impose an oil embargo. Sadaam Husayn, vice-president of the Revolutionary Command Council, later stated that "nationalization is the most efficacious means of using oil as a weapon in the Arab nationalist battle."[24]

The Iraqis continue to associate America and Europe with support for Israel to which they refer as "the Zionist aggressor." Following the war, however, some moderation has resulted, in part due to the better showing of the armies of Egypt and Syria, which salved the wounds of Arab nationalism. Due to the continuing problem of underdevelopment of the Iraqi industrial sector the Iraqis have been forced to seek assistance from foreign companies who, in view of the balance-of-payment difficulties, are only too happy to inaugurate projects for the government.

More important, the Iraqis have shown an increasing level of moderation in their rhetoric on Western states. A fine example is an interview with Saddam Husayn. On July 13, 1973, he stated that the opposition of Iraq to the United States is mainly based upon her support for Israel and he stressed that American interests would likely be better served by developing closer contacts with the Arab states. Husayn was extremely concerned with the American policy of supplying vast quantities of arms to the Shah of Iran, which by his seizure of strategic islands in the Arab Gulf is perceived by Iraq as threatening her interests.[25]

The role of oil in the Iraqi economic boom is not hard to find. To look at 1973 alone is useful, as it was in this year that oil prices approached their current level. In January a new 600-km pipeline from Hadithah to the Persian Gulf was announced; a group of Soviet oil experts also arrived to assist in Iraqi exploitation of a rich new oilfield in al Rumalah. In February a 10-year oil supply deal with France was announced as was a similar deal with Spain. In July a settlement with the oil companies was announced through which in exchange for 150 million tons of oil they would waive all rights in Mosul, pay £141 million, and sell the key Lebanese pipeline to Iraq. In July an Italian oil company and a French steel company agreed to establish plants in Iraq. In September and November a giant project to increase tourist facilities and public works was announced, costing in the tens of millions of dinars.

Economic progress in Iraq continues, fueled by increasing oil revenues and investment capital. This progress has been translated to the population in terms of social services and a higher standard of living. In this way, the government is attempting to alleviate some of the social cleavages that exist in Iraqi society by a more equitable allocation of services and resources, and by bringing all elements of the population into the mainstream of economic life. Many great problems remain: The resources of Iraq are distinctly finite and industrial development has not yet reached "takeoff" point; the spread of primary education has been slow; in spite of progress in the agricultural sector, the improvement of the quality of life in rural areas, particularly in the south, is slow. Nevertheless, the revolution of 1968 has initiated change in the Iraqi social and economic milieu and continues to accelerate this process.

THE KURDISH QUESTION SINCE 1968

The Baath pressed for a reconciliation with the Kurdish Democratic Party. By a manifesto issued March 11, 1970, it achieved a temporary cessation of fighting. The manifesto took the steps of recognizing the Kurdish nationality and placing this in the Constitution, establishing Kurdish universities and studies in Kurdish prose and poetry, promulgating a general amnesty for all members of Barzani's insurgent army, and most important, promising implementation of local autonomy for the Kurds in at least four years from the day of the issuance of the manifesto. The government further pledged itself to recognize the right of Kurds to their own language and their right to be instructed in it in areas of Kurdish majority. The Kurdish Democratic Party (KDP), however, was not unified on acceptance of the manifesto. Deep cleavages within the Kurdish movement became apparent as it divided along tribal and economic lines. While Barzani opposed the manifesto, one group in opposition to his continuing obstruction was led by Shalphh Uthman, a prominent member of the Barzani clan.

After declaration of the manifesto most of its provisions were soon acted upon. Five members of the KDP were admitted to the cabinet, a general amnesty was issued, and a Kurdish newspaper and magazine were set up; also several new cultural organizations were brought into existence. The Baath, however, did not appoint a Kurdish vice-president and the proposed university was not yet established. In 1972 there was considerable disagreement over the boundaries of Kurdish territory, inclusion of the Pesh Merga into the Iraqi army, and border patrol. The Baath also protested what it termed the "coercion of Kurds" by Barzani into the ranks of the KDP.

In September 1973 the Baath Party drafted a proposed regional autonomy plan. The party reported that the Kurdish problems of the past were the result of failings of previous leaderships to understand the Kurdish national mind and the role of forces of "reaction and imperialism."[26] It proposed full regional autonomy for the Kurds as the solution to their national problem.[27] Widening strife in Kurdistan was also alluded to and attributed to "imperialist and reactionary circles" trying to exploit the divisions in Iraq over the Kurdish question.[28]

In December 1973 a report from northern Iraq in the German publication Die Welt indicated that the war would soon resume. The chief point of contention appeared to be control of the cities of Kirkuk and Kanaquin. In fact, this proved to be a point of irreconcilable difference, and fighting resumed in March 1974.

A new manifesto issued on March 11, 1974 gave to the Kurds full local autonomy in the fields of taxation, education and cultural matters, and Kurdish radio and television stations, as well as full licensing powers. In addition, it guaranteed to the Kurds their own executive council for economic planning and legislative assembly.[29] Barzani, however, rejected these items and went into the mountains with his supporters. This time they were much fewer in number. The tribal rivalries and clan disputes had diminished his support drastically. Furthermore, the KDP broke with Barzani over the issues of the manifesto and his leadership.

With arms and support from Iran, however, Barzani was able to sustain heavy fighting against the strongest armored units of the Iraqi army throughout the summer of 1974. But in a dramatic shift in March 1975, Iran withdrew support from Barzani as part of a comprehensive agreement with the Baath government that settled perennial border disputes. With its main artery of support withdrawn, the Barzani rebellion collapsed. The Baath government guaranteed amnesty to the rebels, and a majority surrendered. Barzani fled the country.

MOBILIZATION OF THE MASSES

In many ways the most difficult problem faced by the Baath was to establish their legitimacy and mobilize the population. Iraq had suffered 10 years of coup and countercoup, each new regime making flamboyant promises to the people, but sapping its time and energy and the nation's wealth—willy-nilly—on internal power plans and self-aggrandizement. The masses, then, had been conditioned by a decade of corruption, instability, and strife to expect little from the succession of military cliques in control and to fear much. The Baath, indeed, appeared just another chain in the succession.

Having had a brief taste of power in 1963, however, and armed with a fully developed ideology, the Baath moved quickly to consolidate power. At the same time a carrot of conciliation was offered by freeing all political prisoners of previous regimes and rehiring all civil servants dismissed for political activity.

With power consolidated, the Baath took bold steps in the areas of agrarian reform and solution of the Kurdish problem. The Kurds were offered a far-reaching plan for autonomy and reconciliation.

The Baath moved to broaden the popular base of the party and mobilize the masses around Baathist ideology. Three umbrella organizations were established to encompass the greater part of the Iraqi population—General Federation of Labor Union, General Federation of Peasant Associations, and National Union of Iraqi Students. Their function is to mobilize the masses and provide a line of communication between the masses and the government. These organizations are Baathist-controlled, and function in conjunction with cells of the Baath Party for recruitment of party members and popularization of party goals. These three major associations are buttressed by the organization of professional, occupational, cultural, ethnic, and recreation associations that function in a similar manner. The net result then was to create a network of mobilizing and politicizing organizations that encompassed the people in their daily rounds of life. In addition, mass media are all government-controlled, and are organized to serve the goals of mobilization.

These organizations were established with several purposes in mind: to provide channels of communication between the party and the people, to recruit party members from the ranks of the organizations, and to organize the populace for program implementation. The organizations, then, form the core of the political process. The governmental structure is triangular, with the masses forming the base, and the Revolutionary Command Council and popular organizations the sides. The Baath Party leadership is at the apex of the triangle. Running through the center of the triangle is executive action. The Revolutionary Command Council is the legislative body, yet it is not directly connected with the popular organizations. The popular organizations act as a link between the Baath Party leadership and the masses.

The popular organizations themselves are organized in a similar triangular structure, with Baath Party members at the apex, and the sides consisting of the legislative and executive functions. The base is provided by the rank and file. Within each organization is an agency of the party known as the bureau. The bureaus, then, form a direct link between the party and the organizations. Their purpose is similar in function to that of the leadership of Soviet labor unions and Komsomol (Communist Youth League).

By mid-1973 the Baath had broadened political participation in the government to include Communists, Kurdish parties, and nationalist elements. A "National Front" of all progressive forces was created to participate in government under the guidance of the Baath Party.

CONCLUSION

In summary, it is not an exaggeration to state that the Baathist coup of 1968 has been transformed into a revolution under the banner of a viable and dynamic ideology. Indeed, fueled by rising oil revenues, the Baathist government of Iraq, the first socialist government in the nation's history, has undertaken the social, political, and economic reorganization of the nation along socialist lines. The immature socialist ideology brought to the helm of power in 1968 by a military clique has evolved into a concrete program of socialist action and has transformed the military clique into the apex of a revolutionary force as the Baathist government has attempted to contend with the heady problems of the Iraqi social milieux, broaden the base of political participation, and mobilize the population. The Political Report of the Eighth Regional Congress of the Baath Party (Iraqi region) held January 1974 (Al-Taqrir Al-Syasi) indicated this maturity by proposing stages of socialist transformation and critically and analytically identifying obstacles to it. This report represents the basis of future government action in the social, political, and economic spheres and presents a clear conception of the social order envisioned by the Baathist regime after almost a decade of hard, pragmatic experience.

NOTES

1. One dunum = 0.62 acre.
2. Europa Handbook: The Middle East, 1965-1966 (London, 1967), p. 235.
3. Ibid.
4. New York Times, June 30, 1966.
5. Ibid., August 4, 1968.
6. Ibid., August 19, 1968.
7. Sylvia Haim, Arab Nationalism: An Anthology (Berkeley: University of California Press, 1964), p. 235.
8. Ibid.
9. Ibid.
10. Nidhal Hizb Al-Ba'ath Al-Arabi, U'ibr Motamaratih Al-Qawmiyah (The Struggle of the Arab Socialist Party, Through Its National Congresses) (Beirut: Dar Al-Tali'a, 1971), p. 57.
11. Michel Aflaq, Fi Sabil Al-Ba'ath (For the Sake of the Baath) (2d ed.; Beirut: Dar Al-Tali'a, 1963), pp. 153, 158.
12. Nidhal Hizb Al-Ba'ath Al-Arabi, op. cit., pp. 64-65.
13. Ibid., p. 108.
14. Ibid., pp. 205-11.

15. Iraq, President's Speech, June 17, 1969 (Baghdad: Public Institution for Press and Printing, 1969), pp. 8-11 (in Arabic).

16. Al-Tatawor Al-Iqtisadi Fi Al-Iraq (Economic Development in Iraq) (Baghdad: Al-Thawrah Publications, 1972), pp. 53-54.

17. One I.D. = $3.37.

18. Al-Thawrah (Baghdad), August 29, 1969.

19. Ibid., August 27, 1973, p. 4.

20. Ibid.

21. As related to the author by an official of the ministry in October 1973.

22. Middle East Economic Survey 18, no. 13 (January 17, 1975): 1.

23. Ibid.

24. Al-Thawrah, December 27, 1973.

25. New York Times, July 13, 1973.

26. Al-Thawrah, November 2, 1973, p. 3.

27. Ibid.

28. Ibid.

29. "The Kurdish Problem in Iraq," Al-Thawrah, 1974, pp. 186-89.

PART

III

NORTH AFRICA

5

**LIBYAN
SOCIALISM**
Valerie Plave Bennett

LIBYAN SOCIALISM AND QADDAFI'S POLICIES

The September 1969 military revolution immediately ended the image of Libya prevalent in the international environment as a conservative monarchy drowning in petroleum wealth—wealth that was being siphoned off by the domestic elite into European banks or squandered on Western pleasures.

The coming to power of the socialist, nationalist, and austere Islamic fundamentalist regime led by Muammar al-Qaddafi changed Libya's image to that of a radical socialist military regime following the lead of Syria, Egypt, Algeria, and the Sudan. Qaddafi quickly made it apparent, however, that his policies and image were unique, outdoing all his brother Arab officers in religious traditionalism, economic nationalism, international influence and devotion to Arab unity. Qaddafi's obvious admiration for Nasser helped to create the impression that Libya was merely a rich Egypt. This image is somewhat off the mark. Libya's history and culture diverge significantly from Egypt's.

POLITICAL CULTURE

In the sixteenth century the Ottoman sultans extended their control to North Africa but left Libya's internal administration to local rulers. Early in the eighteenth century the Qaramanli family made Tripolitania virtually independent, eventually extending their control to Fezzan and Cyrenaica, although the family continued to pay tribute to the Ottomans. In 1835 the Ottoman Porte removed Qaramanli and restored Ottoman rule.[1]

99

The rise of the revivalist Sufi missionary movement under Muhammad Ben 'Ali al-Sanusi led to a resurgence of Koranic fundamentalism. About 1840 Muhammad Ben 'Ali settled in Cyrenaica. Ten years later the Grand Sanusi died, but his son, Sayyid al-Mahdi, came to be regarded as the overlord of the desert sheikhs. After Italy declared war on the Ottoman Empire in 1911 and occupied Libya, Sanusi resistance was considered valuable to the Sultan, but the peace treaty of 1912 forced the Sultan to surrender his sovereignty over Libya. In 1916 Sayyed al-Mahdi's son, Sayyed Idris, took over control of the Sannusaya, leading to a peace settlement between the Italians and Idris. This settlement recognized that the Italians and the Sanusis held sway in different parts of Libya, but the accession of Mussolini to power in Italy ended this conciliatory policy toward the Sanusis. In 1923 the Italians dissolved the joint army and took prisoner half the Sanusi army. When World War II began, Idris, who had fled to Cairo in 1923, approved the organization of an Arab force to serve under British command. Britain occupied Cyrenaica in November 1942, and the following month took control in Tripolitania while Fezzan was administered by the French.

After the war agitation began for self-government under the Emirate of Sayyed Idris al-Sanusi. The United Nations, responsible for the general problem of the disposition of the former Italian colonies, called for the establishment of an independent Libya in November 1949. Libya became independent, under the Sanusi monarchy, on December 24, 1951. Its foreign policy was pro-Western, and both American and British military bases were erected on her soil. Domestic policies in the postindependence period were marked by jockeying among clan leaders of the three regions—Cyrenaica, Fezzan, and Tripolitania. Cyrenaica was the base of Senusi power, Tripolitania the business center, while Fezzan was a sparsely populated desert province. At the time of independence there were less than a million Libyans, the vast majority of whom were poor rural nomads and farmers.

Petroleum was discovered in Libya on January 10, 1958; little has been the same since then in that desert nation.

Three changes had notable impact on the future of politics in Libya: urban-rural migration; the growth of an indigenous elite whose wealth was based on petroleum; and the influx of Tunisians, Egyptians, and Palestinians into jobs in the burgeoning modern sector.

Even under the traditional Idris, modernization was apparent: educational and health facilities were begun, the bureaucracy expanded, housing was built for urban migrants (estimates put Libya's urban population at 85 percent of the total today). The Libyan army and the Cyrenaica Defense Force—the latter represented Idris' personal army—were both modernized with petroleum revenues.

Although King Idris was a religious, ascetic leader, the families close to his throne were the real beneficiaries of the growing oil revenues. Political parties and trade unions were banned, but antigovernment sentiment within the army grew nevertheless among the young officers, who were influenced by the assorted modern political philosophies current in the Arab world—Nasser's Arab socialism in particular. The youthful officers, led by Captain Muammar al-Qaddafi, were disenchanted with the corruption surrounding the aging king, the prominence of foreigners in the Libyan economy, Idris' pro-Western foreign policy, and the colonial mentality displayed by the Italians still residing in Libya.

THE COMPONENTS OF LIBYAN SOCIALISM

On September 1, 1969 a handful of officers led by Qaddafi and his principal lieutenant, Abdal Salam Jalloud, overthrew the Libyan king (while the latter was vacationing in Turkey) and proclaimed the arrival of the socialist revolution in Libya. Point number three of the five-point declaration issued by the Revolutionary Command Council (RCC) on September 1 stated that

> The RCC wishes to make it clear to all citizens
> that it is striving with firm determination and stiff
> resolve to build the Libya of revolution, the Libya
> of a socialism which springs from the heart of our
> nation, avoids ideological expectation, and believes
> in the inevitability of irrevocable historical devel-
> opment which will transform Libya from a backward
> country with a sick administration and policy into a
> progressive country opposing colonialism and rac-
> ism and striving to liberate oppressed peoples af-
> fected by the same problems of backwardness and
> social oppression.[2]

Two weeks later, during a speech in Benghazi, Qaddafi explained his version of socialism to his countrymen:

> As for the socialism in which we have announced
> our belief . . . it is the participation of all in pro-
> duction. It is the participation of each individual
> in producing what he consumes. Socialism is un-
> tiring collective work leading us to the society of
> equality and justice. The solidarity of the working
> forces of the people—workers, farmers, non-exploi-

tative capitalists, intellectuals, and soldiers—will
build socialism. Our socialism is the socialism of
Islam. It is the socialism of the true faith. It is
the socialism which springs from the heritage and
beliefs of this people.[3]

These two ideas—socialism as social justice and Islamic socialism—dominated Qaddafi's view of Libya's socialist revolution.

His perception of socialism as a fundamentally Islamic philosophy enables him to view socialism as an indigenous Libyan ideology,
not one imported by the RCC.

Journalists have questioned the compatability of Islam and socialism, but Qaddafi sees no incongruity between the two sets of beliefs. In the same way that some European socialists see the roots
of socialism in Christian charity, Qaddafi sees the precursor of socialism in almsgiving—admitting, however, that it cannot be described
as modern socialism. Because almsgiving blurs the differences between classes, "it can be said that the spirit and basic principles of
Islam are not incompatible with socialism, even if they are not clear
like the socialism of today."[4]

Qaddafi professes to see support for his views on private property and nationalization in Muslim tradition.

Individual private ownership is sanctioned by Islamic law and
tradition, but nationalization is not incompatible with Islam if individuals are not injured. Qaddafi reminds Libyans that the Prophet Mu-
hammed converted a salt mine owned by some of the Companions into
joint property of all Muslims.

Since Arabs are already spiritually united through the Koran in
Qaddafi's view, there is a connection between Arab unity and Islam.
Only artificial boundaries, created by imperialist powers and "coun-
terfeit" thrones occupied by reactionary Arab kings prevent the realization of total Arab unity. Once boundaries and kings are removed,
unity will solve "all the difficult problems of the Arab nation." According to Qaddafi, "Arab unity is an inevitable necessity. Unity is
necessary to protect the Arab people from enemies. . . . Unity is
the secure frame and final image of the struggle of the Arab Nation."[5]

ANTIBACKWARDNESS

Qaddafi's socialism is the socialism of social justice and modernization, not the socialism of class warfare and state ownership
of the means of production. Qadaffi summed up this belief eloquently:

Socialism means social justice. Our objective is to
make progress, build aircraft and ships, manufacture

> cars and medicines, produce and build. We want to
> rid the people of hunger, poverty, backwardness
> and ignorance. We call this socialism.[6]

Qaddafi's socialism derives from a postcolonial situation, caus-
ing him to differentiate between domestic and foreign capitalists. Foreign capitalists are incompatible with Libya's well-being and should
be nationalized or strictly regulated; domestic capitalists are only bad
if they are exploitative. According to Qaddafi, foreign capitalists exploit Libya; Libyans lack technical skills and knowledge, and the industrialized countries take advantage consequently of Libya's backwardness.

Qaddafi nevertheless realizes that the small Libyan bureaucracy
lacks the education, expertise, and manpower necessary to modernize
the nation. Consequently, nationalization is not the whole answer
to either imperialism or backwardness. Agricultural cooperatives
are unnecessary because the country had much land and few farmers.
Qaddafi envisions a Libyan agricultural and industrial economy that
will achieve the complete exploitation of Libya's economic potentiali-
ties, while ensuring the control of the people over the basic means of
production. Libya's great wealth lies in her petroleum resources,
and these assets belong to the Libyan people, not to the foreign oil
companies; the revolution is meant to liberate the people from the
domination of the foreign oil companies and the international capitalists.

Qaddafi charged the monarchy with keeping Libya poor and backward while sitting on top of monumental oil wealth. Petroleum wealth
should be used, rather, to modernize Libya and improve the life of
all her citizens, not to enrich foreign capitalists or a few Libyans.

The fear that oil wealth could become a means of creating new
class distinctions, rather than a means to modernization and socialism, is ever present. Qaddafi often warns Libyans that vigilance
must be exercised to ensure that petroleum income fosters development.

We have seen the basic components of Qaddafi's socialism:
social justice, Islam, anti-imperialism, nationalism, antibackward-
ness, unity of all Libyan classes, and equality. All of these ideas
have been components of either of the two major currents of socialism
in the Arab world—Syrian Baath socialism and Nasserite socialism.
Although Libyan socialism owes its intellectual origins to both these
movements, the impact of Nasserism is paramount. Qaddafi's admiration for the late Egyptian leader verges on hero worship; even
the names of the major governmental bodies are borrowed from the
Egyptian revolution, including the Revolutionary Command Council,
the Free Officers, and the Libyan Arab Socialist Union. Qaddafi told
the Libyan Congress of the Arab Socialist Union that "Nasserism is

the only and the genuine course for Arab development."[7] The first foreign minister in Qaddafi's Cabinet, Salih Bousseir, lived for many years in Egypt on an Egyptian government pension. But Baathist influence was also apparent in the Libyan revolution when the Libyan officers adopted the old Baath motto of unity, freedom, and socialism, and turned it around into freedom, socialism, and unity. Suliman al-Maghribi, the first Prime Minister under the RCC, grew up and lived for many years in Syria where he was reported to have adopted Baath socialism.

Anti-Idris feeling in Libya before the revolution was limited almost entirely to the small intelligentsia who had received their education in the Arab world. Regardless of whether they were educated in Egypt or Syria they imbibed Arab unity, socialism, and nonalignment. There were, however, differences between the Baathist and Nasserist strains of socialism.

THE ORIGINS OF LIBYAN SOCIALISM

Although the nature of both Syrian and Egyptian socialism is discussed in depth elsewhere in this volume, it is nonetheless important to place Libyan socialism in its proper historical, geographical, and intellectual setting.

The father of Baath socialism is considered to be Michel Aflaq. Aflaq, a Syrian Christian (Greek Orthodox) became interested in Marxism while a student in Paris and upon his return to Syria in the mid-1930s he absorbed the concepts of Arabism and humanitarian socialism prevalent in Damascus.[8] Aflaq and Salah al-Din Bitar formed the Baath (Renaissance) Party in 1947; the former as a Christian was "compelled to establish his nationalism on a secular basis."[9] Nationalism and socialism were to unify the Arab world rather than Islam. Aflaq's socialism differed from both communism and European socialism, envisioning socialism as the product of cooperation among classes, rather than as the final outcome of class struggle.

According to Aflaq, the Arab world was in the throes of decadence and nothing short of a total transformation of Arab society would bring an end to this decadence. Socialism was not viewed as an economic order but as a value system "designed to achieve dignity for man through his participation in the activities of society and by means of ensuring a minimum standard of living."[10] Aflaq's socialism was Pan-Arabic rather than Syrian, seeking the creation of a single Arab state based on Arab nationalism. These, then, are the bases of Qaddafi's views of socialism as a system of social justice leading to class cooperation and Arab unity. The cultural and spiritual values of the Arab world had been forgotten, according to Aflaq, but the socialist revolution would result in a transformation of spirit, outlook, and values of individual Arabs and a transformation in the social and cultural organization of Arab society.

Being primarily a program of social and economic development derived from Egypt's own experience, rather than a call for the fundamental transformation of Arab spiritual and cultural values, Nasserite socialism differed from Baath socialism. Aflaq's Christian beliefs necessitated the nonreligious basis of the Baath appeal; Nasser, however, was able to employ the appeal of Islam in the service of Arab socialism. In contrast to the secular nature of Aflaq's thought, Egypt's 1956 Constitution clearly stated that "Islam is the religion of the state." Unlike Aflaq, the Egyptian Free Officers "understood . . . the importance of Islam as a link between their movement and the majority of a tradition-bound public. In the absence of any other strong or fully developed political link, the religious-national bond of Islam appeared . . . the most efficacious for political purposes."[11]

Islam had instrumental value for the Egyptian military leadership. In 1954 an Islamic Congress was established to further Islamic education, research, and scholarship; spread Islam and distribute the Koran; teach Arabic; and mobilize Islamic youth. Although Nasser was unwilling to strengthen Islamic institutions—Islamic courts were abolished and women were given juridicial rights—he did encourage the cultural and Pan-Arab aspects of Islam.

Nasserite socialism progressively changed the attitude toward Arab unity; by the late 1950s Baath Pan-Arabism was adopted.

> The Arab fatherland is an indissoluble political and
> economic unity; no Arab territory could meet the
> very conditions of its existence if it remained iso-
> lated from other territories. The Arab Nation, the
> umma, constitutes a spiritual and cultural unit; all
> existing differences among its members are super-
> ficial and false and will entirely disappear when the
> Arab consciousness reawakens.[12]

Although he adopted Pan-Arabism in theory, the failure of the Egyptian-Syrian union in 1961 made Nasser wary of Arab unity in practice—Mohammed Hussanein Haykal wrote that year that "the Arab people in Egypt had not yet reached the stage of total perparation for Arab unity."[13]

Egyptian socialism concentrated on agrarian and administrative reform, nonalignment, modernization of the army, and industrialization under the aegis of the state. Nasserite socialism, which was fundamentally antiparty, did not find its institutional expression in a political party, as did Aflaq's Baath socialism, but manifested itself

in a series of rallies and unions that were supposed to unite Egyptians. Unlike parties that were "divisive," unions such as the Arab
Socialist Union were more easily controlled by the military leadership, guiding the masses. From Nasser's Arab socialism Qaddafi
adopted the focus on Islam and the antiparty stance, although the importance placed on Arab unity by Qaddafi exceeded either Aflaq's or
Nasser's emphasis. The paramount role of Islam in Libyan socialism
was quite different from Aflaq's secular socialism, or Nasser's instrumental use of Islam as a unifying force. The Islamic component
of Libyan socialism was a consumatory value for Qaddafi.[14]

ECONOMIC DEVELOPMENT IN LIBYA

The RCC is cognizant of the fact that petroleum is a "wasting"
asset: If Libya does not employ petroleum income to foster economic
growth in areas other than petroleum, she will scarcely benefit from
her petroleum wealth, remaining a backward nation when her petroleum reserves are exhausted. Qaddafi's economic policies have
three aspects: petroleum policy, agricultural development, and social investment. Agricultural policy seems the most urgent; the
Minister of State for Agricultural Development has warned that "unless we turn oil revenues into tractors and turn the desert green we
will be plowing in the sea."[15]

Petroleum

Libya began exporting petroleum in late 1961, at the rate of approximately 20,000 barrels a day. In a buyer's market, such as
existed in the early 1960s, there was little incentive for the major oil
companies to invest in Libya, who was seen as a Johnny-come-lately
to the petroleum market. Nevertheless, the Libyan government was
able to exploit Libya's petroleum through the encouragement of drill-
ing by independent companies; one company, Occidental Petroleum,
eventually produced half of Libya's total output.

The Six-Day War in the Middle East had a substantial impact
on Libya's petroleum prospects because the closing of the Suez Canal
to all traffic greatly increased shipping costs for Middle Eastern
oil. The lengthy trip around the Cape increased time, and therefore
costs, for the European petroleum importing nations. Between 1967
and 1970 Libya's petroleum production doubled (from 820 million to
1,960 million tons per annum). Libya's sudden desirability (due to
her position on the Mediterranean, obviating the need to use the Cape
route) led to enthusiasm for investment in Libya's oil petroleum in-

dustry: by 1969 there were 42 oil companies from eight nations exploiting Libya's petroleum reserves.

Libya's petroleum policies have received most attention; Qaddafi has pressed for higher prices, participation and nationalization, and the development of indigenous petroleum expertise.

Shortly after the 1969 revolution, the RCC opened negotiations aimed at securing higher rates for the government with the oil companies operating in Libya. Although they initially resisted Libyan demands, two events beyond Libya's borders led to a victory for Qaddafi: The growth of the European demand for petroleum, coupled with the closing of the Trans-Arabian Pipeline. At the beginning of 1970 European petroleum demand shot up while the production of coal declined. Shortly thereafter the Libyans switched their negotiating tactics from discussing a new agreement with all the oil companies to concentrating on the two largest exporters: Occidental and Exxon. By the end of April Exxon was offering an $.11 rise in rates with a $.10-.12 barrel freight differential. On May 3, Syria suddenly closed the Trans-Arabian Pipeline to force higher payments for transit rights, depriving Europe of much-needed oil. Companies were shipping an extra half-million barrels a day around the Gulf and tanker rates shot up. The Libyans immediately took advantage of Europe's discomfiture by imposing production cutbacks on most of the companies while cutting Occidental's daily production by half.

Prime Minister Jalloud, the negotiator for the Libyan government, adopted the strategy of attacking the weakest link first, rather than dealing with the petroleum companies as a single unity. In 1970 Occidental Petroleum was considered the weakest link. Because Occidental's main production facility was located in Libya, the company's stock was very susceptible to rapid downward movement due to adverse news from Libya. The report that Occidental was ordered to reduce daily petroleum production by half, coupled with carefully cultivated rumors that Libya was contemplating annulling Occidental's concession because of irregularities pertaining to the granting of its concession, was enough to force a new accord with the Libyan government. After the Occidental settlement the other oil companies doing business in Libya fell into line one after another. Libya also insisted on a conservation agreement limiting daily production; Libya's yearly output, which was 160 million tons in 1970, was 107 million tons two years later.

In 1971 the RCC announced that they were planning to begin a new round of negotiations with the oil companies. In April 1971 the Libyans gained a new five-year agreement, calling for an increase in the posted price from $2.55 a barrel to $3.45, and tax increases set uniformly at 55 percent with a protective clause forcing the oil companies to pay the price difference from 1965 to September 1970. In addition, the permanent posted price was to increase 2.5 percent annually. Successive evaluations of the dollar led Libya to demand and receive a total of 15 percent increases in all taxes, royalties, and charges. Price increases were relatively easy to wrest from the oil companies for two reasons: increased costs could be passed along to the consumer, with little impact on profits, and the horizontally integrated petroleum industry has a vested interest in high oil prices that make coal and natural gas more competitive fuels. But if price increases were relatively easy to negotiate, because they could be passed along, the negotiation path to participation agreements was not as smooth. Involving no change in authority patterns, minority participation was agreeable to the petroleum companies, but majority participation would remove day-to-day control of operations from the hands of the operators.

Under the impetus of Libyan prodding, the Organization of Petroleum Exporting Countries (OPEC) passed a resolution at their July 1971 Vienna meeting, calling for "immediate steps towards effective implementation of the principle of participation in existing oil concessions." But in September the Libyans found themselves in total disagreement with OPEC's decision to seek only 25 percent participation, opting unilaterally for majority control.

The nationalization policy, designed to achieve majority control for the Libyan government dates from the December 1971 nationalization of British Petroleum (BP), supposedly in retaliation for British acquiescence in the Iranian occupation of Abu Musa, the Tunbs Islands in the Straits of Hormuz at the entrance to the Persian Gulf. Less than a year later the Libyan government demanded 50 percent participation in the Bunker Hunt operation (Bunker Hunt was BP's partner in its Libyan operations). Close on the heels of the Bunker Hunt nationalization the Libyan government announced that it would seek 50 percent participation in all foreign oil companies doing business in Libya. The only public explanation was Jalloud's statement that "Libya's oil belongs to the Libyan people."

In June 1973 Libya took over Bunker Hunt, proclaiming that the United States needed "a slap in its cool, arrogant face" because of its support for Israel.[16] American arrogance is symbolized in the support of the monopolistic oil companies. It is high time the Arabs take serious steps to undermine American interest in our region."[17]

Negotiations between the "majors" and the Libyans were fruitless; the majors threatened to pull out completely from Libya, seemingly preferring nationalization to a majority participation agreement. In August 1973 Jalloud tried to teach the majors a lesson on the danger of refusing to negotiate, by nationalizing two of the independents, Oasis and Occidental. This action did nothing to improve the outlook for an agreement with the majors. Consequently, on September 1,

1973, exactly four years after the Libyan revolution, goaded by the
failure to achieve union with Egypt, Jalloud announced the nationalization of 51 percent of the remaining oil companies as an anniversary
present to the Libyan people. Compensation would be paid based on
the decision of an all-Libyan three-man committee that would hear
each individual case, but the petroleum companies refused to accept
this unilateral action. Whatever thoughts the oil companies may have
entertained of fighting the nationalization were quickly dispelled by
the Arab oil boycott that followed the outbreak of war in the Middle
East in October.

In Jalloud's September 1 press conference, he gave a hint of
future events, informing the world that the Libyans had discovered
the virtues of vertical integration. Before 1969 Libya received $2.30
per barrel; income by September 1 had doubled, but the current price
of a refined barrel was $27. Libya planned to refine, ship, and market
her own oil in search of a larger share of that $27 price. Jalloud also
announced plans to establish two large refineries and to double the
Libyan tanker fleet.

But the brake on vertical integration and export restriction is
Libya's lack of skilled manpower. Libya is scarcely capital-shy.
According to Libyan law every expatriate employee in an oil company
must have a Libyan understudy who certifies in writing that he is being prepared to assume the expatriate's duties. However, the Libyans complain there has been enormous abuse of this regulation. In
the past it has been the average Libyan laborer that has been selected
as an assistant to a chief of a technical section; only Exxon appears
to have a significant number of senior Libyans in positions of responsibility. The Libyan Petroleum Ministry simply lacks the personnel
to monitor oilfield practices; consesequently the Libyans cannot even
be certain how many barrels are being produced a day. In an effort
to remedy these problems Qaddafi asked President Boumedienne of
Algeria for petroleum experts but was refused. Although Qaddafi has
established an oil institute at Tobruk to teach Libyans the skills necessary to run their petroleum industry, a realistic estimate indicates
that it will require another five to ten years for Libyans to gain the
expertise necessary to control their petroleum wealth.

Agricultural Development

Libya, which was the wheat center of the ancient world, still
produced foodstuffs in the late 1950s but now imports almost all her
food. The discovery of petroleum, which led to mass migration to
the cities, also resulted in large numbers of Libyans deserting their
farms and herds, leaving the encroaching sands to cover cultivated

areas.[18] In an effort to reverse the situation, the RCC is encouraging agricultural development. Presently Libya imports wheat, barley, beans, onions, fruit, and milk; only in potatoes is Libya self-sufficient. Qaddafi hopes that substantial capital investment in agriculture can change the food situation, but only about 1 percent of the country's land area—along the Mediterranean Coast—is suitable for farming. In the desert and oasis areas of the south there is less than three inches of rainfall each year.

The RCC allocated $2.1 billion for an agricultural development plan with five major agricultural projects undertaken: the Jafara Valley project; the Kufra land reclamation project and the Sarir cereal project; the Green Mountains project; and a project in Fezzan.

In the Jafara plain, near the Tunisian border, 6,000 new farms and a number of new industries are planned, while the Kufra land reclamation project involves tens of millions of dollars for irrigation with water from huge underground wells for wheat cultivation. In addition, a stock-farming area to foster meat production is planned.[19] Some of these reclamation projects have been undertaken by Egyptian companies.

As is the case with the petroleum industry, the real impediment to agricultural development is not capital but manpower. In a country with less than 2 million inhabitants, the number of potential farmers is quite small, so that much of the work on the land is presently being done by foreigners—Egyptians and Tunisians in particular. One of the factors influencing Qaddafi's efforts to merge Libya with Egypt is the desire to gain Egypt's surplus agricultural manpower. The lack of administrators, technicians, and infrastructure prevent the RCC from spending the funds allocated in the development budget.

In an effort to return Libyans to the land, urban migration has been restricted and landowners face loss of their property if they fail to occupy it. Social investment is being undertaken in the countryside to affect the urban-rural imbalance because the RCC recognizes that some of the motivation behind the tidal waves of urban migration is the lack of facilities in the countryside. When the carrot failed, the RCC moved to the stick, announcing a decree giving the government the power to introduce compulsory labor in the spring of 1972.

In "Industrial Development," Libya's first Five-Year Development Plan for 1963-68, most of the emphasis was on construction of infrastructure: highways, ports, airfields, terminal facilities, sewage systems, and power stations were all begun on a small scale. Under Qaddafi, as under Idris, infrastructure development has continued. Dams were built near Tripoli and Benghazi, and desalination and electric power stations were constructed. But Libya's infrastructure is still in need of further development.

Industrialization has many faces: a petrochemical industry was established, food-processing plants were built, Libya's resources that could be used in the construction industry were developed, and some consumer goods industries were begun to reduce Libya's dependence on Western imports. In addition to a large petrochemical complex under construction at Mausah near Benghazi, which includes plants to produce ammonia, black coal, and methanel, there are several oil refineries being built. In spite of food processing plants built for flour, dairy products, dates, and sardines, the major portion of industrialization appears to be in the construction area where plants to manufacture cement, bricks, steel pipe, asbestos, plastic pipe, cable wire, and glass have all been built or are on the drawing board. On the other hand, there seems a dearth of consumer industries, with a few factories under way in textiles, shoes, woolens, paper, drugs, and matches. These factories are being built or managed with assistance from East and West Europe, Egypt, India, the United States, and Britain. Little has been done in the area of heavy industry; lacking raw materials and skilled manpower, Libya has eschewed heavy industry with the exception of a single scrap-iron plant.

Nationalization and Investment Policy

Upon seizing power, the RCC moved gingerly in the area of nationalization. In the first few months only foreign banks had 51 percent of their shares nationalized. At a later date, import and export companies as well as wholesale and retail trade were restricted to companies whose capital was wholly owned by Libyans. Then came the turn of commercial banks that have to be completely owned by Libyans, with shares owned by non-Libyans transferred to the state. In March 1970 an industrial policy decree was issued, permitting foreign-owned capital investment for some industrial projects with the proviso that the government will control any major scheme that involves key natural resources. Both public and private sectors are able to start medium-size projects based on agricultural produce, building materials, and goods produced from local raw materials, but no loans are available in this category. In case financial assistance is necessary, joint shareholding companies, in which the state owns the majority share, will be formed. The private sector is still responsible for minor projects based on local raw materials and aimed at local consumption.[20] Capital, as previously noted, is allowed to be privately owned and invested by Libyans under Qaddafi's socialism. Although in theory some foreign private investment is also welcome, in actual fact the government has had to furnish almost all the funds for development in the industrial sector, since foreign investors understandably fear nationalization.

SOCIAL SERVICES

In Qadaffi's urgent desire to modernize his nation, substantial developments funds have been allocated for improved schools, health facilities, and housing.

Independence found Libya with staggering educational deficiencies. There were only 14 Libyans with university degrees, and only 32,000 students in both primary and secondary school. By 1968 there were 300,000 students but Libya's illiteracy rate is almost 75 percent. As late as 1972, Qaddafi bemoaned that there were only 60 Libyans holding doctorates and only 83 Libyans among the staff of 500 at the university, 60 of whom were abroad. Because of the staggering lack of trained professionals (there were only 114 Libyans among the 1,560 doctors in the country)[21] Qaddafi recruited almost 4,000 teachers from Egypt and the Sudan and from among the Palestinians. Seven thousand students were sent abroad to study, many of whom show little inclination to return home, leading Qaddafi to identify a new disease sweeping Libya's intelligentsia—the desire for an American doctorate.

New housing is being constructed at a rapid rate; on the outskirts of Tripoli modern apartment houses are rising to replace an entire shantytown. Hospitals and dispensaries are also being constructed, but the by now familiar manpower shortages limit substantial improvements in the health field.

POLITICAL PARTICIPATION IN LIBYA

After the revolution Qaddafi immediately established his own version of the Egyptian Arab Socialist Union. The Libyan ASU was meant to unite the military, the intellectuals, the workers, and the peasants. Major Bashir Hawadi, a member of the RCC who is the Minister of National Guidance, is also the General Secretary of the ASU. One of the leading intellectuals of the ASU, Ibrahim el-Ghwail, is considered a Marxist. In addition to the ASU, there are two other mass organizations, trade unions, and the Call of Islam society. Trade unions, which were banned under Idris, were formed under the RCC after a labor law was enacted providing for one union covering each trade, and establishing reconciliation and arbitration committees that must be consulted in labor disputes. Until the committees have been consulted, strikes are prohibited.[22] The other mass organization is the Call of Islam Society led by the Islamic scholar Mahmoud Subli.[23] Both these organizations are institutions for mobilizing public energy and channeling ideological discussion, rather than decision-making bodies: Ultimate power rests with the Revolutionary Command Council.

Qaddafi has used the ASU and the Call of Islam society to propagate the theory of the Third International, which has been described as a "kind of Islamic Comintern." The colonel has "explained" his vision of Islamic socialism by drawing two small vertical blocks filled with dots on a sheet of paper, representing the Communist and Capitalist systems, where "wealth is concentrated at the top." Qaddafi then draws a third horizontal block in which "the wealth is distributed evenly."[24]

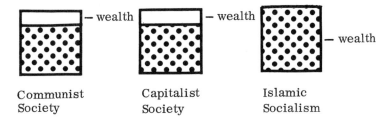

Communist   Capitalist   Islamic
Society   Society   Socialism

If the Libyan colonel fears the appeal of communism for the uneducated Libyan masses in general, he particularly fears the Libyan intellectuals who were educated in the Soviet Union before the September coup d'etat. Qaddafi described a scenario of growing Communist influence in Libya for the 1972 Congress of the Arab Socialist Union:

> Soon you will hear these intellectuals telling the rank-
> and file of the Arab Socialist Union that unless they
> become Maoists like the Chinese they will not be able
> to develop industries or defeat Israel or anything
> else. An ignorant person hearing this would at once
> become a Maoist if that enabled him to defeat Israel.
> The masses will be deceived: they will be told that
> in order to liberate the Arab world, build industries
> and invade the moon, they must become Communists.
> This happened in the Sudan. I saw it myself.[25]

The Arab Socialist Union was the type of organization that could be established throughout the Arab world, leading to spontaneous linkages joining all the Arabs together in one movement. While Qaddafi fears the appeal of communism to Libya's uprooted masses, he also opposes the hold the Muslim Brotherhoods have on his still traditional countrymen. "Islam," according to Qaddafi, "has no room for conspirators who live in the past and who like monkeys imitate each other." He threatened the Muslim Brotherhood with imprisonment, treason trials, and death sentences.[26]

The Minister of National Guidance opened the 1972 meeting of the Arab Socialist Union with the statement "that in a period of revolutionary transformation personal freedom must be sacrificed for the sake of the national interest."[27] This statement led to a debate between Qaddafi and Ali Ben Lashgar on the role of democracy in Libyan society, Ali arguing that freedom and democracy must come first and that Libya needed a people's assembly. Qaddafi replied that he accepted the right of citizens to full freedom, but how were they to operate this in the "extraordinary stage in which Libya finds itself, in which the country seeks to cover a great distance in a short time? If we discuss endlessly the most insignificant rights we shall create obstacles to progress. How can we overcome this problem?"

It was not possible to harmonize government by people's assembly with a revolutionary situation, Qaddafi argued. They might have to take 20 decisions in a night; if they had to get the approval of the assembly every time it could take them two or three years.

Qaddafi lamented that the RCC had sought to reconcile the need for revolutionary transformation with democratic practice, but alas without success. "The more we edge toward democracy, the more we want to broaden its base," but this creates insoluble problems for the revolutionary executive. "The more people we consult, the less revolutionary transformation we shall achieve. Much as we want to hear the views of the majority, we shall continue to implement our own decisions which we consider to be interests of the Arab society of Libya without heeding the views of the majority."[28] On the other hand, Qaddafi opposed those who argued that "during the period of revolutionary change there is no room for democracy. We cannot abolish democracy or the freedom of individuals in the name of revolutionary transformation. If we did, our regime would be no better than a military dictatorship."[29]

On April 15, 1973, the young Libyan colonel made one dramatic effort to expand political participation announcing in response to a variety of problems the institution of an Islamic cultural revolution. The immediate problems were the unpopularity of the 300,000 Egyptians living in Libya and growing opposition to the proposed merger with Egypt. Although Egyptians serve as advisers and technicians in the army, the police, the service administrations, and every government ministry except foreign affairs, and although they are contractors, teachers, doctors, workers, they have never been entirely welcome. Qaddafi seemed stunned at first by the anti-Egyptian riots in Benghazi in February 1973, then became determined to rout out anti-Egyptian feeling. Six weeks later Qaddafi announced the "cultural revolution." The idea for the cultural revolution supposedly originated with Mohammed Hassarein Heykal, the former editor in chief of the Cairo daily Al-Ahram, and Nasser's alter ego. Heykal

visited Peking in January 1973, later writing extensively about the
Chinese "cultural revolution." The Libyan "cultural revolution" had
six components: The distribution of arms to the people; the suspen-
sion of the outmoded Libyan legal system; mobilization of Arab energies in the coming Egypt-Libya union to prepare for "vengeance"
against Israel; a purge of "those who are politically sick"; an administrative revolution; and a cultural revolution inspired by Islamic
teachings "against libraries, universities and school curricula."
Slogans and wallposters appeared, such as, "Our small nation which
wields the Koran and the sword today preaches the Koran and victory,
and issues a call to violent popular revolution."[30] Some arms were
distributed, "not to 'the people' as a whole but to those most trusted
by the regime," with the chosen few given initial training in the use
of arms. Qaddafi said that "anybody who is against the revolution
will not be given weapons, but the weapons will be aimed at his
chest."

The engine of the cultural revolution were People's Committees
composed mostly of young blue-collar workers and students elected
by fellow workers, that became "the controlling force in each town
and hamlet, in government agencies, state-run utilities, factories,
farms, hospitals, schools, university departments—and foreign oil
companies."[31] The committees dismissed, demoted or transferred
thousands of officials in an effort to shatter the bureaucratic complacency and purge the ideologically unreliable.

Qaddafi decreed on April 15, 1973 that "we must suspend all
the laws now in force." In practice this has meant that any law or
local regulation that gets in the way of a people's committee can be
lifted at the committee's request; any new regulation, however, must
be endorsed by the Council of the Revolution.[32] The purge of "devia-
tionists" who are politically sick, according to Qaddafi, was supposed
to rid Libya of those who talked of "Communism, atheism, who make
propaganda for the Western countries and advocate capitalism. We
shall put them in prison."[33] Several hundred people were arrested,
including "lawyers, educators and people with past political party
association, ranging from the highly conservative Muslim brotherhood
to the Communist Party."[34] Many of those arrested were known opponents of the proposed merger with Egypt; a few detainees were "reformed" in prison and then brought to appear on television to admit
their past guilt.[35]

The desire for an administrative revolution seems to have been
one of the prime factors encouraging Qaddafi to undertake the "cultural revolution." He urged the people "to trample under foot any
bourgeois bureaucrat who slams the door in your face, refusing to
respond to your needs."[36] People's committees immediately set
out to dismiss the bourgeois bureaucrats with vengeance: The offi-

cials dismissed read like a Libyan Who's Who including the head of
the Libyan radio, the director of a Tripoli hospital, the chief of operations of Mobil Oil Libya, the assistant general manager of American
Overseas Petroleum, the president and vice-president of Libyan Arab
Arilines, professors at the national universities, the top management
of the state-owned Libyan National Oil Company, the vice-dean of education at the Tripoli campus of the University of Libya, the chancellor
of the university, and the dean of law and the dean of medicine at the
Benghazi campus. Some of these men were later reinstated by the
RCC, which acted to ensure that critical services were not disrupted.
The government clamped down on hospital committees by requiring
that at least 60 percent of the members of a popular committee at a
hospital must be doctors. The council also reversed some of the
popular committees' decisions, restricted other actions, and prevented the "cultural revolution" from disrupting the armed forces,
key government ministries, and the oil fields.

The most useful group of People's Committees for the regime
were those that formed in the foreign oil companies, at a time when
delicate negotiations concerning nationalization were taking place.
"At the headquarters of foreign companies, the committees' first
action was to abolish executive secrecy. They put guards on the
Telex rooms and forbade the use of the companies' coding machines.
They made sure that the executives' offices remained open, in some
cases by knocking off the doors, and moved the executives' secretaries to the secretaries' pool so that dictation could be overheard."[37]

The xenophobic attitude toward books, education, and school
curricula received the most attention in the Western press. Qaddafi
explained that "we live by the Koran, God's book. We will reject any
idea that is not based on it. Therefore we enter into a cultural revolution to refute and destroy all misleading books which have made
youth sick and insane. These books must be burned. Tear up all the
imported books that do not express Arabian or Islam socialism and
progress. Burn and destroy all curricula that do not express the
truth."[38] Students removed books from university libraries; crowds
invaded commercial bookstores and carted off stacks of foreign language books, books believed to be pornographic by Islamic standards,
and economic textbooks embodying capitalist ideology. By the fall of
1973 Qaddafi was preoccupied with the Libyan-Egyptian merger and
the Middle East war—and interest in the people's committees seems
to have petered out.

The RCC dissolved many of the committees that had engaged in
"aimless dismissals for the sake of making new appointments." But
the committees were strengthened and encouraged as local government institutions.

Like other revolutionary military regimes, the Libyan RCC has been unable to share political power on a sustaining basis, or create institutions to function as pressure groups or parties. The military has been more successful at organizing mass displays of carefully orchestrated progovernment opinion.

SOCIALISM AND LIBYAN FOREIGN POLICY

Libyan foreign policy has four significant aspects: the search for Pan-Arab unity; support for anti-Israeli, pro-Islamic guerrilla movements; an Arab counteroffensive against Israel in Africa; and organization of Pan-Islamic rallies. (Qaddafi's policies in the petroleum arena have been discussed previously.) All of Qaddafi's foreign policies ventures are directed toward Arab unity, Israeli defeat, and the revitalization of Islam.

Qaddafi's primary foreign policy goal is Pan-Arab unity, a theme last sounded in the Arab world by Nasser. Qaddafi has encouraged union with his Maghrebian neighbors to the west and the Arabs to the east. Although Qaddafi began in 1970 working on a plan for an Arab federation, including Egypt, Sudan, Libya, and Syria, nothing substantive grew out of the talks. After Sadat expelled Russian military advisers in August 1972 he began a search for new foreign policy options. One of these options was encouragement of union with Libya. The Egyptian leader gave Qaddafi a pledge that the next year would bring union between the two countries in exchange for Libyan financial support, but as the September 1973 date for union neared, Sadat hesitated. Qaddafi first attempted to force unity by launching a march of 40,000 Libyans to Cairo; later he accepted Sadat's plan for a gradual step-by-step merger. Since the Yom Kipper War led to strained relations between Egypt and Libya because Sadat did not consult Qaddafi before launching the attack or agreeing to cease-fire terms, Qaddafi then tried an abortive union with Tunisia. All of Qaddafi's potential suitors agree that his oil wealth is vast but fear that he would be an exceedingly difficult partner to cohabit with.

Qaddafi has used his oil wealth to deny Israel diplomatic allies in Africa. Beginning with Uganda's General Amin in 1972, he launched a diplomatic offensive against Israel, exchanging Libyan financial aid for the severing of diplomatic relations with Israel. Before the Yom Kippur War led to almost total rupture of relations between Israel and Africa, Qaddafi succeeded in encouraging eight African states to break relations with Israel (Uganda, Chad, Niger, Congo, Mali, Guinea, Zaire, and Burundi).

The history of Libyan support for guerrilla movements in the last five years has been checkered: On the one hand Qaddafi has sup-

ported the Palestinian guerrillas with financial assistance and berated
his Arab brothers such as King Hussein who lack enthusiasm for guerrilla activity; on the other, he has constantly expressed his disgust
with both the fractious nature of the guerrilla movement and those
groups that are Marxist oriented. Qaddafi, who is believed to have
made a particular commitment to Black September, the clandestine
wing of Al Fatah, has also supported guerrilla Muslim groups in
Eriterea, Chad, Syria, Morocco, Tunisia, Thailand, the Philippines,
and Panama. "Libyan transhipped guns have been sent to the Irish
Republican Army because the British had 'to be taught a lesson' after
a Persian Gulf dispute."[39] Qaddafi's support for the Chadan rebels
ended when the Chad government broke relations with Israel. The
extent or importance of Libyan support to these movements is difficult to gauge because all these movements existed before Qaddafi began handing out his largesse, and none had had new, striking success
since receipt of Libyan money. Qaddafi's rhetoric may well exceed
his actual support or influence in this as in many other areas. Beginning in 1970, Qaddafi has sponsored a series of Islamic Missionary
Conferences in Tripoli, after the first of which a permanent Islamic
Bureau was established in the Libyan capital. In the summer of 1973
the RCC convened an International Islamic Youth Conference to discuss ways of binding the "society of the Koran" in the twentieth century and to push their Third International theory. Regardless of the
intellectual value of the Third Force theory, Qaddafi's commitment
to an Islamic revival has won him sympathizers and supporters
throughout the Muslim world.

The success of Qaddafi's foreign policy is difficult to estimate,
but he has isolated Israel diplomatically, politicized petroleum, encouraged the Palestinian guerrilla movement, and revitalized Pan-
Islamic sentiment. On the other side of the balance sheet, vast military expenditures have been of little value in destroying Israel, and
real Arab unity is still a long way down the road. One result of Qaddafi's appeal may be to encourage young officers in Morocco, Jordan,
and Saudi Arabia to adopt the Arab Socialist Revolution.

THE FUTURE OF LIBYAN SOCIALISM

The long-term prospects for a leader as mercurial as Muammar
al-Qaddafi are not promising because the tensions, instability, and
near chaos brought by the attempted merger with Egypt, the cultural
revolution, and Qaddafi leadership style seem to contain the seeds of
their own destruction. But even the eventual downfall of Qaddafi
will probably have little effect on Libyan socialism. There is no
chance for a return of the monarchy, for example; future governments

are likely to consist of Libyan army officers with a commitment to modernization, socialism, anti-Zionist activity, and Pan-Arab sentiment. Even if Qaddafi's Islamic fundamentalism and attempts at mergers are played down, the impact of Muammar al-Qaddafi on the Arab world will be substantial.

NOTES

1. Majid Khadduri, Modern Libya: A Study in Political Development (Baltimore: Johns Hopkins, 1963).

2. Middle East Journal 24, no. 2 (Spring 1970): 207.

3. Ibid.

4. Ibid., p. 208.

5. Ibid., p. 216.

6. Jon Kimche, "Libya's Qaddafy," Midstream, June/July 1972, p. 42.

7. Ibid., p. 39.

8. Amos Perlmutter, "From Obscurity to Rule: The Syrian Army and the Ba'ath Party," Western Political Quarterly 22, no. 4 (December 1969): 833.

9. Gordon Torrey, "Ba'ath Ideology and Practice," Middle East Journal 23, no. 4 (Autumn 1969): 449.

10. Majid Khadduri, Political Trends in the Arab World: The Role of Ideas and Ideals in Politics (Baltimore: Johns Hopkins, 1970), p. 156.

11. P. J. Vatikiotis, The Egyptian Army in Politics (Bloomington: University of Indiana Press), p. 193.

12. Anouar Abdel-Malek, Egypt: Military Society (New York: Vintage, 1968), pp. 252-53.

13. Ibid., p. 274.

14. For a discussion of the difference between instrumental and consumatory values, see David Apter, The Politics of Modernization (Chicago: University of Chicago Press, 1968).

15. New York Times, July 29, 1973.

16. Washington Post, September 2, 1973.

17. New York Times, August 8, 1973.

18. Ibid., July 29, 1973.

19. Ibid.

20. Africa Research Bulletin (Economic, Financial and Technical Series), March/April 1970, p. 1648 A and B.

21. Kimche, op. cit., p. 41.

22. Africa Research Bulletin (Political Series), May 1-31, 1970, p. 1769 A.

23. Kimche, op. cit., p. 41.

24. Washington Post, May 20, 1973.
25. Kimche, op. cit., p. 41.
26. Ibid.
27. Ibid., p. 43.
28. Ibid., pp. 43-4.
29. Ibid., p. 44.
30. The Guardian (London), May 23, 1973.
31. New York Times, May 22, 1973.
32. Ibid.
33. Ibid.
34. Washington Post, May 20, 1973.
35. The Guardian, July 26, 1973.
36. Baltimore Sun, August 3, 1973.
37. New York Times, May 22, 1973.
38. The Guardian, April 27, 1973.
39. Samuel Decalo, Present Tense, March/April 1974, p. 53.

6

ALGERIAN SOCIALISM:
NATIONALISM,
INDUSTRIALIZATION,
AND STATE-BULDING
Jean Leca

POLITICAL CULTURE

Algeria's political culture presents itself in such a way that we run the risk of overestimating the cultural process of national unification while neglecting the society's structural divisions. We therefore assert at the outset that, in our opinion, the existence of a political culture must not divert our attention from the political and social struggles inside the society. Nevertheless political culture does provide these struggles with a certain language and can thus be an important analytical tool for certain political processes.

Algerian political culture is characterized by two basic features —populism and segmentarity—which at first glance should prevent a socialist political system from functioning altogether. (By "socialism we refer to a centralized structure concerned with allocation of resources whose objective is the control and utilization of national economic wealth so as to prevent one class from monopolizing the products.) We propose that it is precisely the combination of these two aspects that allows the Algerian system to function.

Populism

Populism[1] consists of two fundamental principles: the supremacy of the will of the people, which is identified with justice and morality, over all norms; the importance of a direct parainstitutional relationship between the people and their leaders. The main components are: (1) a quasi-religious belief in the virtue of the common man who is healthy and uncontaminated by the city, its temptations, and its more or less corrupt leaders; (2) an incoercible mistrust of those who hold the monopoly of power and display that "sacrosanct technicity" that Ahmed Ben Bella, first leader of independent Algeria, declared must be "avoided like the plague because it only serves to strangle the socialist revolution"; (3) contempt for the politician and the civil servant.

People with very different ideas and vested interests all hold these elements in common. The masses had experienced colonization as a sort of hidden virtue, represented according to circumstances by the Europeans, the administrators, the "Spaniards," and similar groups.[2] These feelings combine with a general mistrust of those who "know" or "have" something to produce a feeling of hostility toward the ill-defined guilty parties (the bureaucrats and the imperialists) who are preventing the people from self-realization. The leaders, meanwhile, aver that one must always "go back to the people" so as not to be contaminated and so that the people may experience the solicitude of those in a governing position. For example, Ahmed Ben Bella admitted how with a false ingenuousness, the "little shoeshine boys"—poor children destined to a life of polishing the shoes of the passers-by in the street—were sent to specialized educational centers:

> We held these campaigns because they responded
> to a deep-seated hope of the Algerian masses. Com-
> ing out of a 130-year long night, after being scorned
> for so many years, these people needed to feel, to
> see, to touch the Algerian authorities' concern for
> them. Just as a child asks for reassurance and
> cuddling after waking from a nightmare, the Alger-
> ian people expected affection and attention from
> their first government.[3]

Colonel Boumediene, the current head of state, could not be farther from this kind of style, which is a mixture of sensitivity and political cunning.[4] But then populism is related neither to temperament nor to platform. When the so-called "June 19" regime* expresses its concern with morality and the "human factor" in a party corrupted by "career politicians," it is expressing the very same deep-rooted populist feeling. As Peter Worsley wrote, populism is a "syndrome" rather than a "doctrine"; it evolves on a continuum ranging from a "left wing" defined by an anarchist ideal of political self-determination at the grass-roots level, to a "right wing" that is char-

---

*The day in 1965 that marks President Ben Bella's overthrow by the army and the accession to power of the Revolutionary Council.

acterized by mass political noninvolvement.[5] Thus Ben Bellism represented the left wing and the "June 19 regime" the right wing of
populism.

Of course both wings of populism have been present inside the
two regimes precisely because they both relate to the same political
structures (weak political organization of the different social categories) and the same culture (mistrust of the state and demands on
the state). In fact, if populism seems to resist the establishment of a
well-organized state, it also has the tendency to reinforce that state
for two important reasons. First, populism is egalitarian: It asks
that the national wealth be shared equally and that all have the same
access to social mobility.[6] Therefore, while the people mistrust the
state, they insist on satisfaction from it. Consider, for example, the
"Fellah's (peasants) Congress" organized by Ahmed Ben Bella in 1964,
which demanded further technical and financial aid but refused "the
civil servant dictatorship" and the "colonist-state" represented by its
directors.[7] The Algerian citizen is an aggressive consumer who expects from the national state all that the colonial one had refused.
The urban petty bourgeoisie demands political power and the same
standard of living as the former colonizers, the technicians want the
means to industrialize better and faster than the developed countries,
and the urban proletariat insists on job security and par raises.
Apart from the technicians, all other categories hold a position of
"nonparticipatory expectation." The workers in self-managed agriculture maintain a stand of claim-satisfaction excluding all political
options, above all socialist;[8] the uprooted and regrouped peasants
combine this claim-satisfaction mentality with a refusal to participate.[9] The traditional peasants feel that the fruits of the independence
for which they made such huge sacrifices have gone almost entirely
to the colonized cities that fought less than they did.[10]

These feelings reinforce, at one and the same time, the mistrust of and the demands on the civil servants from the city who do
not correspond to standard criteria of respectability (old age, morality, wisdom, and conciliation).[11] The civil servants are deluged
with claims and then held as scapegoats for all problems. In this
way, the more the society complains about the state, the more it demands government subsidy, and the further the state—the sole direct
body capable of "doing something valid for the country"—is reinforced.

Populism reinforces the state in yet another way. Given that
it represents the reaction of an outlying "province" against the center
(the periphery being the whole of the underdeveloped world, and the
center the industrialized capitalist world), the underdeveloped country's state appears as a workers' international. Anti-imperialism is
not only a political platform of foreign affairs but also a powerful
element of unification rallying around the state the different sectors

of society. The leaders, whatever their former socialization, have
conditioned anti-imperialist reflexes as a result of the liberation war
when they thought that the Algerian nation could only realize itself at
the expense of an opposition toward the whole of the West (and not
only France, as was the case in Tunisia).[12] They now consider an
agreement with imperialism impossible; rather, it is necessary to
gather strength in order to fight it. As Mohamed Khider, one of the
first initiators of the armed rebellion against France, said in 1954:
"[We cannot] believe in persuasion. There is a logic to violence and
it is necessary to carry this logic to its conclusion."[13]

This feeling is shared by the "industrialists," those in economically responsible positions. They build their empire by fighting private enterprises established in Algeria, and then by directly fighting
the French state during the oil crisis in 1971. The whole of their experience makes them see international capitalism not as a partner
but as an adversary with whom one may compromise but never cooperate. The intellectuals agree with the official ideology on this: The
"francophones" spontaneously share the radical ideologies of their
European or Latin-American counterparts while the "arabophones"
find in anti-imperialism the necessary outlet for their frustration at
being replaced by the francophones.[14] The working class, the peasants of self-managed agriculture, and the poor peasants react alike
to the same theme, either because those who emigrated to Europe—
about 800,000 of them—daily experience racism, or because they cannot succeed in selling their wine in France, or simply because it sim-
plifies matters to find the root of one's frustration in an external
enemy. Algeria considers herself to have been pillaged from top to
bottom and demands the "payment of the Western societies' debts for
their odious exploitation."[15] Only the state, a complex and centralized political administrative organization, can exact such repayment.
In this way, anti-imperialist populism reinforces the state and those
who hold power.[16]

We would like to point out that one by-product of this system of
thinking is the rejection of Marxism as an internal ideology.[17] Internal Marxism is the ideology of a society divided by class antagonisms,
while populism is one of a society unified by the general will and in
conflict with other societies that it accuses of domination.[18] Populism offers "nationalism with Marxist tendencies" as a symbolic
framework for an alliance between nationalists (whose anti-imperialism brings them closer to Marxism as an analytical economic method)
and Marxists (who after having experienced the force of nationalism
have approached it without subscribing to its cultural myths and religious ideology).[19]

Segmentarity

The term segmentarity is used to systematically describe those
social relationships that do not fit into the convenient mold of relationships based on national citizenship and political integration; one could
even extend it to the intergroup competition for power among hose
who do not accept the legal authority.[20] The most common terms in
Algeria are "clannishness" or "cousins' solidarity" with automatic
reference to the concept of acabiyya used by Ibn Khaldoun to indicate
kinship or blood ties.[21] While Ernest Gellner held to a vigorous analysis in his study of the Moroccan Atlas,[22] his more precise and probably more exact conceptualization will not be adopted since we are
trying to outline Algerian political culture on the macrosociological
level of the current system as well as on the microsociological level
of local societies. Therefore we will use only two of the features,
pointing out how the evolution since the colonial period has modified
them.

The first feature is the simultaneous recognition of primordial
ties and global ties. This corresponds to what Southall called a pyra-
midlike political structure: The sovereignty of the center coexists
with peripheral centers of power that are relatively autonomous.[23]
This was the case during the nineteenth century when the main structure of the nonurban world was the coexistence of tribes led either
by juads (war chiefs) or by mrabtin (religious chiefs) and linked by
vast religious parties: the brotherhoods. The only other possible
structure was provided in the 1830s by Abd-el Qader's attempt at
creating a modern state by using his religious status. But the French,
aware of the potential danger such a state represented for their colonial endeavors, did their best to undermine and destroy Abd-el Qader's
power.[24] Therefore, while the segmentary feature persisted, the
native brotherhoods, and the juads and mrabtin likewise, became
anachronistic and politically and socially ineffective as the colonial
system changed its form of domination.[25] A new religious movement
appeared, puritan and individualist, capable of organizing isolated individuals not bound by a tribal framework, capable also of borrowing
the colonizer's organizational models.[26] The reformist Islam
preached by the Ulema replaced the ecstatic religion that had blended
so well with the segmentary pattern of behavior. But segmentarity
has not yet withered away; primordial ties still serve to make the
state reward a region or group seeking government aid or contacts.
Segmentarity becomes an indicator of discontent, especially in the
regions where local or functional elites are not powerful nor social-
ized enough to play a significant role within the central bureaucracy.[27]

The second feature is such that there cannot be any legitimate
political process based upon an official pluralism.[28] Segments can-

not lose their identities in cooperating within an organization. They can bargain but not collaborate. Compromise is possible, but never participation in some kind of process in which each segment may gain some advantage. As in most segmentary systems, Algerian actors have a zero-sum concept of power. The origins of this concept lie in the colonial period when the political system did not offer Algerian politicos the opportunity to play a significant role. Because important issues were excluded from the legal political process, the Algerian elites were unable to coalesce and to give a common meaning to their political activities. The people acquired the habit of calling this caricature of politics boulitik (nonsense), a game without any relation to social issues. Accordingly, a strong mistrust of any centralized political process spread over the masses and segmentarity was reinforced among elites unable to share common symbols and institutions of national identity. Each successive political generation, noting the failure of its predecessors, developed new symbols expressing the same basic demands while accusing the preceding generation of being merely "collaborators" manipulated by the colonizer.[29] The absence of a common political culture among the elites explains the foundation, in 1954, of the National Front of Liberation (FLN), which has been the sole political institution since the eve of independence.

However, in 1962 the party was nothing more than a military organization divided into many centers of power and nominally ruled by a government vested with only international competence. Everything was ready for the "summer of shame" of 1962, when the political elites displayed their inability to work out a viable single-party system while making clear that there was no alternative to this system. The pattern of crisis that developed has been repeated often.

1. All parties in the conflict are represented on the arbitration board; there is almost no opposition outside the system that has any influence.

2. The factions never contest the basic principle of the arbitration board since they all recognize its conflict resolving capacity.

3. As each faction calls for a meeting but never at the same time, a spontaneously willed meeting about the official political process never takes place.

4. Each faction claims legitimacy and tries to prove it by asserting that the arbitration board is on its side and that the others are betraying the arbitrator.

5. The "rules of the game," which thus involve de facto exclusion of arbitration, consist of a group of bi- or multilateral negotiations destined not to eliminate the other party entirely but rather to weaken its negotiating position.

6. The "rules" exclude arbitration by a third party claiming
to be impartial. Only goodwill missions from members of a camp on
good terms with the other side are admitted. Effectively, by ac-
knowledging a mediator, each party would be admitting that it is not
the sole possessor of the legitimacy it attributes to the arbitration
board and its supposed support.

In this way, the segments defend not only their own particular
interests but also claim to be the guardian of the general welfare:
they do not claim to preserve their own power and autonomy inside
their own particular system, but rather to have a decisive influence
on the global system—which is why they cannot remain neutral nor
accept the fact that others do so by holding themselves above all factions. Thus even when compromise among the different factions ac-
companies the outcome of a crisis, the solution is never presented as
a compromise but as unification of political forces inside the supreme
symbolic body that is the party. It is not the conflict that is functional
for the system but the unity reaffirmed in its resolution. Segmentarity illegitimizes pluralism, because confrontation of the two would
render the political system incapable of responding to the needs of
the society.

A tentative explanation of such a situation can be outlined by
drawing on the general theory of conflict worked out by Ralk Dahrendorf:[30] if a society's general principles of organization are "subjus-
tice" because of the rapid changes that are going on in its development,
there can be authority structures, latent interests, and quasi-groups
but no interest groups endowed with coherent forms of organization,
and no patterned and normalized recruitment to the relevant positions
of authority. If one does not know who is going to replace the colonial
landowners, the European factory directors, and the civil servants,
if social authority is to be based on belonging to a marabout family,
the technical competence acquired in the colonizers' schools, the position of being a veteran, subscribing to a certain ideology, owning
the means of production, or simply controlling the armed forces,
then it is not surprising that one does not know any more about what
specific type of resources the political authority will be connected
with.

The explanation provided by Abdelkader Zghal, more appropriate to the Maghrebian conditions, is not very different. Dealing
with the reactivation of segmentary structures within a contemporary
political context, he contends that it

> can be explained by the existence in Maghrebian
> society of a structural imbalance between the mass
> of the population who has been torn from its tradi-

tional way of life, and the modern sector which is unable to offer it any possibility of coming to terms
with its new situation. In such circumstances, the
social stratification arising from modern economic
activity loses its coherence, and even at times its
meaning. Nobody knows who represents whom, or
who are the real allies or real enemies in public
life; those who were friends ten years ago have been
enemies for the last five, but continue to meet socially on the occasion of the traditional feast days. [31]

The Algerian political system has handled the problem by reducing
the official ruling elite to a group of very close allies bound together
by a common past political activity; the system has also transformed
the state bureaucracy into a channel of political demands and responses.
An "administrative state" has gradually emerged that incorporates the
political symbols that are the main ingredients of the political culture.
The populist symbols are the "militant" and the "fellah" (peasant) as
actors, brotherhood as the supreme value, and being heir to the mar-
tyrdom of the chouhada (fighters who died during the liberation war)
as the privileged political way to acquire legitimacy. Meanwhile,
the segmentary symbols are the "careerist politician," inequality,
and possession of a good deal of pull to get what one wants. The populist symbols are celebrated; the segmentary ones are strongly criticized. However both of them coalesce to make the state the symbolic
representative of the will of the people, while actually providing goods
and services through a bureaucratic process blending vast impersonal
decisions (such as planning) and particular bargains to satisfy single
groups or individuals.

MOTIVATIONS FOR ADOPTING SOCIALISM

References to socialism appear rather early in the platforms
presented by the Algerian elites. In 1925 a movement was started in
Europe among Algerian immigrant workers; "North African Star" took
an active part in debates following the Soviet revolution. In 1927 its
leader, Messali Hadj, presented a report condemning colonial oppression to the Brussels meeting of representatives of the colonies. It
called for, among other things, the confiscation of large agricultural
properties and the return of this land to the frustrated peasants.
These references, however, were vague and few in number. Only
the small Algerian Communist Party, founded in November 1936, developed a socialist platform based on Marxism. But it was to remain
forever on the fringes of the Algerian National movement, since the

ACP always tended, more or less clearly, to consider itself as primarily an aid to the world communist movement led by the proletariat of the industrialized countries, and to react mistrustingly toward nationalism expressed in religious terms.[32] In fact, socialism did not appear with any precision in the FLN platform until 1962, in the Tripoli program, and then in 1964 in the Algiers Charter. This late but successful appearance is explained by the relations between the various factions of the Algerian political elite, themselves in contact with the social structure of colonial Algeria.

The Relations among the Elites

Modern nationalist management was made up of three kinds of elite. First, there were the religious elites from the Ulema Association founded in 1931 by Sheikh Ben Badis. Known under the name of reformism, this movement is a scripturalistic Islam (linked with the Nadha renaissance movement, which spread throughout the Moslem world). It surpassed ecstatic Islam, which was better adapted for a tribal society in the process of disintegration, and was able to establish a unified religious sphere throughout the whole territory. Scripturalistic Islam was a purely religious movement, since it directed its violence toward the mrabtin or the "evolved ones" (evolues) who had been tempted by Western culture and fought on the basis of "ethnic nationality" rather than "political nationality" (in Ben Badis' own words). It expressed above all the success of a fraction of the urban bourgeoisie in providing the society as a whole with an ideological identity: to be an Algerian is to be a Moslem (that is, a reformist Moslem) and to speak Arabic. This cultural identity, although open to modernization and the organization of a modern centralized state, is nevertheless indifferent to socialism or capitalism as such. Had the urban bourgeoisie been powerful enough to keep control of important means of production, no doubt it would have elaborated a modern ideology radically hostile to socialism. But as we shall see, the social structure (not to mention the political repression attempted by the colonial authorities) did not permit the bourgeoisie to get hold of the political sphere as easily as the religious one.

The "modernist" elites from the "federation of elected representatives" and the Democratic Union of the Algerian Manifesto headed by Ferhat Abbas were also prominent urban citizens who expressed their desire to participate in the government on equal footing. They used the principles of bourgeois democracy incorporated in the 1789 Declaration of the Rights of Man,[33] and demanded to be assimilated within French society and polity. It was only when their expectations were blocked that they turned to the claim of erecting an "Algerian

State with its own constitution" (Declaration of 1943). Meanwhile, the "men of action" who made up the cadre of the "Algerian popular party" and later the "movement of democratic freedoms" (to be replaced by those who founded the Revolutionary Committee for unity and action in 1954), were all sons of peasants or small shop owners from the small towns, marginal workers or veterans who had no platform other than a belief in the inevitability of armed struggle in order to create a free Algeria, plus a project for putting an end to "sterile divisions" among the nationalist political parties.

Their language was a mixture of that of their two predecessors (which they considered outdated by the necessity of anticolonial struggle). Having tactically accepted or internalized the Ulema's religious idiom and the evolues' references to human rights, they came to the diffuse conviction that the only way to endow the community of Moslem Algerians with a democratic and egalitarian structure was to adopt a "socialist" platform based on nationalizing the means of production, agrarian reform, and industrialization. However, it has never been clear why this socialism could so easily undermine bourgeois or modernist ideologies, or why it was not expressed in terms of the class struggle.

The Algerian Social Structure at the End of the Colonial Period

In 1954 the urban population made up only 12 percent of the total, with the group generally labeled bourgeoisie constituting less than 2 percent. This was a landowning bourgeoisie, for industrial and commercial capitalism were almost nonexistent: only 9 percent of the business jobs were held by salary earners. The middle classes (4.31 percent) included salaried workers (0.5 percent) and small and middle tradesmen and artisans (3.8 percent). Meanwhile, the full-time farm laborers and skilled industrial workers made up 5 percent, the agricultural day laborers (most of them unemployed or underemployed farmers) 14.5 percent, the unskilled urban workers 12 percent. Obviously this so-called "working class" was not homogeneous, and farmers constituted a clear majority (62 percent). Thus, although social inequality was striking, any class struggle inside the Algerian society was almost impossible, for wage earners were the exception and not the rule. Only 2 percent of the population were employed in indigenous enterprises.[34]

The political consequences of such a situation were threefold. First, the class struggle was clearly perceived in terms of an international class struggle, the "employers" being grouped with "colonizers."[35] The wage laborers' consciousness was above all a national consciousness, as was that of the small farmer, who perceived the colonizers only as predatory people, and of the middle class, who perceived them as rivals. Thus socialism could not mean "triumph of a class over another" but "independence and equal allocation of wealth to everybody." Second, the economic weakness of the native bourgeoisie accounts for its being unable to oppose socialism in spite of its relative political strength. It could not aim at replacing the foreign owners of the industrial means of production. The attempt made during the summer of 1962 at keeping the farming estates under the state's provisional control (to be sold later to native landowners) was clearly a failure. As for the industrial firms, no one was ready to take them over. Third, the state was clearly the only actor capable of coping with the problems raised by the mass departure of the European "class" and of setting up a viable economic and political organization.

VARIANTS OF SOCIALISM

Self-Management of State Socialism

From 1962 to 1966 Algeria seemed to oscillate between two socialist models: self-management and state socialism. The takeover of some industrial concerns by the workers and the recovery of formerly colonized land gave rise to the first model; the second was brought about by the growing intervention of state apparatus in economic organization. Self-management, according to the "historic decrees" of March 1963, was viewed not only as a pattern for economic planning, but also as a means of social organization.[36] The Algiers Charter adopted in 1964 by the first (and to this day, only) Congress of the National Liberation Front explains self-management as a tangible demonstration of working-class consciousness, and a proof of the ability of the proletariat to wield political power. As a result of the doctrine of self-management, the workers are not merely a social force at the beck and call of political elites, but a political group with a leading part to play in decision making. Thus there is a solution to the problem of private property, and to the contradiction between the managers and the managed. The concept encapsulates the end of the exploitation, and the realization by each worker of the value of his role, for as a result of the worker's direct share in the profits of production the economic and political functions become inseparable. "From this starting-point the age of liberty will arrive."[37]

In actual fact, self-management has two aspects. The first is
derived from a purely expressive ideology that rejects any political
system whatsoever and purports to bring about the withering away of
the state.[38] The second is more instrumental and advocates the use
of self-management as a weapon against the Algerian political system
of 1964 in order to throw out "reactionaries." Regarding the first aspect, it is presupposed that society has the necessary resources to
get rid of parasitic profiteers, provided that the powers of direction
placed in the hands of a board of producers are used impartially. It
therefore follows that the cause of any trouble must come from the
state (hence the constant criticisms of "bureaucratic control"). It is
believed that the allocation of scarce resources could be accomplished
much more easily if self-management councils were set up everywhere, and if the specialized political machinery only intervened,
like the good fairy in the tales of Perrault, as an indefatigable agency
to help producers, and to oust profiteers, but never to impose on producers is a decision that only they themselves can take, since they are
united in a corporate, democratic body. Compared to the "organizations," which are forever making blunders, the masses will always
find the best course to pursue, provided that they are not blinded by
an erroneous political ideology. This unfailing instinct of the masses
is the key that will open up the era of liberty.

The second aspect of self-management involves regarding this
as a transitional stage before the replacement of the entire political
system. It is held that if, in fact, the political complex were to develop "normally," with state-run enterprises coming to the fore,
with state planning, and with a state monopolizing the public interest,
government would become the private property of bourgeois nationalists and the state bourgeoisie. The working class and intellectual
revolutionaries would have no means of fitting into the pattern. It becomes therefore imperative to use self-management to crack open
the base of the state power pyramid. After this, the state, the Leninist Party, and the centralization would be employed . . . but political
power would have changed hands. Taking a leaf from Gramsci, we
may say that above all self-management gives workers' representatives access to governmental hegemony by replacing an established
state bourgeosie. This is what the Algiers Charter referred to as
"the socialist dynamic."

Taken overall, self-management had decided powers of persuasion, but its discontinuation may be understood if we analyze its components. While such a concept is useful to the simple citizen, who
can thus explain away his political powerlessness (if the masses took
over, everything would be better), it places the authorities in a position of permanent contradiction. How can one wish to bring about the
decline of the state, when, on the contrary, the main objective is to

make it flourish, and when even the safeguard of self-management
(when viewed as a form of managing and running companies), necessarily implies the strengthening of the state bureaucracy?[39] How,
in fact, can public development of industry be promoted without graft-
ing on an economic bureaucracy?

The second aspect of self-management (that it would be used as
a weapon by a new political force) seems, on the contrary, to be logical but proves to have one serious failing: the omission of the producers as a politically organized force. This interpretation was part
of the strategy used by intellectuals who set themselves up as spokesmen for the working class, but who were really outside it. Possess-
ing no really solid organization on which to base themselves (the labor
union was building up its strength and the party had yet to be formed),
they relied precisely on this very dynamism of self-management to
consolidate these organizations.[40] Now they could only have been
able to manipulate this "negative" dynamism ("negative" inasmuch as
it disrupts the state), to their own ends, if they already possessed
the means to replace what they had destroyed. Like all ardent scholars of Lenin, they identified "self-management" with "all power to
the Soviets," forgetting that "power to the Soviets" was only effective
because the Bolshevik Party was already in existence (and had a leader!) and because its opponent (the state headed by Kerensky) had a
cial basis and a material force greatly inferior to that of the nation-
state of Algeria. To rely on self-management to reinforce their political power, when they had neither organization nor the necessary
social basis, was their way of ignoring the political system. A very
good political analysis of industrial self-management maintains that
it may be a consolidating factor for the workers, and may accelerate
the realization of class consciousness provided that it defeats its own
object as far as self-management goes.[41] That is an understatement; the realization of class-consciousness in Algeria could only
have come about with (among other things) the mobilization of the
working class into a political force. This force would then have to
turn its back on self-management.[42]

The ideology of self-management was therefore without operational force; it was "pure" ideology establishing no links between
ideas and their application.[43] Its discontinuation, which began in
1967, relates even more closely to the practice of the political elitism—that is, the organization of the administration as a means of political control and economic animation—and the use of a development
plan and an agrarian reform to create social mobilization that is coordinated by the central government. If enthusiasm and spontaneity
have lost much ground in this change, and if centralization is proving
to be, as is often the case, a source of waste, the new ideology is becoming really expressive of the behavior of the rulers who view the

state and its branches (local communities and national corporations) as the best development agency for the whole society.

The debate between these two forms of socialism was particularly heated from 1963 to 1967. "Marx's socialism" and "Mohammed's socialism" were in conflict on both the ideological and material fronts. The Algiers Charter comes out quite clearly in favor of scientific socialism, based on the doctrine of class struggle whose direction is decided, in descending priority, by the workers' representatives, fellahs, and intellectual revolutionaries. Nevertheless Islam itself is acclaimed as the "Cement of the Nation," and the "liberating social ferment." It is regarded as an ideology whose evolution is dependent on social organization. Islam's significance is derived from socialism and not the other way around. Scientific socialism offers itself therefore as a weapon to Marxist intellectuals and Trade-Unionists for whom workers' self-management is merely an instrumental ideology while at the other end of the spectrum stands Moslem socialism. Even President Ben Bella allowed it house room, seconded by his Minister of Religion (Ministre des Cultes) Tewfik El Madani, the former general secretary of the Ulema.[44] His Minister for Labor, Sofi Boudissa, did not hesitate in encouraging "readers correspondence" in the official journal of the UGTA (Union Generale de Travailleurs Algeriens). For example, we may read: "Why is there all this fuss over the class struggle? This imported commodity of Marx and Lenin has no place in a Moslem Algeria that pins its faith on providence and God's will. Our Arabo-Moslem Socialism rejects the class struggle, prohibits the abolition of the class system, and respects private property."[45]

Contrary to appearances, the debate did not rage over the fundamental industrial policy that Algeria had to follow. This included state development of industry, the battle with foreign capital ("public enemy number one"), the incentive schemes to control and augment capital, the state's initiative in large-scale development plans, and its nationalization of valuable mineral and energy deposits, distribution, commercialization, banks, and insurance companies. This industrial policy, and all these objectives, figured in the national program of 1962-74. These goals have gradually been attained by successive governments, if not with a general consensus, at least with no outright friction on ideological terms between the two schools of "specific" (Moslem) socialism, and "scientific" (Marxist) socialism. The heart of the problem lay in the control of the state by rival political factions (whom we mentioned when discussing self-management), and with the consummatory ideology that goes to make up the deep-rooted values symbolizing the Algerian identity—for the doctrine of class struggle was once again challenged by the ideology of thawra (the spiritual revolution).

Thawra defends the purity of the people, their language and mores against the encroachments of "cultural colonialism." The political leaders were at a loss to choose abruptly between these two types of value, and all more or less followed suit with President Ben Bella. He said, "I will take the economic analysis of Marx, but I reject his analysis of scientific materialism."[46] Kaid Ahmed, who was in charge of the party machine from 1968 to 1973, stated that "because of its scientific approach Marxist analysis sets the problem of methodology into a proper perspective, and consequently resolves it, thus allowing consideration to take place in a suitable setting. "But," he added, "we must be careful to avoid slavist imitation or ideological plagiarisms."[47] Another example is Bachir Hadj Ali, a former member of the Algerian Communist Party, for whom it was possible to "turn to socialism with the Koran in one hand and Das Kapital in the other."[48] We shall see below how these different components have come together to promote an official ideology.

EFFECTS OF SOCIALISM ON LEADERS' STRATEGIES

Image Projection

For a political system that aims to develop itself by mobilizing the masses, the designation of a common enemy is of the utmost importance. Even if the Algerian regime gives top priority to the external enemy (anti-imperialism is something that is "ultrafundamental"), and endeavors to create the image of a national regime unanimous in its fight for the liberation of the entire nation, it must also pick out an internal enemy whose destruction would enhance the image of the rulers at home and abroad. Official attitudes and programs have varied greatly on this issue. The first policy program adopted at Tripoli in 1962 was the most ambiguous, for all social classes were regarded as having participated in the national liberation movement. The bourgeoisie, the "vehicle of opportunist ideologies," only qualified as a "potential threat," and it was hoped that it would rally itself to the popular revolution by "patriotism." Admittedly the Tripoli program is not lacking in criticism of the groups inside the FLN, even devoting a whole section to the "political shortcomings of the FLN and to its anti-revolution deviations," but the document never comes forward with any clear social directives. The ubiquitous enemy-in-our-midst is constantly denounced but never named. It is everywhere and nowhere. The Tripoli program stops those who would oppose it dead in their tracks, but does not state who they are.

In this way, suspicion cloaks each faction of the party and thus tarnishes the image of the collective leadership.

On the contrary, the Algiers Charter specifies the enemy and locates it at the very heart of the state machine. The enemy is the "bureaucratic bourgeoisie" that takes form largely "due to the sensation of power that the exercise of the office of government affords." (Incidentally, notice the pseudo-Weberian terminology that is used in this Marxist text to single out a new social class.) The other social strata of the bourgeoisie and the lower middle class are also seen as targets, since they represent antisocialist forces, but the offensive against them is relatively restrained. "Small private property" must be respected; hence the position of the lower middle class will not be hit hard, and its standard of living will not deteriorate. On the other hand, the offensive against the "state bourgeoisie" will be constantly promoted by "the overwhelming majority of the population (poor peasants and the proletariat)" under the auspices of "manager-producers, urban and rural workers," who will make up the party together with the "revolutionary intellectuals," thus encompassing "the whole of the social strata." From now on the enemy is to be found in the nucleus of the political system.

In spite of all this, the image of leadership was not made any clearer to the average citizen, since the denunciation of state cadres came from other cadres within the same state. The difference between the two, to the man in the street, was not clearly delineated or underlined. Added to this, President Ben Bella had none of the capacities of Mao Tse-tung to unleash a cultural revolution that even those partisan to self-management would not have entirely endorsed.

One of the best descriptions of the current regime, and how it views its mission, may be found in the collectively authored brochure presented in 1970 and 1971 under the signature of Kaid Ahmed.[49] Although its author is now in disgrace, the document has not lost any of its symbolic importance. Kaid Ahmed pinpoints the fundamental contradiction between the "exploiters," both old and new, and the "people." The profiteers-exploiters are composed of a part of the old privileged social layer that did not take part in the struggle for national freedom, together with the "nouveaux riches," who profited during the war for independence and during the ensuing political confusion. To put it another way, exploiters are both those who did not participate in the fight for freedom, and those who seized the opportunity to profit from it.

If we attempt to analyze the ideological mechanism by which the enemy is designated in this brochure, we have to agree that it is rather effective.

1. The enemy is indicated and denounced: "The people witness daily examples of fortunes rapidly made, of the frantic and indecent

desire for lucrative profit and gain, and tendencies that lead to mal-
practice, complicity, and complacency. This kind of attitude could
not and cannot but give rise to a foreign body, belonging to the various
types of consumer society, that will insert itself in the very heart of
a society that wishes itself socialist." If an opponent wished to use
the same terms to criticize and accuse the state, he would thus be
forestalled, for the government denounces profiteers and exploiters
itself instead of covering up for them. [50]

2. The enemy is clearly situated outside the regime, a position
that was not adopted at Tripoli (since the enemy was everywhere),
nor at Algiers (where the enemy had infiltrated the whole of the state
machine). This leaves the senior civil servants as potential allies of
the privileged class; but they can disengage themselves since their
problem is merely one of commitment. The fact that the revolutionary government openly disowns its black sheep ought to reassure the
average citizen that the party line is being adhered to, while supplying him with the necessary information when he cannot easily make
up his mind about those who "blot their copy-book."

3. Moreover, the enemy is no real threat. We are assured
that the enemy only represents 5 percent of the active population,
and that the means of production held by private property owners,
although "relatively important," are "nothing in comparison to the
socialist sectors."

4. Besides, this enemy is effectively opposed by the "revolutionary government," which tends increasingly to hand the means of
production to the people by implanting popular institutions from the
bottom to the top rung of the economic ladder. The economic base,
and hence the political influence, of this privileged social layer is
therefore undermined.

5. Finally, the fact that "secondary" contradictions are acknowledged gives sufficient margin to justify certain difficulties and
to put off dealing with them, should the occasion arise. All this
does not imply that the "principal directive" (ligne principale) is to
be disregarded. We may best sum up this concept as follows: the
voluntary action of the political authorities avoids a transformation
of the advantages enjoyed by the privileged stratum into a political
situation of class domination. In other words, the state intervenes
to adjust the mechanics of the society.

Promotion of an Ideology

The function of ideology is to make an autonomous
politics possible by providing the authoritative concepts that render it meaningful, the suasive images

> by means of which it can be sensibly grasped. . . .
> It is when neither a society's most general cultural
> orientations nor its most down-to-earth, pragmatic
> ones, suffice any longer to provide an adequate
> image of political process that ideologies become
> crucial as sources of socio-political meanings and
> attitudes. [51]

The Algerian case fits into this general framework. Algeria has to
build up a political system within a context that has no longer the re-
motest link with that of
a patchwork of a cultural heritage, a hodgepodge of fragmented
themes. Hence the need for a solid symbolic framework to render
the political universe meaningful. The main themes of this framework are the glorification of the precolonial past (insofar as this period already showed glimpses of Algeria as a nation-state), orthodox
Islam (that of the doctors, not of the saints and brotherhoods), along
with scientific culture, industrialization, self-management and anti-
imperialism.

This may seem a bit of a jumble to someone who considers that
an ideology is a coherent program that should take over from an ob-
solete traditional culture. In practice, however, a traditional culture does not just fall apart, to be then replaced by an ideology. The
same causes that doom tradition make it difficult to incorporate a
new ideology into the culture. In other words, the awareness that
any continuation of the past is impossible because of changes in the
environment coincides with a crisis of mistrust toward new, "imported," and "cosmopolitan" ideas. [52] If from now on the fate of tradition
hangs in the balance, the ideas that doomed it find themselves in a
similar situation, for the whole of society is in a state of confusion.
The only clear way out of the vicious circle of skepticism (which would
result in an increasing demobilization of the society), is to announce
that the new ideology is "rational," "scientific," and therefore above
all discussion. To this could be added religious faith, which,
"cleansed of its impurities," would also escape relativization.

This is why the official ideology, with its composite structure,
is essential to the construction of a viable political system. It
hinges on two seemingly contradictory kinds of language: the religious ideology that bases socialism on Islam, and a variety of Marxist nationalism that bases Islam on socialism, and the latter on the
anti-imperialist struggle. The two modes of expression rarely coincide. The first has more of an effect on man in his private life and
serves to maintain his identity or "authenticity." The second appeals
to the man in public office, especially those involved in the modern
economy, and it helps to provide an answer to the tensions provoked

by change; it is the ideology of the "technophile."[53] The religious
ideology holds sway over the family but allows Marxism a free hand
in everything that concerns the transition to socialism. Marxism returns the compliment and avoids meddling with the family unit, and
more broadly speaking, with matters that concern the status of women.

In fact, no confrontation between the two can be possible, for
otherwise the ideology would cease fulfilling its function in a period
of modernization: to provide an overall response to the stresses and
strains of any harmful disputes. This is why the official ideology
distinctly dissociates "modernism" in social mores from "modernization" of the society by developing industry. Heedful of the "economic
revolution" and of the necessary social reforms needed to build up
industry, the leaders' only real interest in the "cultural revolution"
is to bring science into society (and to root out the Western influences).
They are extremely suspicious of any sudden changes in private social relationships. As a general rule, the demands of modernism
(such as family planning or cultural expression of Algerian youth) are
played down to a minimum when compared to the needs of modernization (the creation of an industrial infrastructure, or pilot schemes to
rationalize agricultural production).

The society that the political regime dreams of is an industrialized one, with full employment and full development of all the activities of a modern society (like those of large public firms, advanced
scientific development, social mobility, and growing job specialization). This vision is to be complemented by the solid moral armor
and austerity of the mores found in the ideal of Islam. The state
holds the reins of the religious as well as the economic means of production. It therefore seeks to gain acceptance for modernization in
the name of Islam while allocating sufficient roles to Moslem Arabist intellectuals. The regime is anxious lest the development of industrial, scientific, and technical activities relegate these intellectuals too quickly to a second-row seat behind the "technophiles."
The tensions between the different Algerian elites are, for the moment, controlled by a judicious distribution of position and roles and
by the manipulation of ideological symbols. (The religious ideology
decides on the Minister of Justice, the Minister of Religion, and on
primary and secondary education; Marxist nationalism concerns itself with industry, higher education, and scientific education.) These
tensions also show themselves among Arabist and French-oriented
students; the two groups have ideological horizons and social perspectives that are very different.

Organization Building

The political organizations all hinge, in principle, around the one and only political party, the "leading institution of the nation," which is an "organization that comes before all because it represents the people."[54]

> [The party is] the innovator, the pioneer, the faithful expression of the deep-felt aspiration of the popular masses, and the driving force that allows the collectivity not only to expand and to reinforce its national consciousness, but also puts it into a position where it can improve its knowledge of, and fight more effectively for, its culture and higher interests. [55]

The mission of the National Liberation Front is therefore to aggregate the social interests represented by the national organizations (such as trade unions, youth organizations, and the Union for Women), and by corporate organizations (such as the medical and teaching professions) that it directs and controls. The party also gives the state general policy directives and presides over the recruiting of local representatives, who must then be proposed for popular ratification (since the number of prospective candidates is double that of posts available).[56] Finally, the party also manages and looks after operations that are begun on a national basis—for example, the program of agrarian reform.

In fact, the part played by the party barely resembles the theoretical position that it occupies in society and the political system.[57] On the level of internal organization, the various reforms instituted since 1965 have not resulted in the holding of a single national congress: since independence, the party has therefore only held one congress at Algiers in 1964. Not one of the official central bodies that it had appointed (the central committee, the political bureau, and the general secretariat), survived after June 19, 1965. Since 1965 the party has, under successive leaderships (Cherif Bel Kacem, Kaid Ahmed, Mohamed Cherif Messadia), manipulated "democratic centralism" in an attempt to maintain a solid grip on its central echelons while encouraging a fuller democratic expression from its base.

"Centralism" has had the upper hand over democracy. For the moment, the party seems to amount more to a political instrument that controls the society, rather than one that voices its needs. This explains the party's recruiting problems: neither the new breed of entrepreneurs, the industrialization agents, nor the young students are in a hurry to join its ranks. Within the party there are essentially

three kinds of militants: the "professional" politicians carefully
selected for their loyalty by the central government; the militants
who are only slightly politicized but who are eager to do the social
work of modernizing the behavior and attitudes of the general public
and ease its relationships with bureaucracy; and finally those who
have not benefited enough from the state, and who expect from their
participation some compensation. We might make similar remarks
concerning the union and national organizations in general. [58]

By contrast, the "organizational weapon" was successfully used
on the level both of the state machine[59] and, above all, of the army. [60]
From a precarious alliance between maverick officers ("the moud-
jahiddine group"), the army has been turned into a highly profession-
alized body whose loyalty to the current government seems beyond
question. Given the low level of political institutionalization, it is
no wonder that several key posts are held by high-ranking officers
(such as Colonel Abdel Ghani, recently named Minister of the Interior
after the death of Ahmed Medeghri, himself a former member of the
General Staff in 1962). Nobody can afford to keep the army cut off
from power. Ben Yousef Benkhedda and Ahmed Ben Bella, the only
leaders who dared to act so foolishly, were promptly removed in
1962 and 1965. When the rules of the political game are at stake,
the bayonets cannot be neglected as a political force. However, to
speak of Algeria in terms of praetorian politics would be a gross exaggeration. The army is nothing but a part of the state bureaucracy
with the same organizational values and the same goals as those of
its civilian counterparts. For example, the army is in charge of all
the students with a master's degree who are subject to the compulsory service rule: they are appointed for two years to various civilian posts while remaining under the control of the military. Furthermore, the "walis" (ex-prefects), often former officers, play a key
role in the maintenance of law and order and in economic development
at the local level. That does not mean that the army is immune from
conflicts.

EXPANDING POLITICAL PARTICIPATION

In this area, the regime's seemingly simple strategy consists
of encouraging "good participation" and suppressing the "bad."
"Good" participation is a total social commitment to building socialism: the civil servant who joins the party, the student who agrees
to do his civil service in the "bled" (the countryside) and the "fellah"
who joins a peasants' union are several examples. The "bad" consists of abandoning constructive criticism in order to articulate political viewpoints that would put the general government line into ques-

tion. In this category are the trade union member who encourages
strikes in a public company, uninformed that special interests and
the class struggle no longer have a place in a socialist society, and
the student who would assert his organization's autonomy with respect
to the party.

In reality, however, the regime's populist rhetoric, as well as
its strategy for economic development (which relies on the consent
of the masses for its effectiveness) impels it to accept something
other than conformist participation. The regime must confront the
necessity of accepting a certain loss of power so that it may share
the responsibility of treating certain demands. A certain extension
of political participation results from the operation of the local col-
lectives. The presidents of the popular communal assemblies,
called together each year by the president of the Revolutionary Council, are informed in detail about the development of national policy.
They then present their observations, which are not always in agreement with it. They also give their opinion on their own regional problems and address the government directly with their demands. One
must note, however, that the resolutions that they adopt are drawn
up with the Minister of the Interior, and that the relations they have
with the head of the government are as much related to subordination
as to participation.

Another experiment has been adopted from the "Socialist Enterprise Charter" of 1971.[61] In order to put an end to normless behavior already noticed in the companies, each production unit has been
given a Workers Assembly elected by all the workers who had worked
in the company for at least six months. The candidates for the Assembly must be in the union; they are appointed by a commission made
up of union, party, and company management representatives. The
Assembly controls the running of the company and participates in the
elaboration of many decisions (regarding personnel policy and training), but it has no power over management and is only consulted on
the development plan, and production and investment programs. The
The Management Council, a collegial agency, has real decision-making powers, but the representatives of the Workers Assembly are in
the minority. Although not as decentralized as in the communes,
power tends however to be more largely distributed inside the company. The government expects an extension in participation, and
consequently a rise in the number of those who actively support its
economic and social policies.

The regime sometimes goes further, and instead of organizing
participation for purposes of control, it can accept political mobilization among the most troublesome sectors in time of conflict. That
appears to be the strategy in the revolutionary process of the agrarian
revolution under way since 1972. Although for the present it affects

a reduced area and population (about 1 million hectares versus 2.5 million in the self-managed areas, out of a total of 43 million hectares—of which, it is true, 35 million are pasture lands and roadways; 50,000-60,000 workers versus 190,000 in self-managed areas out of a total of 1,300,000 active agricultural laborers),[62] this operation has created opposition. Its goals of slowing the rural exodus, modernizing agriculture in order to create a market for national industry, and also mobilizing the peasants for development have evoked discontent on the national as well as local level.

The government then agreed to open up the movement to massive student participation (even though their relationship with the regime was so bad in 1972 that the student majority seemed politically anomic).[63] Repeating oft-used themes, the party newspaper called on the students to "be concerned with the deep mutations appearing in our country today"[64] rather than being "the eternal dissenters."[65] What is new is that the theme of the intellectual's return to the "real land" has acquired—for a time—certain legitimacy in the students' eyes due to its association with the manifestly legitimate theme of the agrarian revolution. The results were spectacular: more than 1,000 student volunteers spent July and August 1972 working in the new socialist villages; there were more than 5,000 in 1973 (representing about one-sixth of the total number of Algerian students).

The students asked for the possibility of doing political work by participating in setting up the peasant unions, which was granted to them in theory by the Chief of State. They also asked for the "institutionalization" of the movement, which means in fact the right to freely recreate the student union under the new name of the "University Committees of the Agrarian Revolution," which was also granted. The "National Commission of Volunteers" was created within the framework of the Ministry of Higher Education; this lessened its political importance but guaranteed greater organizational freedom. A certain unblocking of student political participation could then come about. It would be difficult, however, to conceal the limitations of the movement. One need not go so far as to assert that student integration into the agrarian revolution (where at best they can have only a reduced role, due to their lack of knowledge of the rural world's concrete conditions) is only a convenient way to control protest. However, it is necessary to mention to what extent the student mobilization was carried out under administrative control.

If we compare political participation in the three experiments (the popular communal assemblies, the socialist enterprises, and the student agrarian movement), we discover certain general traits. First, participation is always controlled by the state administration (particularly the "walis"). Second, participating groups are authorized to formulate their opinions in particular sectors. However, they are granted no authority to participate in the political system, nor to defend their professional interests, but may only express their concept of the general welfare. They are "coopted," and can also be rejected. Finally, while complete participation in the central political system is not institutionalized,[66] this participation can be activated at any time when specific problems and basic contradictions confront the regime.

Economic Development Policies

Until 1969 Algeria had not elaborated a national economic program. Her development policy was based at times on a follow-up of the Constantine Project established by the French government in 1960, and at other times on a seven-year preproject from 1967. The options chosen, however, seemed sufficiently clear.[67] Algeria certainly developed her gross national product, which was based almost exclusively on oil resources,[68] but at the same time she developed her material productive forces by taking advantage of basic industry (for example, the building of a metallurgical plant in Annaba), and by using her oil income to finance investments. Thus from 1963 to 1969 the percentage of industrial investment in relation to annual investment went from 23 percent (151 million DA)* to almost 60 percent (3,594 million DA).[69] National economic power developed simultaneously with the creation of national corporations and the state bank, which controlled the mining, industrial, and banking sectors, with the diversification of foreign trade (where France's role noticeably diminished), and by maintaining an equilibrium between the commercial balance and the balance of payments.

The weak spots of this policy, as enumerated by Gerard de Bernis, were the lagging of agricultural policy, which resulted in a decrease in production; the inability of agriculture to offer a surplus for industrialization and creation of a market for Algerian industrial products; a rapid rural exodus (about 100,000 people per year); the absence of qualified skilled labor despite the large-scale educational effort; and insufficient technical and political tools for financial and economic planning. The first Four-Year Plan (1970-73) marked the first real effort at a global economic policy.[70] The enormity of this effort appears clearly upon examination of the general investment structure (Table 1).

The rise in the price of oil ($3.35 per barrel in 1971; $9.25 in December 1973) and the increase in exports (from 23 million tons in

---

*One U.S. dollar plus 4.5 DA (Arabian dollars).

TABLE 1

Algeria: General Investment Structure
(million DA)

	1967-69	Four-Year Plan (1970-73) Estimates	Four-Year Plan Reali- zation	Second Four-Year Plan (1974-77) Estimates
Agriculture	1,606	4,140	4,990.5	12,005
Industry	4,750	12,400	17,653.4	48,000
Transports	—	800	793.4	—
Tourism	177	700	700.0	1,200
Infrastructure	855	2,307	2,024.3	15,521
Education and training	870	3,307	2,982.3	9,947
Housing	249	1,520	1,614.9	15,600
Public services and administration	533	2,566	2,564.0	

Source: Compiled by the author.

1963 to 42 million in 1969 and 46 million in 1972) give Algeria a certain financial latitude for her investments, particularly since a large
portion of her budget (investments not included) is financed through
oil taxes. In 1970 these taxes brought in one-fifth of the total budgetary returns (1.4 billion DA out of 6.6); they now account for more
than one-third (3.7 out of 10 billion DA). The Franco-Algerian crisis
of 1971, which ended in the nationalization of 51 percent of the French
oil companies' holdings in Algeria did not reduce Algerian exports
(except in relation to France) and, since October 1973, has allowed a
substantial increase in resources, which rather extensively compen-
sates for the price rise of industrial materials. The gross national
product went from 22.9 billion DA in 1970 to 27.4 billion in 1973.
The industrial sector and public works have held an increasingly
favorable position while agriculture has declined (9 percent of the
GNP in 1973 versus 13 percent in 1969). Thus, Algeria is "planting
her oil" by using its returns to set up a coherent industrial structure,
which means "a system of interrelated industries dedicated to modernizing what already exists."[71] These investments are poured into

production goods and equipment rather than to the consumer goods sector, but the latter mobilizes only 10 percent of investment and creates 21,000 jobs. The result is that there is a relatively small increase in consumption (31 percent from 1970 to 1973), and, above all, that the rise in employment (Table 2) remains slow despite large-scale investment: 265,000 nonagricultural jobs were created from 1970–73, whereas in 1970 there were 260,000 urban dwellers out of work. Urban unemployment will only be reabsorbed in 1980 but to many people, this prediction seems too optimistic.

There has been considerable expenditure on agriculture (15 percent of the total investment) and an attempt at an agrarian revolution. Meanwhile, however, Algerian industrial policy has one major weakness: it creates few jobs and cannot, for the time being, redress the imbalance between the rural and urban areas. Therefore urban income has risen by 37 percent in four years for a population that has grown by 10 percent, whereas agricultural income has risen by 10 percent as has the population. It is for this reason that the second Four-Year Plan (1973–77) seeks to cut the urban consumption growth rate and increase rural consumption.

TABLE 2

Rise in Employment, Algeria, 1969–80

	1969	1973	1980 (estimate)[b]
Theoretical nonagricultural work force[a] (millions of people)	1.10	1.22	1.5
Nonagricultural jobs (millions of people)	0.84	1.10	1.5
Theoretical agricultural work force (millions of people)	1.54	1.73	2.0
Use of the agricultural work force (millions of days based on 200 working days per year)	308	346	—
Rate of agricultural underemployment, percent	49	42	—

[a]The theoretical work force has been calculated on the basis of one active worker for every four nonactive.

[b]Note that these population estimates—as specified by Algerian demographers—are considered by many to be too low.

Source: Compiled by the author.

The second Four-Year Plan aims to remedy the malfunctions of the first plan, while distrubing neither the absolute preponderance of industry nor the high rate of investment. It proposes to develop consumer goods industries that create many jobs, to fight against regional disparities, to build small and middle sized industries all over the country, and to extend the agrarian revolution in order to give land to 150,000 people actively working (as of now only 60,000 people have benefited), to stimulate national savings, and to struggle against superfluous consumption.[72] The second plan does place a major emphasis on housing—a sphere that had been forgotten by the first Four-Year Plan: the objective for 1980 is 100,000 housing units per year and the construction of 1,000 socialist villages.

ACHIEVEMENTS AND PROBLEMS

It would be tedious to list the various results obtained by the Algerian regime,[73] and it would be as flippant to condemn its shortcomings as to congratulate it for its efforts. In any case, it is worth mentioning at least the most outstanding achievement of the last 15 years—namely the considerable expansion of the educational system. During the first Four-Year Plan 12 percent of the total investment was devoted to education and training. During the same period, public expenditures have reached 10 percent of the GNP, which is one of the highest rates in the world. The growth in total number of pupils and students is particularly impressive (Table 3).[74] Fortunately, the Algerian economy still needs so many skilled workers and trained civil servants that this high rate of educational expansion has not brought about the unemployment of intellectuals often observed in the Third

TABLE 3

Students in Algerian Educational Institutions
(thousands)

	1962–63	1972–73
Primary education	750,000	2,300,000
Secondary education	32,000	286,000
Professional education (agriculture, professional training at the secondary level)	—	58,000
University	3,000	30,000

Source: Compiled by the author.

World. On the contrary, engineers and competent bureaucrats are
in such short supply that, in certain sectors of the economy, they
are able to insist on job benefits and salary terms. The state, which
because of its socialist and egalitarian ideals is usually reluctant to
satisfy such demands, frequently capitulates.

However unquestionable the educational and industrial achievements we have outlined, they pose as many problems as they solve.
The economic, social, and political advancements carried out by the
socialist regime tend to revive old problems that the rulers thought
were solved on the eve of independence. They also give rise to new
problems that require further steps in order to properly solve them.
Let us enumerate them briefly by way of conclusion.

Cultural Identity

Algeria is pursuing two goals at one and the same time: developing a modern industrial economy and integrating the whole country
into the same Arab-Moslem culture.[75] Although these goals are by
no means contradictory and are both widely accepted, the success of
the first may jeopardize the second. The qualifications needed to apply
for the most valued technical positions enable the applicants who have
been trained in French to get the jobs they want and push their Arab-
speaking rivals into the background. This is not to say that Arab education is unable to supply the economy with skilled workers, but for
the time being it is easier to find good teachers in the technical subjects among the French-speaking people. A strong feeling of relative
deprivation may be spreading among those who have not been lucky
enough to get good European training: they are not far from regarding
the spread of Arabization to nontechnical education as a way of giving
the ruling class the material resources (namely, the modern skills)
it needs to perpetuate its domination, and of keeping the poor masses
under control by providing them with symbolic rewards such as "Arab
and Moslem culture," which is illustrious but useless.

Needless to say, the government denies the charge and does its
best not to frustrate the Arab-speaking intellectuals. But precisely
for that reason it has to insist on the authenticity of the Arab culture,
and thus risk alienating the modern elites and widening the gap between elites and masses, and between the elites themselves. To sum
up, engineers, technicians, and Westernized bureaucrats are given
relatively substantial material rewards, but are denied high cultural
status, and the contrary is true for the traditional elites whose status
is praised to the extent that their power is withering away. The only
sensible solution is to extend the training in Arabic to all forms of
training, but this is not yet possible and may never be so.

The Condition of Women

The war of liberation, the socialist ideology, and the ongoing economic changes have all contributed to significant alterations in the condition of women. However, social resistance to this extension of equality has increased proportionately. Religious laws regarding marriage and family still apply to most of the women, and the government is reluctant to pass a bill favoring women's individual rights in these matters. It cannot afford to face the recriminations of the powerful traditionalist groups that are supported by most of the men in the country. Similarly, there are very few women elected to public office or holding some power in the state machinery, despite governmental encouragement of women's participation.[76] These factors explain why birth control is practically impossible in Algeria. Although the women seem to favor it, the decisions are made by men and women's pressure groups are nonexistent. This ensures that the male viewpoint predominates, particularly the distrust of any program seemingly initiated by the West.

Technological Dependency

Like most underdeveloped countries, Algeria is faced not only with economic dependence but also with the constraints stemming from its reliance on the capitalist world's technological progress. For example, in the Algerian world view there is a necessary link between oil, the chemical industry, and rural development. However, the economic dimensions required by modern manufacturing processes run counter to the reality of a rather narrow domestic market.[77] Thus a factory can make no profit unless it produces for a larger market than the domestic one, and the technical processes oblige Algeria, whether it likes it or not, to produce for foreign markets. Moreover, since the government has clearly opted for sophisticated development using the most advanced techniques, it is dependent on the large firms, which alone can keep up with the rapid technological advancement. This problem of "national engineering" will not be solved in the foreseeable future.

The Growth of the Private Sector

After a period of decline, private enterprise has tended to expand faster than the public sector, in connection with the general economic development initiated by the Four-Year Plan. The strategic sectors of the economy are controlled by the state and economic policy

TABLE 4

Employment in Industry, Housing, Energy, Banks, Insurance, Real Estate, and Transportation, 1965–71
(thousands)

	Self-Man-agement	Per-cent	Public Sector	Per-cent	Private Sector	Per-cent	Total
1965	25,202	13.1	66,635	34.5	101,143	52.4	192,980
1966	25,052	12.6	69,248	35.0	103,664	52.4	197,964
1967	27,312	13.2	87,723	42.2	92,563	44.6	207,604
1968	30,756	12.6	128,607	52.6	85,028	34.8	244,391
1969	29,248	11.3	139,116	53.9	89,756	34.8	258,120
1970	24,660	8.0	179,863	58.0	105,583	34.0	310,106
1971	17,482	5.5	161,035	49.0	149,483	45.5	328,000

Source: Compiled by the author.

as a whole depends on the state. Nevertheless, although the private sector is subordinate, it benefits from the collective effort made by the state and it may contribute to the creation of a parasite class hindering any change in the distribution of wealth and income.

To that kind of criticism the Algerian rulers answer that the private sector is not always the evil that socialist theoreticians claim. The regime maintains that the position of private "capitalists" in the Algerian economy is subordinate, and that the economy must be able to rely on this sector's flexibility and efficiency, at least for certain activities. Algerian leaders deny that such a growth in the scope of the private sector may result in an increase of its power. However, the small leftist opposition fears the possible alliance of this new class with the state bureaucracy, and the threat to socialism that such an alliance would represent.

Bureaucratic Development and Political Decay

The burgeoning bureaucracy may be criticized from two different standpoints. First, fast-growing administrative consumption encroaches upon the relative part reserved for "family consumption," which keeps the population from enjoying the fruits of economic growth.

Second, the bureaucracy is suspected of giving rise to a "new class" or "state bourgeoisie" characterized by a high level of consump-

TABLE 5

Administrative Consumption Relative to Total Investment*
(dinars)

	Four-Year Plan Estimate	Four-Year Plan Results
Investment	7,060	9,700
Family consumption	11,900	13,600
Administrative consumption	1,540	9,000
Total	20,500	25,300

*Administrative consumption has been calculated by subtracting the salaries and loans returned to the Central Bank from the total amount of the ordinary expenses of the administration. (See A. Benachenhou, "Chronique economique de l'Algerie," Annuaire de l'Afrique du Nord, 1972, p. 464.)

Source: Compiled by the author.

tion and a tendency to retain political power through alliances (sometimes political but mainly matrimonial) with the old landowning families and the new merchant bourgeoisie. It is hardly possible to substantiate those statements, given the lack of adequate studies of social
mobility in Algeria; mere anecdotes cannot substitute for serious inquiry. In any case it should be noted that the existing shortcomings
in the country's political development may enable an emerging state
bourgeoisie to take over as it did in Egypt. But it should also be noted
that the problem of democratic political organization in a country
that bases its economic system on state socialism has always been
most difficult to cope with.

NOTES

1. See Edward Shils, The Torment of Secrecy (London: Heinemann, 1956), p. 98.
2. "Spaniards," a generic word used to name the "little
whites" (French, Italians, Maltese, or Armenians as well), perceived
as stealing the jobs that should have been given to Algerians. See
Pierre Bourdieu, "La Hantise du Chomage Chez l'Ouvrier Algerien,"
Sociologie du Travail 1962, p. 331; Centre Africain des Sciences
Humanies Appliquees, Recherches sur les Attitudes du Sous-Prole-
tariat Algerien a l'Egard de la Societe Urbaine, Aix-en-Provence,
1963 (mimeo.), pp. 46 ff. Compare with what Robert Cane calls
"Cabalism" (idea that a secular power, remote and un-understandable,
controls people's destiny), Political Ideology (New York: Free Press,
1962), pp. 114 ff.
3. Quoted by Robert Merle, Ben Bella (Paris: Gallimard, 1965),
pp. 171-73.
4. It was President Ben Bella's usual practice. In December
1962, less than six months after the official independence day, a
curious meeting took place in Algiers. Professor Rene Dumont, invited as an adviser for land reform, criticized, as usual, the use of
luxury cars by the high civil servants and politicians. The President
replied that a driver was a necessity for him because he was unable
to drive a car, having had no opportunity to learn how to drive under
the colonial system. An imposing array of populist themes can be observed in that simple dialogue: luxury is illegitimate (the car); the
common man must be praised for his deprivation of technical goods
and skills (how to drive); it is legitimate to possess and use the goods
of which one has been deprived so far.
5. Peter Worsley, "The Concept of Populism," in Ghita Ionescu
and Ernest Gellner, eds., Populism (London: Weidenfeld and Nicolson, 1969), p. 245. Also Peter Wiles, "A Syndrome, Not a Doctrine,"
ibid., p. 166.

6. For a good survey of the land workers' attitudes see Claudine Chaulet, La Mitidja Autogeree (Algiers: Alger Societe Nationale d'Edition et de Diffusion, 1971), pp. 277-79. For a description of the women's demands, see Helene Vandevelde, La Participation des Femmes a la Vie Politique et Sociale en Algerie, These Science Politique, Faculte de Droit de l'Universite d'Alger, 1972 (mimeo.), p. 430.

7. "Colonist state" ("etat-colon") refers to the former French landowners with whom the national state is identified. The term is used to symbolize the replacement of the colonizers by the bureaucrats.

8. The distinction has been made by Claudine Claulet on the following basis: "Political attitude," interpretation, even simple, of the issues put forth by the workers with reference to the country's recent history, the necessity of national discipline, the requirements of economic development, and so on; "socialist attitude," interpretation referring to self-management or society's transformation; "the demanding attitude" criticizing the existing system, but without going explicitly beyond that. This classification does not enable us to sort out "apathy" (high perceived powerlessness—low perceived normlessness) from "dissent" or extreme disengagement (high perceived powerlessness—high perceived normlessness). From the global context of the inquiry, we tend to equate "demanding attitudes" to "apathy." Using Ada Finifter's terminology, we will say that the "political attitude" may lead to a behavior of "political integration" (low powerlessness—low normlessness), the "socialist attitude" to a "reform oriented" behavior (low powerlessness—high normlessness). See Ada Finifter, "Dimensions of Political Alienation," American Political Science Review, June 1970, p. 407. No wonder that political integration and reform orientation are more widespread among the executives of the self-managed farms than among the rank-and-file workers who are predominantly apathetic.

9. Michel Cornaton, Les Regroupements de la Decolonisation en Algerie (Paris: Editions Ouvrieres, 1967), p. 235.

10. Actually, the peasants' feelings have some basis in reality. On the eve of independence, a tremendous number of jobs abandoned by the Europeans were available to Algerian citizens: 200,000 jobs at the very least in the civil service; about 50,000 jobs in the self-managed and state farms. See C. Bobrowski, "Agriculture Traditionnelle en Algerie," Africana Bulletin 6 (1967). Other estimates run as high as 450,000 jobs in all sectors. See Samir Amin, L'Economie du Maghreb (Paris: Editions de Minuit, 1966), vol. 1, p. 285. But most of the people who benefited from such an increase in the job opportunities lived in the cities. The peasants drew some benefits from their urban relatives' help because of the solidarity of the agnatic family. The chouhada's (martyrs: soldiers or civilians killed by the French) parents or relatives were also given state pensions.

11. Jacques Lizot, Metidja, Etude d'Un Village de l'Ouarsenis, These Paris, Ecole Pratique des Hautes Etudes, 1967 (mimeo.), p. 285.

12. The Tripoli Program, approved in June 1962 by the National Council of the Algerian Revolution, states: "During the war, France benefited by the material and moral help of all the Western powers, and in particular the United States."

13. Quoted in Clement Henry Moore, Politics in North Africa (Boston: Little, Brown, 1969), p. 86.

14. "French speaking" and "Arab speaking" people have the same mother tongue: dialectal Arabic or Berber. The schooling makes the difference, especially the attendance at the universities. Science, technics, technology, and medicine are taught exclusively in French; history, geography, sociology, and philosophy are reportedly taught in Arabic (but there are several exceptions). Law and economics are taught in both languages, but not to the same students.

15. Statement made by Colonel Boumediene on the opening of the meeting held in Algiers by the group of 77 underdeveloped countries, to prepare the UNCTAD Conference of New Delhi. Le Monde, October 12, 1967.

16. Oil is the best symbol used in those circumstances. For example, in July 1964, Ahmed Ben Bella, speaking of the "plot against Algeria hatched by those who want to bleed Algeria white," conjured up a striking picture of the Algerian situation. Oil was likened to blood, earth to flesh, and therefore the international corporations to vampires. Quoted by Jean Leca, "Le Nationalisme Algerien Depuis l'Independance," in Louis Jean Duclos, Jean Duvignaud, and Jean Leca, Les Nationalismes Maghrebins (Paris: Fondation Nationale des Sciences Politiques, 1967), p. 66.

17. Kaid Ahmed, Contradictions de Classes et Contradictions au Sein des Masses (Algiers: SNED, 1970). When he made this statement, Kaid Ahmed was a member of the Council of the Revolution and in charge of the party.

18. See Maxime Rodinson, "Dynamique Interne ou Dynamique Globale? L'Exemple des Pays Musulmans," in Marxisme et Monde Musulman (Paris: Le Seuil, 1972), pp. 266-97.

19. The expression "Nationalism with Marxist tendency" ("Nationalisme Marxisant") is borrowed from Maxime Rodinson, "Les Ideologies Revolutionnaires dans le Tiers Monde," in op. cit., pp. 311-36.

20. M. G. Smith, "Segmentary Lineage Systems," Journal of the Royal Anthropological Institute 86, pt. 2 (1956): 48.

21. Newspapermen frequently use acabyia for "clannishness." They fail to recognize that acabyia is not only a process of fission but also of fusion when acabyia leads to mulk, that is, sovereignty.

Sovereignty is caused by the people's search for an authoritative power. Compare Georges Labica, Politique et Religion Chez Ibn Khaldoun (Algiers: SNED, 1968), pp. 77 ff.

22. Ernest Gellner, Saints of the Atlas (London: Weidenfeld and Nicolson, 1969), pp. 41-49.

23. A. Southall, The Alur Society: A Study in Processes and Types of Domination (Cambridge, England: Heffer and Sons, 1954).

24. Alexis de Tocqueville is a precious witness to the French conviction that Abdel Quader was the only real enemy because of the new pattern of organization he was setting up. See his "Ecrits et Discours Politiques," in Oeuvres Completes (Paris: Gallimard, 1962), pp. 222 ff.

25. The crucial role was played, in this respect, by the great land tenure bills enacted between 1871 and 1896. See C. R. Ageron, Les Algeriens Musulmans et la France (Paris: Presses Universitaires de France, 1968), vol. 1; Andre Nouschi, Enquete sur le Niveau de Vie des Populations Rurales Constantinoises de la Conquete Jusqu'en 1919 (Paris: Presses Universitaires de France, 1961).

26. Fanny Colonna, "Cultural Resistance and Religious Legitimacy in Colonial Algeria," Economy and Society 3, no. 3 (1974): 242; Ali Merad, Le Reformisme Musulman en Algerie de 1925 a 1940 (Paris: Mouton, 1967).

27. See the comparison between the postindependence uprisings in Kabylia and in the Aures by Jean Favret, "Traditionalism Through Ultra-Modernism," in Ernest Gellner and Charles Micaud, eds., Arabs and Berbers (London: Duckworth, 1973), pp. 307-25. The persistence and even the revival of brotherhoods in 1974 may be accounted for in terms of the ineffectiveness of the bureaucratic elites at the local level, but we should bear in mind that such a functionalist explanation is too convincing to be quite true. The revival of the brotherhoods may be related to a quite different set of phenomena.

28. By "pluralism" we mean a process granting different groups the legal right to compete for power, and not the situation described by M. G. Smith in which individuals hold their citizenship through segmental or sectional identifications ("Institutional and Political Conditions of Pluralism"), in L. Kuper and M. G. Smith, eds., Pluralism in Africa (Berkeley: University of California Press, 1969), pp. 27-65. It is not farfetched to say that, in Algeria, for reasons examined later in the text, pluralism (in the second sense) is a hindrance to a pluralistic process (in the first sense).

29. William B. Quandt gives a good account of the different attitudes of the members of the Algerian political elite in his Algeria: Revolution and Political Leadership 1954-1968 (Cambridge: Massachusetts Institute of Technology Press, 1969).

30. Ralf Dahrendorf, Class and Class Conflict in Industrial Society (London: Routledge and Kegan Paul, 1959), p. 188.

31. Abdel Kader Zghal, "Nation Building in the Maghreb," in S. N. Eisenstadt and S. Rokkan, eds., Building States and Nations: Analyses by Regions, vol. 2 (Beverly Hills, Calif.: Sage Publications, 1973), p. 338.

32. On the Communist International and colonial issues, see Enrica Colloti Pischel and Chiara Robertazzi, L'Internationale Communiste et les Problemes Coloniaux 1919-1935 (Paris: La Haye Mouton, 1968). See also the memoirs by the first general secretary of the Algerian Communist Party. Excluded from the party in 1948 for "nationalist deviation," he was in charge of the rural problems in the first government of independent Algeria (1962-63). See Amar Ouzegane, Le Meilleur Combat (Paris: Julliard, 1962).

33. The splitting of the urban bourgeoisie into two forms of resistance (ulema, evolues) has not yet been explained satisfactorily. See Mostefa Lacheraf, "Resistance Urbaine et Lutte Nationale Depuis 1830," in his Algerie, Nation et Societe (Paris: Maspero, 1965).

34. 1954 Census cited in Favret, loc. cit., p. 318.

35. We are aware that wage earners made up the major part of the European population but they were perceived as linked to the employers by strong common interests. A common "class consciousness" actually never developed among Algerian and European workers.

36. The opinions of those who were in favor of self-management are fairly well expressed by Mohamed Harbi in "L'Algerie et Ses Realites," Economie et Politique 130 (May 1965); and Michel Raptis, "Le Dossier de l'Autogestion en Algerie," Autogestion (September 1967). On the self-managed farms see Claudine Chaulet, op. cit.; and Gerard Duprat, Revolution et Autogestion Rurale en Algerie (Paris: Armand Colin, 1973). On the self-managed factories, see Damien Helie, "Industrial Self-Management," in I. W. Zartman, ed., Man, State and Society in the Contemporary Maghreb (New York: Praeger Publishers, 1973), pp. 465-75.

37. Algiers Charter, Theses 11 and 37.

38. Colonel Boumediene often came out against that ideology: "We have been independent for only three years and we have heard some advisers call for the withering away of the State, before the State is even built up" (October 20, 1965). Quoted by Michel Camau in La Notion de Democratie dans la Pensee des Dirigeants Maghrebins (Paris: CNRS, 1970), p. 159.

39. This occurs for two reasons. First, the state bureaucracy, constantly called upon to assist self-management firms, is tempted to obtain control over the firms it is supposed to maintain. Second, if the self-managed firms are self-sufficient, however, they may behave as separate units struggling against one another and jeopardizing

the overall economic policy. The state then has to interfere. Repudiated in the name of self-management, the state comes back in the name of planning.

40. The leaders of the trade union, the "Union Generale des Travailleurs Algeriens," appointed in 1965, had built their power on the ideology of self-management. No wonder that they were swept away in 1967 when the ideology of centralized industrialization prevailed over self-management. Compare Francois Weiss, Doctrine et Action Syndicales en Algerie (Paris: Cujas, 1970), pp. 211-28, 292-301.

41. Monique Laks, Autogestion Ouvriere et Pouvoir Politique en Algerie, 1962-1965 (Paris: Etudes et Documentation Internationales, 1970), pp. 310 ff.

42. The workers can organize in two different ways. They can form "strike committees" (comites de greve) or "management committees" (comites de gestion). The two organizations can be mingled only after the working class political has taken over power. The Algerian Marxists obviously did not think that condition was met because they expected the management committees to give rise to such a political organization. They were confined in a vicious circle.

43. This distinction is borrowed from Franz Schurmann, Ideology and Organization in Communist China (Berkeley: University of California Press, 1966), pp. 26 ff.

44. See, for example, Raymond Vallin, "Muslim Socialism in Algeria," in Zartman, ed., op. cit., pp. 50-65.

45. Revolution et Travail (in Arabic), October 26, 1964. Because of that letter, the editor of the journal was sent to jail for 48 hours at the decision of the head of the party's orientation committee, Hocine Zahouane. After the June 19 coup, Zahouane was himself imprisoned.

46. Quoted with mockery by Cerif Belkacem in Revolution Africaine, no. 143 (October 23, 1965).

47. Contradictions de Classe et Contradictions au Sein des Masses (Algiers: Entreprises Algeriennes de Presse, 1970).

48. Interview given to Unita, June 1964.

49. Contradictions de Classe, op. cit., n. 46.

50. The author's strategy may be all the more successful as he is very careful to insist that "the stratum of exploiters have the same feeling as a part of the executives bred in the midst of the western university, liberal and bourgeois." So, executives and exploiters "are split from the poor masses of workers, which is a contradiction both objective and subjective." It may be noticed that such an analysis lacks any logical basis. (The link between the owners of the means of production, the former bourgeois cleared by their participation in the liberation war, some high civil servants, and the Western univer-

sities does not appear crystal-clear to a critical mind.) But it is
precisely that lack of clarity that makes the speech efficient: it focuses upon all the features of the perfect political foe, a rich, liberal, Westernized, revolution-profiteer. A robot-portrait is more efficient than an exact analysis because each one may complete it by
projecting his preferred foe's image.

51. Clifford Geertz, "Ideology as a Cultural System," in David
Apter, ed., Ideology and Discontent (New York: Free Press, 1964),
pp. 63-64.

52. The Tripoli program censures both "the longing for the past,
which means powerlessness and confusion,"and "the cultural cosmo-
politanism and Western influence which instilled in many Algerians
feelings of contempt for their own language and values."

53. On the ideology of the technophile, see Abdallah Laroui,
L'Ideologie Arabe Contemporaine (Paris: Maspero, 1967).

54. For a presentation of "the government by the party," see
Jean Leca, "Parti et Etat en Algerie," Annuaire de l'Afrique du Nord
1968, pp. 13-42; and A. Remili, "Parti et Administration en Algerie,"
idem., pp. 43-56.

55. Note from the party, December 16, 1969, Revue Algerienne
des Sciences Juridiques, Politiques et Economiques, no. 2 (1970):
415.

56. The process must apply likewise to the central political
agencies. However, no national election has taken place since the
1964 elections to the National Assembly. The National Assembly was
suspended in 1964. Since June 19, 1965, the supreme power has been
held by the Council of Revolution composed of military chiefs in active service and former officers of the National Liberation Army (both
from the outside and the inside). The membership of the council has
dropped from 24 to 12 because of ousters, resignations, and deaths.

57. W. H. Lewis, "The Decline of Algeria's F.L.N.," in I.
W. Zartmen, ed., Man, State and Society, op. cit., pp. 330-40.
The membership of the party is unknown. It may amount to 300,000.

58. On the workers' organization see Francois Weiss, op. cit.

59. According to the census of the civil servants in 1969,
there were 197,951 civil servants (Societes Nationales not included),
including about 10,000 aliens; out of 187,000 Algerians, 113,000
lacked any diploma, 2,700 had the "baccalaureat," 2,100 a university diploma, 500 some kind of Ph.D. The rest had diplomas inferior
to the baccalaureat. The first Four-Year Plan (1969-73) estimated
the "administrative employment" (including state bureaucracy, local
communities, and the various staffs of the Societes Nationales and
public corporations) at 275,000 in 1969 (out of 840,000 nonrural jobs)
and forecast 322,000 administrative jobs in 1973 (out of 1,105,000
nonrural jobs). The second Four-Year Plan (1973-77) forecasts that

106,000 new administrative jobs will be created during this period (given a general increase of 456,000 nonrural jobs). The Algerian army would number 63,000 members, the civilian members and the workers in the many military firms not included, according to La Revue de Defense Nationale 1967, p. 155, and Maghreb-Machrek, November/December 1973, p. 66.

60. The best study of the army remains I. W. Zartman's "The Algerian Army in Politics," in C. E. Welch, Jr., ed., Soldier and the State in Africa (Evanston, Ill.: Northwestern University Press, 1970), pp. 224-49.

61. Compare Michel Miaille, "Contribution a une Reflexion Theorique sur l'Entreprise Socialiste Algerienne," Revue Algerienne, no. 3 (1972): 653-93.

62. See Bernard Gaud, "La Participation Ouvriere en Algerie," Revue Algerienne, 1967, p. 829.

63. Pierre Marthelot, "Reflexions sur Certaines Consequences de la Revolution Agraire en Algerie," Maghreb-Machrek, September/October 1974, p. 34.

64. On the relationship between students and political power, see Clement H. Moore and Arlie Rotschild, "Students' Unions in North African Politics," Daedalus, Winter 1968; Donald K. Emmerson, ed., Students and Politics in Developing Nations (New York: Praeger Publishers, 1968); Jean Leca and J. C. Vatin, L'Algerie Politique: Institutions et Regime (Paris: A. Colin, 1975), chap. 4.

65. El Moudjahid, July 13, 1972. On the overall issues raised by the students' mobilization see Jean Leca and J. C. Vatin, op. cit., chap. 8.

66. We are using herein the concept of institutionalization outlined by S. P. Huntington ("process by which organizations and procedures acquire value and stability"), Political Order in Changing Societies (New Haven, Conn.: Yale University Press, 1968), p. 92.

67. Gerard Destanne de Bernis, "L'Economie Algerienne Depuis l'Independance," Annuaire de l'Afrique du Nord, 1969, pp. 13-41.

68. During the four years preceding the first Four-Year Plan (1965-68) the GNP rose from 16.2 billion DA (2.7 billion of which coming from oil) to 18.5 billion (4 billion coming from oil).

69. The oil resources rose from 50 million DA (1962) to 1,450 million DA (1969).

70. Gerard Destanne de Bernis, "Le Plan Quadriennal de l'Algerie," Annuaire de l'Afrique du Nord, 1970, pp. 195-230. Jean-Claude Melki, "Realisation et Financement du Plan Quadriennal Algerien de Development 1970-1973," Maghreb-Machrek, September/October 1974, pp. 16 ff.

71. Gerard Destanne de Bernis, op. cit., p. 201. The Algerian planners prefer to speak of "integration of economy" in the sense that

each economic unit must be a supplier and a buyer for other national units.

72. Note that the increase in imports of industrial consumer goods diminished the potential saving and was likely to throw off the balance of trade at the very moment when the agricultural sector's failures entailed an increase in the imports of cereals (about one million tons in 1971). A. Benachenhou, "Chronique Economique Algerienne," Annuaire de l'Afrique du Nord, 1972, p. 462.

73. See a good tentative account in Gerard Viratelle, L'Algerie Algerienne (Paris: Editions Ouvrieres, 1969).

74. Although all children are not yet eligible to go to school, one must keep in mind that their parents often refuse to send them. This is particularly noticeable in the areas where the traditional religious influences are still strong. In Algiers, 85 percent of the girls go to school, but only 32 percent in Mostaganem and 28 percent in Medca. See Annuaire Statistique de l'Algerie, 1972, p. 53.

75. Jean Leca and Bruno Etienne, "La Politique Culturelle de l'Algerie," Annuaire de l'Afrique du Nord, 1973, pp. 30–55.

76. See Vandevelde, op. cit., passim.

77. See Ahmed Ghozali and Gerard Destanne de Bernis, "Les Hydrocarbures et l'Industrialisation de l'Algerie," Revue Algerienne des Sciences Juridiques, Politiques et Economiques, no. 1 (March 1969).

7

SOCIALIST DEVELOPMENT IN AFRICA: THE CASE OF KEITA'S MALI

Helen Desfosses
J. Dirck Stryker

When Modibo Keita assumed the leadership of independent Mali in 1960, he was confronted with an economic situation of great complexity: a country with a population dispersed over a huge geographical area serviced by very poor transportation facilities, high costs of moving goods to and from foreign markets over the 1,231-kilometer railway to Dakar, a per capita income of $50 that had remained stagnate for decades, and dependency on French aid to a degree that the ruling Union Soudanaise deemed intolerable. The whole shape of the economy, moreover, was oriented around Mali's role in the French colonial empire. Because of its interior location, Mali had served first as a source of labor for the cash crops being developed in the coastal territories and only second as a source of production. Furthermore, most of the growth that did occur was due primarily to increased commercialization of groundnuts, cotton, livestock, and fish and to the expansion of the colonial bureaucracy. There was little improvement in agricultural practices, especially of food crops, or development of industry.

The social perspective was equally difficult. The masses of the population were tradition-bound, while the smaller number of wage earners, teachers and junior civil servants, traders, artisans, reform-minded Muslim intelligentsia, displaced ruling families, and depressed social groups had for years been frustrated in their opposition to the French colonial regime and its Malian allies. Despite this common front, however, there were substantial tensions between these disparate groups, which became increasingly apparent during the decade following independence.[1]

Keita's program of scientific socialism was an attempt to launch a frontal attack on these socioeconomic problems. Scientific socialism encompassed several strains: Keita's conception of the Leninist development model, a form of African socialism, and a loose formation of Malian political culture. The multiple foundations of this ideology allowed for a certain flexibility. Since subscription to each tenet implied certain policy choices, however, the attempt to incorporate all these into a single action program often proved confusing, and at times self-defeating. Furthermore, the regime's effort to derive full benefit from the ideology—to manipulate it as a unifying veneer for a divided elite, a constructive myth,[2] and an action program— also involved contradictions and a strain on the organizational and socializing capabilities of the party.

Scientific socialism, of course, involved several elements, ranging from a reorganization of the judiciary to building a strong trade union movement. There were also ideological constructs directly relevant to Malian rural development—for example, an emphasis on a single-party system, party penetration of rural society, and the cooperativization of agriculture. As implemented in Mali, these elements were to reflect more Keita's perceptions of the society's realities (and eventually the effects of those realities) than a strict adherence to Marxism-Leninism.

A primary feature of the Leninist model is a centralized, one-party system. While Keita's regime adhered to the principle that a single, ruling party was essential, there were certain deviations from the model. The Leninist concept of an elitist party based on the vanguard principle was not accepted. The Union Soudanaise, instead, chose to risk the dilution of its revolutionary energies and potential in exchange for the perceived benefits of a mass party: politicization and socialization of the masses. Another departure from the Leninist model was evident in the U.S. leadership: ethnic and regional factors were at least as important as ideological fervor in determining membership, while class or social origin was of minimal significance.[3] Finally, the party represented its basic equalitarian "concern as an expression of the social values of Islam rather than in the context of Marxist doctrine."[4]

Keita's scientific socialism did mirror the Leninist emphasis on party penetration of society. A mass organization had been the aim since 1946, youth and women's associations were established, and the party strove to replace the chiefs as the primary political authority for the rural masses.[5] To this end, elected party subsections were created in each village to direct socioeconomic activity and to provide a political link between party and people. There was great optimism in the Union Soudanaise that the village comite would serve as an agent of both modernization and mobilization, helping through its efficiency and political work to extend the legitimacy of the party.

The village was a major focus of Keita's scientific socialism. The cooperativization of agriculture was deemed essential both to Malian economic development and to political mobilization. The effort to establish a system of rural cooperatives stemmed partly from a widh to emulate the Soviet model, and partly from the acceptance of a principal tenet of African socialism—the belief that African rural communities are socialist in their traditional form, and that this age-old foundation can be used to construct a uniquely African form of socialism, rather than simply a variant of the Marxist type. Keita's regime seemed hopeful that communal traditions could become a vehicle for modernization, providing, through their familiarity to the peasant, an acceptable method of accelerating the transitional process.

SOCIALISM IN MALI: PLAN AND REALITY

An important instrument for the mobilization of support for a major social and economic transformation was to be the Malian 1961-66 plan. As originally conceived, this plan was to provide for the priority development of agriculture as well as the beginning of industrialization and a systematic exploration for minerals.[6] Rapid growth was anticipated as a result of a massive movement in the countryside to modernize agriculture within a system of village cooperatives and the exploitation of opportunities to create certain light industries. It was clear to the planners, however, that an effort of this magnitude would require austerity in general government expenditures and efficient operation of the public sector in order to provide the resources necessary for directly productive investment.

As the plan was reviewed during 1961, it became apparent that substantial resources were being diverted to relatively unproductive projects, such as relatively luxurious administrative buildings, institutes of higher education, a luxury hotel, and a modern airport.[7] Furthermore, current government operating expenditures were rising at an alarming rate. As a result, the plan began to appear increasingly unrealistic and was scaled down to a projected annual rate of growth of 8 percent. Even to achieve this, however, would require a tremendous effort, especially in the rural sector where a disciplined cadre was largely lacking.

Instead, the tendencies of the first years of independence were continued. The number of government employees was expanded rapidly, as were the recurrent government expenditures required to pay their salaries.[8] State enterprises, which were supposed to contribute to public revenues, became instead a serious drain on the budget. Unproductive investments failed to create the resources necessary for reinvestment and sustained growth. Government deficits were,

consequently, financed by bank credit. This led to inflation and balance-of-payments difficulties, which reduced foreign exchange revenues, increased Mali's foreign indebtedness, and resulted in severe
exchange controls and import restrictions.

Particularly harmful for rural areas were some of the policies
employed in the commercial sector. State monopolies were given control over exports and imports of many basic commodities. Price and
other controls were imposed at all levels. As the government budgetary situation became increasingly severe and as inflationary pressures
mounted, prices to farmers were maintained at artificially low levels,
in effect subsidizing urban consumers and increasing the profits of
the state trading monopolies. In addition, government restrictions on
imports reduced their availability in rural areas and thus limited the
incentives for cash crop production.

MALI'S RURAL DEVELOPMENT PROGRAM

The task of enlisting efficient peasant involvement in the formation of cooperatives was complicated by the difficulties inherent in any
agricultural development program, problems stemming from the regime's perception of traditional communal attitudes as positive values
susceptible to minor "modernizing" adjustment, and by certain peculiarities of the Malian rural sector.

In its plan to promote rural development, Keita's regime had to
make a decision familiar to leaders in all developing countries: to
opt for the primacy of politics or the primacy of economics. Was political mobilization the party's foremost goal, especially since this
might compensate for financial limitations, or was raising the standard of living the priority? Keita chose to emphasize the former,
deeming it imperative to ensure an increase in the level of national
political consciousness. This would serve to increase the system's
legitimacy and spur the population to greater productive efforts in
spite of the (hopefully) short-term absence of economic incentives.

Emphasis on political mobilization also would help to convince
the Malian peasantry that it is the type rather than the level of economic development that is most important. Keita's belief in scientific
socialism impelled him to echo this Leninist-Maoist view. He cautioned that the central focus of his economic development program was
not raising the standard of living. Rather, it was the accumulation of
capital in order to end Mali's economic dependence on France and to
ensure that the "progressive forces" assumed a leading role in Mali's
political-economic structure.

Vis-a-vis the peasantry, a central premise of Keita's ideology
seemed to be that the traditional culture had provided a good schooling

for socialism for the peasant and that it might be used as a foundation
for the building of a socialist society. Keita apparently accepted the
theory that in the context of rural Africa, socialism implied a "modernization" of the old, rather than a concerted attack against the social and political survivals that the African commune sustained. [9]

The question of the relation of African communal values to an
economic development program is, of course, an old one. Soviet and
Western writers, as well as African leaders, have wrestled with the
problem of evaluating the merits and risks of using the traditional—
and the familiar—as a vehicle for rural modernization. Those who
emphasize the merits of this approach note that the African regime
lacks the necessary cadres and legitimacy to attempt a rapid transformation of the peasant way of life without risking widespread unrest.
The commune could provide an acceptable basis for introducing agricultural cooperatives, since the government could assume some understanding of reciprocal obligations and a sense of identity with the
group.[10] Furthermore, age-old cultural and organizational forms
within the village are solid and powerful. "In the Bambara and Maline
villages, the communal tendency, the existence of collective fields,
and the vitality of age fraternities coming from promotions to the
circumcised[11] were presumed to provide unchallengeable and easily
retooled foundations for the agricultural policies of scientific socialism.

Once the premise was accepted that the communal values still
enjoyed almost universal legitimacy, and, more important, could be
adapted to the regime's purposes,[12] then any suggestion that the entire precapitalist formation of Malian agriculture should be quickly
extirpated to facilitate the transition to socialism was untenable. It
was feared that dissolution would be premature, unsuited to Malian
realities, and might result in the conversion of the peasants to capitalist farming. Keita already feared that the peasants were being
crushed by commercial traders. In addition, further intrusion of
capitalism into the rural sector would strengthen the political position
of bourgeois elements, and facilitate neoimperialist efforts to foist
the capitalist system of development on the country.

In 1962 a third of the villages in Mali were placed in a simplified
cooperative plan—a plan that envisaged very broad and definite unit
goals:

> The cooperatives of the Republic of Mali are collec-
> tive organizations of a mass character, set up, ad-
> ministered and managed by the workers, to carry
> out for their profit, at their expense, and at their
> risk, the economic functions pertaining to their com-
> mon needs.[13]

The village formed the base unit, represented by a Groupement Rural de Production et de Secours Mutuel (GRPSM) responsible for the organization of communal labor, marketing and consumer goods purchasing. A second tier was occupied by a Zone d'Expansion Rural (ZER), charged with rural education programs, while a third level consisted of the Societe Mutuelle de Developpement Rural (SMDR), an overseeing credit and provisioning agency. The Party Youth Groups and Women's Associations were in charge of carrying out the ideological and persuasive functions, with the army called on eventually to develop certain showcase projects.

By the end of 1965, however, there were in the entire country only 95 consumption cooperatives and 45 others related to specific trades. A report commissioned by the Mali government commented, moreover, that even "these statistics do not accurately reflect the situation, as among these some were not functioning at all, and a great many were in difficult condition and others in quasi-normal condition."[14] Although these cooperatives had some success in reorganizing the sale of cash crops and purchase of imported staple goods, they achieved much less in their organization of manual labor. The party had intended that collective fields in each village worked by this labor would serve as agricultural demonstrations and would be expanded in size to eventually encompass the entire village. Instead, these fields were given the most desultory attention and would probably have been abandoned entirely if party supervision were not present.[15]

The most unyielding problem stemmed from the unsuitability of the traditional commune as a basis for rural modernization. In the Malian context, there were several factors complicating the general task of transforming institutions based on cooperation in consumption into production cooperatives.

1. The organizational forms of collective production familiar to the peasant generally were based on the extended family, not the village community.

2. Traditional forms of cooperation in consumption did not provide for a group approach to responsibility.[16]

3. While much had been made of the possibility of using as models the association of young men who have been circumcised in a given year and who traditionally have undertaken collective work, the feasibility of this approach was limited by such cultural factors as deference to age.

4. The problem of raising the goal-orientation of peasants was complicated by a traditional setting in which often "the cost of high attainment was socially prohibitive."[17]

Finally, the traditional setting often worked to ensure that traditionally powerful groups, such as chiefs and elders, dominated the new efforts in their attempts to consolidate power. To have overcome these problems would have required an enormous effort, but, as an ILO report stated,

> The cooperative movement in Mali presents a number
> of contrasts: (a) between the dimension and number
> of activities and the means and personnel at their dis-
> posal . . . ; (b) the dispersion of the cooperatives and
> the centralization of the administrative personnel for
> technical assistance and inspection; (c) the pressing
> need for education among the grand mass of coopera-
> tive members and insufficient means.[18]

SCOPE VERSUS MEANS: THE
PROBLEM OF CADRES

Persuading the peasant masses of the utility and advisability of their participation in a cooperative program is a difficult task requiring a substantial number of effective cadres. The cadres must serve as the communication link between party and masses, and, in many cases, as the animators of rural development projects. To discharge this dual role, the cadres must be able to understand the peasants' needs and demands, while never losing sight of the significance of the complex task with which the party has entrusted them. Also, and perhaps, more important, the cadres must be loyal and obedient to the party hierarchy, scrupulously observing the principles of democratic centralism.

Admittedly this description represents an ideal rarely if ever realized in practice. But in Mali, what the Union Soudanaise called "the numerical and qualitative insufficiency of cadres"[19] represented a very serious constraint on the realization of the cooperative program. One of the main qualitative criticisms centered on the cadres' lack of ideological fervor and "commitment." Party militants were criticized for not being prepared "to give the lie quickly to all the deceits and tendentious rumors capable of assaulting Malian opinion, whatever their source might be or the rank of those responsible for them."

> A party cadre who does not manage to convince a live-
> stock-raiser that the Soviet Union has never said that
> Mali should nationalize livestock does not deserve
> the name of cadre. If peasants in certain corners
> of Mali can still think that our Government is going

> to steal their grain, plunder their barns, confiscate
> their goods and put them to work on roads [cadres
> have been inefficient]. If merchants still manage
> to intoxicate our masses [not mentioning] that all,
> without exception, have doubled or quadrupled their
> business in relation to the colonial era [cadres have
> been inefficient].[20]

The response of the Union Soudanaise to cadre inefficiency was to
threaten to eliminate such cadres, and, more realistically, to establish a network of party schools. The year 1966 witnessed a drive to
set up basic institutions in several regions of the country, while an
upper school for cadres was projected for Bamako. (The establishment of the Higher Party School was assisted by a Soviet loan of approximately 500 million CFA [Communaute Financiere Africaine]
francs.) To supervise the party's renewed emphasis on military and
ideological consciousness, the National Committee for the Defense of
the Revolution (NCDR) was created in March 1966. Efforts were also
made to decentralize the party structure, to provide cadres with military training, and to create statutory labor commissions that would,
in Keita's words, help "administrative comrades to feel more involved in the affairs of their circonscriptions, and consequently, more
militant and responsible."

The fact that the enactment of these measures in no way resulted in a diminution of party attacks on the cadres suggests that the
steps were ineffective and that the cadres were used as scapegoats
for the cooperative program's more general failures. Between 1966
and 1968, attacks on the cadres in the party press increased in
stridency: their self-serving attitude was criticized, as was their
overall unreliability as animators in the rural development program.
As Keita noted in his speech on the sixth anniversary of Mali's independence,

> We cannot help but mention some evidence which, al-
> though it is not widespread, still creates problems
> in certain districts. Some political comrades wish
> to be in charge of administrative work only. . . .
> The National Committee receives the most optimis-
> tic reports confirmed by the absence of open con-
> flict, while, in fact, nothing functions according to
> the Principles of the Party.[21]

Aside from their lack of ideological fervor and commitment,
party cadres suffered in another way: they lacked the technical knowledge required to introduce any important improvements into farming

methods. Traditional agricultural techniques in Mali have been developed over centuries to provide farmers with modest yields to their land and labor and with a reasonably high degree of protection against the risk of drought. Interventions in this sector are likely to be greeted with skepticism until they have proved themselves. But during the early 1960s the only important agricultural innovation that has been proven successful was the use of animal power in the cotton-growing areas. This innovation was introduced by the Compagnie Francaise pour le Developpement des Fibres Textiles (CFDT), a French-owned company that benefited from previous research that had fully tested the new techniques. CFDT's extension service was developed quite independently of the party or village cooperative system, and members of these two organizations were relatively ignorant of the methods employed. Since no other comparable research had been performed in Mali, party cadres had little advice to give the farmer, and village cooperatives in the cotton areas were reduced to "the rather nominal role of selling supplies and equipment to farmers under the general supervision of the CFDT."[22]

THE PROBLEM OF OVERCENTRALIZATION

Once the decision to embark on a major rural development program was made, Keita's regime was faced with an important choice: to set up a program that would allow for local initiative and control, or to maximize central direction over this radical project. Arguments could be marshaled to justify either decision. If the local unit were made the most important link in the organizational plan, this would encourage peasant participation and unit responsiveness to local conditions. Furthermore, the villager would feel involved in the creation of "the new Mali" and would develop a consciousness about his role in developing this society. Finally, cooperative members would have some knowledge about financial conditions, and have some real personal interest in making the cooperative pay.[23]

A strong case could also be made for constructing a pyramidal structure that would vest information, decision making, and, most important, power, in central government organizations. This would help to preserve some uniform standards of output and performance from the cadre corps. It would also mitigate against the transformation of cooperatives into power bases for rural potentates.[24] Governmental expertise could compensate for the ill-preparedness of parochial village societies for such a transformation of social and economic organization. Finally, cooperatives could become instrumentalities of the efforts of the Union Soudanaise at system consolidation and system expansion. This was an important incentive toward the centralization of control over the cooperative program, for, as Keita states, "the objective was and still is an increased mobilization capacity for the Party."[25]

There were, on the other hand, important dangers in centralizing the cooperative system within the party structure.

> Cooperatives that become an instrumentality or an extension of a political party rest on potentially unstable foundations and run the risk of forfeiting their members' support by becoming involved in political strife. When the political party is also the ruling party, there is the danger that cooperatives will become virtually an agency through which the government implements its policies without consulting the members. It aggravates the tendency of farmers to regard the cooperatives not as their own organization but as another "external" agency.[26]

The Union Soudanaise leadership was aware of the problems of alienation and elite-mass gap, but it was not until 1968 that there was an effort to effect organizational changes that would increase elite responsiveness to the demands and supports among the population. These included the dissolution of the National Politbureau and the local leadership bureaus, and the assumption of their duties by the NCDR and related organs on the local level.[27]

RURAL EDUCATION

In order to forestall a loss of the rural support that had been a hallmark of Keita's political genius during the independence struggle, the regime relied on a two-pronged rural education effort: exhortative (propagandistic), and practical. The exhortative consisted of reports that Keita helped till the fields, that he had converted his farm into a socialist production unit, and that the army had participated in the rice harvest to show that it was "dedicated to the cause of the people."[28] Then there were chiding speeches by Keita, reminding the people of "a Malian adage: the glutton is a slave of his stomach."[29] Finally, there were attempts to remind the people of the benefits of cooperativization, such as the "comfortable standard of living that has currently been provided for the peasant masses,[30] and the fact that 'developed' countries, which some nostalgic people today envy, have known difficulties worse than ours. . . . Others, who have followed a different course, are experiencing more difficulties. . . . The difference lies in the Malian's dignity, his confidence in the future, and his attachment to the Party and its leaders."[31]

Increasing the confidence and party-orientation of the peasantry was also a goal of the rural education curriculum. The idea behind the establishment of a network of seasonal agricultural schools was that if certain young men could learn the techniques and implications of successful cooperativization, they would absorb, and could instill in others, a real commitment to the program and to the party that originated it.

To correspond to the Zones d'Expansion Rurales (ZER), the Five-Year Plan envisaged the creation of 150 seasonal schools that would educate a projected 7,000 students. Each pupil would attend a school for one agricultural season, learning all the techniques of farming and some comprehension of the merit of the cooperative concept. He would then return to his village with two bulls, one cart, one plow, and a fixed government credit, to become the animator of his village.

It is clear from articles in the Malian press, as well as from Western reports, that this plan fell short of its qualitative if not its quantitative goal. Keita complained that the nine-month program sent "still illiterate and unequipped young peasants back to their villages."[32] De Wilde notes that many people had to be pressured to enter the schools, especially since the tradition of receiving land only after one's marriage meant that they would not get land to cultivate for a long time. Furthermore, some of the schools had "practice" fields of such low fertility that the results of the modern methods were often worse than those achieved through traditional practices at home.[33] In 1966, the program was expanded to two years in order to provide a more intensive literacy and farming training. However, this change in duration could do nothing to alter the factors in the students' social environment that served to hinder the program's success. Nor did the Malian version of the Cultural Revolution[34] effect any significant changes in the rural social sphere, especially since the United States had to temper cadre enthusiasm in order to save its dwindling base of peasant support.[35] Mali's UN-supported functional literacy program could have been expected eventually to wreak some attitudinal changes, but not in time to save the increasingly vilified regime or its cooperativization effort.

THE DETERIORATING RURAL
ECONOMIC SITUATION

By 1967 it was becoming clear that the policies of the Keita government were meeting substantial resistance among the peasantry. Wasteful investments and expanding government employment and recurrent expenditures financed by deficit spending were taking their toll in inflation. The retail price index of food products increased from 100 in 1962-63 to 200 in July, 1967.[36] Yet, official prices paid to farmers rose during the same period by only 50 percent for millet and rice.[37] As a result, scarcities developed in the official markets as black marketeering increased. This was dealt with increasingly by the use of the army to forcibly confiscate stores of grain, which were then sold at low official prices to those few urban consumers with influence enough to obtain the limited supplies.

In addition to the low grain prices paid to producers, imported goods became increasingly expensive and scarce as import restrictions were tightened to deal with rising balance-of-payments deficits. Furthermore, prices paid to farmers for the two most important cash crops rose only 22 percent for peanuts and not at all for cotton during the same period.[38] Thus the incentive for farmers to produce for other than their own needs declined markedly.

In 1967 the government devalued the Malian franc by 50 percent. Prices of peanuts and cotton were raised substantially with the devaluation, but those of grains were not. This resulted in a considerable disparity between official prices in Mali and prices prevailing in neighborhood countries, and led to an increase in smuggling activity. Peasant support for the government's rural development program was at an all-time low.

CRISIS FROM WITHIN, CRISIS
FROM WITHOUT

It is of course relatively simple in retrospect to list the evidence of growing conflict within the Union Soudanaise in the months before the coup. There were signs of a generation gap within the party, with certain younger leaders like Seydou Badian Kayate espousing a pro-Chinese orientation, while Keita had inaugurated a rapproachment with France. There was also the double postponement of the Congress of the Union Soudanaise-RDA, originally scheduled for September 1965 and not held until late 1966. Finally, there were the numerous organizational changes, almost invariably accompanied by references to "insufficient militancy" and the failure of certain leaders to perceive the party's duty clearly.[39] There were frequent references to the overemphasis on criticism in the party—criticism that could be equated with opportunism: "Within the Party, complacency cultivates this state of affairs. Bereft of ideological unity, one encounters resultant difficulties which sap and impede far-ranging action."[40] It seemed that Keita was caught in the center of concentric vicious circles: (1) the lack of ideological unity impeded the adoption of effective policies, while policy failures only served to increase the rhetoric and tension;

(2) at various junctures, Keita found himself at odds with one wing of the party (for example, the moderates in 1966, the radicals in 1968). However, any effort to compromise with one group would only exacerbate tensions with the others, and the conflict would begin anew.

At the root of these struggles was not only ideological wrangling and policy confusion but also the advocacy of frequently conflicting programs to stave off the alienation of increasingly restive urban interest groups. The workers, who represented a very small, yet vocal segment of the population had been hard hit by the combined effects of inflation and Keita's wage control policies. According to Diop, while the guaranteed minimum wage increased five times between 1947 and 1958, and almost one and one-half times between 1957 and 1959, in the following decade it fell in real terms by 50 percent.[41] The 1967 devaluation, which was accompanied by a wage freeze, obviously hit the workers hard. Even though Keita attempted to reduce the growing discontent by promises of low-cost housing programs for workers in 1968, the probability of any early realization of this project was minimal.

The civil service shared many of the workers' complaints regarding inflation and shortages. Certain high functionaries also objected to the regime's policy of subjecting them to military training and requiring that they go to the countryside on weekends to cultivate their fields and "keep contact with the masses." Many also objected to the regime's attempt to lay a good deal of the blame for inequities and policy failures on the civil service. Thus during the devaluation controversy Keita chose the occasion of a November 1967 mass rally in Bamako (organized by the workers and youth groups under the sponsorship of the NCDR) to announce severe penalties for misappropriating public funds.[42] The same month also witnessed charges being brought against 200 civil servants for complicity in a "cultural revolution" used as a cover for their varying degrees of responsibility with respect to the bad administration of past years.[43]

The charges of complicity in a pseudocultural revolution could indicate that the civil service, which had always provided a strong base of support for scientific socialism, was agitating for more leftist policies than the current center of gravity within the Union Soudanaise leadership would allow. It would not be surprising if the bureaucracy advocated a continuation of state socialism—an ideology that, under Malian conditions, meant little more than expanding the public administration. "In the absence of a true proletariat to uphold his socialism, Keita had to form an artificial class from among the state's employees."[44] Perhaps the other cornerstone of Keita's support was the youth organization, which was originally set up as a "transmission belt" for the U.S.-RDA. Eventually, it became more and more important in the arena of socialist politics, as other groups and policy, in general, became bogged down in contradictions and over-

bureaucratization. Part of Keita's solution to these difficulties was
to bypass many of the established organizations, assigning a key role
to the youth association in "providing impetus, stimulation and animation" for scientific socialism.[45] Eventually, many young activists
were coopted into the People's Militia, which not only antagonized the
peasants by its undisciplined forays into the regulation of smugglers
and black marketeers, but which also angered the army by its arrest
of several officers in 1968.

The reaction of the army command to this indignity and others
that it had suffered at the hands of Keita's regime (such as tilling the
soil where the peasants refused to do so) was to install Colonel Sekou
Traore at the head of a new military government in November 1968.
Appalled by a foreign debt over five times the national budget, by
widespread corruption and the bad harvests of that year, the military
deemed the forcible removal of Keita's regime essential.

CONCLUSION

Keita's collectivization program foundered on two obvious but
significant problems: lack of money, and the disintegration of relations between leadership and people. The financial difficulties that
Mali shared with many countries were compounded by the political aspects of the scientific socialist path to development—namely, a basic
emphasis on ending the dominant position of capitalist (French) investment.

This necessitated substituting in its place a state bureaucracy
and party organization that were required both to provide daily management of the economy and to launch a massive campaign designed
to develop the rural sector along the lines of scientific socialism. The
success of this effort demanded a cohesive elite, a well-disciplined and
indoctrinated cadre, several limitations on consumer aspirations, the
elimination of wasteful public investments, and the active cooperation
of the peasantry. In the absence of these, the result was an inflated
government bureaucracy, budgetary and balance-of-payments deficits,
upward pressure on prices, stagnation of production, controls and
shortages throughout the economy, and increased indebtedness not
only to France but to the Soviet Union and the People's Republic of
China as well. Given that the Union Soudanaise "attempted to superim-
pose solidification of mass support onto the long-range goal of economic advance,"[46] difficulties with one aspect of the nexus threatened
the viability of the other. Keita's problems in both areas meant that
the success of scientific socialism was moved from the realm of the
improbable to the realm of the impossible.

NOTES

1. Thomas Hodgkin and Ruth Schachter Morgenthau, "Mali," in James S. Coleman and Carl G. Rosberg, Jr., eds., Political Parties and National Integration in Tropical Africa (Berkeley: University of California Press, 1966), pp. 234-35.

2. Carl G. Widstrand, "Efficiency and Cooperatives," in Cooperatives and Rural Development in East Africa (New York: Holmes & Meier, 1970), p. 35.

3. According to Mamadou Diop, the 19-man Politburo elected by the Sixth Party Congress of the US-RDA included ten members of the intelligentsia, seven clerk-functionaries, one worker, and one businessman. Histoire des Classes Sociales dans l'Afrique de l'Ouest I: Le Mali (Paris, 1971), p. 214.

4. Hodgkins and Morgenthau, op. cit., p. 252.

5. Frank G. Snyder, One-Party Government in Mali: Transition Toward Control (New Haven, Conn.: Yale University Press, 1965), p. 100.

6. Samir Amin, Trois Experiences Africaines de Developpement: Le Mali, La Guinee et Le Ghana (Paris, 1965), p. 100.

7. Amin, ibid., pp. 111-12.

8. In 1959 there were about 17,000 government employees; by 1967 approximately 45,000 people were working for the administration or for state enterprises. J. Dirck Stryker, "The Malian Cattle Industry: Opportunity and Dilemma," Journal of Modern African Studies 12, no. 3 (September 1974): 445.

9. Le Mali, p. 9; compare V. G. Solodovnikov, ed., Africa in Soviet Studies, 1968 (Moscow, 1969), p. 63, cited in Helen Desfosses Cohn, Soviet Policy Toward Black Africa (New York: Praeger Publishers, 1972), p. 194.

10. John de Wilde, Experiences with Agricultural Development in Tropical Africa I: The Synthesis (Baltimore: Johns Hopkins Press, 1967), pp. 213-14.

11. Emile Leynaud, "Age Fraternities and Cultural Societies in Upper Niger Valley," Cahiers d'Etudes Africaines 6, no. 21 (1966): 41-68.

12. One aspect of traditional social relations was, however, ignored in this line of agument. Over a large part of Mali "traditional co-operation within a patrilineally organized household is based on status differences between non-equals, whereas socialist co-operation is based on a presumed contract between equals." Nicholas Hopkins, "Socialism and Social Change in Rural Mali," Journal of Modern African Studies 7, no. 3 (October 1969): 460.

13. Law No. 63-121, January 25, 1963.

14. Rapport au Gouvernement de la Republique du Mali sur l'Organisation et le Developpement du Mouvement Cooperatif (Geneva: Bureau International du Travail, 1967), p. 2.

15. Hopkins, op. cit., p. 466.

16. S. M. Makings, Agricultural Problems of Developing Countries in Africa (Lusaka, 1967), p. 9.

17. I. S. E. Migot-Adholla, "Traditional Society and Cooperatives," in Widstrand, ed., op. cit., p. 21.

18. Rapport au Gouvernement de la Republique du Mali, op. cit., pp. 2-3.

19. General Resolution of the Fourth Conference of the Koutiala Section of U.S.-RDA, L'Essor Hebdomadaire, December 5, 1966.

20. L'Essor, December 7, 1965.

21. Ibid., September 26, 1966.

22. De Wilde, op. cit., p. 159.

23. Rene Dumont, African Agricultural Development (New York, 1966), p. 53; compare L'Essor, October 10, 1966.

24. L'Essor, October 10, 1966.

25. Ibid., September 26, 1966.

26. De Wilde, op. cit., p. 218.

27. L'Essor Hebdomadaire, March 11, 1968.

28. L'Essor, January 19, 1967.

29. Quotidien Information (Bamako), September 23, 1965.

30. Mamadou Gologo, "Speech at the Conference of Cadres at Nioro," L'Essor Hebdomadaire, June 21, 1965.

31. L'Essor Hebdomadaire, February 21, 1966.

32. L'Essor, September 26, 1966; see also Pierre Morlet's interview with Keita in L'Humanite, October 6, 1966; compare interview with Seydon Tale, Minister of Education, L'Essor, September 8, 1967.

33. De Wilde, op. cit., pp. 189-90.

34. L'Essor, September 7, 1967.

35. Note the admonition in L'Essor Hebdomadaire, April 1, 1968, that "ideological fervor does not mean attacks on religion, as have occurred in certain sections of Bamako and at Nioro."

36. Mali, Service de la Statistique Generale, de la Compatabilite Nationale, et de la Mecanographie, Annuarie Statistique 1970 (Bamako, 1972), p. 185.

37. Mali, ibid., p. 187.

38. Ibid.

39. See, for example, L'Essor Hebdomadaire, June 3, 1968.

40. L'Essor Hebdomadaire, January 10, 1966; June 21, 1965.

41. Diop, op. cit., p. 203.

42. L'Essor Hebdomadaire, November 27, 1967.

43. Le Mois en Afrique, no. 25 (January 1968): 27.

44. Colin Legum and John Drysdale, eds., Africa Contemporary Record 1969-1970.

45. L'Essor, November 5, 1966. Note that young militants were opposed to the 1967 reentry into the franc zone and the expansion of French influence that this implied.

46. Synder, op. cit., p. 111.

CHAPTER

8

SOCIALISM AND
POLITICAL ECONOMY
IN GHANA
Jon Kraus

In the first half of the 1960s the small West African state of Ghana, under the leadership of Kwame Nkrumah and the Convention People's Party (CPP), was the focus of considerable attention as it articulated and sought to pursue a socialist path to development. The first sub-Saharan colony to achieve internal self-rule (1951) and then independence (1957), by 1959-60 Nkrumah and some portions of the CPP turned their priorities to effecting rapid economic development and social change by building a "socialist" state. In February 1966, with the economy in desperate straits, the army rose up and over-threw the Nkrumah regime, met active resistance only from the Presidential Guard, and was greeted with visible widespread jubilation by Ghanaians in the main cities. The short-lived attempt at socialist transformation was denounced by many observers with left as well as liberal orientations, inside Ghana and out, as a fraud, a failure, or both.[1] Where was the popular support for this Socialist regime? Where was the "mass Party" with whose support Nkrumah ruled? Nkrumah's international reputation as a Socialist and vigorous anti-imperialist brought him the support of the more radical African leaders for awhile, and he found a home with Sekou Toure in Guinea, but the regime was finished.

The successor National Liberation Council (NLC) government, composed of the army and police, strongly and repeatedly denounced Nkrumah and his regime for its undoubted tyrannical abuse of power.

The author gratefully acknowledges a valuable critique of this chapter by Professor David Apter, Yale University, and a State University of New York Research Foundation grant, which provided time for writing.

But there seems no doubt that it was primarily the regime's disastrous economic performance that provided the basis for extensive popular disaffection and hence support for the military's coup d'etat; the
army coup leaders had their own institutional grievances as well. [2]
The new NLC regime moved quickly to restore good relations with
the capitalist Western regimes, literally kicking Eastern European
personnel out of the country. It pronounced almost as much scorn for
Nkrumah's socialist pretensions as it did for his socialist economics.

> In spite of his extravagant pretensions to being an intel-
> lectual, Nkrumah was never able to explain satisfac-
> torily the theory of this socialism. It was variously
> Marxism, Marxism-Leninism, Scientific Socialism,
> or Socialism "conditioned" by Ghanaian and African
> traditions and institutions, African Socialism, Marx-
> ism-Leninism-Nkrumaisn, or, for short, Nkrumaism.
> But if one asked, "What is Nkrumaism?" there are a
> thousand and one answers, all equally absurd. [3]

It was further argued, with more interest in its political effect than
its accuracy, that Nkrumah was a clandestine capitalist, having acquired some £2.5 million assets and property. [4]

Under the guidance of an Economic Committee of trained economists and senior civil servants, the NLC jettisoned as rapidly as
possible numerous of the Nkrumah regime's economic policies and
state enterprises, selling off many of the more profitable state industries to foreign and domestic businessmen. It looked to the Western
countries for technical assistance and relief from a staggering burden of external indebtedness, and invited in the International Monetary
Fund (IMF) and a Harvard Advisory Group to assist in restoring the
economy and reintegrating it in the international liberal capitalist
network. This very deliberate policy involved a perception distinctly
different from the Nkrumah regime's on how to generate economic
growth—the "exports as engine of growth" model—and of the dynamics
of interaction between the industrial capitalist societies and the underdeveloped preindustrial societies. Despite a sharp rise in the world
price of cocoa, which helped the new regime, a reduction in the rate
of inflation, and close adherence to the IMF deflationary cure, the
NLC was unable to induce the Ghanaian economy to achieve any significant growth in GNP in its three and a half years in power.

After elections in mid-1969, a new civilian regime came to
power in September, whose leaders were largely composed of Nkrumah's old opposition, drawn from the new middle class of lawyers,
businessmen, and civil servants, and closely tied to certain traditional
states. This Progress Party (PP) regime was as devoted to a capital-

ist path to economic development as Nkrumah was to a socialist route.
When the economy failed to respond by 1970-71, the government introduced further measures of import and exchange liberalization, sought
to curtail some government expenditures (antagonizing, in turn, students, civil servants, the army, and workers) while simultaneously
attempting to expand the economy through new development projects
and higher private spending. Imports soared; severe new balance-
of-payments problems arose; a withering devaluation of 44 percent
(increasing the dollar costs of goods by 90 percent) was undertaken;
and, within a month, the Progress Party government was overthrown
in a new military coup in January 1972. The capitalist path and close
dependence upon Western creditors having relieved none of Ghana's
problems or animated renewed growth or employment, the new military National Redemption Council (NRC) reversed direction again.
And, armed with a highly nationalistic orientation, the NRC renewed a
number of the Nkrumah regime's policies, going so far as to nationalize gold mines, banks, and timber firms, though with a dedicated and
righteous scorn for ideology.

Ghanaian regimes pursuing both primarily socialist and capitalist
economic strategies have experienced grave problems. If Ghana's socialist rhetoric was previously taken at face value by the Nkrumah
regime's supporters and detractors, it has also been dismissed too
readily, as were its efforts, performance, and problems. This study
attempts to reevaluate and cast new light on the development, meaning, and impact of socialism in Ghana.

In doing so, one must first ask, What does one examine in
studying "socialism?" and, second, How can one most adequately analyze the subject? One may study socialism (or, for that matter,
capitalism) in terms of several distinct, but generally interrelated,
dimensions that embody certain social and economic relationships:
first, as a mode of economic production and distribution that entails
certain economic and social relations among a population, and that
usually gives rise to a limited range of probable political relationships; second, as a more or less integrated political belief system or
ideology; and, third, as certain policies or programs.

Of these dimensions, the one most frequently analyzed and confused is ideology. This is so, in part, because of the prominence of
a formalized Marxist ideology and its contemporary varieties but also,
in Africa, because formal ideological statements are more accessible
and easier to evaluate than actual political beliefs or behavior. Moreover, the study of ideology is subject to many abuses. As was the
case with the articulation of socialist goals and values in Ghana, an
ideology is often attacked as dogmatic and unreal if it is coherent and
tight in its vision, disdained for its inadequacy and inelegance if
poorly integrated or the whole lacking in clarity. This is so despite

our knowledge that (1) political beliefs or ideologies held by most people are neither highly explicit nor integrated, but consist largely of schematic cultural symbols and fragmented idea clusters; and that (a) the interrelatedness and centrality of political ideas, and (b) the range of objects involved in belief systems all tend to sharply decline as one moves from the social and political elites down through the social hierarchies;[5] (2) certain ideas, expressed by idioms or slogans (such as imperialism, socialism, capitalism) have the capacity to evoke distinct political values and attitudes that are meaningful and shape orientations and behavior.[6]

A distinction between a system of values or beliefs and an ideology is useful. A belief system will refer to a more or less stable set of established beliefs shared by a given social or political community; its ideas may be more or less closely interrelated, and many are not commonly articulated but held at the level of social assumptions. These beliefs, social and political, perform a variety of functions in a social system, providing individual role identities and community solidarity by explaining the social and physical universe, in political terms justifying and legitimating a particular social structure and political system.[7] An ideology is characterized here as an alternative belief system that challenges and seeks to supersede the existing one, by laying claim to a more moral and effective basis of social behavior. It almost invariably develops during periods of social or political change and tension, when existing beliefs no longer seem as capable of comprehending new behavior or social needs. It usually must be more explicit and integrated than the beliefs it challenges.

In Ghana a large number of quasi-traditional African belief systems survived colonial rule; British colonialism introduced certain modern social, economic, and political beliefs, some of which were adopted quite widely in modified forms, while others, concerned with the norms of modern social and political institutions, were internalized only partially and only by those strata involved in these institutions. A new nationalist government that sought new forms of political power and significant shifts in political beliefs found it necessary to formulate at least a partial ideology in order to assert and sustain the moral basis of its authority and induce compliance. The very fact that the nationalist movement was built upon new social strata and political structures compelled it to articulate its claim to political authority through new political ideas.

Our focus on the political economy of socialism seeks to avoid a specter that haunts the corridors of academe—functionalism and systems analysis. While these approaches identify some common political problems and processes, they tend to assign political phenomena a role by definition and to systematically ignore the conflicts by which new social and political forces and ideas emerge (however haphazardly and ambiguously), crystallize, and come into conflict with others. This is an historical process and can be comprehended only in terms of the changing political economy—national and international —which summons up new social forces and ideas, constrains them, and also renders possible new political choices. [8]

Last, it is important to stress that socialism was only one of the ideological perspectives of the Nkrumah regime, and neither the earliest nor most salient focus of it. Strategies for winning and holding political power stressed first nationalism and then the single-party state. Neither was necessarily linked to a socialist perspective, but the single-party state came into being in a fashion that gave a peculiar cast to Ghana's (and, generally, African) socialist perspectives and policies. For Kwame Nkrumah in Ghana also Pan-Africanism was a much more important and intensely pursued goal than socialism. And while it was variously characterized over time and to diverse audiences, it ultimately involved a relatively integrated ideology characterized by an essentially socialist political-economic perspective.

POLITICAL ECONOMY, SOCIAL AND POLITICAL GROUPS, AND POLITICAL CULTURE

Ghana is a former British colony (known as the Gold Coast) in West Africa. In appearance on the map it is like a rectangle standing on its short side—the side bordering the Atlantic. During the colonial period, which formally began in 1875 in the coastal area, the Gold Coast was composed of four parts: the colony, the southern part; Ashanti (named after the powerful African kingdom that held imperial sway in the nineteenth century until its defeat by the British in 1899), which occupies the central two-fifths of the country; the Northern Territories, which cover the upper two-fifths; and the British Togoland trusteeship territory, acquired after World War I, a strip in the east running from south to north, which was linked permanently to Ghana after a 1956 plebiscite. In 1960 Ghana had a population of 6.7 million people, with the former colony area the most populous (44 percent), Ashanti next (25 percent), followed by the Northern Territories (19 percent) and the Volta region (11.6 percent). Since British colonialism came by sea, the impact of colonialism, capitalism, and diverse forms of socioeconomic change tended to be highly skewed regionally and ethnically from south to north. The colony area and southern British Togoland (part of which became the Volta region), in the coastal strip and forest zone, have had the longest and largest amount of exposure and change; Ashanti, also a forest area, has changed somewhat less and later; the Northern Territories in the dry savannah zone have altered least in virtually all aspects. Modern distinctions

in terms of education, wealth, social mobility, and secularization—
all of which provided access to wage employment, material resources,
and high modern status—tended to compound and exacerbate older intergroup distinctions based on language, customs, social and political
institutions, and historical enmities.

Several other factors shaped decisively the types of social and
political groups that emerged in Ghana and their orientations to politics (or their political culture): the diverse types of traditional social,
cultural, and political institution; the impact of colonial policy on economic change and African political institutions; and the structure of the
colonial economy.

First, within the Gold Coast there were a large number of diverse precolonial traditional groups, states, or chiefdoms that helped
establish the basis for different political orientations and values.
The many Akan-speaking states in the colony and Ashanti shared a common culture and social-political organization. They were essentially
centralized chieftaincies. Chiefs were selected from royal lineages
and had substantial but limited powers, hedged by the councils of extended family elders from commoner and royal families, and by some
commoner prerogatives concerning the enstoolment (or selection) and
destoolment of chiefs. These societies were stratified socially in terms
of royal, commoner, and slave families, and social mobility was low.
There was a low level of specialization of labor among these sedentary,
agricultural groups, but social status, political office, and military
achievement provided opportunities for the accumulation of wealth.
The most important kingdom was Ashanti in the eighteenth and nineteenth centuries, a confederation of Ashanti chieftaincies for defensive
and warmaking purposes. During the eighteenth and nineteenth centuries many formerly autonomous states in the colony area and the
north were conquered by the Ashanti armies and became part of the
confederacy or tributory states. Ashanti military prowess was the
foundation for a strong sense of Ashanti identity and of fear by southern people and formerly subordinate chieftaincies in modern politics.

In the colony there were some 62 separate states in the colonial
period; in Ashanti some 24, many of which seized the occasion of
British defeat of the Ashanti—and subsequent colonial rule and party
politics—to free themselves from Ashanti ascendancy. There were
also several dozen separate states in the Northern Territories. The
most powerful and centralized were the conquest states of the Gonja,
Dagomba, and Mamprussi, whose paramount chiefs and subchiefs exercised an unfettered power. The Ga-Adangbe, in and around Accra,
the coastal capital, and the Ewe in the Volta region were originally
unintegrated beyond the village level but banded together periodically
for their common defense.

These groups shared certain value traits: a very high level of deference to authority, sustained by social organization and sanctified by religious injunctions; a high regard for age, which granted status and authority to lineage elders; an enormously strong corporate identity, where the lineage (and village and chiefdom) was a coherent unit that provided the individual with his social identity and roles, gave him land by usufruct, bound him to his people—living, dead, and unborn—and fostered a profound sense of status and propriety, which flowed from social rules and roles generally regarded as unchanging. Theses traits are stressed, especially the powerful corporate family bonds, because they have survived for many, have been reinforced by modern political competition, and have influenced political beliefs and behavior.

Colonial power was exercised largely through indirect rule, with the chiefs at various levels utilized as agents of colonial rule. In the north this tended to reinforce the chiefs' power. Among the Akan, where the powers of the chiefs were circumscribed by councils of elders, this use of chiefs violated traditional constitutional constraints; it maintained abusive chiefs in power. Mounting dissatisfaction with chiefs and colonialism tended to undermine the legitimacy of both chieftaincy and the chiefs. New social status and economic hierarchies developed, based upon education, cash crops, wage labor, and new skills, and these hierarchies precipitated new grievances with the colonially protected political hierachy. Younger, educated commoners formed ethnic associations to attack their chiefs' unconstitutional and abusive practices and to destool them.

The structure of the colonial economy was an even more important animator of new groups and grievances. Wholesale and large retail commerce, the export-import trade, the banking industry and access to capital, the enormously profitable gold mines (the companies paid a pittance in royalties to chiefs), and the timber enterprises were all firmly in British hands. Africans who had become established as merchants were actually displaced; those who sought to enter the businesses above were continually frustrated. Racism buttressed colonial rule. Economic changes were encouraged that corresponded to the interests of the colonial administration (which had to finance itself locally) or that of Great Britain. The large merchant companies that purchased and exported cocoa—the major crop—entered into collusive price-fixing agreements on how much was to be paid to the cocoa farmers, and these companies were put in charge of the wartime cocoa marketing board. The government maintained a notoriously low minimum wage for unskilled workers in government so as to keep wages in private gold mines low.[9]

The distribution of the work force shows how the political economy structured socioeconomic change and new social and political groups. First, some 62 percent of the population was engaged in the primary sector in 1960, 57 percent in agriculture. (There is no longer a subsistance sector wholly detached from the market economy.) One-third of those in agriculture, or 522,350, were engaged in cocoa; eliminating family workers, there were two nonowner workers to every five farmers.[10] Cocoa had developed rapidly in the early twentieth century, spread by rural capitalist farmers, first in the eastern region, then in Ashanti.[11] The swollen-shoot disease decimated the cocoa plants in the eastern region in the 1930s. By 1954-55 Ashanti produced 51 percent of Ghana's cocoa crop, and 56 percent by 1960-61.[12] Its cocoa interests were one focus of opposition to the Nkrumah regime. Cocoa constituted Ghana's most important source of foreign exchange (about 60-65 percent since 1930), and an important part of domestic income. Thus cocoa and cocoa farmers became crucial factors in Ghana's political economy. Capable of organization and knowledgeable about world cocoa prices, cocoa farmers were at various times politically active and potent. They organized to oppose the colonial regime (for cutting out diseased, still-bearing cocoa trees), foreign companies (on matters of price collusion and control of the market), traditional leaders, and the nationalist government (on control of cocoa prices). The source of much of this political activity lay in the restratification of rural society and the emergence of a class of rich and middle-income cocoa farmers who demanded some control over the cocoa market. In Ashanti in 1956-57, for instance, 7.7 percent of the cocoa-producing families earned 29.2 percent of the gross earned income, 24 percent earned 56 percent, and the poorest 53 percent received only 24 percent of gross income. Income differentials created a rural quasi-bourgeoisie that hired labor, reinvested earnings in cocoa and urban rental housing, possessed incomes larger than most wage/salary earners, and consumed in ways that brought these farmers status and influence.[13]

The industrial or secondary sector engaged only 14 percent of the employed population (over 15 years in 1960). The mining sector, wholly British-owned (except for some diamond digging), had declined as an employer by 1960 but had previously been the largest employer of wage labor in the Gold Coast, the base for the largest and most militant trade union (with long, effective strikes in 1947-48 and 1955-56). The manufacturing and construction sector in 1962 had a few large firms and many small family workshops with no employees or only family members; only 38 percent of the 329,249 workers in 1962 were paid employees.[14]

The service or tertiary sector was very large, and, outside of government services (railway, postal service, electricity, teachers, and civil servants), largely composed of women petty traders who provided a relatively economic retail distributive system. The European stores handled the bulk of the wholesale and export-import trade, and Lebanese, Syrians, and Indians tended to dominate the smaller retail trade. Although there was a significant merchant class in the Gold Coast in comparison with other West African countries, African merchants had small sales as compared with Levantine firms.[15] But the fastest growing service employment was governmental—local, national civil service, and in state enterprises, which comprised 38 percent of all wage/salary employment in 1960, over 50 percent of nonagricultural wage employment. This sector continued to grow rapidly, spurred by the Nkrumah regime's attempts to prevent unemployment.

There were moral, political, and socioeconomic dimensions to the Ghanaian nationalist movement. If morally and politically the nationalists rejected colonial as well as traditional political authority (the latter only in modern matters), in socioeconomic terms the nationalist revolt expressed the contradictions of the colonial political economy, a demand for the opportunity to acquire the economic resources and opportunities that the Europeans possessed. This expressed a limited revolt, one in behalf of socioeconomic resources that could be employed to satisfy the extraordinary drive for social status among Ghanaians. Ghanaians attempt to achieve "big man" status, to avoid being referred to as a "small boy." In this sense, Ghanaian society is highly competitive. While this status drive is by no means unique to Ghanaians, its dimensions in Ghana are striking; in contrast to neighboring African countries, bicycles or motor bikes are seldom seen in Ghana, both being regarded as lowly; the only acceptable personal vehicle is a motor car. This characteristic reflects a limiting and powerful orientation of the nationalist movement.

One can depict several clusters of political values or ideas that occur in Ghana: liberal, nationalist, socialist, quasi-traditional, and technocratic. These diverse idea clusters overlapped in various political groups and expressed themselves in responses to such issues as rapid political change, attitudes toward capitalism, inequity in distribution of resources, centralization or decentralization of power, popular political participation, and the perception of social cleavages.

Ghana's subsocieties, while responsive to change, were in many ways quite conservative; people born in villages, not unnaturally, had rather parochial orientations. The British connection introduced liberal values, not radical ones. Ghanaians who went to Britain for an education were not exposed to even a quasi-radical political left, as in France. British universities were liberal in substantive political orientations, conservative and elitist in tone. Ghanaian graduates returned as "been-to's": they had "been to" Britain and returned with high status degrees. Ghana was markedly without a radical intelligentsia; its lawyer intellectuals adopted the values of nineteenth-century

liberals, proudly wearing their woolen frock coats in Ghana's tropical
heat.

TOWARD SOCIALISM: FROM THE REJECTION OF COLONIALISM TO THE STRUGGLE OVER THE POLITICAL ECONOMY OF DEVELOPMENT

From 1947-48, when an aggressive nationalism first stalked
the Gold Coast, until 1959-60, when the CPP government in an independent Ghana felt that it had consolidated its power and reduced
threats to its rightful authority and to the political system, the attention of Ghana's political leaders tended to focus almost exclusively on
political problems, especially that of independence. There were certainly critical economic issues, and several involving development
patterns. Nonetheless, political crises and political dimensions of
economic choices preoccupied political leaders. A high international
demand for cocoa helped the economy to grow during these years;
government expenditures leaped forward; critical choices were not
required. This had changed radically by 1960-61. Moreover, CPP
government leaders had neither the economic advice nor knowledge
on which to predicate sharp policy changes. A relatively nonradical
economic policy, in addition, reassured the British. The British who
headed the civil service were also economic innocents to whom experi-
mentation was anathema. And, critically, Nkrumah was seeking foreign investment for building the Volta Dam and alumina complex.

The nationalist movement drew together a host of economically
aggrieved groups: the coastal merchant-professional bourgeoisie that
launched the United Gold Coast Convention (UGCC) to rally support
for self-rule "in the shortest possible time"; ex-servicemen without
jobs and urban dwellers suffering an enormous postwar inflation;
cocoa farmers; trade unionists, constantly on the verge of launching
general strikes, until they did so in 1950; and educated commoners
in urban and rural youth associations seeking jobs and status, led by
those who had achieved petit bourgoise positions—teachers, journalists, clerks, and pharmacists. The CPP, led by the charismatic
Kwame Nkrumah, broke with the merchant-lawyer-dominated UGCC,
gathered aggrieved groups behind it, racing to keep in front of them
with the demand for "self-government NOW," and quickly came to
power in 1951 under a constitution providing internal self-government.

The CPP was a nationalist movement more than a party, a
fragile national coalition whose appeals varied from one region, ethnic group, and incipient class to another. To its core supporters in
the colony and Ashanti, it derived its legitimacy from several dominant ideas that received wide currency through what Nkrumah later

referred to as "our patch-up nationalist political education." First
was its militant nationalism—"we prefer self-government with danger
to servitude in tranquility," said the CPP's Evening News, and Nkrumah
reiterated, "Seek ye first the political kingdom, all other things shall
be added unto it." Then there was its role as the "common man's"
party, as against the lawyers and chiefs, which legitimated a political
revolution at the grass roots. The CPP has "only one ideology," said
the CPP General Secretary Welbeck, "and that is to raise the common
man from the bottom of the ladder to the top."[16] To these must be
added Nkrumah's charismatic appeal, which drew upon a strong strain
of Protestant messianism in African churches—he was the one who
had "come," for whom they had been waiting. Although it began as a
populist, antichief, antibourgeois, common man's nationalist movement, the CPP had to hold its coalitional support together in the 1950s
in a democratic framework. Thus its dominant ideological emphasis
was organizational and heavily nationalist in a country where most
people identified themselves in ethnic and parochial terms. After
1951, multiple groups demanded material resources, influence, and
status and, when unsatisfied, commenced to abandon the coalition.
The expansion of political participation in a culturally diverse community, where patterns of socioeconomic development tended to reinforce these cultural cleavages, rendered the CPP vulnerable to ethnic-
regional fragmentation. Because of this the CPP stressed an undif-
ferentiated nationalism and sought to consolidate itself as a mass
party, whereupon fragmentation of a different kind—ethnic-communal-
regional fragmentation—occurred nonetheless.

   In the face of a centralizing nationlism, opposition movements
developed which drew upon socioeconomic grievances and primordial
communal ties, linking them in powerful sets of countervalues and
beliefs to those of the CPP. A Muslim Association Party (MAP),
formed in 1953, drew off Muslim urban support from the CPP, animated communal religious passions, and indicted the CPP for failure
to rectify the socioeconomic neglect of the Muslims (14 percent of the
population). The Togoland Congress (TC), an ethnic coalition set up
in 1951 by the Ewe in the southern Togoland trusteeship, sought to
secede and join with French Togoland, and thereby sparked a powerful
Ewe subnationalism. The nonparty Legislative Assembly members
from the Northern Territories formed in 1954 an ethnically diverse
Northern People's Party (NPP) to represent the seriously underdeveloped north; the NPP crystallized regional, quasi-traditional, strongly
antisouthern sentiment. Although the CPP won the 1954 election
handily, with 56 percent of the votes and 72 of 104 seats (plus 7 "CPP
rebel" seats), the CPP's vulnerability to local-ethnic demands was indicated by the large vote, 14 percent of the total, for "CPP rebels"
who failed to get the CPP nomination. The National Liberation Move-

ment (NLM) in Ashanti, which arose explosively in late 1954, stimulated an aggressive Ashanti subnationalism and raised a crisis in
Ghana's politics with its demands for severely decentralized power in
a federal constitution and a delay in independence to allow a new election on this issue. It drew together in the name of Ashanti autonomy
cocoa farmers who protested the government-set cocoa price, the
unsuccessful "CPP rebels" in Ashanti who denounced "southern
stranger" domination, and Ashanti chiefs, who smarted under their
sharp reduction in status and power brought by secular, democratic
local councils. While the CPP won the 1956 election, the result
showed a substantial erosion in CPP strength: when one includes the
"CPP rebel" vote (14 percent) with the CPP vote (56 percent), the
CPP declined from 70 percent in 1954 to 57 percent in 1956; the drop
was sharpest in Ashanti, where the CPP (59 percent) and "CPP rebel"
(25 percent) vote in 1954 was 84 percent (with 20 of 21 seats), in 1956
only 43 percent.[17]

The polarization of political conflict and the sharp ethnic-com-
munal consciousness etched in sharp relief the contrasting tendencies
in political beliefs between a national, centralizing, future-oriented
CPP and opposition political movements (not parties, they said), which
fused socioeconomic grievances with ethnic-regional-communal sentiment. The strength of the latter orientations raised the critical, recurring problem of nationality. It enabled the CPP to regard itself as
the embodiment of the nation, to consider as intolerable and illegitimate the political expression of ethnic cleavages. It induced the CPP
to be wary of broad participation, to see therein the unraveling of its
authority. It spurred the CPP to organize under its own auspices support groups of cocoa farmers (the United Ghana Farmers' Council,
UGFC), businessmen (Chamber of Commerce), market women (CPP
women), veterans (Ex-Servicemen's Union), and many of the trade
unions. After independence in 1957, the CPP government emphasized
national unity as an overriding need and implemented measures that
substantially undermined the opposition movements: constricting the
chiefs' power, destooling many; politicizing and extending the colonial
administrative structure of district and regional commissioners with
party appointees, combining party and government roles; employing
carrot-and-stick tactics to win over opposition members; and, ultimately, following an abortive plot, employing repressive measures,
such as preventive detention, which CPP leaders themselves came to
fear.

During the 1950s the CPP was implementing a vigorous economic
program, with populist egalitarian characteristics, but one within
the existing, essentially colonial economy to which Ghana was bound
by educational, financial, commercial, and industrial ties, and by
consumer and value preferences. It greatly expanded primary, secon-

dary, and teacher training education, increased employment and Africanized government positions (gradually replacing colonials), provided greatly increased social services and government employment, encouraged cocoa marketing cooperatives, and its own organization, the UGFC, in this area, supported African businesses, and increased wages to workers in an egalitarian fashion.[18] It tended to accept the liberal, move-slowly economic recommendations of economist Arthur Lewis to develop its infrastructure to attract foreign investment. But it also took the politically costly move of fixing cocoa prices below world market levels, to prevent inflation and accumulate funds for development.

The CPP's populist capitalism and gentle statism were not distasteful to the bulk of the CPP leadership. Few other CPP leaders would have identified themselves as Nkrumah did in 1951 as a "Marxist socialist." Nkrumah's university studies, reading, and political observations in the United States (1935-45) and political organizing in Great Britain (1945-47) had given him a substantial familiarity with Marxist and Leninist thought, which he regarded as tactically useful, made him an ardent Pan-Africanist, and gave him leftist perspectives rare among Ghanaians.[19]

However, it was nationalist themes and tactics that Nkrumah considered imperative priorities. The CPP's vague socialism in the 1950s served as a goal for a small faction, a symbol of the moral order for a much wider number, for whom it expressed egalitarianism and a view of colonial capitalism as highly exploitive. An egalitarian, nationalist capitalism in practice met the passionate need of many CPP leaders and followers, formerly denounced as "verandah boys" (too poor to sleep in a house), to attain socioeconomic success. For CPP leaders represented a petit bourgeoisie in skill (as in education) rather than property terms, without high social status or economic means by either British or quasi-traditional standards or beliefs. The CPP political elite in the 1950s were CPP parliamentarians and government ministers. While a small but increasing number of this elite was university trained, the largest number had either primary school education (1951—18, or 46 percent; 1954—16, or 22 percent; 1956—23, or 32 percent) or two- or four-year teaching training or secondary school (1951—13, or 33 percent; 1954—45, or 62 percent; 1956—49, or 68 percent). By occupation the largest single group were former schoolteachers (a mobility route in all societies), evenly divided between primary and secondary school; second in frequency were traders or storekeepers, though by 1956 a larger number could properly be called businessmen (merchants, contractors); several others were pharmacists, clerks, local government workers, or politicians; and a small number were lawyers (3-5), distinct in social class or traditional elite status from the other CPP leaders.[20]

In their majority, then, initially the CPP leaders were, and represented, a nonpropertied, mobility-oriented, somewhat educated "middle" stratum that saw in political and state power the means for acquiring, for themselves and others, socioeconomic status and opportunity. The propertied elements—many rural cocoa farmers and urban merchants and contractors—had dropped out of the CPP's coaliation of active support by 1959-60 or earlier. The rest had neither an economic base nor high social status outside of state power, which made them receptive to a powerful state economic role. However, the impetus to socialism came from those whose political and organizational interests and values were also met by renewed political change.

IN SEARCH OF SOCIALISM: THE IDEOLOGICAL EXPRESSION OF CONFLICT BETWEEN POLITICAL GROUPS, INSTITUTIONS, AND ECONOMIC DEVELOPMENT STRATEGIES AND INTERESTS

After independence and the consolidation of CPP government power, Nkrumah sought to turn the party and government to two closely linked further struggles: (1) Pan-Africanism, involving common efforts to liberate the rest of a still wholly colonial Africa, and then political unification to achieve political equality and economic power and (2) Ghana's own economic independence and development. Ghana's foreign policy and its economic rationales for Pan-Africanism have been well documented.[21] It suffices to emphasize that (1) Nkrumah's vision of Africa's development was for him inseparable from Ghana's (much as in Trotsky's notion of the need for "permanent revolution"); (2) his ego, emotional, and intellectual involvement with this vision of a united, powerful, and purposive renascent Africa dominated his preoccupations and energies, diminishing his tendency to employ highly nationalistic appeals; and (3) Ghana's early, generally pro-Western if nonaligned foreign policy changed after 1960-61 due to a conjunction of clashes with Western cold war and imperial interests in Africa, especially in the Congo crisis, frustration in his Pan-African politics among the balkanized independent African states after 1960, and internal economic and political changes. This study focuses on internal political changes, but these changes acquire their coherence only within the frame of Nkrumah's broader and keenly accurate understanding of international political forces. The Organization of African Unity is itself certainly a living monument (if far less than Nkrumah desired) to the persistency and power of his Pan-African and anti-imperialist values, which compelled African leaders basically uninterested in African unity to support the creation of the OAU.

The socialist values ultimately championed by the CPP government during 1960-65 contained elements of traditional socialist values
insofar as they embodied (1) an increasing rejection of private capital
as the major producer of goods and services (including agriculture),
and the price mechanism as the dominant allocator, (2) an attempt to
prevent gross class inequalities in income and status, and (3) an emphasis on collective rather than individual welfare and goals. They
differed from traditional socialist values in: (1) rejecting the class
struggle on the grounds that classes were incipient, not established,
that national unity and the mass open nature of the CPP must be emphasized; (2) focusing on the production of wealth as well as its distribution; (3) rejecting the relevance of formal democratic institutions,
less because of "revolutionary" than "national" political imperatives
(although the parliamentary norms remained); (4) failing to radically
expand substantive political participation, since the CPP government's
fragile authority and power self-interests inclined it to opt for order
over change when there was tension between the two.[22] (This charac-
terization represents the CPP government's actual goals and practices, not their varying ideological expression.)

Socialism as a Response to Image
or Actual Needs ?

The CPP's and Nkrumah's attempts to institute socialist ideas
in political and economic practices were not initiated in order to develop the CPP's popularity among the elite and nonelite, and did not
have this consequence. Certainly the regime argued that the socialist option would permit rapid economic development in terms of new
jobs and social services. But an increasingly wide segment of the
public came quickly to appreciate the costs involved in the government's enormous development expenditures. The 1961 "austerity"
budget included a range of heavy taxes plus a compulsory savings
law for wage earners, cocoa farmers, and businesses (5-10 percent).
Some traditionally militant unions staged an unsuccessful general
strike to protest compulsory savings.

The most elaborate effort to project a favorable image of the
regime involved promoting the leadership of Osagyefo Kwame Nkrumah. The attempt to reinforce Nkrumah's declining charisma with a
personality cult started in the 1950s. The cult did not associate Nkrumah with a specific politicoeconomic ideology. The cult was a means;
the ends were to give Nkrumah unique authority within the CPP and to
bolster the authority of Nkrumah, the CPP, and the government within
this multiethnic society in which traditional values were disintegrative
and legal-rational modern values ineffective in inspiring loyalty to

either system or government. Like Ghana's ideologies, the cult had
to address itself to various constituencies and hence had to provide
Nkrumah with multiple values—traditional (Osagyefo = victorious
chief) and mystifying, radical and socialist, benevolent, and Pan-African. However, the personality cult posed real problems to the Socialists: it accented a leader rather than historical analysis and program.
It became a focus of factional conflict between a Marxist faction and
the CPP Old Guard, which emphasized nationalism and retained Nkrumah's confidence by demonstrable loyalty to his personal leadership.
A characteristic if untypically explicit compromise was that announced
after a 1965 meeting of party and government leaders:

> This monolithic foundation of the party's organiza-
> tional might and philosophy can best be expressed
> in the fusion of the party's ideology with the person-
> ality of the founder of the ideology himself. . . .
> All party cadres are agreed on the need to express
> the ideology of the CPP in the personality cult be-
> cause all comrades realized that in our situation
> the people need a charismatic leadership, a beacon
> light to look up to in their development.[23]

Why did the Nkrumah regime opt for socialism, here defined
minimally as an active if not dominant public sector role in the (modern) economy, egalitarian values, and an explicit mobilization of people for socioeconomic change? Certain political conditions were necessary but not sufficient: a profound suspicion of foreign economic
interests and essentially noneconomic socialist ideals concerning human and social development; a belief, unprofaned by experience, in
the efficacy of planning and public enterprises versus the uncontrolled
workings of private capital; the crystallization of class interests
around an active use of state power; and, critically, bids for power
within the CPP of previously uninfluential groups—leaders in the
unions, Farmers' Council, and party ideologues. The economic conditions were the sufficient ones: the conclusions drawn by 1960 that
neither foreign nor indigenous private capital would be sufficiently
forthcoming, and a financial crisis in 1960-61 that forced Ghana to
make some new economic choices. With the Ghana currency tied to
the pound sterling, the rate of growth of national income was limited
by the growth rate of export earnings (and hence imports). After
1959, export earnings were flat, imports soared, and currency reserves were depleted. The regime's choice was (1) declining growth
or (2) breaking the link between external balances and money supply,
establishing exchange and import controls, and starting to borrow
internally (from itself) and externally. The government chose the

latter route. This opened the way to independent control over monetary
policy and policy changes and to higher government expenditures—but
also to external indebtedness and internal inflation, both of which occurred.

Organizational and Group Formation
and Conflict

The participants in the organizational changes and conflicts involved in the rise of socialist ideology and programs can be construed
as the conflicts of groups—institutional, class, ethnic, factional (personal, ideological), elite, and nonelite. All these participated—some
actively, some defensively. With several exceptions, most of the
major participants were institutional groups, whose power resources
were the real or perceived support of certain constituencies (local,
labor, farmer), or the ability to carry these constituencies along.
While elite factions are the most visible in political conflicts, virtually
all the groups involved had constituencies that were conscious of and
had stakes in the conflicts, which were much more than intraelite
squabbles and involved sharp changes in power, status, and resources.
(The leading groups or individuals, policies, and conflicts will be
identified, and some important group conflicts analyzed.) Not all
participants in these conflicts were ideologically conscious; indeed,
the level of ideological thinking in the CPP was quite low. Hence,
personal power and institutional interests, which are always present,
help to account for shifts in group and factional alliances, but these
interests reflected ideological assumptions.

Kwame Nkrumah was undoubtedly the most important participant
in the drive for socialism in Ghana, as an individual and as president,
with the ability to distribute resources, authority, and status. After
the 1966 coup it became popular to ridicule his socialist convictions,
in view of the clear evidence of his economic policies, [24] on the basis
of Nkrumah's personal corruption, that which he permitted among
other CPP ministers, and the looseness and variety of the regime's
socialist ideas. During 1959-62 Nkrumah took substantial political
risks in providing access to power for young Turks who supported
socialism and forceful shake-ups of the self-satisfied CPP Old Guard
and new political changes in power distributions and development strategies. Other tendencies competed with Nkrumah's socialist desires
in determining his strategies and tactics: his perception of the primacy of the "nationality question," holding Ghana's divergent people
and the CPP's distinctive groups together; his related desire as ruler
to maintain himself and his party in power; the availability of bureaucratic means to deal with problems. For instance, Nkrumah firmly
believed that a socialist society required, above all, industrialization,

largely carried out by the public sector. For this and the pursuit of his Pan-African policies he could and did rely increasingly on bureaucratic machinery, some of which was assembled within the Office of the President and responsible directly to him. But it was the constantly recurring problems of national integration and political power preservation that were most significant in depoliticizing his socialist concerns and reducing radically the meaningfulness of his socialist intentions: the political conflicts provoked by the CPP socialist militants led to intense factional disputes, personal abuse, and demoralization among the Old Guard and others, which led Nkrumah to curtail open group conflicts, reduce popular participation, and reemphasize the CPP's openness to all, Old Guard and new. Several assassination attempts on Nkrumah's life (1962, 1963) narrowly missed, the first of which, he came to believe, involved his chief "socialist" lieutenant (Adamafio). Nkrumah thereafter tended to be more preoccupied with personal loyalty and containing those with a capacity to evoke participation than with attitudinal and program changes. In these ways Nkrumah undermined substantive participation and resorted to continuous manipulation among contending groups and interests, permitting those who were politically safe and loyal to retain positions of power.

If Nkrumah's solution to the nationality question was unity, "the CPP is Ghana, Ghana is the CPP,"[25] he was equally conscious that "the composition of our Party has become socially quite heterogenous," and "we cannot build socialism without socialists."[26] Hence Nkrumah was compelled to acknowledge an increased political role for various groups, including (1) a small body of socialists who were grouped in NASSO (National Association of Socialist Students Organizations), composed of the CPP's small group of ideologues, journalists, and trade unionists, (2) a new national party leadership, which had to invigorate the increasingly parochial local branches, and (3) two groups [the Trades Union Congress (TUC) and United Ghana Farmers' Council (UGFC)] with strong, ambitious leaders and large constituencies, which opposed foreign private companies in Ghana, demanded a larger role for their organizations in development, and had the growing capacity to animate change. During 1959-62, the groups noted above (most of whose leaders were allied) reanimated criticism and debate of CPP's policies and some degree of popular participation. By their attacks against corruption and the self-satisfaction of government ministers, they drove Nkrumah's leading Old Guard lieutenants from office, placed existing institutional leaders of the National Assembly and civil service on the defensive, and successfully pushed for more thoroughgoing socialist measures (especially state industries) and new ties to the Communist countries.

The rise to power of the TUC and UGFC both forced and reflected a new set of politicoeconomic exchange relationships between Nkrumah and the coalition of groups that were the core basis of CPP support.

In the 1950-57/58 period, when elections mediated power relationships and the goal was CPP power and independence, the CPP's local constituency base was the core basis of support and in a position for its leaders, Assembly members and ministers, to demand status, influence, and material resources. With the shift in priority goals to economic change, Nkrumah became more responsive to allied institutions controlled by CPP leaders, the TUC and UGFC, which represented, channeled, and restrained the demands of major producers—wage/salary workers and cocoa farmers. However, the TUC and UGFC were not simply government tools, extracting surplus value for government investment or the politicians' pockets. As part of their exchange relationship with the CPP government, they demanded, and at least initially received, certain material, power, and status benefits for both their organizations and their constituents.

The new and rising bourgeois elements (contractors, timber companies, large merchants) reached the zenith of their influence during 1957-60, when their organizations bargained successfully with the government for benefits (credit, contracts) for African businessmen and spokesmen for their interests held posts as ministers and deputy ministers. After 1960 socialist politics made their interests illegitimate and drove their advocates from office, though they continued to do business and obtain government contracts and import licenses. However, the development of a powerful nationalist bourgeoisie was temporarily halted, to be revived under the successor military and civilian Busia regimes. Its development policies were the displacement of foreign capital with Ghanaian private capital and the reservation for Ghanaians of many areas of business, especially commerce—a very popular policy, later implemented by Busia.

During 1959-60, NASSO developed from a small discussion group of the CPP intelligentsia, which met privately, into several very large CPP Study Groups that operated under Nkrumah's direct sponsorship and led the open attacks against the party Old Guard, corruption, and political careerism. Its leading participants were the new CPP general secretary, Adamafio, Tettegah (TUC), Appiah-Danquah (UGFC), some young technocrats, and the party's ideologues and others who espoused or supported socialism. It was these activists who formulated the CPP's socialist program, "For Work and Happiness," adopted in 1962.

Tawia Adamafio was a late convert to the CPP (1953), enormously articulate in the colorful and abusive rhetoric of Ghanaian politics, an energetic and ambitious organizer, and a Ga—the main ethnic group in Ghana's capital, Accra. In 1960 he was brought back from London law studies by Nkrumah to become CPP general secretary. In close alliance with Tettegah, Adamafio set out to invigorate the CPP, win over former opponents, roll up a large CPP majority in

the 1960 constitutional plebiscite and presidential election, and build
up the party machinery with new, better-educated, and higher-paid
regional party secretaries and District Commissioners. Under the
slogan "the Party Is Supreme," Adamafio initially sought to assert
party power and that of the new activists against government power,
that of the ministerial Old Guard and the National Assembly. However,
Adamafio moved quickly from party organizing to bureaucratic roles
where the power was more substantive; the CPP nationally after 1961
was "administered"; its roots took on local coloring and preoccupations. By mid-1960, Adamafio, Tettegah, and Appiah-Danquah were
members of the Cabinet (having been appointed "ministers extraordinary") as well as the CPP Central Committee. Soon Adamafio was
given ministerial responsibilities in the president's office, controlling
CPP affairs and the civil service commission, introducing change-
oriented technocrats into the upper reaches of a staid bureaucracy.
New state sector programs and projects were pursued as Adamafio
helped subordinate government departments, with their independent
institutional interests, to government and party policies. Politically
Adamfio facilitated the linkage to the new CPP groups. He was the
leading sponsor of Nkrumah's famous April 1961 "Dawn Broadcast,"
in which Nkrumah (1) criticized National Assembly members as
"tending . . . to become a new ruling class of self-seekers and ca-
reerists"; (2) announced that being a CPP parliamentarian and businessman were incompatible—they must choose; (3) dismantled several
ministries, turning part of their functions over to the UGFC, which
acquired the lucrative monopoly right to market cocoa; and (4) criticized the TUC's growing militance and independence.[27] Adamafio engineered the demotions of Nkrumah's long-time chief lieutenants Bot-
sio and Gbedemah, and in important ways came to control access to
Nkrumah, which led to enormous antagonism toward him by senior
ministers and National Assembly members. Adamafio was not an
ideologue, and he spoke as an "African Socialist," not a Marxist.
This ardent but ambitious servant to Nkrumah's leadership was the
most outlandish embellisher of the Nkrumah cult; in 1961 he argued
that "we must look upon the Osagyefo as our Saviour and Messiah.
Let us exploit him for the benefit of the nation . . . institutionalize
him."[28] One of the most forceful and effective of the CPP political
leaders, Adamafio used his power ruthlessly to displace others and
build up a predominantly Ga faction to support his own leadership.
He attracted enormous enmity and, ultimately, Nkrumah's suspicions
after the mid-1962 assassination attempt at Kulungugu, after which
he was arrested. Henceforth Nkrumah was chary of too ambitious
lieutenants, recalling to service members of the CPP Old Guard who
had been retired.

The TUC and UGFC provide fascinating contrasts in the roles, power, and fate of the productive sectors under a socialist-oriented regime. Tettegah was ambitious, dynamic, widely regarded along with the TUC unions as a political threat; Appiah-Danquah was ambitious and quiet, and the UGFC perceived as nonthreatening. The TUC leadership acquired substantial power and had it quickly curtailed; the UGFC kept acquiring power in one area after another until the 1966 coup. The TUC did propose some radical changes, wanted to mobilize workers into power centers, and was conflict-oriented; the UGFC did not pursue radical changes (with one exception), did not overtly challenge CPP groups, and sought primarily to bureaucratize and rationalize cocoa marketing and other agriculture pursuits. The TUC articulated an explicitly socialist ideology, including the idea of workers' control; the UGFC expressed nationalist, only slightly egalitarian, beliefs.

After several years of intense struggle between one group of trade unions that wished to be apolitical, bread-and-butter oriented, and autonomous and another group that were politically oriented and saw the advantages of close ties to the CPP, a highly fragmented and weak trade union movement was centralized by legislation under the pro-CPP John Tettegah in 1958. This TUC-proposed legislation—opposed by almost all CPP ministers, supported by Nkrumah—amalgamated 85 unions into 24, required employers to bargain collectively with these unions (previously they had refused), mandated a check-off (which provided the TUC and individual unions with a strong financial base), and in 1960 established union shops. In exchange, the Nkrumah government obtained CPP leadership over the unions and a prohibition on strikes until a lengthy conciliation-arbitration procedure was exhausted, though the prohibition was not strongly enforced. By this exchange, the unions and TUC leadership had political authority, status, and economic resources; if the TUC was now linked intimately to the CPP, most of the national unions had leaders from their own rank and file and could run their own affairs.

Tettegah's aggressive leadership alarmed the CPP Old Guard, which worked to remove him from the TUC; in mid-1959 he was temporarily forced to leave the TUC to head the Workers' Brigade (for unemployed school dropouts) but soon returned. With Adamafio, Tettegah subordinated the Labor Department, briefly bringing it into the President's Office. As a result of his new influence Tettegah used worker dissatisfaction to induce the government to establish a national minimum wage and increase the government minimum by 18-30 percent in 1960. But opposition was constant. As an ideologue Tettegah tried to articulate a multifaceted role for the workers, running cooperatives and establishing people's stores to eliminate middlemen.[29] The industrial coops were completely abortive (unions had no manage-

ment); fearful of too much TUC power, the meager people's stores
were absorbed into a new, government Ghana National Trading Corporation (GNTC). When the TUC sought to establish local workers'
councils, CPP members saw them as threats, forerunners of a labor
party; they were discontinued. The traditionally militant workers of
Sekondi-Takoradi opposed Tettegah's leadership and the CPP government's compulsory savings in 1961 with an attempted general strike,
which was effective locally, demonstrating the TUC's less than full
worker support. The attempts to develop a workers' role in the management of state enterprises were strongly opposed by managers and
came to nil. To offset Tettegah, Nkrumah assigned him to Pan-African activities, building up the All-African Trade Union Federation.
The TUC was lost to the unions as their advocate when, first in 1962
and then again in 1964, former unionists who were uninterested in
strongly articulating worker-union needs and grievances were appointed from outside as TUC secretary generals. As a consequence
of this erosion of TUC power in the regime and the drastic inflation
that brought a substantial decline in real wages during 1962-65, socialism and the notion of union-party ties were widely rejected by
union leadership in the post-Nkrumah period. However, the "collective consumption" through public expenditures greatly benefited workers, as did the rationalized union structure, collective bargaining,
the check-off, and attempts by the Nkrumah regime to maintain employment, which dropped sharply after 1966. These benefits of the
TUC-CPP link, and the political status it brought, were increasingly
acknowledged by union leaders after harsh experiences with the NLC
military and Busia regimes; the latter tried to destroy the union movement in September 1971.

The UGFC developed from a nationalist coalition of cocoa farmers' groups, exchanging support of the CPP for representation of
farmer grievances, to become in the 1960s an extremely powerful,
multifunctional organization run by CPP cocoa farmers and a 6,000-
man bureaucracy. In the 1950s it was a financially weak organization
that pursued several farmer demands: to market cocoa, bypassing the
European buying firms; and a loan scheme for the many heavily in-
debted cocoa farmers. The UGFC serviced these roles for a new,
CPP-controlled state agency to the CPP's partisan advantage.

While the UGFC was led by CPP partisans at all levels, it was
not simply a controlled, CPP wing; indeed, before 1957 it resisted
cooptation. In return for its support for the CPP, it demanded in
1957-58 that the CPP government provide it with certain authority,
resources, and status. The UGFC was licensed by the state Cocoa
Marketing Board (CMB) to purchase cocoa and was advanced credit
to do so—which put it in direct competition and conflict with the autonomous cooperatives. Next, the government recognized the UGFC as

the spokesman of Ghana farmers. Then the CMB was directed to give the UGFC an annual grant of £100,000 and to build the UGFC a new £100,000 national headquarters.

The UGFC's role was to organize and maintain cocoa farmer support for the CPP and spur economic development—important but not necessarily socialist roles. It is normally considered that the UGFC's chief role was to sanction larger government taxation of cocoa farmers' earnings. The UGFC openly supported the following reductions in price per 60-pound load of cocoa: 1959, from 72 shillings to 60, the 12 shillings being farmer support for the second Development Plan; 1961, the reduction of 6 shillings, to 54, for compulsory savings; June 1965, a reduction from 54 to 50 and in August from 50 to 40, as the price had dropped out of the world cocoa market and the Cocoa Marketing Board was paying the farmers much more than it was getting. However, the UGFC also bargained hard for programs for itself and the farmers—payments for cutting out diseased trees, heavily subsidized insecticides, an end to school fees, and the like— and may well have forestalled the CMB and government's well-known interest in reducing the price earlier than 1965.

Between 1959 and 1961 the UGFC led a strong campaign to oust the European companies from cocoa buying. In 1961 it succeeded and was made the monopoly buyer of cocoa, but against the sustained opposition of the cooperatives, the Department of Cooperatives (which was abolished), many outspoken CPP parliamentarians, and ultimately, the CPP Minister for Cooperatives and Labor. Why did Nkrumah take this decision? Two reasons, probably: first, the alternative of a state agency clashed with Nkrumah's criticisms of civil service unresponsiveness, while the UGFC would provide political organization; second, satisfied that the UGFC could do the job (and it did), the UGFC's Appiah-Danquah promised to use UGFC resources for rapid economic development in the agricultural sector. And rapid change was central to Nkrumah's perception of Ghana's needs.

The UGFC proceeded in the next years to take on important new economic roles, in the process dismantling the Department of Agriculture. It established over 1,000 producer cooperatives, which farmers developed in addition to their own farms, and a huge mechanization program that provided rental tractors to producer coops (though few paid the fees), and was developed so quickly and managed so poorly that most tractors were soon useless; it marketed other crops poorly. The producer coops were not animated by socialist ideas, as were some efforts at worker participation in the separate state farm program. One genuinely egalitarian measure was the UGFC's successful pressure for a land rent act, which set an annual limit of five shillings per acre, undercutting exorbitant rent rates. This measure unleashed a storm of rural class conflict, led by owner-farmers; the CPP stopped trying to enforce the law by 1963; the military government quickly repealed it in 1966.[30] The UGFC, whose internal structure was oligarchical, became so powerful that it was able to resist numerous efforts in 1964-65 to reform it and to reintroduce democratic coops. It was accountable to no ministry. Despite major UGFC efforts to prevent abuses of farmers, its local agents engaged in many acts of "dishonesty, intimidation, victimization, extortion, theft, and outright roguery" against the farmers, alienating them from the regime.[31] While this was not unique to the UGFC, and occurred in the restored coops after 1966, it still meant that the UGFC failed to provide the government with legitimacy and status. It also failed to give government returns on its huge investments.

The context in which group and ideological conflict occurred was an increasingly oligarchical one at the national and local levels, with the demise of non-CPP groups, government-party control of newspapers and radio, and the movement toward a single-party system. Politically, Nkrumah was involved in a holding action, an effort to balance off and integrate diverse groups into the CPP omnibus. Hence, in the 1965 parliamentary "nonelection," both old Assembly members and leaders of new groups became members. This political compromising manifested itself in economic and ideologic ways. Economically, Nkrumah continued to insist on structural change policies but refused to respond with reforms to evidence of economic inefficiency and incompetence. Ideologically, Nkrumah vacillated between (1) an African socialism or Nkrumaism, emphasizing his leadership, Ghana's diverse traditions, and evolutionary change, and (2) more programmatic Marxist socialist positions, stressing conflict and a vanguard party. Attempts to summarize "Nkrumaism" did lead to confusion, but major socialist positions were clear.

The CPP Old Guard and Parliament made a comeback after 1962. Nkrumah was content to have the CPP nationally "administered" by an ineffectual Old Guard lieutenant. Others were restored to ministerial office, like Krobo Edusei, who was irrepressible, antisocialist, and corrupt. Most Old Guard ministers had neither the energy nor power to demand higher performance levels; for example, Edusei's many attempts to make the UGFC and State Farms accountable to the Ministry of Agriculture floundered. In adversity during 1960-62 parliamentarians had discovered an institutional interest. Their predominant conception of socialism was simply more benefits and their equitable distribution to constituents. Not incidentally they sought to safeguard their own positions; many, but not all, feathered their own nests (as post-coup commissions documented). However, it was quite legitimate to criticize the gap between rhetoric and reality in government performance in "socialist" terms. During 1963-65 the Assembly was often a highly critical body. Members openly criticized the

grossly inadequate performance of many state enterprises, especially
those affecting food and import prices (UGFC, State Farms, Ministry
of Trade).

With the exception of Finance Minister Kwesi Amoaka-Atta, the
few Marxist Socialists did not hold government office. However, they
had substantial influence. The two most articulate ideologues, Kofi
Batsa and S. G. Ikoku (a Nigerian exile), ran The Spark (a weekly),
which took a "scientific socialist" position, publishing analyses often
at variance with government-party policies. They argued for a reformed, ideologically homogeneous vanguard party to staff government
and party positions and mobilize social energies for disciplined participation in and support for socialist policies. The training of cadres
was to take place at the Kwame Nkrumah Ideological Institute (KNII),
directed by one of the few Marxist-Leninists, Kodwo Addison. The
KNII started two-year courses in 1962. Its students were primarily
lower level civil servants and CPP, TUC, and UGFC officials. The
serious CPP ideologues at KNII grappled with trying to articulate a
distinctive Marxian socialist ideology for Ghana. That the official
and innocuous definition of "Nkrumaism" that emerged once in 1964
was meaningless reflected the power struggle between the Marxists
and the Old Guard nationalists, not analytical poverty. The CPP Old
Guard's strength was demonstrated in its ability to prevent the placing
in key positions of many of the KNII's graduates.

However, socialist ideas and policies were articulated widely
by the regime, its officials, and media from 1960 on. The variations
in its substantive expression involved both group conflicts and Nkrumah's own unresolved perceptions of the tactical and the possible.
At its broadest range, socialism was expressed as a welfare state and
anti-imperialism. Its African socialist expression emphasized Africa's unique qualities, its communalism, and "Nkrumaism as the embodiment of the life and thought of Kwame Nkrumah," which gave rise
to much ambiguity, confusion, and nominal devotion. Nkrumah himself affirmed an African socialism, evolutionary rather than revolutionary and based on Africa's communal values (Consciencism, 1964),
but then emphasized a Marxian anticolonial aspect in the ghostwritten
Neo-Colonialism (1965). Despite these disparities, however, there
is little doubt that some notions of socialism penetrated society as
idea-clusters of slogans meaningful to some: socialism as egalitarianism ("one man, one car," was heard in anticorruption campaigns but
conflicted with Ghanaian status aspirations; many CPP officials rode
in Mercedes Benzes), anticapitalism and profiteering, solidarity with
"socialist" countries, a position widely disliked because of powerful
pro-British sentiment, and a dominant state sector pursuing rapid
development. But it was also associated with poor economic performance and the CPP's monopoly of power.

The technocrats in power were few but important, holding positions in banks, the Finance Ministry, Planning Commission, ad hoc commissions, and secretariats in the President's Office. The most important were economists who liked or accepted the socialist option and were interested in economic rationality. Their weakness was that most were apolitical, nonideological, and believed that Nkrumah could be persuaded to support economic rationality in procedures and programs. They found their counsel bypassed by political considerations, their Seven-Year Plan not followed. Occasionally one was caught out ideologically, as was J. H. Mensah, head of the Planning Commission, who lost Nkrumah's attention and a role for the Planning Commission in 1964-65 after he was attacked for not being a Socialist.

Economic Development Policies

Between 1959-60 and 1966 Ghana under Nkrumah mounted a massive effort to structurally transform the economy. It failed, and rather massively. While Ghana had achieved an average compound rate of growth of 4.8 percent in gross domestic product (GDP) during 1955-62, between 1958-59 and 1964-65 (the period of the major effort to implement socialist policies) the average increase in GDP was only 2.5 percent (in constant prices), less than the 2.6 percent population growth. There was no real per capita growth (although, after Nkrumah, during 1965-68/69, per capita GDP actually declined). And this occurred despite an incredible increase in development spending: gross fixed capital formation rose from 16 percent of GDP in 1958-59 to 23 percent in 1964-65; Ghana's capital stock increased by 80 percent between 1960 and 1965.[32]

If the economic crisis of 1961 forced certain decisions, the series of policy choices behind Ghana's development program involved a strategic option. If this option meant different things to Ghana's politicians (more jobs, services), ideologues (destroying the iniquity, inequity, and dependency of capitalism), and economists and technicians, it did involve certain common assumptions: real, rapid economic development, equitably distributed, was desirable; this required ending Ghana's role as a dependent agricultural producer and becoming industrialized; and only the state had the necessary resources and capacity to bring this about.

Central, then, to Ghana's socialism was an entrepreneurial role for the state sector, with room for joint state-private enterprises, an equitable distribution of resources, and Ghanaian control and popular mobilization in this effort.

The results of Ghana's socialist option are clear, although the debate over why Ghana's attempt failed is unsettled, in Ghana (wit-

ness the NRC's policies) and elsewhere. As of March 1966, Ghana
had created 53 state enterprises (some predated 1960), 12 joint state-
private industries, and 23 public boards with economic roles. An
overwhelming number of the state enterprises were operating at losses
—but of course many industries were new, had not yet become fully
productive, or were near the breakeven point. The state enterprises
with the largest investment losses—State Mines, State Farms, CMB,
and Ghana Airways—were either specifically designed to maintain employment levels (as were other losers) or regarded as a necessary foreign policy expenditure (Ghana Airways). That is, the expressed policy that state enterprises were to be profitable development projects
and supply capital for further investment was violated by other politicoeconomic policies. This contradiction in objectives in state enterprises is common. Moreover, private companies in the same businesses were profit-making, and, compared with public enterprises
elsewhere, Ghana's showed a markedly low profitability and productivity.[33] The joint state/private companies, in which the state was
little involved, were profitable.

The standard of living of Ghanaians declined, in terms of per
capita GDP. Additionally, as the government mobilized resources for
investment, public consumption increased markedly, private consumption decreased. There was, however, a 50 percent increase in "collective consumption" during 1960-69 (for education, health, and housing),
35 percent of which occurred during the Nkrumah period (1960-66),
but it is doubtful that this offset the reduced private consumption.
Moreover, because of the resources devoted to state agricultural enterprises (UGFC, State Farms), food production could not keep up
with population increases, which led to sharply higher food prices,
especially in 1963-65. And a postcoup survey indicated that the single most important reason why Ghanaians were happy with the overthrow of the Nkrumah regime was the shortages of goods and high
prices.[34] This sharp inflation occurred in the context of import
shortages of basic consumer goods and reduced significantly the real
wages of wage/salary workers, though less than is usually argued.[35]
The inflation was partly fueled by a tripling of government expenditures
during 1957-65 (in current prices), or annual increases of 17 percent;
capital expenditures rose most quickly, at an annual rate of 24 percent. Through new and increased forms of taxation, the CPP government substantially increased revenues during 1957-65, at an average
annual rate of 13 percent, which was insufficient to cover expenditures.
To finance the development effort, Ghana engaged in heavy deficit
spending internally (it "printed" money). Due to a sharp decline in
cocoa prices during these years, Ghana's export and foreign exchange
earnings were flat, despite large increases in the cocoa tonnage exported. Since foreign reserves had been eroded by previous import

demand (pre-1962), and efforts to attract foreign private investment
were unavailing, Ghana was increasingly forced to rely upon Western
supplier credits or Eastern European credits and bilateral trade arrangements to finance needed capital imports. The supplier credits
proved disastrous: there was no coordination and control of supplier
credit deals, which quickly led to an incredibly high external indebtedness, too much of which wasted; supplier credits were advanced for
two- to five-year periods—insufficient time for the projects financed
to generate profits for repayment.

Last, Ghana's import controls, while necessary, were employed
for too many purposes and had severe economic consequences. Except
in 1965, the controls did tend to contain the level of imports but in a
highly erratic fashion, giving rise to consumer and raw material
shortages and the shutdown or underutilization of industries. Controls
did not succeed in balancing imports and exports, since when shortages
developed the politicians felt pressured to import more goods. Controls did facilitate the policy decision to expand trade (to open new
cocoa markets) with communist countries (from an average of 4 percent of Ghana's imports in 1959-61 to 20 percent in 1964-66). Controls
also permitted a change in the relative composition in imports to emphasize capital goods (as a percentage of imports, producers' equipment increased from 12 percent on the average during 1959-61 to 28
percent in 1964-66, while nondurable consumer goods dropped from
42 to 28 percent); it is doubtful whether they did so efficiently, but
the use of market mechanisms worked no more efficiently in 1969-71.
And crucially, Ghana's administrative capacity to allocate import licenses was weak and the process itself tended to give rise to corruption, which the public began to perceive as the main problem. There
was lower-level corruption in 1961-63 in license administration, and
in 1964-66 the last two Nkrumah government Ministers of Trade engaged in wholesale corruption in distributing licenses.

By 1966 Ghana was more dependent and economically weaker
than in 1960. But it was also a more advanced, complex, highly capi-
talized economy with the potential for rapid growth if there were
fewer constraints.

Two alternative conclusions are drawn from Ghana's experience.[36]
The conservative conclusion, which takes into account the complexity
of economic development and the likelihood of human error, argues
that the structural transformation route to development in small developing countries, in which the state plays a leading economic role,
leads to disaster. This is because the state tries to do too much too
quickly, given its limited resources, and that import-substituting industrialization in a small country does not work (which of course is
why Nkrumah favored Pan-African economic linkages). The second
conclusion argues that the basic transformation strategy was sound

but failed for a number of reasons: (1) the sharp drop in the world cocoa price during 1962-65, which created import constraints; (2) poor project design, implementation, and coordination, caused by poor or indifferent management, lack of skilled workers, and, critically, the predominance of political over economic considerations; (3) inadequate political will and discipline in implementing the socialist option (failing to stick to a development plan's priorities, failing to hold state managers strictly accountable). The conservative conclusion says all these things are bound to happen, even with a firm political will and low levels of corruption, that there must be a trade-off between some continued dependency and external resources (capital, management skills) necessary for development. The radical transformationist argues (1) that not all the weaknesses manifested by the Nkrumah regime's economy are necessarily inherent in this strategy; (2) that the gradualist, capitalist approach creates a class stratified society, increases rather than decreases dependency, and hence creates and perpetuates a new exploiting class and the real disadvantages developing, one-crop economies have vis-a-vis industrial economies.

There is substantial truth in both positions. And in the case of Nkrumah's regime, there is little doubt that pervasive, short-run political considerations regularly undermined economic criteria in the design, implementation, and evaluation of economic projects. Nkrumah himself was often responsible for this and did not demand high economic performance from state sector managers. The sociocultural beliefs and attitudes in Ghana made it difficult to exact high economic performance and accountability (one begged forgiveness, and was forgiven). The blatant gap between high ideals and the corruption, routine ineffectiveness, and deteriorating conditions created a corrosive cynicism.

On the other hand, it may be argued that Ghana's socialism was a generic expression of the traditional socialist impulse as well as of African communal values, both of which argue for production for use, not profit. The economic data employed above are accurate and meaningful only for production and economic exchanges that enter the modern sector, with only rough estimates of those that do not. It seemed clear to this observer at the time that a certain amount of production among state enterprises, especially the agricultural ones, was exchanged through local markets and within the enterprises and among relatives, and not only at the top of the hierarchies in state enterprises. The widely distributed state farms and UGFC tractor stations may well have given rise to higher levels of private consumption than the data suggest.

All this suggests that the Nkrumah regime made substantial contributions to undermining its economic strategy, one which has led to developing national economies elsewhere. External factors, such as the low world cocoa price, make it clear that Ghana's possible choices were in any case narrow, as economic performance during 1966-71 demonstrated. The Nkrumah regime's economic strategy was immod-

est in its scale, given its small market, low level of management
skills, and inability to form a larger economic market with surrounding former French colonies, which are linked to France and the European Economic Community. But it was certainly not irrational: to reject agricultural exports as the primary engine of growth, given their
poor terms of trade with industrial imports; to decline an open-door
strategy for foreign private capital, which is uninterested in Ghana's
small market, primarily attracted to extractive industries, with little
direct contribution to permanent growth, and tends to repatriate, not
reinvest, profits; or to control imports, which tend to be largely consumer goods. Given the small capital and trading interests of Ghana's
capitalists, the overwhelming economic power of Western multinational
corporations, and international economic constraints upon an "open"
economy, politicians pressed to fulfill popular needs will find it difficult to discover an alternative to control over monetary policy and
the state as an important (but not only) economic entrepreneur.

CONCLUSIONS: ON THE PROSPECTS FOR
SOCIALIST OPTIONS IN GHANA

The prospects for socialism in Ghana depend on whether socialism refers to (1) a central role for the state as producer and allocator;
(2) equitable distribution policies; (3) a political alliance of nonpropertied middle-class elites with workers and farmers, with their participation in economic management and political choices; (4) values that
stress egalitarianism and collective goals and means in development;
or all of these. Two limitations on any politicoeconomic strategy are
inherent. Ghana is still a culturally conservative country, prosperous
by African standards, whose most politically articulate groups have
not been so aggrieved as to support radical changes in socioeconomic
and status relationships. National integration remains a problem, as
the resurgence of tribal-ethnic perspectives in politics during 1966-71
showed. Second, it is necessary to produce economic wealth before
it can be distributed. And any economic strategy—capitalist or socialist—requires extracting investment capital from workers and
cash crop farmers; reliance on foreign private capital only marginally
relieves this need in building a national rather than an enclave economy. A nonpropertied middle-class-worker-farmer alliance will always be under pressure to distribute resources and relieve discontent,
as was the Nkrumah regime that launched a wide range of public services and had the highest rate of job creation (some of it make-work)
in black Africa. Although the regime was dictatorial after 1960, it
was also populist and not terribly harsh.

The near-term prospects in Ghana are for a state role as producer and allocator to some degree, and some emphasis on equality of distribution, but little on the political alliance and broad participation that lie at the core of socialism. The National Redemption Council (NRC) government has moved in many directions simultaneously; it has demanded participation in the ownership and management of foreign firms, encouraged Ghanaian businessmen, maintained business sectors reserved for them, revived state sector projects dropped after 1966 and the primacy of public goals, reinstituted price and import controls, unilaterally repudiated some international debts, extracted more favorable terms on others, and returned to a nationalist emphasis on developing Ghana internally—best exemplified by the energetic "Operation Feed Yourself" program. However, the anti-ideological NRC military, which gives no indications of restoring civilian rule soon, has shown little interest in developing alliances with civilian Ghanaian groups, whether the merchant-professional bourgeoisie (the NLC's ally) or the unions, but it has actively sought the support of all groups. It has felt compelled to maintain its popularity by distributing wage-price benefits to workers, farmers, and the numerous state bureaucrats. But without alliances with civilian groups, which might accept economic constraints in exchange for power and status, and with no coherent development strategy, the NRC will become increasingly dependent upon the large, resource-consuming bureaucracy, whose devotion to economic development and popular participation is slight.[37] While the NRC has not increased the size of the military since its coup (unlike the NLC), it is likely to lead Ghana toward an increasingly bureaucratized state sector economy, ruled by a military, technocratic, and administrative bourgeoisie, though with substantial room left for Ghana's growing commercial-industrial class. Nonetheless, since the 1972 NRC coup, sectors have reemerged that articulate socialist policies and beliefs, some of which coincide with NRC perceptions of economic strategies. These sectors include some trade union leaders (who also supported John Tettegah's attempt to become TUC secretary-general again), left-wing intellectuals and journalists (The Spokesman, Palaver), and many former students during the Nkrumah period, especially those trained abroad under government programs. They will keep alive socialist political alternatives to a military-bureaucratic alliance.

NOTES

1. For an analysis of the Nkrumah regime from a liberal perspective, see Dennis Austin, Politics in Ghana (Oxford: Oxford University Press, 1964); and the more analytical David Apter, "Nkrumah,

Charisma, and the Coup," Daedalus 97 (Summer 1968): 757-92; from
a socialist and radical perspective, see Roger Genoud, Nationalism
and Economic Development in Ghana (New York: Praeger Publishers,
1969); the Fanon-Maoist interpretation by Bob Fitch and Mary Oppen-
heimer, Ghana: End of an Illusion (New York: Monthly Review Press,
1966); and Ruth First, Power in Africa (New York: Pantheon Books,
1970).

    2. On the military's motives and grievances, see Jon Kraus,
"Arms and Politics in Ghana," in Claude Welch, ed., Soldier and
State in Africa (Evanston, Ill.: Northwestern University Press, 1969),
pp. 179-86; Robert Price, "Military Officers and Political Leadership,"
Comparative Politics, April 1971, pp. 361-66; Major-General A. K.
Ocran, A Myth Is Broken (London: Longmans, 1968).

    3. Broadcast, Radio Ghana, March 1966, reprinted in Ghana,
Broken Myths, 1966, p. 11.

    4. See Ghana, Report of the Commission to Enquire into the
Kwame Nkrumah Properties (1967), which regards the properties and
funds of several party organizations as belonging to Nkrumah personally.

    5. Philip Converse, "The Nature of Belief Systems in Mass Pub-
lics," in D. Apter, ed., Ideology and Discontent (New York: Free
Press, 1964), pp. 214-19.

    6. See Clifford Geertz, "Ideology as a Cultural System," in D.
Apter, ed., Ideology and Discontent, pp. 47-76.

    7. See Chalmers Johnson, Revolutionary Change (Boston:
Little, Brown, 1966), pp. 13-39, 82 ff; Apter, op. cit., "Introduction," pp. 16-26; Geertz, op. cit., pp. 47-76.

    8. History has recently been reintroduced to comparative poli-
tics, this time in a more systematic fashion. See Barrington Moore's
Social Origins of Dictatorship and Democracy (Boston: Beacon Press,
1966); Gabriel Almond takes "the historical cure," in Almond, et al.,
Crisis, Choice, and Change (Boston: Little, Brown, 1973). For
other historical-sociological approaches see S. Huntington's Political
Order in Changing Societies (New Haven, Conn.: Yale University
Press, 1968); Eric Wolf, Peasant Wars of the Twentieth Century (New
York: Harper & Row, 1969); E. Allardt and Y. Littunen, eds.,
Cleavages, Ideologies and Party Systems (Helsinki: Academic Book-
store, 1964); S. M. Lipset and S. Rokkan, eds., Party Systems and
Voter Alignments (New York: Free Press, 1967); A. G. Frank, Capi-
talism and Underdevelopment in Latin America (New York: Monthly
Review Press, 1967).

    9. Documentation on government mine-owner maintenance of
low wage rates was found in Department of Labor files. Data on the
problems of early Ghanaian merchants can be found in David Kimble,
A Political History of Ghana (Oxford: Clarendon Press, 1963); colon-

ial attitudes toward business and Ghanaians in G. B. Kay, ed., The
Political Economy of Colonialism in Ghana (London: Cambridge University Press, 1972); and aspects of the colonial structure of the
Gold Coast economy in W. Birmingham, I. Neustadt, and E. N. Oma-
boe, ed., The Economy of Ghana (Evanston, Ill.: Northwestern University Press, 1966).

10. Ghana, 1960 Census Advance Report, vols. 3 and 4, pp. 43,
51, 69, 84.

11. See Polly Hill, Migrant Cocoa Farmers of Southern Ghana
(London: Cambridge University Press, 1963).

12. Ghana, 1961 Statistical Yearbook, p. 32; 1962 Statistical
Yearbook, p. 38.

13. Ghana, Office of Government Statistician, Survey of Cocoa
Producing Families in Ashanti, 1956-57, Statistical and Economic
Papers, no. 7, pp. 16-17; and Survey of Populations and Budgets of
Cocoa Producing Families in the Oda-Swedru-Asamankese Area, 1955-
56, pp. 72-77; Ghana, Ministry of Trade and Labor, Annual Report
of the Labor Division, 1956-57 (1959), p. 66.

14. 1960 Census: Advance Report, vols. 3 and 4, p. 43; A. Killick, "Manufacturing and Construction," in Birmingham et al., eds.,
op. cit., p. 275.

15. Peter Garlick, African Traders and Economic Development
in Ghana (New York: Oxford University Press, 1971), pp. 42-43.

16. Daily Graphic, September 9, 1953.

17. "CPP rebels" voters are assessed as CPP voters since "CPP
rebels" said they would be CPP if they won, and were. Data derived
from: newspaper reports on identity of "CPP rebels"; "Report of the
Gold Coast General Election, 1954," government report (mimeo.);
"Report on General Election, 1956," government report (mimeo.).

18. Jon Kraus, "The Political Economy of Trade Union-Govern-
ment Relations in Ghana under Four Regimes: Its Iₐ pact upon the
Minimum Wage Worker" (manuscript; publication forthcoming).

19. See Kwame Nkrumah, Autobiography of Kwame Nkrumah
(London: Nelson & Sons, 1957).

20. Data in J. Kraus, "Cleavages, Crises, Parties and State
Power in Ghana," unpublished Ph.D. thesis, 1970, pp. 538-40.

21. On Nkrumah's Pan-Africanism, see K. Nkrumah, Africa
Must Unite (London: Heinemann, 1963); I. W. Zartman, International
Relations in the New Africa (Englewood Cliffs, N.J.: Prentice-Hall,
1966); R. Green and Ann Seidman, Unity or Poverty? The Economics
of Pan-Africanism (Baltimore: Penguin Books, 1968); W. Scott Thompson, Ghana's Foreign Policy, 1957-1966 (Princeton, N.J.: Princeton
University Press, 1969).

22. For a differentiation between European democratic socialism
and African socialism, which varied from Ghana's, see M. Roberts,

"A Socialist Looks at African Socialism," in W. Friedland and C. Rosberg, eds., African Socialism (Stanford, Calif.: Stanford University Press, 1964), pp. 80-96.

23. Evening News, October 2, 1965.

24. See Tony Killick, Development Economics in Action: A Study of Economic Policies in Ghana (Cambridge, Mass.: Harvard University Press, forthcoming).

25. Nkrumah speech in 1959, quoted in K. Nkrumah, I Speak of Freedom (New York: Praeger Publishers, 1961), pp. 161, 163.

26. Ibid.; Kwame Nkrumah, "Building of a Socialist State," speech to CPP Study Group, April 22, 1961, p. 12.

27. Kwame Nkrumah, "Broadcast to the Nation," April 8, 1961.

28. Ghanaian Times, April 10, 1961.

29. See John Tettegah, Towards Nkrumaism: The Role and Tasks of the Trade Unions (Accra: TUC, Report to First Biennial Congress, March 26-30, 1962).

30. Material on the UGFC is from J. Kraus, "Political Economy and the Politics of Planning: The Case of Farmers," unpublished paper presented to 1971 African Studies Association meeting, 1971.

31. Ghana, Report of the Committee of Enquiry on the Local Purchasing of Cocoa, 1967, p. 14.

32. Unless otherwise noted, economic data are from Killick, Development Economics in Action, op. cit.

33. Ibid., chap. 9, "The State as Entrepreneur."

34. Data from an unpublished survey by Professor Norman Uphoff, Cornell University.

35. See Note 18.

36. For conservative and transformationist views in comparing the Ghana and Ivory Coast economies, see Eliot Berg, "Structural Transformation Versus Gradualism: Recent Economic Development in Ghana and the Ivory Coast"; and Reginald Green, "Reflections on Economic Strategy, Structure, Implementation, and Necessity: Ghana and the Ivory Coast, 1957-67," in Philip Foster and Aristide Zolberg, eds., Ghana and the Ivory Coast (Chicago: University of Chicago Press, 1971).

37. See the excellent critical study of Ghana's bureaucrats and their attitudes by Robert Price, The Social Basis of Administrative Behavior in a Transitional Policy: The Case of Ghana (Berkeley: University of California Press, 1975).

SUGGESTIONS FOR FURTHER READING

On Ghana

Apter, David. Ghana in Transition. 2d rev. ed.; Princeton, N.J.:
    Princeton University Press, 1973.

Austin, Dennis. Politics in Ghana. New York: Oxford University
    Press, 1964.

First, Ruth. Power in Africa. Baltimore: Penguin Books, 1970.

Foster, P., and A. Zolberg, eds. Ghana and the Ivory Coast. Chica-
    go: Chicago University Press, 1971.

Friedland, William, and Carl Rosberg, Jr., eds., African Socialism.
    Stanford, Calif.: Stanford University Press, 1964.

Genoud, Roger. Nationalism and Economic Development in Ghana.
    New York: Praeger Publishers, 1969.

Green, R., and A. Seidman. Unity or Poverty? The Economics of
    Pan-Africanism. Baltimore: Penguin Books, 1968.

Kay, G. B., ed. The Political Economy of Colonialism in Ghana.
    London: Cambridge University Press, 1971

Killick, Tony. Development Economics in Action: A Study of Eco-
    nomic Policies in Ghana. Cambridge, Mass.: Harvard Univer-
    sity Press, forthcoming.

Nkrumah, Kwame. Africa Must Unite. London: William Heinemann,
    Ltd., 1963.

_____. Neo-Colonialism. New York: International Publishers,
    1965.

ON Economic Development

Emmanuel, Arghiri. Unequal Exchange: A Study of the Imperialism
    of Trade. New York: Monthly Review Press, 1972.

Rhodes, Robert, ed. Imperialism and Underdevelopment. New York:
    Monthly Review Press, 1970.

Seers, Dudley, and L. Joy, eds. Development in a Divided World.
    Baltimore: Penguin Books, 1971.

9

UJAMAA: AFRICAN SOCIALIST PRODUCTIONISM IN TANZANIA
Frances Hill

> TANU is involved in a war against poverty and op-
> pression in our country; the struggle is aimed at
> moving the people of Tanzania (and the people of
> Africa as a whole) from a state of poverty to a
> state of prosperity.
>
> Julius K. Nyerere
> Arusha Declaration (1967)

As the first decade of Tanzanian political independence drew to
a close, President Nyerere was trying to mobilize his people and his
polity for "the second great task of TANU" (Tanzania African National
Union)—Ujamaa. Nyerere calls not merely for economic development
but for a pervasive socialist transformation culminating in both prosperity and democracy. Nyerere's Ujamaa, unlike pre-Bolshevik
Marxism, is consciously designed as a socialism of production, for
low production is perceived as a more urgent problem for Tanzania
than is inequitable distribution. These productionist imperatives
have been elevated to the paramount position in Tanzanian ideology
and policy. Ujamaa may truly be called a productionist socialism.

At the same time, Nyerere seeks to reconcile these productionist imperatives with his concept of an African humanism. African
"familyhood" or "communalism" is seen by Nyerere as not merely establishing norms of social justice but also as providing a basis for a
socialism appropriate to African conditions.

At this very general level, most Tanzanians share Nyerere's
ideals. However, specific policies promulgated in the name of Ujamaa
raise a number of difficult questions. These questions center on the
feasibility of Tanzania's economic strategies and goals as well as on
the political implications of these goals and strategies. What level

of production is possible? Does this assessment of a feasible increase
sustain an ideology of inevitable and imminent prosperity? What is the
relation between the individual as citizen and the individual as producer? What leader-citizen relation is implied in the leader's call for
dedication to the goals and strategies of socialist transformation?
In short, how does African socialist productionism relate to democratic socialism?

Nyerere's writings on Ujamaa, several of which appeared as
TANU party documents, provide the best insight into official Tanzanian concepts of democratic socialism—what it is and how it is to be
achieved. The ambiguities and internal contradictions in the official
ideology are one guide to understanding contradictions in policy formulation and implementation.

UJAMAA: AN IDEOLOGY OF PRODUCTION

Ujamaa means familyhood. This basic definition is crucial to
understanding the quality of interpersonal relations Nyerere invokes
as both the means and the end of socialist transformation. Ujamaa
has a far broader and more humanistic meaning than does the other
possible Swahili translation for socialism—Ujima, or communal work.
The use of a Swahili term for socialism emphasizes the African character of the ideas, values, and policies associated with socialism in
Nyerere's Tanzania.

Ujamaa posits a peaceful transition to socialism. Contemporary
socialism will grow out of the African communal past. Unlike European socialism, it is not the product of class conflict. Nyerere denies
the relevance of any concept of class in Africa, claiming that Africans
never even had a word for "class" in their indigenous languages.[1]
Contrasting Ujamaa with European socialism, he wrote:

> Ujamaa, then, or "familyhood," describes our social-
> ism. It is opposed to capitalism, which seeks to
> build a happy society on the basis of the exploitation
> of man by man; and it is equally opposed to doctrin-
> aire socialism which seeks to build its happy society
> on a philosophy of inevitable conflict between man
> and man.
>
> We, in Africa, have no more need of being "con-
> verted" to socialism than we have of being "taught"
> democracy. Both are rooted in our own past—in
> the traditional society which produced us.[2]

He thus claims that it is the essence of "scientific socialism" in
these conditions to transcend European concepts of class differentia-

tion, stratification, and antagonism. Nyerere suggests that Marx, had he been an African, would have certainly done so, concluding:

> If he [Marx] had lived in Sukumaland, Masailand, or Ruvuma, he would have written a very different book than Das Kapital, but he could have been just as scientific and just as socialist. [3]

Nyerere thus urges Tanzanians to analyze their heritage and their present circumstances in developing a realistic and appropriate socialism. In rejecting any claim to universal validity and applicability of one socialist orthodoxy, he asserted:

> It is imperative that socialists continue thinking. And this thinking must be more than an attempt to discover what any so-called socialist Bible or socialist Koran really says and means. It is necessary that those who call themselves scientific socialists should be scientific! In that case they would accept or reject socialist ideas and methods in accordance with the objective circumstances of time and place. They would certainly not be hampered or inhibited by the irrelevancies of a socialist theology. [4]

This is not to imply that socialism is coterminous with or results spontaneously from communalism. Changes imposed by colonialism diverted Africans from their own past and began to convert them to European ways. Colonialism did not, however, remedy the main defect of precolonial Africa—poverty. Nyerere rejects any ideology that seeks merely an egalitarian poverty. He calls instead for intensified efforts to overcome poverty, emphasizing that respect for the African past

> does not mean that we have in any way accepted our present poverty. On the contrary, the Arusha Declaration calls for a tremendous human effort for change. We are saying what has taken the older countries centuries should take us decades. What we are attempting is a telescoped evolution of our economy and of our society. [5]

He told the TANU National Conference in 1967,

> Our task, therefore, is to modernize the traditional structure so as to make it meet our new aspirations for a higher standard of living. [6]

Nyerere finds no contradiction in a socialist ideology that emphasizes not merely progress but wealth. He wrote in 1962,

> There is nothing wrong in our wanting to be wealthy;
> nor is it a bad thing for us to want to acquire the
> power which wealth brings with it. But it is most
> certainly wrong if we want the wealth and power so
> that we can dominate somebody else.[7]

Nyerere's emphasis on increased production is clear and pervasive. Ujamaa assigns greater importance to questions of production than to questions of distribution. Nyerere asserted that Tanzania does not suffer from a fundamental crisis of inequitable distribution. As he graphically put it,

> The real problem in Tanzania is not redistribution
> between rich and the poor, but a fair distribution of
> wealth, and of contribution to national expenses, be-
> tween the very poor and the poor, between the man
> who can barely feed himself and the man who can
> barely clothe himself.[8]

Since Tanzania has no class inequalities to overcome, unity for increased production replaces conflict over more equitable distribution. Production is so vital to Nyerere's concept of socialist transformation that he urges Tanzanians:

> Our major preoccupation must be to increase our
> wealth, and the amount of time and energy we spend
> on squabbling over what we now have should be very
> limited indeed.[9]

Increased prosperity is possible only through increased effort. Work (kazi) is a central tenet of Ujamaa ideology. Nyerere constantly tells Tanzanians that "we in Tanzania have to work our way out of poverty."[10] This work ethic is closely identified with Nyerere, who is generally acknowledged to be the hardest worker in the country. The president would be the last to dispute such an image, for he insists that

> The type of social organization we adopt affects both
> the distribution of the goods we produce and the
> quality of the life our people can lead, but it is ir-
> relevant to the central fact that our output of goods
> has to be increased. Each person has to produce
> more by harder, longer, and better work.[11]

In 1962 Nyerere had written that "there is no such thing as socialism without work."[12] This was as true in traditional Africa as in independent Tanzania. The work ethic grows out of African customs:

> Not only was the capitalist, or the landed exploiter,
> unknown to traditional African society, but we did
> not have that other form of modern parasite—the
> loiterer, or idler, who accepts the hospitality of so-
> ciety as his "right" but gives nothing in return! Capi-
> talistic exploitation was impossible. Loitering was
> an unthinkable disgrace.[13]

Only if Tanzanians work can they hope to develop by their own efforts. Nyerere emphasizes the need for Tanzanian self-reliance (kujitegemea). While foreign aid can be helpful, it must not be the basis for economic development. As Nyerere wrote in the Arusha Declaration, "A poor man does not use money as a weapon."[14] He told Tanzanians flatly: "The only people we can rely upon are ourselves."[15] Self-reliance is not merely a development strategy; it is to become a way of life.[16] It is essential for the return to the African heritage that forms the basis for socialist transformation.

Work cannot lead to socialist self-reliance unless it is organized. Socialist leadership is crucial. Nyerere outlines a humane nonauthoritarian leadership consistent with African "familyhood." According to Nyerere, Ujamaa

> calls for leadership, but not for orders to be given;
> it directs the people along the socialist path, but ex-
> cludes any attempt to whip them into it—saying
> clearly that you cannot force people to lead socialist
> lives.[17]

Nevertheless, good leadership is imperative. At one point Nyerere stated bluntly that "Progress in socialist rural development does in fact depend almost entirely on leadership at all levels."[18]

However, leadership must be based on discussion and education, not on coercion. Nyerere told an audience of future leaders at University College, Dar es Salaam:

> Let me emphasize that this leadership I am now
> talking about does not imply control any more than
> it implies bullying or intimidating people. A good
> leader will explain, teach and inspire. In an ujamaa
> village he will do more. He will lead by doing. He
> is in front of the people, showing them what can be

> done, guiding them, and encouraging them. But he
> is with them. You do not lead people by being so far
> in front, or so theoretical in your teaching that the
> people cannot see what you are doing or saying.
> You do not lead people by yapping at their heels like
> a dog herding cattle. You can lead the people only
> by being one of them, but just being more active as
> well as more willing to learn—from them and others.[19]

The ambiguities in these portraits of leaders are fundamental to
the ambiguities of the entire ideology. Such a concept of leadership
is fairly easy to envisage and even to implement at the village level
where leaders are local men or women selected by and in daily contact with their peers. These are the types of leader Nyerere chooses
most often for examples of proper leadership in action. It is much
more difficult to envisage and implement such leadership among professional leaders whose roles impel them to produce "results." How
does an Area Commissioner or Regional Commissioner or Agricultural Officer justify his leadership, his commitment to socialism,
and his right to receive a salary without tangible results? How can
such officials convince a touring president that socialist attitudes are
being nurtured if there are no socialist villages to substantiate their
assertions of their own energy and effectiveness? Nyerere seems to
be asking similar questions when he notes:

> Indeed, there are two opposing dangers at the outset;
> on the one hand there is a danger that enthusiastic
> TANU members and others might rush out and bully
> people into artificial communities which will collapse
> with the first breath of adversity, and on the other
> there is a danger that nothing will happen at all.[20]

While actual events in Tanzania are now closer to the first problem, the ideology of Ujamaa suffers from the second problem. This
ideology of socialism as humanism or communalism lacks any sense
of historical forces making socialism inevitable. In this sense,
Ujamaa is closer to Eduard Bernstein's revisionism than to Marx's
and Engel's dialectical materialism. Socialism is desirable but not
inevitable.[21] It may be congruent with selected elements of the past
but nothing in the political-economic-cultural past or present serves
as the motor for an inevitable transition. Since Nyerere identifies
no historically dynamic forces responsible for the transition to socialism, he must rely either on Marx's idea that the elimination of
false consciousness will solve the problem of political commitment
and political action,[22] or he must edge toward the Leninist vanguard

solution.[23] Since Ujamaa is a rural socialism, a peasant communalism,
Nyerere is caught, wittingly or unwittingly, in the dilemma of which
socialist view of peasants is more accurate—that of Marx on India[24]
or that of the elderly Marx tentatively exploring the socialist potential
of the Russian communal village.[25] Resolving this dilemma in the
spirit of Tanzanian democratic socialism is especially difficult for
Nyerere, for he must solve the problem both Marx and Bernstein were
only too glad to leave to the bourgeoisie—the historic task of solving
the problem of scarcity. As Nyerere said in his state visit to China,
"Tanzania's Long March is economic."[26]

BACKGROUND TO SOCIALISM: TANZANIAN ECONOMY

In translating ideology into policy, Tanzanian leaders must take
account of numerous economic realities. Tanzania is a very poor
country. It is one of the 16 African countries included on the UN list
of the world's 25 least developed countries. Tanzania has few known
mineral deposits and those once in production are nearly exhausted.
Gold and diamonds were never central to the Tanzanian economy.
Neither is manufacturing, which in 1971 accounted for only 9.7 percent of gross domestic product in the monetary sector.[27]

Tanzania's is an overwhelmingly agricultural economy. Although the second Five-Year Plan spoke of long-term industrialization, the next two decades will see continuing dependence on agriculture.[28] Taking the monetary economy and excluding the subsistence
sector, agriculture accounted for almost 39 percent of gross domestic product in 1971.[29] The next largest sector is trade, including
hotels and restaurants, which accounted for 13 percent.[30] However,
these figures underestimate the true importance of agriculture by excluding the subsistence sector, which accounts for an estimated 28
percent of the total GDP.[31] Agriculture is essential not only to feed
the population but for the exports earning the bulk of Tanzania's foreign exchange. Tanzania's currency is negotiable only within the
country. After the March 1971 export controls, it could not even be
spent in the East African Community partners (Uganda and Kenya).
Thus foreign exchange is fundamental to most government economic
transactions. For foreign exchange, Tanzania relies on three crops
—cotton, coffee, and sisal. The market for sisal all but collapsed
shortly after independence as synthetics replaced natural fibers.
The 1971 price is approximately half of the 1962 price.[32] The Tanzanian economy weathered this crisis due to increases in the production of cotton and coffee. The price of coffee has increased since
1962, while the price of cotton has held almost steady.[33] Unlike sisal,

which is grown on large plantations most of which are now state enterprises, both coffee and cotton are peasant crops and have always been
grown primarily by African producers. Two other peasant cash crops
—sesame seeds and cashew nuts—have seen price increases on international commodity markets. Local production has increased along
with price increases, but the basic price remains far below that of
cotton and coffee, the two principal earners of foreign exchange. The
outlook for coffee is uncertain, and Tanzanian planners hope that production of other crops like cashews and other oilseeds can be stimulated to replace its foreign exchange earnings.[34]

Food crop production lags behind production of cash crops.
Tanzania imports foods it could produce locally, including cereals and
dairy products. In 1970 Tanzania spent 176 million shillings (or almost $30 million) on food imports.[35] The cost is not merely mone-
tary. Tanzania pays a price in an undernourished population. Under-
nourishment means both human suffering and low productivity of labor.
In discussing the food problem, Nyerere told his countrymen: "Our
present attitude to food is the result of ignorance, indifference, and
indolence."[36] Even so, the government cannot afford to invest resources in food production. What resources are available for stimu-
lating agricultural production are to be channeled into production of
cash crops.

This means that the government is dependent on particular areas
and designs its investment pattern accordingly. The crucial cash
crops are each grown only in particular regions. Coffee is grown
only in Kilimanjaro and Bukoba, and cotton is grown only in Mwanza
and Shinyanga. This pattern emerged early in the colonial era and
has persisted for ecological reasons until the present. Colonial governments were as dependent on foreign exchange earned by cash crops
as is the government of independent Tanzania. These areas benefited
from colonial investment and social services, to the extent that any
were provided. At independence Tanzania's regions showed a differential pattern of economic stratification.

Stratification patterns among local areas depended essentially
on only one characteristic—the ability to provide the colonial power
something it needed, valued, and was willing to "pay for." Thus unskilled labor for porterage could be compelled and did not confer any
advantage within the colonial system. Growing those cash crops on
which colonial finances depended was an entirely different matter.
These areas received benefits that could be provided only at the expense of the peoples of other areas. Areas that were ecologically
unsuited for cash crop production were not ignored so much as they
were exploited to sustain a colonialism of selective incentives. Such
regions paid more than their share of taxes and received far from a
commensurate return in government services.[37] During the entire

colonial era, such areas became increasingly relatively "underdeveloped."[38]

This economic stratification pattern has had marked political consequences in independent Tanzania. These areas, especially Kilimanjaro and Bukoba, have produced the bulk of Tanzania's educated manpower and most political leaders. Tanzanians from the relatively underdeveloped regions resent these advantages and feel that independence has brought little change.[39] Regional imbalances thus pose a serious political problem for the national government.

The independence government has been reluctant to acknowledge the full import of this problem for fear of unleashing "tribal" hostilities inimical to "national integration." It is true that geographic-ecological production areas are also ethnic homelands, but Tanzania's 120 tribes or peoples have lived in remarkable peace since colonial occupation put them into one administrative-economic unit. It is also possible that the problem received little recognition because reliable statistics were not available. Information is still sparse for both political and technical reasons.[40] However, the second Five-Year Plan presented an exceptionally candid delineation of the problems.[41] Equally candid was the government's admission that little could be done to mitigate, let alone overcome, these problems in the near future. Nevertheless, the government pledged itself to treating regional imbalances as a serious problem that could not be allowed to continue indefinitely.

The other areal stratification pattern is the rural-urban imbalance. Urban areas, especially Dar es Salaam, have since colonial times enjoyed a far greater level of social services than those available in the most prosperous rural areas. While the services available even in Dar es Salaam are far from a desirable level, imbalances are great enough to cause political concern. Nyerere has warned of dangers in this intensifying imbalance, saying:

> If we are not careful we might get to the position
> where the real exploitation in Tanzania is that of the
> town dwellers exploiting the peasants.[42]

The Annual Plan for 1971-72 called for special efforts for "rectifying the rural-urban imbalance of the development effort. So far, it has been heavily weighted towards urban areas."[43] Despite these expressions of official concern, investment in urban areas continued to increase relative to investment in rural areas. Direct expenditures on urban areas rose from 16.6 percent of the total development budget in 1969-70 to 23.9 percent of the total development budget in 1970-71.[44] The Ministry of Development Planning also computed a measure of rural or urban impact of expenditures based on a project's effect rather than its precise location. In 1969/70 urban impact expenditures were estimated at 40 percent of the total development budget compared to 45 percent in 1970/71.[45] Urban areas had about 7 percent of total national population and produced about 35 percent of GDP.[46]

This trend reinforces the increase in urban in-migration, especially into Dar es Salaam, where there is insufficient wage employment for those leaving rural areas. The government became so concerned about this trend, that it began a highly unpopular attempt to "round up" the unemployed from the streets of Dar es Salaam and repatriate them to their home areas.[47]

Even more serious, perhaps, was the effect on investment in rural areas. In 1970/71 only 48.3 percent of government expenditures were devoted to rural impact projects.[48] This is considerably below the level projected in the second Five-Year Plan.

By 1971 the entire economy was clearly "under strain, as the rate of expenditures by government and parastatals began to exceed the resources available."[49] Between 1967 and 1971 GDP had grown at 4 to 4.5 percent per year, a third below the growth targets of the first and second Five-Year Plans.[50] During this period exports failed to reach the record levels of 1966, while investment increased by 37 percent in both 1969/70 and 1970/71.[51] This investment went into large projects undertaken by foreign contractors and "was not accompanied by a similar growth in directly productive—especially rural—investment."[52]

The overall development budget of the ministries had to be decreased by 11 percent for 1971/72.[53] The 1971/72 Annual Plan noted:

> Thus overall financial resources are falling short of plan targets while expenditures are increasing faster than planned. Thus a period of consolidation is required as expenditures are brought back into line with available resources. Virtually no new programmes or projects can start this year but investment actually will still be at a high level due to the large number of continuing projects.[54]

Constraints established by ongoing projects in the urban sector meant that little attention could be devoted to such specifically rural problems as regional imbalances. Noting that the pattern of public expenditures had increased some of these differences and calling for increased emphasis on the poorer regions and districts, the 1971/72 Annual Plan nevertheless concluded: "The reduction in the size of the development budget in 1971/2 compared with the previous year had left very little room for maneuver in reallocating expenditures between projects, regions, or sectors."[55]

The emphasis would remain on production. The 1971/72 plan listed the following criteria for evaluating rural expenditures: "Ministries should evaluate their rural programmes to determine average rates of return, and their impact on recurring revenue and expenditures, and should channel more funds to the programmes showing the best result."[56] As the second Five-Year Plan noted in justifying the emphasis on aggregate growth, all areas of Tanzania are poor in an absolute sense and therefore "economic policy must remain constantly concerned to produce productive results."[57]

The other economic reality is the fact of class. This has been faced much less candidly than the question of geographic imbalances. When it has been recognized, it has been discussed primarily in racial terms. This was not a total misperception. The colonial legacy meant that race and class coincided. Colonial stratification among individuals was based on the same factors as stratification among areas—a colonial judgment that particular individuals could provide desired services. This colonial perception was based not on individual ability primarily but on ingrained prejudices about appropriate positions for individuals of the white, brown, and black races. Such prejudices meant that whites were not allowed to hold positions below a certain level and blacks were not permitted to rise above a certain level. The space in between was reserved for browns, who became traders and middle-level clerks. Africans staffed only the lowest levels of administration, while policy-making positions were reserved for whites. Since government was the main employer of skilled manpower, these distinctions were basic to stratification patterns. Colonialism created a class system correlated with race and based on cash earnings. In short, it created a salariat. The primary African beneficiaries were chiefs, whose salaries were enhanced by manifold opportunities for graft provided by their positions as magistrates and tax collectors. While African cash crop producers earned more than some low-level clerks, they faced the problem of translating cash into skills necessary for dealing with the alien administration. They had to pay for their children to acquire the literacy and knowledge of British ways that the salariat possessed. Income alone was insufficient. The main distinction was between those earning steady cash income, primarily the salariat, and those who were not, primarily peasants. Colonialism created a class system appropriate to an administrative state: a class system based not on direct control of the means of production but on control of the means of management.[58]

During the nationalist struggle and the early years of independence, attention was focused on racial inequalities, not on the problem of class itself. Since there has never been a large white settler problem in Tanzania and since white administrators who remained or arrived after independence served an African government, African hostility was directed primarily at resident Asians, whether or not they were citizens. Government efforts centered on allowing Africans to catch up with Asian employment in administration. Until 1964, Africans were given preference over Asian citizens in civil service employment. [59]

These efforts consolidated an African salariat employed by the government without decreasing racial tensions. [60] In 1967 Nyerere had to remind Tanzanians that "socialism is not racialism," but he did not deal directly with the problems of class. [61]

Since the main class cleavage turned on government salaries, Nyerere perhaps felt that any such discussion would weaken the structures he had worked so hard to establish and on which he pinned his hope for socialist transformation. As the economic realities of limited production, continued dependence on foreign exchange, and inability to overcome geographic imbalances impinged on the planning effort, it became imperative, in Nyerere's eyes, to gear Tanzanian organizations to the tasks of socialist economic development. The inherent productionism of Ujamaa worked to focus attention on problems it hoped to solve and to exclude those that might somehow interfere with productionism. The assumptions linking elite consolidation to economic development seem vague to the outside observer, but they were fundamental to political engineering efforts of independent Tanzania.

FOUNDING A SOCIALIST PARTY-STATE

The Ujamaa ideology suggested that socialism was culturally appropriate but identified no dynamic socioeconomic factors that could account for a socialist transformation. Economic realities offered little room for maneuver. Thus, Nyerere relied on political organization to move Tanzania toward socialism. He needed political organizations that could formulate and implement socialist productionist policies. As Tanzania took a more determinedly socialist course, the organizational heritage of colonialism was replaced and that of the nationalist era was modified.

Nyerere, the nationalist hero, took on a more complex role as founder. His work of founding involved both creating new organizations and defining relations among them. He has never been able to rule unopposed but he has had an outstanding record of success in translating his ideas into the policies and institutions of independent Tanzania. [62] As founder, he enjoys the power of initiative. He has been much less successful at controlling the subsequent course of the policies and organizations that he initiated.

It proved fairly simple to change the organizational legacy of colonialism. [63] Tanzania became independent as a theoretically multi-

party parliamentary system. In fact, TANU was the only viable political party. The only non-TANU candidate ever elected to the National
Assembly soon rejoined the nationalist party. At independence, Nyerere was Prime Minister, a post he resigned within six weeks. By December 1962 the Constitution had been changed to remove the Queen's
representative, the Governor-General, and to replace a Prime Minister directly responsible to the National Assembly with a president
elected directly by the entire citizenry. Julius Nyerere was elected
president with only token opposition. His role as founder was thereby
given insitutional expression. The subsequent decline in the relative
importance of the National Assembly was not a marked change, for
the parliament had never been the heart of the Tanzanian polity. Implications for the future were more important.

The administrative apparatus had been the core of the colonial
regime. In independent Tanzania the administration was redesigned
locally and nationally to enable government to take a more positive
role in directing economic development efforts. Locally, administrative chiefdomships were abolished. Chiefs could enjoy their local
status but were no longer part of government. Nationally, new policies necessitated new components of the administration. Ministries
were added with specific responsibility for development. Thus the
administration increased dramatically in size. This increase posed a
serious question for the regime. How were these organizations to
be supervised by a democratic government? What was to distinguish
the independent from the colonial administrations? The relative unim-
portance of the National Assembly meant that such questions depended
on the role of party in the new state. National independence did not
automatically resolve these questions. Even Africanization of the
civil service did not resolve questions of political accountability and
the relation between citizens and administrators.

During the nationalist struggle, citizen participation had been
used to destroy an administrative regime. TANU had been designed
as a channel of citizen participation. At independence, political
leaders faced the difficult question of the role that citizen participation
was to play in the new state and then of redesigning the nationalist
movement for its new role. TANU itself had to be adapted and its relations with the numerous new components of the administration defined. Designing the national role of TANU proved difficult for two
reasons. First, although TANU was supported in all areas of the
country and was a mass party in intent and formal organization, its
actual organization throughout the nationalist era had been multilocal. [64]
Uhuru meant freedom from a variety of local problems that were often as important as national independence in sustaining nationalist
loyalty. Second, just when TANU had to become the most important
party of a new state and thus a national institution in its own right, it

lost most of its educated cadres to the expanding administration.[65] Prominent politicians, including Nyerere, retained their party positions, but their energies were devoted primarily to the new state. TANU was left without strong central leadership capable of devoting its energies to defining the ongoing daily role of the party in these changing conditions and to consolidating the party's grass-roots organization as nationalist militancy was made irrelevant by political independence. Nyerere called attention to this problem when he resigned as Prime Minister in early 1962. At that time he pledged to devote his efforts to rebuilding the party.[66] However, this was one of the founder's periods of withdrawal and reflection rather than a period of active organizational work. The result was Nyerere's first major statement on Ujamaa, the TANU pamphlet "Ujamaa—the Basis of African Socialism" and not any appreciable change in the party as an organization.[67]

When Nyerere became president he urged that Tanzania become a constitutional party-state.[68] Nyerere suggested that the change would do more than make TANU's de facto role official; it would provide an organizational framework for Tanzanian development.

Nyerere maintained that party competition was irrelevant to African ideas of democracy.[69] The party itself would resolve opposing policy preferences and maintain leaders' accountability to followers. As an official component of a party-state, TANU's relations with administrative organizations would be clarified and it would take a more active, responsible role in the entire political process.

TANU's dual role as both a partner in government and a channel of citizen participation were not necessarily compatible and problems were not resolved by the decision that TANU should continue as a mass party. In 1965 when the new constitution came into effect, TANU lacked the capability for either role. It did not have a professional staff necessary for its government role, its own experts who could deal with planners in the administration. Nor did it have an effective grass-roots organization linked to national decision makers through a party hierarchy capable of making democratic centralism a reality. The party could not be ignored because of its nationalist legitimacy, but it could be circumvented by "expertise." Citizen participation via the party seemed to have a little role. The party's main role is as a forum for Nyerere within the national levels of the party-state. Neither Nyerere nor the party can guarantee that these policies will be implemented as intended.

Even when the founder is as committed to citizen participation as is Nyerere, the dynamics of a presidential party-state tend more easily toward elite initiative than toward a vigorous citizenship. These dynamics are reinforced by the specifics of a "modernizing" and productionist ideology, whether or not it is socialist. The presidential

party-state tends toward paternal government.[70] For many party-state
initiatives an active citizen commitment is superfluous. They need only
be assured by the legitimating founder that the action or policy in question is appropriate. Leaders need citizens only sporadically, even in
innovative systems. For many major changes they require only lack
of opposition.

The Tanzanian presidential party-state's move toward socialism
shows the difference between initiatives that require citizen participation and those requiring merely tolerance. There have been two major
types of ostensibly socialist initiative in Tanzania since independence:
the 1965 nationalization of the "commanding heights" of the economy
and the 1970s mobilization for rural socialism. The relation between
the two phases is by no means clear. Neither is the relation of either
separately or both together to democratic socialism at all unambiguous.
Each initiative has created its own institutions. Nationalization produced the parastatal enterprises, an alternate bureaucracy in uneasy
relation with other party-state structures. Rural socialism created
Ujamaa Villages. Parastatals involve elite interests; Ujamaa Villages
may or may not involve peasant interests. The relation between organizations resulting from nationalization and those resulting from
rural socialist transformation remain ambiguous and potentially con-
flictual. The president as founder could resolve these tensions on an
ad hoc basis during the Nyerere presidency, but even Nyerere cannot
control the entire party-state apparatus. If Tanzanian socialism were
to be democratic socialism, TANU would have to face the challenge
of becoming a true ruling party. Thus socialist initiatives are interwoven with central organizational modifications designed primarily to
strengthen TANU within the party-state. Any hope for democratic
socialism depends on these efforts.

SOCIALISM AND NATIONALIZATION

Nationalization is an expression of economic nationalism but it
does not necessarily create a momentum for socialist transformation.
The Nyerere government felt that in Tanzania nationalization was a
requisite fundamental for socialism. Nyerere argued that socialism
meant Tanzanian control, while capitalism necessarily involved foreign control. He maintained that Africa lacked a bourgeoisie and
therefore in Africa:

> The choice is between foreign private ownership on
> the one hand, and local collective ownership on the
> other. For I do not think there is any free state in
> Africa where there is sufficient local capital, or a
> sufficient number of local entrepreneurs, for locally-

> based capitalism to dominate the economy. Private
> investment in Africa means overwhelming foreign
> private investment. A capitalistic economy means
> a foreign dominated economy. [71]

The socioeconomic legacy of British colonial occupation left Tanzania with no African bourgeoisie and with its important economic enterprises in British or Asian hands. The list of nationalized enterprises reveals the colonial racial-economic pyramid and how little there was to nationalize in Tanzania.

The major target of the nationalizations announced the week of February 5-12, 1967, were foreign-owned banks, which were primarily British.[72] The second targets for total nationalization were food processors, which were primarily Asian-owned. The government took complete control of insurance businesses. To form the nucleus of the State Trading Corporation, the government nationalized eight wholesale or import-export firms previously owned by both Britons and Asians. There were no African enterprises in any sector.

Before these dramatic nationalizations of existing private firms, the government had established the National Development Corporation (NDC) to oversee and expand industrial enterprises. By 1967, the NDC controlled 21 firms totally and held at least 50 percent of the shares of 17 others.[73]

Expansion of the public sector posed two sets of challenges. Government control of the "commanding heights" may be nominal in the absence of the technical expertise needed to oversee economic enterprises. If this technical expertise remains the sole property of a small group, whether citizens or expatriates, problems of political direction and accountability become paramount. Tanzania faced both problems as a result of the 1965 nationalizations, although the problem of political control over "experts" proved the most acute and tenacious.

The banks were nationalized with a minimum of dislocation. A group of young Tanzanian economists from the Economics Department of University College, Dar es Salaam, replaced the British directors. The NDC and other parastatals, with their lucrative salaries, attracted skilled managers and were allotted by manpower planning the bulk of university graduates not trained as teachers. There were inevitable inefficiencies, especially in the State Trading Corporation. Rampant inefficiency could, of course, undermine efforts for socialist transformation, but this was not the main problem.

Much more troublesome was the relationship between nationalization and socialism. This abstract question became in practice a matter of relations between the party and the new national enterprises. This is not to say that TANU was a militant socialist party but it was the only organization Nyerere could use in his efforts to make nationalization the basis for socialism rather than state capitalism.

The relation between the nationalizations and the new political arrangements remained ambiguous. Did nationalization aid party-state institutionalization by increasing the scope of its responsibility, or did nationalizations undermine the party's contribution as a channel of citizen participation by making decision making the preserve of "experts" whose actions were protected and legitimated by the mantle of a "national" enterprise? There is certainly evidence that national-ization facilitates increased self-determination in planning, thereby increasing the party-state's scope for effective action for socialist development. At the same time, nationalization created an entirely new sector within the party-state without creating any countervailing structures of political accountability. This "new class" of managers fell outside the existing structures of both party and state. The para-statals became "states within the state" in terms of planning and ex-penditure and evaluation of performance. Performance was evaluated in terms of efficiencies in increasing the rate of turnover, not in terms of the contribution to a broad socialist transformation. The resultant repercussions on the entire "development" effort were monumental, since the parastatals quickly became the major consumers of increas-ingly scarce and expensive foreign exchange. [74] Lack of political con-trol thus resulted in inefficiencies. Both were inimical to socialist transformation.

The true nature and dimensions of the problem were only slowly perceived. Nyerere had proved acutely aware of the need for a strong socialist-oriented party, but he had only slowly seen that threats to so-cialist transformation are structural and not merely, or even primarily, personal. The 1967 Arusha Declaration clearly treated personal corrup-tion as the major barrier to socialist transformation. [75] The Arusha Declaration Leadership Code meant that a political leader could no longer use his political position to enhance his personal business pros-pects. The individual must choose between political leadership in the struggle for socialist transformation and personal aggrandizement in the struggle for individualistic capitalist success. The Arusha Declaration did not condemn capitalism but merely demanded that the individual choose between capitalism and politics. The Arusha Declaration clearly posited that removing capitalists from the party-state and establishing them in a restricted capitalist sector would remove the major impedi-ment to socialist transformation. Nyerere clearly felt that the danger of personal corruption grew out of the rapid expansion of elite roles and functions.

In February 1971 another major party policy document dealt more directly with the consolidation of a nonsocialist national elite outside of both party and state. Mwongozo, or the TANU Guidelines, called upon the party to take a more active role in supervising every facet of the development effort, especially the quasi-independent para-statal sector. [76] But TANU was not to become merely an alternative

bureaucracy. It must consolidate a mass base for socialism. Nationalization must be hedged by other initiatives.

The ambiguous relation of nationalization to socialism and the
continued weakness of TANU, a weakness compounded by the increase
of new organizations staffed by "expert" managers, put Nyerere in a
difficult position. He was a leader without a reliable political base
despite his role as founder of Tanzania's political and economic organizations. He had no constituency of truly committed socialists to support his efforts to discipline the elite and make it socialist. He thus
turned his attention to consolidation of a peasant political base. Peasants were not socialists either, but Nyerere felt they were closer to
the ethos of socialism than was a privileged urban elite. Nyerere,
the founder, had to balance a nonsocialist elite against nonsocialist
peasantry in hope of getting each to move the other toward Ujamaa.
He thus gambled that no sector was so antisocialist that they were
willing to become overtly anti-Nyerere.

In this complex effort, Nyerere is circumscribed by Tanzanian
economic realities and the productionist imperatives of Ujamaa.

UJAMAA VILLAGES IN NATIONAL PERSPECTIVE

Ujamaa Villages are the third phase of Tanzanian efforts to increase rural production. The first phase focused on "progressive
farmers" organized into marketing cooperatives.[77] The second phase
emphasized resettlement schemes with the capital-intensive techniques then deemed essential to large-scale agricultural production.[78]
Each approach was, in turn, declared a failure shortly after it had
been launched. The Tanzanian economy remained dependent on small-
scale rural producers who are also the majority of Tanzania's population and of TANU's membership.

However, there is no guarantee Ujamaa will be a peasant-oriented
socialism or an indigenous peasant initiative. Indeed, the relation of
Ujamaa Villages to Tanzanian socialist transformation remains unclear.
The lack of clarity reveals a political struggle over the definition of
Ujamaa. This struggle is not and cannot be conducted in an idiom
other than the Ujamaa idiom. The dynamics of a party-state headed
by a nationalist founder and the importance of ideology as a basis of
power within the elite both preclude an open challenge in the form of
an alternate rhetoric. The debate asks the fundamental question:
What is the purpose of rural socialist transformation? There are two
possible answers, each suggested by different facets of existing plans
but each involving a very different role for the rural producers.
Ujamaa Villages either provide the economic basis for a total Tanzanian economic transition from an agricultural to an industrial econ-

omy, or they solve specifically rural problems in an economy that remains predominantly agrarian. The basic difference—in economic patterns, in the social relations of production, and in political consequences—centers on the nature, origin, and extent of demands for increased production.

Any full-scale attempt to create an industrial economy would require a maximal mobilization of the currently most productive sector of the national economy—rural smallholding producers. Tanzania's policy of self-reliance certainly does not preclude accepting foreign aid and external private investment. Indeed, both have increased steadily since enunciation of the self-reliance policy in the 1967 Arusha Declaration.[79] However, the level of aid and investment will remain inadequate to finance domestic industrialization on even a modest scale. The only alternative remains increasing domestic production of cash crops earning foreign exchange. Any attempt to accelerate the tempo and extend the scope of industrialization will require increased production of cash crops and of marketed food crops. Peasants will have to feed and finance the workers and managers of an urban industrial economy.

The productive capacity of Tanzanian agriculture is not infinitely expandable. It is presently limited by both ecology and technology. In the absence of the basic research necessary to overcome these constraints, one must ask how industrialization would affect both the standard of living and the political role of the Tanzanian rural population. The answer suggested here is that such a strategy of moving Tanzania toward industrialization through internally generated surpluses would necessarily involve the economic proletarianization and political exclusion of the rural population. Proletarianization has little to do with the productivity of labor. It deals with the organization of production, and especially with the denial to the producers of the right to affect decisions about either the organization of production or the allocation of the product. Ujamaa Villages could easily be used by an unaccountable and extractive national elite to impose this kind of "factory discipline" on the rural producers.[80] Should this occur, the mass of Tanzanians would be stripped of their citizen rights along with their economic rights, for the two are inextricably mingled in a developmental and productionist party-state in which the party is mass only in rhetoric and there is no founder to serve as arbiter and protector.

The alternative is a peasant socialism within the framework of a national but predominantly agricultural economy. Instead of proletarianization Ujamaa would bring peasantization—the political-economic consolidation of participant rural producers aware of their own sectoral needs and able to press their own justifiable claims in national decision-making circles. Peasantization does not necessarily

mean reliance on household decision making. It could be consistent
with Ujamaa Villages. It merely means that the members of Ujamaa
Villages would have some meaningful input into the management of
their own villages and into decisions of the party-state affecting them.

The alternatives of peasantization and proletarianization necessarily involve different attitudes toward citizen participation. This
question is often obscured by suggestions that citizens are incapable
of participation. Treating the Tanzanian rural producers as unincor-
porated parochials is misleading in the 1970s. The most relevant
question is not whether rural producers will be "socially mobilized"
but what will be the terms of their incorporation. [81] This is precisely
the question that states seek to avoid by discrediting their citizenries.
Efforts become especially intense when leaders deal with peasants,
not because peasants are incapable of dealing with their governments
but because governments are unwilling to deal with peasants as a sector with its own legitimate interests. Peasants are generally perceived as an unreliable economic sector because decisions about production are made with reference to the needs of the producing unit
rather than with reference to the needs of an external consuming
unit. [82] The anxiety increases as the state becomes the paramount
consumer. Inthese circumstances the state will rapidly arrogate to
itself the appearance of responsibility for "modern" production. The
Tanzanian party-state followed the same pattern, becoming modernizing paternal before it became overtly productionist.

At the same time, Nyerere's concern about the premature consolidation of an antisocialist elite meant that this move toward productionism could not take the form of a straightforward state putsch
against the peasantry. Nyerere needed both the peasants and the leaders, each as a means of controlling the other. An uneasy tension between the two would have to be maintained by the active intervention
of the president-founder. The task was all the more delicate since
neither group was unaware of this tension. Each hoped that its own
version of compliance with this plan would provide the opportunity
to "capture" Nyerere, and with him the control of the party-state.

This trend toward productionism and the complex political calculations involved meant that Ujamaa could not be left to be implemented in the voluntaristic manner set out in the official ideology.
Instead, the party-state would assume active direction of rural socialist transformation. That is, various sectors would seek an active
role in the process in an attempt to redefine rural change in a manner
consistent with particular nonrural sectoral interests in the interest
of consolidating the position of particular groups within the loosely
articulated party-state. The questions logically arising out of the
ambiguities of the Ujamaa ideology are not necessarily resolved in
practice. Nevertheless, the experience with Ujamaa to date has clar-

ified the de facto direction that their resolution seems to be taking.
This pattern nationally suggests that citizen participation has accounted
for less of the existing pattern of Ujamaa Villages than has party-state
direction. Government mobilization has been circumscribed less by
local inputs than by constraints imposed by the productionist purpose
of Ujamaa. Thus Ujamaa Villages are a feature of economically marginal regions where the central party-state can experiment with socialism without disrupting the production of export crops or the production of the local urban food supply as the table of Spearman correlation coefficients suggests[83] (see Table 6).

    This pattern became even clearer when in 1970-71 the govern-
ment began to choose entire regions for total transformation. The
Annual Plan for 1971 notes that Dodoma, Kigoma, Mara, Mtwara, and
Singida would be the focal points of government initiatives.[84] All except Mtwara rank in the lowest third of all indicators of economic performance. Thus any disruption to production caused by mobilization
for socialist transformation would have minimal national impact.
These same regions were politically marginal when the central party-
state took responsibility for their transformation; they had supplied
neither outstanding national-level leaders of the nationalist movement
nor the bulk of the middle-level cadres of the party-state.

    Even in these marginal areas, local Ujamaa initiatives were
seen as inconvenient. These local experiments do not give the central
levels of the party-state sufficient control over the national economy,
nor do they give the competing sectors of the party-state the political-
economic advantages sought. In this context, it is clear that Ujamaa

TABLE 6

Spearman Correlation Coefficients for Ujamaa Villages

	Ujamaa Villages	Percent of Regional Population in Ujamaa Villages
Subsistence agriculture	.238	−.111
Export agriculture	−.319	−.590
Market agriculture	−.302	−.556
Food crops marketed	−.047	−.007
Livestock sales	.391	.161
Primary school enrollment	−.560	−.715
Government per capita expenditures on medical services	−.264	.106

Source: Compiled by the author.

expresses national power relationships more directly than it suggests
solutions to local problems.

The test case setting the pattern for the latest phase of the rural
"development" effort was the short history of the Ruvuma Development Association.[85] This case is still discussed in hushed tones by
those whose faith in Ujamaa and the president is troubled by the story
of the demise of a local experiment with socialism. The full story of
the rise and demise of the RDA remains to be told. This lack of knowledge and the barriers to acquiring it trouble young Tanzanian planners.
The contemporary controversy centers on the demise of the RDA: why
was a promising local experiment disbanded by the central government? No one expects a purposive party-state led by a founder with a
sense of destiny to wait for peasants to reorganize themselves along
lines consistent with the mobilization of national resources for national
transformation. Nevertheless, the RDA case does raise serious questions about the central party-state attitude toward local initiatives.
What is the citizen's role in Ujamaa?

VILLAGE SOCIALISM

Until 1970 Ujamaa Villages were nationally approved local experiments. During 1970-71 Ujamaa became a top priority effort by
the central organizations of the party-state to mobilize the rural populations. These efforts centered on Dodoma Region as a potential
showcase for the benefits of socialist transformation. Nyerere hoped
to show that rural socialist transformation would increase local production and consolidate a peasant constituency for Tanzanian
socialism. In March 1970 he ordered that the entire population of
Dodoma Region should form socialist villages within 14 months.

Dodoma is truly marginal to the national economy. Its recurrent
famines are considered a national embarrassment and resented as a
drain on the national treasury. Table 7 shows how Dodoma ranks
among the 17 regions on the main production sectors.[86] National mo-
bilizers clearly felt that they had nothing to lose by redoing Dodoma.

Rural socialist transformation can mean either Ujamaa Vijijini
(socialism in the villages) or Vijiji vya Ujamaa (Ujamaa Villages).
These two strategies do not necessarily differ in the ultimate degree
of socialist transformation, the actual effect on production, or the
consolidation of a constituency of peasant socialists. They do differ
in the degree of initial perceived change, leaving open the question of
the relation between change and socialist transformation. Ujamaa Villages involve resettlement. Ujamaa Vijijini changes the social relations of production within existing settlements. In Dodoma Region the
government began by encouraging Ujamaa Vijijini, but soon committed

its full resources to creating Ujamaa Villages. The change was a
classic example of bureaucratic enthusiasm spurred on by the president. If Nyerere wanted Ujamaa Villages the bureaucracy would produce them. It is less clear that administrators were as committed to
socialism as they seemed to be to resettlement.

The only area of Dodoma Region to make a serious effort to foster socialism in the villages was Irangi in Kondoa District.[87] The
Rangi are, by Dodoma standards, good farmers and astute politicians.
Since colonial times their leaders have learned to interact successfully
with whatever government was currently in power to extract benefits
and to avoid reprisals. Both motives were involved in the attempts to
foster Ujamaa in the Rangi villages during 1969 and 1970.

Although the Rangi have a nonnucleated settlement pattern, there
are identifiable villages. People live close enough to each other to
cultivate a communal field, but this was not a living tradition by 1969.
Instead, groups of kin and neighbors helped each other prepare their
fields for planting. Each household head would provide meat or beer
for these helpers. Under no circumstances did this aid give claim to
part of the harvest. The useright over land was absolute, as was control of the crop produced. Thus even the early experiments with
Ujamaa could not grow directly or spontaneously from the African communal heritage.

The early Ujamaa experiments differed widely and generaliza-
tions are apt to be misleading. At this early stage it is more useful
to explore the process of socialist transformation than to try to generalize about results. Since the process involved all party-state organizations and nonofficial local power systems, it would be impossible to discuss Ujamaa in all of Irangi. Instead, I shall trace the
change from Ujamaa Vijijini to Vijiji vya Ujamaa in one Rangi village
that was at the center of the controversy over rural socialist transformation.

Mnenia is a ward headquarters and thus the base for government
services. Villagers had agreed to cultivate a communal field in 1969.
Drought and then floods had meant famine in 1969. Mnenia had been
more fortunate than some other areas of the district, but rumors
that, in the future, government famine relief would go only to Ujamaa
Village members provided an incentive for socialism. Rangi in this
area were also positively disposed toward Ujamaa because it was a
TANU-Nyerere policy, and TANU had been strong and militant in the
area during the independence struggle. Nevertheless, the people of
Mnenia were not prepared for complete socialism transformation.
Citizens and leaders alike were experimenting with a new way of life.
At the very least the experiment could serve as a defensive compli-
ance with government policy that would protect the existing way of
life from government sanctions.

TABLE 7

Dodoma Region Production Rankings

	Regional Rank	Percent of total
Manufacturing	11	0.9
Commerce	13	1.2
Export agriculture	17	0.0
Market agriculture	16	1.0
Subsistence agriculture	6	6.0
Food crops marketed	10	5.5
Stock sold	1	18.4
Gross domestic product	13	3.4

Source: Compiled by the author.

The first year 55 workers, far less than 1 percent of the population, cultivated about 30 acres. After troubles organizing work on the Ujamaa field, 65 bags of corn were harvested and the entire crop sold to the cooperative for 22 shillings per bag, or a total of 1,430 shillings to be divided among the 55 workers. If it were divided equally, each person would get 26 shillings, a sum the Mnenia wajamaa dismissed as paltry, a certain indication that Ujamaa did not lead to prosperity. Dividing the cash caused severe strains among the members of Mnenia Ujamaa Village, some demanding equal shares, some demanding women's shares go to their husbands, some demanding pay according to work as recorded in the Ujamaa Village log. Finally, there was an equal division, confirming the widespread fear that Ujamaa was a social security scheme for the lazy. The Rangi, who invariably refer to Ujamaa in terms of wealth, saw little evidence of Ujamaa's connection with it.

Party-state leaders were also dissatisfied with the production levels reached in these early Ujamaa experiments. Under pressure from a new regional commissioner and from the political head of the President's Economic Planning Team, the Kondoa area commissioner began to push for larger Ujamaa Villages that promised greater economic returns. This necessarily meant that local Ujamaa experiments would come under increasing pressure to conform to national expectations. Since national Ujamaa policy was by no means clearly or adequately specified, there was considerable confusion and mutual suspicion.

Tensions had been rising in the area since the President's Economic Planning Team began work in Kondoa. In every district the team head was a politician, a member of the TANU National Executive Committee. The head of the Kondoa team was a Bukoba and hoped to use his service in Kondoa as a stepping-stone to a high-level, well-paid government position. He thus demanded maximum results and sought to ascertain that full credit for these results devolve not on the area commissioner but on himself. As in other districts with similar teams, the team head and the area commissioner were soon locked in a political duel marked by reciprocal allegations and denunciations. Based on the president's March 1970 call for total socialist transformation of Dodoma region within 14 months, Karagho condemned the extent and nature of Ujamaa in Kondoa, calling for Ujamaa Villages with at least 250 families, with each adult worker responsible for a minimum two acres of Ujamaa field. [88] These demands necessarily meant amalgamation of numerous Ujamaa Villages. Technicians on the teams, under severe strain and unhappy about the Rangi's reluctance to aid their work, began denouncing villagers, telling them that soon recalcitrants would be jailed. At this point the area commissioner ordered the entire team to a remote corner of the district, where local complaints would have less direct impact on the district party-state. This was tantamount to banishment for technicians accustomed to larger cities. In their own words, many "despaired." They nevertheless produced plans for numerous Ujamaa Villages calling for greater production.

These plans caused apprehension among the local population. Those not living in Ujamaa Villages feared the government would take their land even though President Nyerere had repeatedly said Ujamaa was voluntary. Even members of Ujamaa Villages regarded these plans as either threatening or ludicrous. The plans made erroneous estimates of both population and land area, set unrealistic targets of economic production, and expected fledgling Ujamaa Villages to assume a heavy burden of debt. The area commissioner, too, knew these plans were worthless, but felt impelled to change from voluntary Ujamaa that was a mere addition to the prevailing system of production to a more encompassing rural socialism. He chose Mnenia as one of the high-priority targets for this new approach because he believed the local leadership was cooperative and effective. He did not expect the furor that soon erupted.

The area commissioner and the President's Economic Planning Team decided that Mnenia should enlarge its Ujamaa field to 170 acres, a change requiring collectivization of adjoining private plots. In this effort, the area commissioner relied on the ward executive officer and the TANU chairman to continue relatively smooth operation of local government. He totally misjudged the people of Mnenia and its party-state leaders. In the ensuing crisis the ward executive officer and TANU chairman opposed collectivization openly and actively, while the Ujamaa village chairman maneuvered for advantage in the ward power structure by allying himself with the area commissioner. This gamble failed, leaving Ujamaa and the Ujamaa village chairman weakened.

Public discontent surfaced in a special meeting called by the opponents of collectivization, led by the Mnenia Moslem sheikh. At this meeting no one except the Ujamaa village chairman supported collectivization. All demanded instead that they clear new land, although no one had any idea where such could be found. They successfully insisted that Ujamaa coexist with socioeconomic patterns the Rangi now regard as normal, neither encroaching upon nor disrupting them. Those with little land were as insistent as those with more to lose. TANU leaders and Ujamaa Village members opposed collectivization as strongly as ordinary citizens not in Ujamaa Villages. Even a delegate to the ward development committee and member of the Mnenia Ujamaa Village Committee opposed collectivization because his private plot would have been among the first taken.

Opponents of collectivization all claimed to be good socialists intent upon building a "proper" form of Ujamaa. No one opposed Ujamaa openly. Such debate was characteristic of the entire party-state. As long as a person limits his criticism to details of Ujamaa implementation he can make plausible claim to being a good socialist. Anyone who suggests otherwise incurs general wrath. The young ward agricultural officer undertook to lecture the meeting on Ujamaa, telling people of Mnenia that they did not understand Ujamaa. He asserted that Ujamaa was no longer a matter of discussion—Ujamaa was mandatory and all-encompassing; citizens must follow the orders of "leaders" like himself. This produced a furor and the agricultural officer was ignominiously expelled from the meeting. The people then agreed to draft a letter to the area commissioner stating categorical opposition to changing either their way of life or Ujamaa as it currently existed. The letter was signed, "People of Mnenia."

This show of united opposition convinced the area commissioner that the situation was serious. He could do little to discipline the recalcitrant citizens since the entire local party-state apparatus was in disarray. In an effort to reassert his control, he transferred all ward executive officers. The man assigned to Mnenia resigned rather than face an aroused populace. The area commissioner also sent the district TANU chairman, both members of parliament, and the district council executive officer on tours to calm the situation and laud the virtues of Ujamaa living. Irangi gradually became calm but not socialist. The district government had spent over $200,000 to produce this impasse. [89] The Rangi continued a minimal level of defensive compliance, but their enthusiasm for Ujamaa and trust of the party-state were shaken.

The Rangi had been able to turn aside a mobilization effort by district officials. The Gogo of Dodoma district had to capitulate to a mobilization effort by national officials led by the president himself. Operation Dodoma was conducted with the active opposition of numerous local officials, but TANU had never been strong in Dodoma district and the Gogo had never taken control of the local party-state the way the Rangi had. There were few leaders around whom they could rally in a confrontation with the government.

The Gogo live in scattered homesteads surrounded by their cattle. They are generally poor farmers in a harsh environment. [90] When there is adequate rain, the Gogo produce enough food for themselves. Droughts and famines are so regular that Gogo date their age grades accordingly. [91] Gogo society is characterized more by mutual suspicion than by cohesion and interaction. Everyone fears witchcraft; most leaders are thought to be wizards. Gogo from one ritual area do not readily interact with Gogo from another area.

Unlike the Rangi, who protect themselves from the government by interacting with it, the Gogo ignore the government. Until Operation Dodoma the government generally reciprocated by ignoring the Gogo. The only exception came during famines. Even the colonial government would have been embarrassed by mass starvation. The independence government also grudgingly kept the Gogo alive during such crises. The 1969 famine in Dodoma cost the government over $1 million. [92]

The costly and traumatic famine had numerous repercussions. The people had again faced starvation and some had died. Large numbers of stock had also died or been sold at very low prices to get money for food. While everyone recognized the Gogo's suffering, the regional commissioner and other officials also blamed the Gogo for their plight. The alcoholic area commissioner told the Gogo that the famine resulted from their tendency to prefer drinking local beer to cultivating their fields. [93] The 1969 famine created fear and uncertainty making people receptive or vulnerable to mobilization. The district party-state was too weak even to contemplate taking the primary responsibility for a serious mobilization effort. In both 1969 and 1970 area commissioners lost their postings for inadequate attention to Ujamaa and for misleading President Nyerere about the true state of socialist transformation. Party leaders opposed Ujamaa openly. The district council-TANU chairman was warned about his opposition to Ujamaa by President Nyerere during his November 1969 tour of Dodoma. A year later the chairman was removed from office and put under fairly lenient house arrest. The member of parliament for Dodoma South opposed Ujamaa as openly as had the district TANU chairman. He was not allowed to stand for reelection to parliament and was also put under continual security surveillance. Other elected officials opposed socialism but were far less vocal or visible. At the Regional Development Committee they voted in 1969 that leaders should not join any particular Ujamaa Village but take general responsibility for all Ujamaa Villages, [94] an ingenious means of dissociating themselves from socialism. Others whose opposition was less subtle were jailed under preventive detention by the area commissioner in late 1970.

By early 1971 the new regional commissioner and new area commissioner were under intense pressure from Nyerere to make Dodoma both productive and socialist. The area commissioner was acutely aware that his two predecessors had been transferred and demoted. The regional commissioner, a former Cabinet minister defeated in the 1970 general election, faced a bleak political future if Dodoma region continued its reputation as a center of famine but not of Ujamaa. Both undertook to mobilize their staffs to produce results consistent with the new idea of large, nucleated Ujamaa settlements.

At this point the field staff began to circulate the rumor that during any future famine only those in Ujamaa Villages would receive government food. Ujamaa was not voluntary; it was required. All land would be allotted to Ujamaa Villages and there would be no place for those not joining Ujamaa Villages. These threats seemed especially menacing in 1971. The early rains had failed and another serious famine seemed imminent. The Gogo had no food reserves, for the 1970 harvest, coming after the 1969 famine, had been barely adequate. The Gogo were entirely dependent on the national government. In this atmosphere, they decided to become socialists. Some began moving into Ujamaa Village sites on their own; others waited for government trucks to transport their goods. Those who initially refused to move had government "help" in demolishing their homes. At this point Dodoma district became the focus of the nation as President Nyerere chose to make Dodoma district, and especially Chamwino Ujamaa Village, a demonstration of his policy.

Presidential commitment meant mobilization of any resources Nyerere felt necessary. Thus, at Chamwino Ujamaa Village the National Service built a dispensary in two weeks even though there was a dispensary within two miles of the village center. Everyone from secondary school students to members of parliament came to Chamwino to make bricks for modern houses. Tractors cleared the Ujamaa Village plot. Three hundred trucks were called from other regions to move people into Chamwino. When the president was living at Chamwino, there would often be as many as 25 government Land Rovers there. Subsequently, the village was electrified, a convenience not enjoyed by Kondoa Town, a district headquarters. As

Dodoma members of Parliament noted, things can always be financed
if the president so orders. The total amount of aid given to Chamwino
in this early phase is unknown. Neither are there reliable figures for
the total cost of Operation Dodoma.[95] One Tanzanian economist estimated $7 million for Chamwino alone.

The relationship between this enormous resettlement effort and
either socialism or economic development remains uncertain. There
was no attempt to introduce improved agricultural methods or even to
adapt methods to the changed human-resource relationship caused by
population concentration. Tractors merely meant that more land
would be cultivated in the same way. There was also no attempt to
limit stock numbers or to collectivize cattle. In response to prior
rumors about cattle collectivization, some politically aware owners
of large herds had discreetly sold stock on the assumption that no government could collectivize cash. However, most Gogo sought to re-
plenish their herds after the drought. They thus demanded and received assurances from Vice-President Kawawa that stock would remain private property. Stock owners also bargained successfully for
larger plots so they could have adequate room for cattle kraals attached
to their new Ujamaa Village houses. Thus Ujamaa Villages would not
impinge on the basis of economic stratification but would openly legitimate it from the outset.

The same was true for social stratification. At Mvumi Ujamaa
Village, where about 600 families were living in temporary grass
shelters, there was a neat line of brick houses being built up to deceased Chief Mazengo's home and headquarters. The wajamaa of
Mvumi Ujamaa Village were building suitable accommodations for the
deceased chief's close kinsmen.

There was a similar lack of change in the political sphere. If
anything, Operation Dodoma intensified the party-state tendency toward elite initiative at the expense of participatory citizenship. During the initial phase of Operation Dodoma no official had time for questions of the future of these villages, for ensuring that they became
self-reliant nuclei of democratic socialism rather than government
relief operations. It was impossible to find officials who even thought
questions of the composition of the Ujamaa Village Committee, modes
of intra- and intervillage decision-making, channels of communication
from Ujamaa Village to district and regional bodies, especially the
District Development and Planning Committee and the Regional Development Committee, were relevant. When important meetings were held,
one could find Ujamaa Village chairmen and TANU chairmen at their
homes. Only government officials had been invited.

The experience with Ujamaa in Dodoma and Kondoa districts
reveals certain problems of inducing fundamental change in rural Tanzania. The relatively uniform poverty of Dodoma region eliminates

expropriation as a tactic of inducing and financing at least the intial phases of the revolutionary dynamic. Unlike the early phases of the Chinese revolution where redistribution of economic assets within the villages provided the initial predisposition to revolution, the early phases of Ujamaa mobilization could only be financed by government aid. [96]

Such a dependence on government aid brings its own problems and imposes its own limitations. The Tanzanian economy cannot finance many Chamwinos. The attempt to provide aid on that scale will only increase anti-Ujamaa sentiment among the salariat entrusted with mobilizing and managing peasants. In the extreme, the managers could turn on the founder and stop any pretense that peasant proletarianization is a step toward Tanzanian socialism. In such a confrontation it is highly unlikely that the peasantry could save Nyerere. Ujamaa has become linked with proletarianization and productionism rather than with building the reliable socialist constituency that Nyerere still lacks.

Nyerere has not been able to convince Tanzanian peasants that their way of life will change even without socialist transformation and that nonsocialist change would make conditions even worse than they are now in rural Tanzania. Population pressure on land has already exhausted the frontier that each of the local socioeconomic systems relied on for economic survival and social flexibility. Slash-and-burn agriculture requires a continuously expanding resource base. Since no individual can play a full part in community affairs until he is an established household head, access to land is crucial to continued social flexibility. Until recently, there have been marked differences of wealth and status but no permanently landless and thus powerless class. Now, even within the poor but relatively equitable societies of Dodoma region, one sees the beginnings of a class of landless laborers unable to find secure employment in any sector of the economy. Ujamaa could solve the problems of impending rural change by establishing a new relationship between people and resources, thereby ensuring economic survival and continued social flexibility. The failure of Nyerere's African socialism would create the preconditions for European socialism. It would be unduly romantic to see this as a positive opportunity to build socialism in Tanzania. European history has shown that the preconditions for class conflict do not produce socialism. African managerial elites, both civilian and military, have shown little tendency to let citizens threaten their privileged positions. If Tanzania is to become a socialist state, it will do so through Ujamaa. The experience with Operation Dodoma suggests that the socialist content of rural change is being sacrificed to productionist imperatives that are economically unrealistic. A productionist Ujamaa that sacrifices citizen participation to elite management will merely be a state capitalism that uses the rhetoric of "modernization" and "development" to legitimate elite consumption of the fruits of peasant labor.

NOTES

1. Julius K. Nyerere, "The African and Democracy," in Nyerere, Freedom and Unity (Uhuru na Umoja) (Dar es Salaam: Oxford University Press, 1967), p. 103.

2. Julius K. Nyerere, "Ujamaa—the Basis of African Socialism," ibid., p. 170.

3. Julius K. Nyerere, "Introduction," in Freedom and Socialism (Uhuru na Ujamaa) (Dar es Salaam: Oxford University Press, 1968), p. 77.

4. Julius K. Nyerere, "The Varied Paths to Socialism," in Ujamaa: Essays on Socialism (London: Oxford University Press, 1968), p. 77.

5. Julius K. Nyerere, "The Purpose Is Man," ibid., pp. 93-94.

6. Julius K. Nyerere, "After the Arusha Declaration," ibid., p. 171.

7. Julius K. Nyerere, "Ujamaa—the Basis of African Socialism," in Freedom and Unity, op. cit., p. 166.

8. Julius K. Nyerere, "After the Arusha Declaration," in Ujamaa: Essays on Socialism, op. cit., p. 163.

9. Ibid., p. 162.

10. Julius K. Nyerere, "Education for Self-Reliance," ibid., p. 65.

11. Julius K. Nyerere, "Socialism and Rural Development," ibid., p. 119.

12. Julius K. Nyerere, "Ujamaa—the Basis of African Socialism," in Freedom and Unity, op. cit., p. 165.

13. Ibid.

14. Julius K. Nyerere, "The Arusha Declaration," in Ujamaa: Essays on Socialism, op. cit., p. 18.

15. Julius K. Nyerere, "The Tanzanian Economy," in Freedom and Socialism, op. cit., p. 167.

16. Julius K. Nyerere, "Education for Self-Reliance," in Ujamaa: Essays on Socialism, op. cit., pp. 44-75.

17. Julius K. Nyerere, "Progress in the Rural Areas," ibid., pp. 178-79.

18. Ibid., p. 183.

19. Ibid., pp. 183-84.

20. Ibid., p. 179.

21. Eduard Bernstein, Evolutionary Socialism (New York: Schocken Books, 1961). For a study of Bernstein that distinguishes

revionist socialism from Marxism, see Peter Gay, The Dilemma of Democratic Socialism: Eduard Bernstein's Challenge to Marx (New York: Columbia University Press, 1952).

22. Karl Marx and Frederick Engels, The German Ideology, edited by C. J. Arthur (New York: International Publishers, 1970).

23. V. I. Lenin, What Is To Be Done? (New York: International Publishers, 1932), and Organizational Principles of a Proletarian Party (Moscow: Novasti, 1972).

24. Shlomo Avineri, Karl Marx on Colonialism and Modernization (Garden City, N.Y.: Doubleday Anchor Books, 1969).

25. See especially Marx's 1881 letter to Vera Zasulich, presented and discussed in E. J. Hobsbawn, ed., Pre-Capitalist Economic Formations (New York: International Publishers, 1964).

26. Julius K. Nyerere, Freedom and Socialism, op. cit., pp. 33-34.

27. United Republic of Tanzania, The Economic Survey, 1971/72 (Dar es Salaam: Government Printer, 1972), p. 6.

28. United Republic of Tanzania, The Second Five-Year Plan for Economic and Social Development, 1969-1974, vol. 1, "General Analysis" (Dar es Salaam: Government Printer, 1969), p. 202.

29. United Republic of Tanzania, The Economic Survey, 1971/72, op. cit., p. 6.

30. Ibid.

31. Ibid.

32. Ibid., p. 19.

33. Ibid.

34. United Republic of Tanzania, The Second Five-Year Plan for Economic and Social Development, vol. 1, "General Analysis," op. cit., pp. 42-50.

35. United Republic of Tanzania, The Economic Survey, 1971/72, op. cit., p. 21.

36. Julius K. Nyerere, "Speech by the President to the TANU Conference—28th May, 1969," in United Republic of Tanzania, The Second-Five Year Plan for Economic and Social Development, 1969-1974, vol. 1, "General Analysis," op. cit., p. vxi.

37. Colonial authorities were reluctant to reveal any information on taxation, but scattered evidence forms a convincing pattern. See especially, Great Britain, Colonial Office, Annual Report on the Administration of Tanganyika for 1927, Appendix I, Charles Dundas, Secretary for Native Affairs, "The Effects of the Policy of Indirect Rule Introduced into Tanganyika Territory in 1925," Tanzania National Archives File No. 19176, "Statistics Regarding Direct Taxation of Natives and Expenditure Thereof." The Member for Local Government, The Secretariat, Dar es Salaam, to all Provincial Commission-

ers, May 18, 1950, "Division of Native Tax Between the Central Government and Native Authorities," in Tanzania National Archives File No. 46/C.5/38, "District Commissioners' Meetings."

38. Andre Gunder Frank, Capitalism and Underdevelopment in Latin America: Historical Studies of Chile and Brazil (New York: Monthly Review Press, 1967).

39. Interviews in Kondoa and Dodoma districts 1970/71. People in these areas consistently identified themselves as less well-off than people in Kilimanjaro and Mwanza.

40. The only source of comprehensive local data is United Republic of Tanzania, Ministry of Economic Affairs and Development Planning, District Data, 1967.

41. United Republic of Tanzania, The Second Five-Year Plan for Economic and Social Development, 1969-1974, vol. 3, "Regional Perspectives" (Dar es Salaam: Government Printer, 1970).

42. Julius K. Nyerere, "The Arusha Declaration," in Ujamaa: Essays on Socialism, p. 28.

43. United Republic of Tanzania, The Annual Plan for 1971/1972 (Dar es Salaam: Government Printer, 1971), p. 3.

44. Ibid., p. 51.

45. Ibid.

46. Ibid.

47. The Standard (Dar es Salaam), November 16, November 18, and December 16, 1970. The Standard, now the Daily News, is a government newspaper, but letters to the editor printed during the ensuing three months were generally unfavorable. The government argued that the unemployed were not making their fair contribution to national development and should return to Ujamaa Villages in their home areas where their labor would be an economic asset, The Standard, November 18, 1970.

48. United Republic of Tanzania, The Annual Plan for 1971/1972, op. cit., pp. 55-56.

49. Ibid., p. 1.

50. Ibid.

51. Ibid., pp. 1-2.

52. Ibid., p. 2.

53. Ibid., p. 21.

54. Ibid., p. 12.

55. Ibid., p. 55.

56. Ibid., p. 71.

57. United Republic of Tanzania, The Second Five-Year Plan for Economic and Social Development, 1969-1974, vol. 1, "General Analysis," op. cit., p. 179.

58. Milovan Djilas, The New Class (New York: Praeger Publishers, 1957).

59. Julius K. Nyerere, "Africanization of the Civil Service," in Freedom and Unity, op. cit., pp. 99-102, and "Tanganyika Citizenship," ibid., pp. 258-60.

60. For a profile of the first generation of Tanzanian national-level civil servants, see Raymond Hopkins, Political Roles in a New State (New Haven, Conn.: Yale University Press, 1971).

61. Julius K. Nyerere, "Socialism Is Not Racialism," in Ujamaa: Essays on Socialism, op. cit., pp. 38-43.

62. John S. Saul, "African Socialism in One Country: Tanzania," in Giovanni Arrighi and John S. Saul, Essays on the Political Economy of Africa (New York: Monthly Review Press, 1973), pp. 237-335.

63. William Tordoff, Government and Politics in Tanzania (Nairobi: East African Publishing House, 1967).

64. There are surprisingly few studies of Tanzanian local politics in any era. One of the best descriptions of a local area is Gene Andrew Maguire, Toward Uhuru in Tanzania (London: Cambridge University Press, 1969). See also Goren Hyden, Political Development in Rural Tanzania (Lund: Scandinavian University Books, 1968). Tanzania's political multilocalism is especially apparent during national elections since local factors are the primary determinant of the voting decision. See Frances Hill, "The Electoral Moment in the Local Political Context," in The Tanzanian General Election of 1970 (Dar es Salaam: Tanzania Publishing House, 1974).

65. Henry Bienen, Tanzania: Party Transformation and Economic Development (Princeton, N.J.: Princeton University Press, 1967), provides a general overview of the party and its problems.

66. Julius K. Nyerere, "Resignation as Prime Minister," in Freedom and Unity, op. cit., pp. 157-58.

67. Julius K. Nyerere, "Ujamaa—the Basis of African Socialism," in Freedom and Unity, op. cit., pp. 162-71.

68. Julius K. Nyerere, "Guide to the One-Party State Commission," in Freedom and Unity, op. cit., pp. 261-65.

69. Julius K. Nyerere, "Democracy and the Party System," in Freedom and Unity, op. cit., pp. 195-203.

70. Alexis de Tocqueville, The Old Regime and the French Revolution (Garden City, N.Y.: Doubleday, 1955).

71. Julius K. Nyerere, "Economic Nationalism," in Freedom and Socialism, op. cit., p. 264.

72. A complete list of nationalized enterprises is available in Julius K. Nyerere, "Public Ownership in Tanzania," in Freedom and Socialism, op. cit., pp. 251-56.

73. Ibid., p. 254.

74. United Republic of Tanzania, The Annual Plan for 1971/1972, op. cit., pp. 16-17; and "The Guidelines to the Plan," The Standard, March 15, 1971.

75. Julius K. Nyerere, "The Arusha Declaration," in Ujamaa: Essays on Socialism, op. cit., pp. 17 and 36.

76. Mwongozo Was TANU (Dar es Salaam: Mpigachapa Mkuu wa Serikali, 1973). An English version was printed in The Standard of February 22, 1971.

77. Tanganyika, Development Plan for Tanganyika, 1961-1964 (Dar es Salaam: Government Printer, 1964). The main proponent of this approach outside of government is Rene Dumont, who urged this approach in his report prepared for the Tanzanian government under the title Tanzanian Agriculture after the Arusha Declaration (Dar es Salaam: Ministry of Economic Affairs and Development Planning, 1969).

78. Government of Tanganyika, Tanganyika Five-Year Plan for Economic and Social Development, 1964-1969 (Dar es Salaam: Government Printer, 1964).

79. United Republic of Tanzania, The Economic Survey, 1971/ 1972, op. cit., p. 31.

80. E. P. Thompson, The Making of the English Working Class (Harmondsworth: Penguin Books, 1968).

81. Karl Deutsch, "Social Mobilization and Political Development," American Political Science Review 15 (September 1961): 492-514, is typical of the "modernization" literature that suggests that the citizens of the new states are incapable of using their current forms of social-cultural organization to deal with the "modern" world.

82. A. V. Chayanov, The Theory of Peasant Economy (Homewood, Ill.: Richard D. Irwin, 1966) is the pioneering study of peasant economic calculations in terms of household needs and priorities. Chayanov, his analytical approach, and his agricultural policies were all casualties of the Soviet approach to agricultural policy after 1917.

83. Based on data from United Republic of Tanzania, The Economic Survey 1970/1971, p. 54, and District Data, 1967.

84. United Republic of Tanzania, The Annual Plan for 1971/1972, op. cit., p. 58.

85. For a discussion of the operation of this project see Ralph Ibbott, "Ruvuma Development Association," Mbioni 3, no. 11 (July 1966): 3-43. Analysis of impact of Nyerere's decision to disband the RDA is based on personal interviews with Tanzanian officials 1970-71.

86. Based on data from United Republic of Tanzania, District Data, 1967.

87. All data on Kondoa and Dodoma districts based on field research during 1970 and 1971. For a fuller treatment of these themes see Frances Hill, "Mobilization and Participation in Tanzania," unpublished Ph.D. thesis, Harvard University, 1973.

88. This fit the national policy guidelines of June 1970 proclaimed by the Dodoma regional commissioner when introducing the President's Economic Planning Teams.

89. Figure based on allocations in District Development and Planning Committee, Kondoa district, February 26, 1970, in Kondoa district Council File No. C.40/7.

90. Peter Rigby, Cattle and Kinship among the Wagogo (Syracuse, N.Y.: Syracuse University Press, 1969).

91. C. Brooke, "The Heritage of Famine in Central Tanzania," Tanzania Notes and Records, no. 67 (1967): 18-25. H. A. Fosbrooke, "A Note on the Dating of Age Sets and Famines in 'Historia, Mila na Desturia za Wagogo wa Tanzania,' by Mathias E. Mnyampala," in Tanzania National Archives File No. 435/A2/24, "Gogo History, Land Tenure and Cattle Tenure."

92. Figure from a special report prepared by the regional development officer, Dodoma region, for the purpose of briefing President Nyerere during his tour of Dodoma, February 19, 1970 ("Taarifa ya Maendeleo ya Mkoa wa Dodoma kwa Ajilia ya Mazungumzo na Mh. Baba wa Taifa") in Dodoma region, Development Department File No. CD/RE/DO/1.

93. "Speech of Area Commissioner for the People of Dodoma District for the Purpose of Increasing Agricultural Effort in 1969-1970," at the October 30, 1969 meeting of the District Development Committee in Dodoma district Council File No. C.40/7, vol. 1, "District Development and Planning Committee."

94. Dodoma Regional Development Committee meeting of May 16, 1969.

95. United Republic of Tanzania, The Annual Plan for 1971/1972, op. cit., p. 57, and The Economic Survey, 1971/1972, op. cit., pp. 62-64.

96. William Hinton, Fanshen (New York: Monthly Review Press, 1966).

10

SOCIALISM IN
SRI LANKA
A. Jeyaratnam Wilson

HISTORICAL BACKGROUND

The origins of the Sinhalese, the majority ethnic group of Sri Lanka (Ceylon), date back to about the sixth or fifth century before Christ and the coming of Buddhism around 247-207 B.C. Tamil invaders from across the south Indian mainland marauded the island, at intervals, from around the first century B.C. until the arrival of the Portuguese in 1505. In time a separate Tamil kingdom of Jaffna in north Sri Lanka came to be established in 1325 and remained an independent entity, except for a 17-year pause (1450 to 1467) when it was subjugated by a Sinhalese prince, until its conquest by the Portuguese in1618. The record of wars is a potent cause of contemporary friction between the two ethnic groups.

Western interest in the island began in 1505 with the arrival of the Portuguese. They occupied a fair stretch of the western seaboard and their rule lasted till 1638 when the Dutch replaced them. The Portuguese left behind their Roman Catholicism, their mixed descendants called Portuguese Burhers, some of them to this day speaking a pidgin Portuguese language, and an educational system made up of churches, churches, convents, and schools.

The Dutch were ousted in 1796 by the British. Their legacy was the system of Roman-Dutch law (still in operation), schools, some converts to Dutch Protestantism, and a mixed Dutch-Sinhalese community referred to as the Burghers.

The author wishes to acknowledge the helpful comments and criticisms of Professor Dennis Austin, Dr. Valerie Plave Bennett, and Dr. C. A. Woodward.

Britain was the first conquering power to bring the whole island under a single administration, a task accomplished with the annexation of the interior kingdom of Kandy in 1815. The island thereafter, with the exception of two major rebellions, that of 1817-18 and 1848, went through gradual and peaceful stages of constitutional development. The Colebrooke-Cameron reforms of 1833 introduced nominated legislative and executive councils, which were progressively expanded, democratized, and Ceylonized in 1909-11 (McCallum reforms), 1921, 1924 (Manning reforms), 1931 (Donoughmore reforms), and 1947 (Soulbury reforms). In 1948 Ceylon obtained independence by an act of the British parliament.

British rule brought the English language, British justice especially the rule of law and trial by jury, a measure of economic progress, and a demand for parliamentary institutions. In the last quarter of the nineteenth century both indigenous and Western-style nationalist trends became manifest culminating in the formation of the Ceylon National Congress in 1919, more a middle-class, English-speaking, elitist organization.

The Congress ceased to be national for long. Differences arose between its Western-oriented Sinhalese and Ceylon Tamil leadership, and thereafter it became a political machine of the Low Country Sinhalese landed, commercial, and professional interests. Subsequently there proliferated a number of ethnocentric political societies. The Muslims formed themselves into a Malay Association in 1922, a Ceylon Muslim League in 1924, and a Ceylon Moors' Association in 1935. The Burghers launched their Political Association in 1938. Interethnic rivalries came into sharper focus when the Sinhala Maha Subha (the Great Council of the Sinhalese) under S. W. R. D. Bandaranaike (later to become Prime Minister, 1956-59) came into being in 1937, followed by the Ceylon Indian Congress in 1939 and the All Ceylon Tamil Congress in 1944. The last mentioned persisted in an unsuccessful agitation for "balanced representation" in the legislature (that is for 50 percent of the seats to be reserved for all the minority communities) at the time that power was being transferred by Britain to Ceylon.

The 1930s witnessed a more significant development, the beginning of a Marxist movement, which was to later split into Trotskyists and Moscow Communists. Partly it was because Britain sensed the possibility of these Marxists leading a strong anticolonial protest nationalism that the decision was made to transfer power to the premier conservative Sinhalese statesman of this time, Don Stephen Senanayake.[1]

THE PLURAL SOCIETY

Ethnic divisions, social barriers, and religious rivalries based on primordial sentiments of race, language, religion, and caste characterize Ceylonese society. The Sinhalese form the majority comprising 71.9 percent of the population (9,146,679). They form two groups, those of the Low Country, 5,445,706 (42.8 percent of the island's population), somewhat different from their tradition-bound conservative highland counterparts, the Kandyan Sinhalese (3,700,973, 29.1 percent of the island's population). The latter were less exposed to Western influences. The largest ethnic minority is the Tamils, Ceylon, and Indian. The indigenous Ceylon Tamils constituting 11.1 percent of the population (1,415,567) are very middle-class-oriented and in competition with the Sinhalese in the professions and in the public and private sectors. The Indian Tamils[2] (1,195,368 or 9.4 percent of the population), who until recently were stateless, are mostly indentured labor brought by the British from south India to work their tea and rubber plantations. The Muslims comprise Ceylon Moors (824,291 or 6.4 percent), Malays (41,615 or 0.3 percent), and Indian Moors (29,416 or 0.2 percent). The tiny Burgher minority number 44,250 (0.3 percent).

Religionwise, the majority of Low Country and Kandyan Sinhalese are Buddhists (8,567,570 or 67.4 percent) and the Ceylon and Indian Tamils are mainly Hindu (2,239,310 or 17.6 percent). The Muslims (909,941) are 7.1 percent of the total, while the Christians subdivided into Roman Catholics and Protestants (Sinhalese, Tamil, and Burgher) constitute 7.7 percent of the population.

The stratifications of caste among the Sinhalese and Tamils have still to be completely eroded.[3] Though occupation is no longer ordained in terms of caste, marriage tends to be endogamous, there rarely being cross-unions. However, education, employment opportunities, and urbanization have promoted social mobility.

A majority of Sinhalese are goigamas (farmers) while the karavas (fishermen), salagamas (cinnamon peelers), duravas (toddy tappers) in that order count for much among the Low Country Sinhalese. The navandannas or achariyas (artisans and smiths of all types) come immediately after. Further down are various underprivileged low caste groups. Caste follows similar patterns among the Kandyan Sinhalese except that the radalas (goigama feudal landlords) among them wield considerable influence. There are huge underprivileged caste concentrations in some Kandyan Sinhalese areas.

Among the Ceylon Tamils, there are the "clean" castes—the brahmins (a priestly minority), the majority vellalas (farmers), the karaiyars and mukkuvars (fisher folk), and the koviyars (cooks and domestics to the vellalas) in that order. There are then various craftsmen such as the thattar (goldsmiths), nadduvar (musicians), and vannar (laundrymen). There is finally a category of "unclean" castes.

POPULATION AND INCOME DISTRIBUTION

The population in 1972 (after the latest census) stood at approximately 12.8 million.[4] The rate of increase is still high. It was 2.8 in 1953, 2.4 in 1968, and 2.3 in 1971. State-sponsored population planning programs have still to yield tangible results.

Eighty percent of the population lives in the rural areas and 60 percent of the total is concentrated in the southwest quadrant of the island with population densities of over 1,000 per square mile along the coastal strip. Put in a different way 75 percent of the people live and earn their livelihood within a radius of 80 miles of the capital city, Colombo. This can be a problem for governments having to impose unpopular economic or other measures. Its opponents can mobilize maximum pressure against it within a short locus.

In 1963 (the last published figures) 51.8 percent of the population was engaged in agriculture, the wholesale and retail trade employed 7.9 percent, industries and crafts, 7.3 percent, transport and communications, 4.6 percent, and government services, 2.3 percent. Employment in the public sector is the highest aspiration of most Ceylonese giving rise to sharp and bitter competition between the island's ethnic, religious, and sometimes caste groups.

Agewise there is a marked imbalance. Fifty-two percent of the population is under 19 years and 40 percent under 14. This implies greater dependence of the young on the old and additional strains on the nation's already stretched welfare system.

Unemployment and underemployment has reached uncontrollable proportions. The work force is expected to be about 7 million in 1981. Already between 17 to 18 percent of the existing work force are unemployed including large numbers of graduates and youths with senior school certificates.

The income distribution indicates disparities and poverty levels. For example, 84.14 percent receive salaries of between Rs 125 and Rs 200 a month (Rs 6 = approximately U.S. $1), and as many as 45.9 percent of the workers obtain between Rs 25 and Rs 75 a month. The gap between urban and rural incomes is wide, those in the former category earning more than double those in the latter (1963 figures). A Central Bank survey in April 1972 showed that over 9 million of the 12.8 million Ceylonese receive no income, and of the 3.5 million who have incomes, about half receive monthly incomes ranging from Rs

100 to Rs 400, while the other half obtains less than Rs 100. There
were only 175,000 in the population who earned over Rs 400 a month.

THE WELFARE STATE

These income differences could give rise to an explosive situation but for the maintenance—beyond the country's means, of course—
of a liberal welfare system. It worked reasonably well when the population was at an optimum level and the island's export produce fetched
competitive prices in markets abroad. With population almost doubling
itself between 1946 (6.7 million) and 1972 (12.8 million) and prices of
exports fluctuating, the island's successive governments have barely
been able to sustain the extravagant welfare system brought into being
in an earlier age of relative prosperity.

The social services are on a par with, and sometimes more
liberal than, those in Britain or the Scandinavian countries. All education from kindergarten through the university is free; health services are virtually free, housing is subsidized, the state-owned rail
and omnibus transport system provide some of the cheapest services
in the world; generous assistance is given to persons wishing to settle
in state-sponsored agricultural schemes, and a free grant of two
pounds of rice per week is made to each and every adult member of
the population. These services take 35-38 percent of total government expenditure per year, leaving hardly any savings for capital development.

THE ECONOMY

The island is an underdeveloped export-import economy with
tea, rubber, and coconut (in that order)—and in recent times gems,
precious stones, and tourism—planing the dominant role of foreign
exchange earner and the country's principal single source of income.
They account for over 90 percent of total exports and nearly one-third
of the national income, and sustain a number of other economic activities as well.

A good part (about 45 percent) of the tea business is owned by
British companies, and 13 percent by companies locally registered,
where ownership is divided between Ceylonese and non-Ceylonese.
About 33 percent of the rubber business is in the control of British
capital. Most of tea and rubber is in large estates of a hundred acres
or more, while coconut is a smallholders' crop and is almost entirely
in Ceylonese ownership. The management and supervision of the large
tea, rubber, and occasionally coconut estates are vested in agency

houses that are mainly British-owned. Furthermore, an important
segment of the commercial banking system is also under British control.

Prices of agricultural exports are dependent on the vagaries of
the foreign market. Tea alone accounts for some 63 percent of total
exports and provides 65 percent of foreign exchange earnings, the
main buyers being Britain, the United States, Australia, New Zealand,
and South Africa, with the Middle East countries concentrating on the
purchase of low- and medium-grown teas. But tea prices have been
fluctuating in the last two decades and prices of rubber (exported
mainly to China and the United States) and coconut will fall because
of competition from substitutes. The result is a serious and continuing balance-of-payments crisis. To worsen matters, British investors are withdrawing their capital from tea, owing to the uncertain political climate and the frequent threats of nationalization.

The largest cultivated area is, however, paddy land (1,313,239
acres in 1966) and it is here that the pressure of population is felt
most. Population per acre of agricultural land rose from 1.56 in
1946 to 2.24 in 1962. About 64 percent of holdings are below one acre
each and about 31 percent below half an acre each. All in all about 85
percent of paddy land is below two acres each. Only about 60 percent
of this land is owner-cultivated, with 25 to 30 percent cultivated by
tenants. Consequently heavy rural indebtedness, fragmentation of
existing landholdings, and low levels of production characterize the
paddy economy.

THE POLITICAL SETTING

In comparison to all other South and Southeast Asian countries,
Sri Lanka is more of a nation-state than a geographical expression of
an artificial administrative entity. Despite the absence of consensus
among the island's rival ethnic and religious groupings, there is still
a basic loyalty to the concept of a Ceylonese nation, evidenced particularly by the willingness of dissenting minority communities to have
their differences settled within the national framework.

The island's literacy rate (85 percent) ranks highest in Asia
next to Japan. It is also next to that country the most experienced
in the exercise of universal franchise. There have been nine general
elections held since universal suffrage was introduced in 1931. On
five occasions the electors turned out governments, the transfer being effected in a peaceful and orderly manner. Only in a single instance (the general election of March 1960) was the outcome inconclu-
sive. On every other occasion the electors returned to parliament a
party or a readily identifiable coalition with a clear mandate. In the

span of some 25 years only two major political parties, the United
National Party (UNP) and the Sri Lanka Freedom Party (SLFP) have
dominated the political scene.

On balance, there is evidence of a transit to modernity on the
part of the island's polity. The diverse roles suggestive of modernization are clearly manifest.[5] The island has the strong framework of
an efficient administrative service; it has agitators, transmitters, and
ideological propagandists from Marxist and socialist populist parties,
and amalgamates in the form of political leaders like the prime ministers Don Stephen Senanayake (1947-52), Dudley Senanayake (1952-53,
March 1960—July 1960, 1965-70), Solomon West Ridgeway Dias Bandaranaike (1956-59), and Sirima Ratwatte Bandaranaike (1960-66,
1970-), and the usual quota of political brokers trying to forge united
fronts both of the left and the right.[6]

The variables relative to political change are also prevalent.[7]
This is evident in the degree of structural differentiation of institutions
performing political functions, the high ratio of political activity vis-
a-vis all other activities, achievement orientation in terms of political recruitment and role differentiation, and in the reasonable degree
of secularization that persists in the performance of numerous (but
not all) political functions.

Modernization is not unilinear, however. There are other
forces operating that encourage obscurantist political ideologies and
narrow ethnocentrism. They have not succeeded so far in overwhelming the political system, but they have nevertheless had their impact.
Opportunities to political parties whose appeal is to narrow nationalism are provided by the system of electoral demarcation, which gives
undue weight to the rural areas where a majority of the conservative
and tradition-bound citizenry lives, and by the Sinhalese Buddhist
sense of grievance regarding the centuries of neglect of their language,
culture, and religion.

The 52.3 percent of the population engaged in agriculture hardly
provides, at the higher levels, recruitment opportunities for political
parties in search of personnel.[8] At the middle and lower levels some
farmers are involved in local government and constituency politics.
But even here the big and small shopkeepers and traders, the local
legal profession, Buddhist monks, native physicians, swabasha (which
means "one's own language") schoolteachers, and trade union workers
form the component of local bodies and the constituency organizations
of the political parties; while at the higher levels, political leadership comes from a relatively small category of professional people—
mostly lawyers, retired public servants, a few physicians, industrialists, and businessmen. Finally there is a miniscule group of full-
time professional politicians who generally form the top layer of leadership in all parties, drawn mostly from the affluent class.

The unfulfilled rising expectations of voters in an underdeveloped and impoverished economy, added to the incremental radicalization of the electorate by the left-wing movement that began in the 1930s, has made of socialism a sine qua non for political parties vying for parliamentary power.[9]

Socialism therefore covers a wide ideological spectrum. At one end are the Marxist parties—the Trotskyist Lanka Sama Samaja Party (LSSP, the Ceylon Equal Society Party) and the pro-Soviet Communist Party (CP). In the middle is the Sri Lanka Freedom Party (SLFP) with its declared objectives of a socialist democracy. Right of middle is the United National Party (UNP), claiming to be democratic socialist but really practicing a kind of benevolent paternalism that aims at containing social discontent.

The Tamils have their own political organizations, all of them protesting adherence to socialism or socialist objectives, but in reality (with one exception) committed to a rightist position. The leading organizations of the Ceylon Tamils, the Tamil Federal Party (FP), and the All Ceylon Tamil Congress (TC), are middle-class-oriented, drawing their support mainly from the high caste vellalas (farmers), most of whom disapprove of the Marxists because of their stand on behalf of the underprivileged castes. Both parties also oppose nationalization measures on the ground that these are devices for providing greater employment opportunities for the Sinhalese. The leading Indian Tamil trade union-based party, the Ceylon Workers' Congress (CWC), is contolled by a right-wing politician. Its rival, the Democratic Workers' Congress (DWC) is led by a sympathizer of the CP. It must, however, be noted that the Left as well as the UNP and SLFP have some support among the Ceylon and Indian Tamils.

Outside the system, and refusing to accept its framework, are the revolutionary Marxist parties—the Maoist CP, the LSSP (Revolutionary), the Revolutionary Workers' Party (RWP), all of which count for little, and the influential Janatha Vimukthi Peramuna (JVP, People's Liberation Front). Wavering between revolution and parliamentarism is the Mahjana Eksath Peramuna (MEP, People's United Front) founded by the late Philip Gunawardene.[10]

The low levels of income, the landlessness as well as fragmentation of land, heavy rural indebtedness, underemployment and unemployment referred to earlier—adequate in themselves to engender a revolutionary situation—have their effects on the political process. Governments must intervene in view of the wide disparities in income, the concentration of property in few hands, and the control of the commanding heights of the economy by British capital. Social discontent in such a situation is kept at a safe minimum by a scheme of redistributive justice operating through a graded system of heavy taxation and the reckless welfare system that operates across the board without taking into account the needs of particular individuals or groups in the low income levels.

Since the welfare system is precariously balanced upon a shifting base of fluctuating export income, a drop in prices produces an instability characterized by hartals (a general stoppage of work, which in the Ceylonese situation is sometimes accompanied by violence), massive strikes, deterioration in interethnic relations, and the defeat of governments at general elections. Successive governments have been obliged to fall back on the international credit agencies (IMF and IBRD) or foreign governments and foreign banks for credit accommodation. Few loans are granted for welfare purposes. In fact, in most instances the precondition is that loans must be directed toward economic development. The debt service and repayments are a heavy drain on the country's exchequer.

The conservative UNP relied on deference to social privilege and the industry of vote-brokers operating within a closely linked social hierarchy to bring it electoral support. The SLFP, on the other hand, aims at a different clientele that is underprivileged or at any rate feels neglected and/or inferior. This clientele includes the swabasha schoolteachers, Sinhalese native physicians, Sinhalese petty shopkeepers and traders, Buddhist monks, Sinhalese dancers, musicians, and craftsmen, as well as large sections of educated and undereducated youths.

Caste is a pertinent consideration. The UNP has always veered in the direction of the dominant goigama (farmer) caste, drawing its leadership and leadership potential from the wellsprings of the urban and rural middle- and upper-level strata of a group that is in a majority situation and that claims for itself the topmost position in Sinhalese society.[11] It has had the support of Buddhist clerical feudalistic elements and their retinue among the goigama and the monkish siam nikaya (Siamese sect). The UNP no doubt has its strengths among the other caste groups, but its patronizing attitude toward them and its focus on their upper layers has tended to alienate the rank and file who live in stratified isolation despite attempts on their part to become socially mobile. All UNP cabinets have had representatives from the non-goigama castes—especially from the karavas (fishermen) and salagamas (cinnamon peelers) as well as on occasion from other groups further down.[12] But an examination of their economic and educational backgrounds proves what we stressed earlier—they are professionals who have had their education in elitist institutions.

By contrast, the SLFP tends to be more flexible in its efforts at leadership recruitment.[13] A thin layer at the top comes from among the privileged goigama, but the remainder of its goigama component is from the middle or lower-middle levels. And the same could be said of its non-goigama component—its karavas and salagamas. It tends also to pay greater attention to castes beyond the pale. The present SLFP-led UF government illustrates the point that it is a cabinet of many caste talents while its electoral nominees have a liberal distribution of lower caste elements. The drift to socialism is doubtless accelerated by the mounting expectations of lower-caste groups who have in the SLFP leadership a sympathetic patron.

The traditional left (LSSP and CP) leadership follows nonetheless the general tendency of establishment politics—it is affluent and elitist. And although not as goigama-centered as the other two groupings, both the LSSP and CP have always taken care that their leaders should be from the goigamas. This is an obvious concession to the electorate's predilections, as there are other leaders in the LSSP who could just as well fill key positions.

Egalitarian goals have in fact a powerful appeal to the non-goigama castes. This partly explains the support the JVP received from the frustrated youths of the depressed bathgama and wahumpura castes in the south central districts and from the karavas and duravas in the southern parts of the island during the April 1971 insurrection. [14]

LEADERSHIP STRATEGIES

Political thinking and activity tend to converge toward the center. This arises partly from the Sinhalese Buddhist ethos of tolerance and its willingness to accommodate and seek what are called middle-path solutions. However, it should be noted that this Sinhalese Buddhist ethos has been infused with the ideas of British liberalism and parliamentarism—ideas that gained currency among the intelligentsia and elites as a result of their secondary and university education. The process of indoctrination also applies to those educated in the national languages, Sinhalese and Tamil, for national texts are inevitably translations of standard English works, and teachers are invariably transmitters of knowledge obtained from Western sources.

The cumulative effect of the Sinhalese Buddhist ethic and British traditions is to produce a setting unusually conducive to the functioning of a local variant of the Westminster model. This version of parliamentarism has recruited to itself parties and politicians of not merely the Right and the Center but also of the traditional Left. The latter, however, see parliament more as an instrument for the implementation of socialism than as a mechanism for obtaining consensus. Nevertheless, the Left professes to want a Westminster-type parliament operated by a "workers' and peasants' government," and not a government based on the Soviet model.

Political leadership in the established parties has to cope, as Eldersveld remarked, with "widely varying local milieus of opinion,

tradition and social structure" and in the process they have been obliged to diversify the sources from which they recruit their members.[15]
The effect has been to broaden their bases through the creation of new
elites. However, of all three groupings—the UNP, the SLFP, and the
traditional Left—it is the SLFP that has provided the greatest opportunities for lower-income groups, classes, and castes to find their way
into Parliament.[16] Whereas the LSSP and CP parliamentary leadership still remains vested largely in professional Western-educated
elitist personnel (with the occasional odd exception), and whereas the
UNP puts up poor candidates mostly for exhibition, or brings to the
fore a few "men of the people" simply as its front-line leaders, the
SLFP has endeavored to encourage leaders from among the economically and socially depressed classes. The present leader of the UNP
tangentially confirmed this view in a memorandum he circulated to
its working committee in February 1971 (when he was its deputy leader) in which he stated that his party was considered by the majority
of voters "to represent the "haves," the affluent and the employer,"
while its opponents are accepted as the spokesmen of "the have-nots,
the needy and the employed."[17]

The UNP and SLFP illustrate in a qualified form Taketsugu
Tsurutani's typology of stable conservative and attenuated modernizing leaderships.[18] Elements of the one are certainly to be found in
the other, but there does appear a line of demarcation to validate
this classification. Tsurutani argues that in the former case, society
is well governed and enjoys general peace and order. However, the
pace of progress may be slow though the economy may be prosperous:
increases in national wealth are not likely to be distributed outside
the normal channels, thus continually favoring "the politically powerful and socially entrenched." This is more or less what happened
during the first phase of UNP rule from 1947 to 1956 and was continued
in a modified form during its second phase, 1965-70.

On the other hand, the SLFP with its LSSP and CP allies fits
into Tsurutani's category of "attenuating modernizing leadership."
During the first two phases of SLFP or SLFP-oriented rule (1956-59
and 1960-65), and in the present phase of SLFP-LSSP-CP rule (1970-),
powerful opposition from opposing national and subnational elites undermined (and continues to undermine) developmental programs and
policies. In such a situation "the level of stability shifts and sometimes even sinks below the safe minimum," but "progress in the direction of modernization takes place," although "usually at slow, uneven, diluted paces." This in fact has been Sri Lanka's experience
during the three phases of SLFP-led rule.

It was an accident of circumstance that resulted in the socialist
movement drawing its leaders from among the Western educated and
the affluent. It is reasonable to argue that Social Democrats such as

S. W. R. D. Bandaranaike and Sirima Bandaranaike, Trotskyists like
N. M. Perera, Colvin R. de Silva, Leslie Goonewardene, and Bernard Soysa, and Communists like S. A. Wickremasinghe and Pieter
Keuneman, given their social, economic, and educational backgrounds,
might have found themselves part of a broad middle formation that
could very well have been the UNP had it been willing to shift a little
to the left of center. In fact Dudley Senanayake, the late charismatic
leader of the UNP, attempted this exercise during his term as Prime
Minister, 1965-70. Furthermore, he had intended to include some of
the Trotskyist leaders in a government had he been successful in the
general election of May 1970.[19] Entrenched right-wing elements in
his party, however, thwarted his attempts in this direction. S. W. R.
D. Banaranaike would have pursued similar objectives had he remained
in the UNP and become its leader on the demise of D. S. Senanayake.
Indeed he would, however, have probably taken the UNP in a more leftward direction than Dudley Senanayake had intended. Sirima Bandaranaike is just as conservative, if not more conservative, than either
her late husband or Dudley Senanayake. However, the will to power
and to be free of political embarrassment makes her tread a more
leftward path.[20]

The Trotskyist LSSP had high hopes for office in 1956 when
S. W. R. D. Bandaranaiki's MEP rode to power at the April general
election. The vain belief was that they could push the MEP in a leftward direction—a well-nigh impossible task because of the strongly
entrenched right wing within it. Bandaranaike gained sufficient
strength not to have to depend on the LSSP and CP, but within his centrist formation was another version of Trotskyism, the VLSSP of
Philip Gunawardene. Gunawardene obtained the key portfolio of Agriculture and Food while his colleague, William Silva, was assigned the
equally important Ministry of Industries and Fisheries. Philip Gena-
wardene was ambitious but overanxious to expand his area of influence,
and was unable to agree with his rightist colleagues. Eventually a
strong reaction from the MEP's right wing ended in his VLSSP being
elbowed out. Even the moderately socialist reforms Gunawardene introduced, such as the Paddy Lands Act of 1958 and the Cooperative
Development Bank Bill of 1959, were emasculated by the collective
endeavors of his rightist opponents in the cabinet.

Despite its condemnation of Philip Gunawardene's attempts at
"building socialism in one ministry," the LSSP anxiously hoped for
office in a projected SLFP-led coalition government headed by C. P.
de Silva in April 1960. However, they were disappointed when Parliament was dissolved. At the ensuing general election in July 1960 they
nurtured similar hopes, but the SLFP, led by Sirima Bandaranaike's
wife gained an overall majority. The LSSP finally achieved its objective in June 1964 when it joined with the CP and Philip Gunawardene's

MEP (formerly VLSSP) to form the United Left Front (ULF). The
ULF, with its 21 demands and threat of massive strike action endan-
gered the stability of the SLFP government and led Ms. Bandaranaike
to reconstitute her cabinet with a LSSP component. Once again the
SLFP's right wing reasserted itself and a section led by the party's
deputy leader, C. P. de Silva, engineered the defeat of the SLFP-
LSSP government five months later at the division on the debate on the
throne speech on December 4. The defeated SLFP-LSSP coaliation
(with support from the CP) fought the general election held in March
of the following year (1965), suffered defeat, went into opposition,
formed a United Front (UF) based on a Common Program in 1968, and
swept the polls at the general election of May 1970.

   The central figure in all these maneuvers since 1947 has been
N. M. Perera, the leader of the LSSP and its principal electoral asset. Perera hails from the goigama caste group and is steeped in
British, European, and American constitutionalism having been a
student at the London School of Economics.[21]

   This constitutionalism has influenced Perera throughout his political career. In 1947 he sought the leadership of Her Majesty's loyal
opposition in the Ceylon Parliament as the leader of the largest opposition party but did not obtain it till 1950.[22] His party sought the office
for him in the 1952 Parliament but it went to S. W. R. D. Bandaranaike because the CP-VLSSP combine supported the latter. In the
1956 Parliament he was leader of the opposition once more. Perera's
national prestige was at its peak in the few months after the assassination of Bandaranaike when he led the parliamentary opposition's demand for a proper investigation into the circumstances surrounding
the assassination, and forced his former Trotskyist colleague, now
Prime Minister W. Dahanayake, to dismiss two of the ministers suspected of being connected with the conspirators.

   The goodwill that accrued to the LSSP from Perera's leadership
in the 1956 Parliament encouraged his party to make a bid for parliamentary power at the general election of March 1960. But it fared
disastrously. It was clear, as it had been evident on earlier occasions, that the LSSP was viewed more as a useful and vigilant opposition than as a party that could be entrusted with governmental power.
But by this time the LSSP leadership was beginning to weary of its
oppositional role and was increasingly becoming impatient for office
—a goal realized for a brief span in June 1964, finally reaching frui-
tion in the formation of the United Front government in May 1970.

   The key personality in the building up of parliamentary socialism, however, was S. W. R. D. Bandaranaike. Essentially a prag-
matist, he campaigned for a political program that was a mix of social conscience and Buddhist revivalism. While his UNP rivals
skimmed the electoral surface, Bandaranaike delved somewhat deeper

in his pursuit of power. It was expected that his middle-of-the-road
politics would result in his being salvaged both by the political Left
and Right. However, there were certain factors that gave him unexpected advantage. His wealth and upper-class social inheritance appealed to the electors. His skills in avoiding the Scylla of UNP cons(
vatism and the Charybdis of extreme left-wing materialism struck th
correct note among electors influenced by the Sinhalese Buddhist eth'
of moderation. In the end Bandaranaike was able to win sections of
support that usually went either to the UNP or to the traditional left.

Bandaranaike's eclecticism divested his socialism of any final-
ity. In the absence of defined goals, it was possible for his party to
adapt itself to the Right or the Left. There were, therefore, no sev(
strains created by the exit of the Marxist VLSSP component from his
government in 1959. Shortly thereafter, Bandaranaike readily rever
to a centrist position, which he clearly articulated at the Kurunegala
sessions of his party. The SLFP government of 1960-65 headed by
his widow, Sirima Bandaranaike, more or less followed this centrist course. However, the flexibility of the party's eclectic sociali:
enabled Ms. Bandaranaike to shift to a left-of-center position when
she entered into an alliance with the traditional Left on the basis of a
common program hammered out with the LSSP and the CP.

Beyond the pale of parliamentary socialism are the revolutionary parties—the Maoist CP, the LSSP (Revolutionary), the RWP, an(
the powerful JVP. Leadership of the first three remains in the hand
of Western-oriented politicians and their activity is confined to the i:
suing of press communiques and embarrassing the government by us
ing for strike purposes the trade unions that the first two control.

It is the JVP that posed the greatest threat. In their insurrection of April 1971 they reduced the armed forces to desperate straits
by their organized widespread violence. On the one hand, their up-
rising cast the traditional left leadership in a poor light. On the
other, it left the UF government with a sense of urgency regarding tl
implementation of a radical program of economic reform. In effect,
the UF leadership was compelled to move further to the left. This
process was accelerated by the emergence of a strong Maoist-orient
group within its ranks, the Janavegaya (the People's Force), which i:
led by the Prime Minister's son-in-law, Kumar Rupesinghe and her
daughter Sunethra Rupesinghe.

The failure of the JVP showed the futility of a conspiratorial
organization seeking through violence and surprise insurrectionary
tactics to achieve its objectives in the face of the armed power of the
state, which was also able to command military assistance from foreign powers. Division among its leaders, infiltration of its ranks by
Moscow Communists, and the absence of a widely accepted leader
placed the JVP at a disadvantage. (Rohana Wijeweera, who commands

much influence in its ranks, is a karava who has to prove himself in a
goigama-dominated society.) Furthermore, the party has been pro-
scribed under emergency regulations since March 1971 and is thus at
a disadvantage because it cannot engage in open political activity.

PARTY ORIENTATIONS

The unwitting prophet of a flexible and elastic left-of-center socialism was S. W. R. D. Bandaranaike. When he launched his party
in September 1951, he emphasized that it would be "a middle party between the UNP on the extreme right and the Marxists on the extreme
left."[23] By temperament and political orientation, Bandaranaike preferred a dead center position in politics. Yet presumably expecting
that at some time he would have to enter into a coalition with the traditional Left, he fashioned a program that gave him enough room to
shift to a left-of-center position should the need arise. Hence his
party's program as outlined in 1951 was a catchall one, a hodgepodge
of Sinhalese Buddhist populism and radical social and economic reform.

In its 1951 policy statement, the SLFP affirmed its commitment
to Parliament. But it condemned unrestricted free enterprise and
declared that it would gradually nationalize all essential industries,
transport, banks, insurance, and plantations, impose a super tax on
all incomes in excess of Rs 50,000, and promote industrial development with a view to eliminating unemployment. On the religious and
cultural plane, the party demanded (1) the adoption of Sinhalese and
Tamil as the official languages (later changed to Sinhalese as the only
official language with provision for "the reasonable use of the Tamil
language"), and (2) the taking of all necessary steps by the public and
the government "to revive and assist religion and make it a living
force among our people." In effect this meant providing special facilities and recognition to Buddhism. This broad program, though
oriented in the direction of Sinhalese Buddhist populism, provided
enough leeway for other parties to support it.

Partly these developments can be attributed to the anxiety of
parties to outbid their opponents. In part there is, as mentioned earlier, a pull to the center. More specifically, the system of electoral
demarcation, with preponderant weight assigned to the conservative
rural and sparsely populated areas, placed the traditional Left at a
disadvantage (their support bases are in the more densely populated
southwestern seaboard and in the Kelani Valley district). They were
consequently left with one of two alternatives. They could advocate
revolution and overthrow of the existing social and political order—
which they did, from the 1930s to 1951. Or they could adapt them-

selves to the parliamentary system into which in fact they were rail-
roaded from 1951 onward after the inauguration of the SLFP.

However we should not conclude that the traditional Left has committed itself completely to the "bourgeois democratic framework."
They have their escape routes. This can be illustrated from various
pronouncements of their leaders.

For example, after the defeat of the UNP at the general election
of 1970, Philip Gunawardene's Marxism was reiterated in his pamphlet The Present Political Situation, which he presented to his party in
January 1971.[24] He rejected the UNP as being in "the grip of capitalists and monopolists," condemned "the system of electing governments by the ballot," poured scorn on his former colleagues in the
LSSP as being "saviors of both the local and foreign capitalist classes,"
and declared his support for the JVP.

The CP has a section in it headed by its veteran leader, S. A.
Wickremasinghe, that is critical of the collaboration extended to the
SLFP by the section led by Pieter Keuneman. If at any time the CP
decides to withdraw support from the SLFP-oriented UF government,
the Wickremasinghe wing could refurbish the image of the party and
dump the Keuneman group.

The LSSP, being the strongest of all the left parties, finds itself in a more difficult situation. On the one hand excuses have to be
produced for the party leadership's inability to push the UF government faster on the road to socialism. Hence N. M. Perera has stated
that "instant socialism" is not possible because people want "changes
within the framework of the law,"[25] while Colvin R. de Silva has
stressed the difficulty of speedy change because of "the pressure of
circumambient imperialism in Ceylon."[26] On the other hand, the
party must prepare itself for an exit if things go awry. Leslie Goonewardene, the party's general secretary, provided the alternative
strategy when he wrote in December 1970 that the LSSP had "not made
any final judgment" on "how far the journey towards socialism can be
made through Parliament and the parliamentary system," adding that
"the answer to this question does not lie in our hands but in the hands
of our enemies."[27]

However, collaboration with the social democratic SLFP has had
its adverse effects on the traditional Left. The trade unions in their
control are restive and in some disarray. There is turmoil in their
rank and file. Edmund Samarakkody, the leader of the microscopic
Trotskyist RWP, condemned his former colleagues when he wrote
in May 1974 in the Workers' Vanguard:[28]

> The LSSP betrayers and their Stalinist friends have
> so well practiced class collaboration through the
> (UF) coalition government during the last four years

—weakening seriously the working class and politically disorienting it—that the forces of capitalist
reaction have gathered strength and are already
taking the first steps . . . towards the realization
of their new solution: a naked capitalist dictatorship.

THE IMPLEMENTATION OF SOCIALISM

The Ceylonese experience affords an example of Gunnar Myrdal's
"soft state" serving as a catalyst for socialism. The circumstances
of Sri Lanka make such a shift necessary, if not imperative.[29] The
rural population, some 73.7 percent, is impoverished by unemployment and underemployment made worse by a steady drift to the towns
of youth in search of opportunity. Pressure of population on land is
tremendous: land that is fragmented into tiny parcels characterizes
agricultural life. The population is marked by an imbalance in its
age structure, and the birthrate is relatively high (2.3 percent in
1971). Ninety percent of the population lives at subsistence level and
in fact 60 percent is close to the poverty line. The gap between rich
and poor is considerable. Twenty percent of the national income is
lodged in 1.5 percent of the population. Further, a coterie of 40 family groups own a total investment of Rs 273 million, and of this 11 family groups own Rs 205 million or 51 percent of total investment in the
private sector.[30]

Nevertheless, any impetuses toward revolutionary socialism are
moderated by social and religious influences. The Buddhist ethic of
karma (fate, destiny), which leads people to accept without protest
their station in life makes change slow, if not difficult. In addition,
there is the closely knit and interdependent nature of society that
makes hierarchy, deference to all forms of authority, and assistance
by the better-off sections of the community to the socially depressed
and economically impoverished—a normal activity. Socialism in such
a context is bartered away for a benevolent paternalism. Consequently
the economic programs of nationalization and steep taxation put forth
by Marxist parties to equalize opportunities fail to have the desired
impact.

On the other hand, fear of the influence that the traditional Left
can wield obliges the Right (UNP) and the Center (SLFP) to drift toward socialism. The competition between parties is leavened by the
social responsibility that Buddhism enjoins on the privileged—that
merit can best be obtained by the performance of good deeds of which
the giving of alms is a prime duty. This when translated into secular
terms can mean either the paternalistic welfare state or a socialist

democracy. But it cannot easily imply a Marxist totalitarian dictatorship.

In the years 1947-56 the UNP had protested its adherence to an evolutionary type of socialism in opposition to the traditional Left's Marxism and perpetual theme of a "revolution round the corner." But the UNP's attitude to social problems was more that of a distant patron to his client, while its welfarism was designed to ward off discontent in the interests of its upper layers. Consequently, government was Colombo-centered, the administration was looked upon as a cold and remote object by the common man, and the colonial emphasis on benevolent authoritarianism was rigorously maintained.

The advent to power of S. W. R. D. Bandaranaike's SLFP-dominated Mahajana Eksath Peramuna (MEP, People's United Front) in 1956 changed the situation measurably.[31] The SLFP had a social conscience. Its policies on language and nationalization, though populist, were nevertheless directed toward greater democratization and equalization of opportunity. Whereas earlier, English had been the official language (despite its use by little more than 5 percent of the population), with the enactment of the Official Language Act in June 1956 (also referred to as the "Sinhala Only" Act), the administration and the institutions of higher education became accessible to the Sinhalese majority (the change, however, adversely affecting the Tamil minority). The nationalization of omnibus transport and the Port of Colombo in 1958, both constant social irritants, eliminated powerful monopoly interests. The Paddy Lands Act of 1958, the work of Philip Gunawardene, the Marxist Minister of Food and Agriculture, provided some security of tenure to tenant cultivators. However, its more far-reaching radical provisions were clipped by the strongly entrenched right-wing SLFP ministers in the MEP Cabinet, who described themselves as "democratic socialists." The tax structure was overhauled to provide relief to the lower income groups. And a Ten-Year Plan was formulated by 1959 with the assistance of economists from the West and the Soviet Union. The plan provided for some order in economic development unlike the earlier emphasis on private enterprise.

Indirectly, a further step in the direction of socialism was the reform of the laws relating to parliamentary elections. The changes effected—a one-day general election, state assistance to candidates, the imposition of a limit on expenses that a candidate might incur, a ban on the transport of voters in vehicles hired by political parties or their candidates—provided greater opportunities to disadvantaged parties and reduced the chances of parties with large financial resources. Further a new electoral demarcation was effected resulting in an increase in the number of electorates from 95 to 151 while at the same time reducing their sizes. The net effect was that it was no longer possible for a party commanding greater resources, such as the UNP, to have an advantage over other less endowed parties.

In the field of foreign affairs, which was indeed S. W. R. D. Bandaranaike's metier, diplomatic relations were established with the Soviet Union and the People's Republic of China as well as with other countries of the communist bloc. Cultural delegations from a number of communist states visited the island. And numbers of students went on scholarships or short visits to China, the Soviet Union, and other East European communist states. This open-door policy provided a boost to the local Marxist movement. Probably it injected militancy and revolutionary fervor into a new group of insurrectionary Marxist youth in just the same way that young Ceylonese returning from their studies in Britain in the first three decades of the century (the "England-returneds") were infused with the ideas of British liberalism and the practices of Westminster-style parliamentary government. The effects were, however, not to be felt until the mid-1960s and early 1970s.

It was Bandaranaike's view that there would be an "explosion" if attempts were made to "dam up communism." His way of dealing with it was to leave it free to expand in the belief that in time its extremism would wear off and with "the capitalist world moving left," a middle solution of a democratic socialist type would eventually evolve.[32] Such a view of middle-ground Buddhistic socialism is also held by influential members of the Sinhalese Buddhist elite.

While the years 1956-59 broadly indicated the confines of a dead center democratic socialism, Ms. Bandaranaike's first government (1960-65) provided evidence of a slight shift to the left of center. The SLFP of these years claimed to be more social democratic than socialist, with its right wing still in an entrenched position. During 1960-64 the only Socialist of any consequence in the Cabinet was T. B. Ilangaratne, all the others being either to the right or the center. The nationalization measures enacted therefore by individual ministers were more with a view to eliminate UNP supports, reduce inequalities of income, and provide greater opportunities to the indigenous Sinhalese bourgeoisie than to trail a pathway to socialism per se. Left-wing economists criticized this program of "nationalization at random."

Thus the nationalization of schools in 1960-61, a majority of which were owned by the Roman Catholic Church and others by Protestant missionary organizations, satisfied important sections of Sinhalese Buddhist opinion. It also reduced a fortress of conservatism that normally rendered allegiance to the UNP. The nationalization of the major assets of British and American-owned petroleum companies and the nationalization of insurance had similar adverse effects on the UNP. The nationalization of the Bank of Ceylon and the establishment of state-operated people's banks in many towns helped to make available easier credit facilities to local entrepreneurs. The introduction of channeled practice for medical specialists and the imposition of additional tax burdens on the better-off sections of the community were intended to reduce ostentation and redistribute income. The full implementation of the official language (Sinhalese) as of January 1, 1960 pleased the Sinhalese Buddhist intelligentsia and made government and administration more accessible to the common man in the Sinhalese community.

Further amendments to the election law under the Ceylon (Parliamentary Elections) Amendment Act of 1964 completed the process by which no party or individual candidate in affluent circumstances could have a preponderant advantage over their less fortunate counterparts. But more significant, from the left-wing point of view, was the enfranchisement of the 18-year-olds under this amending act. While the conservative UNP opposed the decision, the traditional Left gave it its strongest support in the belief that the young are more "progressive" and oppose the established order. This teenage or youth vote, however, did not go to the traditional Left or the SLFP at the general election of 1965. It was estimated that 70 percent of this group voted UNP in 1965 mainly because they were dissatisfied with the governing SLFP's failure to alleviate unemployment and to bring down the cost of living. However for these same reasons, youth voted for the SLFP-LSSP-CP coalition at the general election of 1970. There was therefore no necessary connection between youth and socialism.

The formation of a SLFP-LSSP coalition government in June 1964 did not help to accelerate the march to socialism. The 14-point program on which the LSSP and SLFP agreed did not indicate a perceptible shift to the left. It was an agreement within the broad confines of the SLFP's own political program. Nor did Ms. Bandaranaike have any serious convictions as to the efficacy of socialism in a situation of near economic bankruptcy. She was mainly motivated by practical political considerations. In her address to the executive committee of her party, she stated, [33]

> [We] cannot expect any results unless we get the co-
> operation of the working class. This could be under-
> stood if the working of the Port (Colombo) and the
> other nationalized undertakings are considered. . . .
> Disruptions especially strikes and go-slows must
> be eliminated and the development of the country
> must proceed. . . . Therefore gentlemen, I decided
> to initiate talks with the leaders of the working class,
> particularly, Mr. Philip Gunawardene and Dr. N.
> M. Perera.

The LSSP, no doubt, hoped that by joining hands with the SLFP they could mobilize the "progressives" within that party. The effort proved futile because apart from the fact that Ms. Bandaranaike's government had only at best a year to go, the LSSP made a number of tactical errors in its premature attempts at "express socialism." Its anxiety to force the passage of a bill to control the press and to nationalize the more influential sections of it unnerved established social interests. Perera's proposal as Minister of Finance to permit the free tapping of toddy (as an antidote to the often poisonous home brew) gave those opposed to the Marxists an opportunity to alert sections of Buddhist opinion to whom temperance was an important religious precept.

The return of the UNP at the general election of 1965 was evidence of the electorate's dissatisfaction with the SLFP government's failure to solve the country's outstanding economic problems—the soaring cost of living and unemployment. Further, it was obvious that important vested interests organized themselves against the divided ranks of the SLFP-LSSP-CP front.

The years in opposition (1965-70) led to the forging of closer links between the SLFP, LSSP, and CP—the United Front based on the Common Program. This program however did not in any way represent a sharp shift to the left. Nor was it in conflict with the basic principles of SLFP policy as detailed in its first policy pronouncement in 1951.

There were aspects in the Common Program, however, and in the UF's election manifesto of May 1970, which the LSSP believed it could use for its own purposes. Colvin R. de Silva stressed a few months before the general election that Parliament must, if the UF was to implement its socialist policies, be characterized "by leadership and not consensus."[34] In other words, it was his view that Parliament must be utilized to implement the mandate that the UF hoped to obtain. A LSSP theoretician, V. Karalasingham, who had earlier condemned his party's "collaborationist policies," now came round to arguing that the Common Program was "not so much a milestone as a springboard . . . not so much a stage in a journey but a springboard from which the journey itself will really commence.[35] Other LSSP leaders nurtured similar hopes.

The right wing in the SLFP is, however, capable of considerable resilience. Thus while the LSSP planned to utilize the UF's socialist orientations to mobilize mass opinion in favor of more socialism, the conservative SLFP ministers took steps to ensure that it would be "socialism within limits." This was evidenced even during the general election campaign of March-May 1970 when Felix Dias Bandaranaike made obvious his dislike of the Marxists, and Ms. Bandaranaike categorically stated that the people's committees that the UF proposed would be purely advisory bodies, emphasizing that they "would not be partisan bodies packed with party cadres."[36] The Left had thought in terms of mass participation in the administration of state enterprises and the machinery of government in the hope that these could generate sufficient enthusiasm to compel the government to move faster in a leftward direction. Their plans were, however, effectively stymied by the Minister of Public Administration, Felix Dias Bandaranaike. While these committees are expected to function as watchdogs over the administration and help in bringing about better understanding between the people and the administration, their members are selected (not elected) by the minister himself from among names submitted by the local MP, local organizations, and the general public, while their chairmen are appointed and can be removed by the minister as well. The end result is that the majority of these committees are more or less lower level SLFP agencies, naturally so, in a government parliamentary group that has 95 of its 120 members drawn from that party (the LSSP has 19 and the CP 6).

There is also provision for workers' councils and advisory committees in government offices. Many of these have been actively promoted by the LSSP Minister of Communications (Leslie Goonewardene) and the CP Minister of Housing and Construction (Pieter Keuneman). But, again, the majority of the advisory committees (being in government offices) come under the purview of the Minister of Public Administration. (There was the unexpressed hope that these advisory committees would be controlled by the LSSP Minister of Finance, N. M. Perera, but his ministry was divested of control over the public services at the time the UF government was formed.)

Nor has the appointment of district political authorities from among senior members of Parliament to each of the island's 22 administrative districts (to oversee the bureaucracy and decide on budgetary priorities), helped in the "march to socialism." The majority of them are from the SLFP and, being politicians, their primary function will be to disburse patronage so as to strengthen their party's position in the areas for which they are responsible.

Furthermore, the LSSP had hoped that, in establishing a new constitution, the existing system of electoral demarcation, which places a premium on rural areas, would be overhauled to bring about a proper balance between the rural and urban areas. Again, this was opposed by SLFP members of Parliament representing the rural population. Consequently no changes were made. A second attempt by the LSSP to gain advantage in 1974-75 when a new demarcation of electorates became necessary because of the census conducted in 1971 was effectively blocked. The increase in population necessitated a greater number of electoral districts than at present and this would have resulted in additional seats being allocated to urban areas. The

Constitution was, however, amended to avoid an excessive increase in the composition of the legislature.

On the other hand, unpopular decisions relating to budgetary policy have had to be taken by the LSSP Minister of Finance. The Minister no doubt has placed restrictions on the private sector and imposed ceilings on income. But the enveloping financial and economic crises compelled him to adopt measures that in effect have meant the dismantling of the island's welfare system.

In its first year, therefore, the measures taken by the UF government to bring about a socialist transformation of society were hardly of significance. These were mainly aimed at bringing about a measure of control over sectors of the economy that were excessively in the control of the private sector. A state trading corporation was set up to handle all foreign exchange transactions involving industry, trade, and major exports; and the state-run Cooperative Wholesale Establishment was invested with control over the entire food import trade. The Business Undertakings (Acquisition) Act empowered the state to take over any business concern employing more than 100 persons if it is in the public interest.

At the same time, the private sector was permitted sufficient leeway. The LSSP Minister of Finance (N. M. Perera) in his first budget speech (October 25, 1970) stated that the public sector expansion he envisaged would also provide an effective infrastructure for cooperative, private, and small-scale industry. He added that "that sector of industry which for reasons of scale, technology and policy do not make state ownership vital in the national interest" would be "left for private enterprise, but would at the same time be subject to regulation by the state."[37] The minister was unwilling, however, to implement the UF's election pledge to nationalize foreign-owned banks, arguing that this would be unwise as the previous government had borrowed heavily from these institutions.

Meanwhile a Five-Year Plan was in the process of preparation by an economist (H. A. de S. Gunasekere) who had formerly been a member of the central committee of the LSSP and had crossed over to the SLFP in 1968. There were many problems, however. He did not see eye to eye with his former mentor, the LSSP Minister of Finance. As permanent secretary (the designation is now "Secretary") to the Ministry of Planning and Employment, a portfolio vested in the Prime Minister, Gunasekere plays an important role in shaping economic policy. But, faced with constant criticism from some of the left-wing members of the UF Cabinet, the ministry that he was in charge of was split in two and a separate Ministry for Plan Implementation was created in August 1973.

It is possible that the Five-Year Plan inaugurated in November 1971 would have taken on a different orientation but for the JVP insurrection of March–April 1971. Presumably it would have done no more than concentrate on immediate objectives of achieving an annual growth rate of 6 percent, of raising domestic savings from the present level of 12.5 percent of national income to 17 percent, of improving the living standards of some 40 percent of the population (who in 1972 were earning less than Rs 200 a month) by raising per capita income from Rs 910 per annum to Rs 1,150 at the end of the plan period (1976) at 1970 prices, and of creating employment for 810,000 persons. There was renewed emphasis on the private sector, which was expected to contribute 52 percent of the anticipated investment of Rs 14,820 million.

But it was the sense of urgency created by the JVP insurrection that compelled the UF government to tack on to the Five-Year Plan what came to be known as the "package deal"—a generous parcel of radical reform. This provided for (1) a ceiling on landholdings— from which, however, foreign and public limited liability companies were exempted—brought into effect by the Land Reform Law of 1972 under which the maximum amount of agricultural land that a person can own is 25 acres of paddy and 50 acres of other land, (2) government acquisition, with compensation, of shares in plantation companies and the appointment of government directors to the boards of such companies, (3) the appointment of government directors to public and private companies, (4) either nationalization or state acquisition of not less than 51 percent of any trade or industry where necessary, (5) the overhauling of the wage and salary structure to reduce disparities between manual and service or clerical occupations, and (6) a charter of workers' rights.

Most of the proposals outlined have been converted into legislation. In addition, legislation enacted in 1973 limited ownership of houses—the total number of houses owned per family should not exceed the number of persons in that family.

The Left hoped that it could exploit the Land Reform Law to create mass enthusiasm to further the progress toward a socialist society. Some 5,500 landowners declared that they owned land above the limit stipulated, the total acreage amounting to 1.2 million acres. Approximately 400,000 acres of this total have been vested in the Land Reform Commission. The popular demand for land and the spiraling expectations that it gave rise to could have created the necessary snowballing effect. The government once more has acted firmly and declared that the changes it has proposed will take place only within the framework of the law.

A danger to the furtherance of socialism from the point of view of the SLFP and the traditional Left was the greater part of the national press, especially the newspapers published by the Associated Newspapers of Ceylon Limited (often referred to as Lake House), and the Times group. The third of the great press combines, the Davasa group, strongly supported the SLFP and its Marxist allies at the 1970 general election but became increasingly critical of the UF government from around 1972. The Lake House newspapers were, until they were taken over, mainly the monopoly of the Wijewardene family, whereas the Davasa group is, for all purposes, owned by the Gunasena family (there are a few outside shareholders). The three groups publish five English, four Sinhalese, and two Tamil dailies, besides many weeklies. Though distribution figures at face value are not very impressive, often a newspaper passes from one hand to another and it is also read aloud in boutiques and other such places to groups of listeners. On this basis, it could be assumed that there is approximately a reading public of 1,400,000 in an adult population of 7,800,000. There is, in addition, a flourishing party press, especially the UNP's Siyarata, and two Marxist dailies, the LSSP's Janadina and the CP's Attha. There are also other party papers. All of them have an extensive reading public.

Attempts had been made by the SLFP government of 1960-64 to enact legislation to control the press, and by the SLFP-LSSP government in 1964 to nationalize Lake House but these failed. With the return of the UF government in 1970, the fate of the national press was sealed.

The first to go was the powerful Lake House group of newspapers. It had fought very hard since 1960 to safeguard its privileges but ultimately went under when legislation—the Associated Newspapers of Ceylon Limited (Special Provisions) Act—was enacted in 1973 to broaden its ownership. For an interim period, 75 percent of its shares will be vested in the government's public trustee who is required to dispose of these in due course to the general public (the other 25 percent is vested in the existing shareholders). However, despite the fact that Lake House was not nationalized as such, it is today virtually a mouthpiece of the government. The Left for its part hopes that when its trade unions purchase a certain number of Lake House shares, such unions will be able to influence policy. But the way in which the shares will be disposed of will only permit the Left a minimal influence. Nevertheless, Lake House no longer obstructs or criticizes the socialism of the UF or the policies and politics of its component partners. But it could turn critical of the Left if at any time the alliance with the SLFP were severed.

The legislation on Lake House was followed by the Press Council Act of February 1973. This act prohibits the press from publishing reports of Cabinet meetings or other related confidential information and it can be disciplined upon a legitimate complaint made against it.

All these actions have had their effect on the other two newspaper combines. The Times group now supports the UF government because it fears reprisals. And the Davasa group, which had commended the UF until around 1972 and then became critical of it, has had its newspapers suspended since 1974 under emergency regulations.

A more serious problem for the UF was the Soulbury Constitution of 1947-72 with its built-in safeguards against the excessive concentration of power in any one branch of government. Efforts to revise the Constitution during the earlier phases of SLFP rule, 1956-59 and 1960-65, failed to materialize. The UF's victory in 1970 ensured immediate priority for the framing of a new constitution.

The Republican Constitution of May 1972 concentrates all power in the National State Assembly.[38] The second chamber, the Senate, along with appeals to the judicial committee of the Privy Council— possible institutional checks on the UF government's socialist legislation—were abolished in 1971 even before the Soulbury Constitution was discarded. The earlier separation of powers, under which the judiciary had the right to pronounce on the constitutionality of legislation, no longer exists. It is therefore no longer possible for interests affected by legislation to impede its implementation by contesting its validity before the ordinary courts. The supposedly independent Public Services Commission under the earlier Constitution stands abolished. Instead, the Cabinet of ministers is now vested with the power of making appointments to important positions in the administration. It was alleged that higher-rung public officials were not always willing to carry out orders of ministers if they thought these were not in conformity with the law, or if they were not in sympathy with the government's policies. Two strong barriers therefore to the exercise of unrestricted authority have been removed and the UF government is now left a free hand to act as it wishes. Furthermore, the Constitution's directive principles of state policy—full employment, equitable distribution of the social product, development of collective forms of property with a view to ending human exploitation, elimination of economic and social privilege, the ensuring of social security and welfare, and the enlisting of maximum participation of the people in the processes of government—make it clear that it is a socialist democracy that is sought.

In the area of foreign policy, there was, in the first flush of victory, a complete reversal of the pro-West stances of the predecessor UNP-led "National Government." Initially, the UF government effected a number of changes that indicated a pronounced anti-West orientation. The American Asia Foundation and Peace Corps were asked to leave. The Democratic Republic of Korea, North Vietnam, the Provisional Revolutionary Government of South Vietnam, and the Sihanouk government-in-exile were recognized. Of greater significance, perhaps, were the decisions to sever diplomatic relations with Israel until issues concerning the Arabs were satisfactorily resolved, and the steps

taken to recognize the German Democratic Republic in spite of repeated protests from Bonn. There was also talk of rejecting the
World Bank loan made to the "National Government" for the Mahaveli
River diversion scheme on the grounds that the terms were an infringe-
ment of the sovereignty of Sri Lanka. The UF government however
did not pursue this.

The simple expectation was that these changes would pay rich
dividends in the form of large-scale assistance from the Communist
states. Yet there was no desire on the part of the UF government to
commit Sri Lanka completely to the Communist bloc. Its policy merely
implied a left-centered nonalignment or a "radical neutralism," as it
came to be called.

In the end, however, only the People's Republic of China proved
a generous aid-giver, whereas there was a distinct cooling off on the
part of Britain, the Federal Republic of Germany, and the United
States. Yet the situation changed when, after the JVP insurrection of
April 1971, the UF government began to retrace its steps. Military
assistance to quell the disturbances came from countries as different
as the Soviet Union, Yugoslavia, the United States, Great Britain,
India, and Pakistan. The People's Republic of China followed later,
but only after the insurrection had failed. Ms. Bandaranaike claimed
that the support received was a vindication of her neutralist policies.
But within her government disillusionment set in: many questioned
the wisdom of Sri Lanka's continuing to be so dependent on the Communist states—a view compounded no doubt by the encouragement al-
legedly given by the North Korean embassy in Colombo to the insurrec-
tionists, and by widespread suspicion of Chinese involvement. In the
months that followed the UF government sought closer links with India. But again the expected returns from closer relations did not
materialize, and by June 1972 Ms. Bandaranaike was being warmly
welcomed when she visited the People's Republic and obtained agreements providing generous financial and economic assistance. However, there was little doubt that the earlier "radical neutralism" had
undergone some revision—as evidenced by the welcome given in early
1972 to both the U.S. Pacific Fleet and the Soviet Pacific Fleet when
these touched at Colombo port on "goodwill" visits. Such shifts and
changes in UF policy reflected the inner contradictions that beset it.

The inclusion of the general secretary of the CP (Pieter Keuneman) in the UF Cabinet did not evoke the expected response from the
Soviets, presumably because of the large Trotskyist LSSP presence
—and the LSSP Minister of Finance has still not visited the capitals
of the Soviet Union and the People's Republic in any of his global aid-
soliciting missions. It was the CP that was most interested in the
granting of diplomatic recognition to the German Democratic Republic, but the action worsened relations with a principal aid-giver, the

Federal Republic of Germany. Nor could CP participation in the UF have made the People's Republic of China overenthusiastic, despite the fact that the leader of the Peking lobby in the UF, R. D. Senanayake, is junior minister of planning and employment, a portfolio vested in the Prime Minister, while the Janavegaya group with strong Maoist leanings is controlled by her daughter and son-in-law, the Rupesinghes. On the other hand, two Maoist stalwarts, N. Sanmugathasan and S. D. Bandaranaike, were detained for several months in the aftermath of the PLF insurrection, the latter in fact convicted by the Criminal Justice Commission.

From another quarter, the SLFP's powerful pro-Arab component, the Islamic Socialist Front, was instrumental in pushing for the decision against Israel and in the matter of support for Pakistan in Bangladesh's war of liberation. Failure here is seen in the Arab states not helping Sri Lanka on the price of oil. And Sri Lanka's friendship with India was strained over Bangladesh.[39]

The end result is that the UF government is constrained from moving further to the left because of adverse reactions that can emanate from the international credit agencies and from the West—Sri Lanka's principal aid-givers and financiers. Neither the Arab nor the Communist world is willing to commit itself fully and unconditionally to Sri Lanka because Sri Lanka is of no great significance to them either economically or in the power balance of international politics. The domestic considerations outlined, however, oblige the UF to walk a tightrope, an exercise that its rival the UNP does not have to subject itself to because of its simple straightforward pro-West stances.

CONCLUSION

There are certain facets of Sri Lankan socialism that come into clear relief in this study. Competition between political groupings has made of socialism a method of social bargaining, the primary consideration being staving off galloping discontent so as to ensure that a party will arrive at or remain in power. If the UNP is benevolently paternalistic, the SLFP is less so if for no other reason than that its objective is to distinguish itself from its main rival by more closely identifying itself with the populist and indigenous petit-bourgeois sections of the Sinhalese majority. The catalog of SLFP-oriented legislation—the national languages, moderate nationalization, primacy for Buddhism, participatory democracy, land reform, heavy taxation—could just as well have been accomplished by a UNP-led government. The latter's record however has been one of missed opportunities or of delaying concessions until they have lost their value.

The SLFP, for its part, realizes that it should not make of it-self an instrument of its Marxist partners. SLFP leaders therefore from time to time affirm their views on what they suppose are the lim-its to socialism. Their recent pronouncements indicate a belief in "pragmatic socialism"; there is no acceptance of socialism as an end in itself, but only as that degree of socialism necessary to retaining power.

The view that socialism is a method of "scientific" social engi-neering is therefore only held by the traditional Left, and, in a more uncompromising form, by their revolutionary counterparts the JVP, LSSP(R), RWP, and the Peking CP. They see the revolutionary trans-formation of society and the rule of the proletariat as their ultimate objective. However, the traditional Left, after years of unsuccessful campaigning, sought alliance with bourgeois parties as a step in the "right direction." The hope was that they could infiltrate the ranks of the SLFP and bend it toward the socialist goal. The exercise has failed and disillusionment has seized their ranks. Already the left wing of the LSSP has been in dialogue with sections of the JVP and the likelihood is that the LSSP will revert to its precollaborationist revo-lutionary stance. This would imply the repudiation of parliamentary goals. But revolutionary prospects are dimmed by competition from the left wing of the SLFP and from the CP itself, and by the fact that a majority of plantation workers is in the control of a right-wing trade union, the CWC. A revolutionary struggle could succeed only if there is a firm alliance between the Sinhalese workers and Indian Tamil plantation labor.

Still another variable is foreign power interest in the domestic situation. The rejection of parliamentary goals implies seizure of power by extraparliamentary action. A lawfully constituted govern-ment will ask foreign powers for military assistance in that event. Such a precedent was set when Ms. Bandaranaike's UF government sought and obtained from various states arms and ammunition to put down the JVP insurrection of March-April 1971.

Socialism in Sri Lanka has labored under several difficulties. First, Marxian socialism is difficult to attain in a fragmented and communally divided society. For example, in 1957-58 sections of the LSSP saw an opportunity for revolutionary action in the discontent among the Ceylon and Indian Tamils over the language and citizenship issues and in the general dissatisfaction of the working classes—ac-tion that they hoped could result in their replacing the MEP govern-ment of Bandaranaike. A working paper on these lines was seriously discussed in certain LSSP circles. The pull however of bourgeois populism so ably manifested in the separatist policies of the Tamil Federal Party and the Sinhalese Buddhist chauvinism of the SLFP and UNP negated such a possibility.

Second, competition between bourgeois parties on the social and economic plane diverts the attention of the underprivileged from the deep underlying problems of poverty, low standards of living, and unemployment. The situation is rendered more difficult by the Buddhist view of earthly existence as the result of the actions and deeds of one's previous birth—a doctrine of quiet resignation if not immobility, which is also a convenient vehicle of frustration tolerance.

Third, a slow and gradual lowering of living standards over a period of time as it has happened over the decades 1940 to 1970 will not readily create the mass drive toward violent protest that could result from a sudden and abrupt imposition of burdens. The hartal of August 1953 activated by the UNP government, which reduced without adequate warning the rice subsidy, illustrates this point. Governments since that time have been cautious, cushioning shocks by increasing burdens in a gradual way.

There is the fact that Parliament is accepted as the basis of political activity. Coupled with this is the right to vote. Over the years Parliament has developed into a recognized instrument of compromise through elected government. It is also the grand inquisition of the nation and in that way relieves social and political tensions.

The Left tried to dismiss Parliament at first as a bourgeois institution. But it has also wished to make use of it. However the system of electoral demarcation gave rural-based and conservative parties an advantage. The traditional Left had therefore no alternative but to become part of the system and utilize Parliament to achieve their objectives. They have not succeeded in this exercise, however, and are still trying to formulate an effective revolutionary posture.

The question arises as to whether an impatient generation of young people angry at the failure of governments to provide employment and reduce living costs will tire of Parliament and seek an alternative to it. The aging leadership of the traditional Marxist parties (a majority of them are well over 60 years old) had, before they opted for parliamentarism, thought in terms of a Communist setup. But their credibility will now be questioned when they—or at any rate sections of them—decide to revert to their former revolutionary stances. To make matters more difficult, their second liners too have been led to believe that Parliament can be utilized to achieve socialist goals. But even they are not of much consequence because the senior men have monopolized their respective parties since the 1930s. These traditional Marxists will therefore not be accepted by the emerging new Left when disappointment and frustration drive many of them to seek admission into their ranks.

The new Left has already been spurned by senior Trotskyists as "putschists" and "dadibidi" (hit and run) revolutionaries who have done more harm than good to the cause of socialism by their unsuccess-

ful efforts at insurrection. But as one writer emphasized, their growing ranks nevertheless pose a "countermodel" that "rejects the old
political game and all the subtle rules that go to support it."[40] In effect this writer argues that the JVP will refuse to be "bourgeoisified"
or lured into Parliament.[41]

The JVP will serve as the nucleus of a constellation of revolutionary socialist forces that will challenge Parliament and "the elite
model of politics"[42] that has sustained it for the last 25 years or so.
But will they succeed in the context of Sri Lankan governments tending to increasingly depend on the expanding military and semimilitary
arm of the state? Furthermore these governments will also, if hard
pressed, seek and certainly obtain military assistance from abroad.

This brings us to the position taken by the Bolshevik splinter of
the LSSP and even of the LSSP itself in the 1940s. The Bolsheviks,
not without reason, called themselves at first the Ceylon Unit of the
Bolshevik Leninist Party of India—later changing the appellation to
Bolshevik Samasamaja Party because of the adverse local connota-
tions of a link with India. They stressed that only if the "revolution"
succeeded in India could they win in Ceylon. As well the LSSP too
scoffed at the idea of "building socialism in one country." Both
groups were aware of the possibility of intervention by hostile foreign
powers. They still have such apprehensions. For example, the
LSSP leader, N. M. Perera, has cautioned that "socialism is a hard
road of social reorganization to be patiently built up stone by stone"[43]
while the party's deputy leader, Colvin R. de Silva has warned of the
pressures from foreign imperialism.[44] It is precisely for these reasons that the LSSP and CP have chosen to ally themselves with the
SLFP in the hope of achieving some of their socialist goals. But they
are confronted here with the insoluble problem of pushing a social
democratic party into adopting Marxist orientations. Either way,
both the traditional Left and the new Left are each caught in a vicious
circle from which they will not be able to easily break loose.

NOTES

1. See Sir Charles Jeffries, Ceylon—The Path to Independence
(London: Pall Mall Press, 1962), p. 112, where he states inter alia,
"the deceptive lull was broken in October 1946 by a series of strikes
and unrest in Ceylon. Communist agitators, who had no desire to see
the island's political problems solved by peaceful means, took advantage of the situation to incite the workers to violence. . . . It became
clearer daily to the Governor, Sir Henry Moore, and to Mr. Arthur
Creech Jones, who succeeded Mr. Hall as Secretary of State in October, that if Ceylon was to be saved for the Commonwealth and the

free world, there would have to be something more positive than the policy of gradual evolution contemplated by the 1945 White Paper." (Note: Jeffries was deputy permanent under-secretary and between 1946 and 1948 was in charge of Ceylon affairs at the Colonial Office.)

2. The vast majority of the Indian Tamil population was deprived of citizenship and voting rights under legislation enacted in 1948 and 1949 by the UNP government of D. S. Senanayake. In October 1964 the issue was partly settled when Ms. Bandaranaike and the Indian Prime Minister, Lal Bahadur Shastri, came to an agreement under which the government of Ceylon agreed to grant to 300,000 of the 975,000 resident Indian Tamils and their natural increase citizenship rights over a 15-year period and the government of India agreed to take back 525,000 of them and their natural increase over the same time period. The question of the remaining 150,000 was left unresolved until 1974 when Ms. Bandaranaike and Indira Gandhi came to an understanding under which each country agreed to absorb 75,000 of this balance.

3. For a detailed description of the Sinhalese caste structure see Bryce Ryan, Caste in Modern Ceylon: The Sinhalese System in Transition (New Brunswick, N.J.: Rutgers University Press, 1953). For caste among the Ceylon Tamils, see Michael Banks, "Caste in Jaffna," in E. R. Leach, ed., Cambridge Papers in Social Anthropology, vol. 2: Aspects of Caste in South India, Ceylon and North-West Pakistan (London: Cambridge University Press, 1960), pp. 61-77.

4. For further details see Wilson, Politics in Sri Lanka 1947-1973 (London: Macmillan Company, 1974), pp. 17-19, 61-63.

5. We have made our assessment on the basis of criteria suggested by Apter, La Palombara, Pye, Rustow and Ward, and von der Mehden. See for example David E. Apter, The Politics of Modernization (Chicago: Chicago University Press, 1965); Joseph La Palombara's chapter, "Bureaucracy of Political Development: Notes, Queries and Dilemmas," in his Bureaucracy and Political Development (Princeton, N.J.: Princeton University Press, 1963), pp. 39-48; Lucian W. Pye's chapter, "Comparative Political Culture," in his and Sidney Verba's, eds., Political Culture and Political Development (Princeton, N.J.: Princeton University Press, 1965), pp. 512-60; Dankwart Rustow's and Robert E. Ward's "Introduction," in their Political Modernization in Japan and Turkey (Princeton, N.J.: Princeton University Press, 1964), pp. 3-13; and Fred R. von der Mehden, Politics of the Developing Nations (Englewood Cliffs, N.J.: Prentice-Hall, 1964), p. 6. For a criticism of theories of modernization and political development, see Dean C. Tipps, "Modernization Theory and the Comparative Study of Societies: A Critical Perspective," in Comparative Studies in Society and History 15, no. 2 (March 1973): 199-226; and R. S. Milne's review article, "The Overdeveloped

Study of Political Development," in Canadian Journal of Political
Science 5, no. 4: 560-68.

6. The categories are Pye's and are mentioned by Apter, op.
cit., pp. 49-50.

7. The variables are those suggested by La Palombara, op.
cit.

8. See my Chapter 5, "The Candidates," in A. Jeyaratnam
Wilson, Electoral Politics in an Emergent State: The Ceylon General
Election of May 1970 (London: Cambridge University Press, 1975).

9. For accounts of socialism, Marxism, and socialist and Marxist parties, see W. Howard Wriggins, Ceylon: Dilemmas of a New
Nation (Princeton, N.J.: Princeton University Press, 1960); Calvin
A. Woodward, "The Trotskyite Movement in Ceylon," World Politics
14, no. 2 (January 1962); Hector Abhayarardhana, "Categories of
Left Thinking in Ceylon," Community, no. 4 (1963); Robert N. Kearney, "The Ceylon Communist Party: Competition for Marxist Supremacy," in Robert A. Scalapino, ed., The Communist Revolution in
Asia: Tactics, Goals and Achievements (Englewood Cliffs, N.J.:
Prentice-Hall, 1965); George J. Lerski, Origins of Trotskyism in
Ceylon: A Documentary History of the Lanka Sama Samaja Party,
1935-1942 (Stanford, Calif.: Hoover Institution of War, Revolution
and Peace, 1968); Calvin A. Woodward, The Growth of a Party System in Ceylon (Providence: Brown University Press, 1969); Robert
N. Kearney, "The Communist Parties of Ceylon: Rivalry and Alliance," in Robert A. Scalapino, ed., The Communist Revolution in
Asia (2d ed.; Englewood Cliffs, N.J.: Prentice-Hall, 1969); George
Lerski, "The Twilight of Ceylonese Trotskyism," Pacific Affairs
3 (Autumn 1970); A. Jeyaratnam Wilson, "Ceylon: A New Government Takes Office," Asian Survey, February 1971; Robert N. Kearney, Trade Unions and Politics in Ceylon (Berkeley, Calif.: University of California Press, 1971); Charles S. Blackton, "The Ceylon Insurgency, 1971," Australia's Neighbours, July/August 1971; A. Jeyaratnam Wilson, "Ceylon: The People's Liberation Front and the 'Revolution' That Failed" (Montreal: Centre for Developing Area Studies,
Reprint Series, No. 23, 1972); Charles S. Blackton, "Sri Lanka's
Marxists," Problems of Communism 22, no. 1 (January/February
1973); Politicus (W. Wiswa Warnapala), "The April Revolt in Ceylon,"
Asian Survey, March 1972; S. Arasaratnum, "The Ceylon Insurrection of April 1971: Some Causes and Consequences," Pacific Affairs
45, no. 3 (Fall 1972); Tissa Fernando, "Elite Politics in the New
States: The Case of Post-Independence Sri Lanka," Pacific Affairs
46, no. 3 (Fall 1973); A. Jeyaratnam Wilson, Politics in Sri Lanka
1947-1973 (London: Macmillan Company, 1974); Gananath Obeyese-
kere, "Some Comments on the Social Backgrounds of the April 1971
Insurgency in Sri Lanka (Ceylon)," Journal of Asian Studies 33, no. 3

(May 1974); A. Jeyaratnam Wilson, Electoral Politics in an Emergent State: The Ceylon General Election of May 1970 (London: Cambridge University Press, 1975).

For an exhaustive bibliography on the JVP insurrection, see H. A. I. Goonetileke, The April 1971 Insurrection in Ceylon: A Select Bibliography (Louvain: CRSR, 1973), especially the author's excellent introduction, pp. i-vii.

For useful party literature see Leslie Goonewardene, A Short History of the Lanka Sama Samja Party (Colombo: Gunaratne and Company, 1960); V. Karalasingham, Politics of Coalition (Colombo: International Publishers, 1964); Pieter Keuneman, October, National Liberation and Ceylon (Colombo: Education Bureau, Ceylon Communist Party, 1967); Basil Perera, Pieter Keuneman—a Profile (Colombo: Co-operative Printers' Society Ltd., 1967); 25 Years of the Ceylon Communist Party: 1943-1968 (Colombo: People's Publishing House, 1968).

10. This MEP was formerly known as the Viplavakari (Revolutionary) LSSP and is not to be confused with the original MEP organized by S. W. R. D. Bandaranaike in 1955 to fight the UNP at the general election of 1956.

11. For a perceptive account, see Janice Jiggins, Family and Caste in the Politics of the Sinhalese 1947-1971, unpublished Ph.D. thesis, University of Ceylon, 1973.

12. See A. Jeyaratnam Wilson, "Ceylonese Cabinet Ministers: Their Political, Economic and Social Backgrounds," Ceylon Economist 5, no. 1 (March 1960).

13. See A. Jeyaratnam Wilson, Electoral Politics in an Emergent State: The Ceylon General Election of May 1970, chap. 5; and W. A. Wiswa Warnapala, "The Formation of the Cabinet in Sri Lanka: A Study of the 1970 United Front Cabinet," Political Science Review 12, nos. 1 and 2 (January-June 1973).

14. See Gananath Obeysekere, "Some Comments on the Social Backgrounds of the April 1971 Insurgency in Sri Lanka (Ceylon," Journal of Asian Studies 33, no. 3 (May 1974); and Charles S. Blackton, "Sri Lanka's Marxists," Problems of Communism 22, no. 1 (January/February 1973).

15. See S. J. Eldersveld, Political Parties: A Behavioral Analysis (Chicago: Rand McNally and Company, 1964), pp. 1-13.

16. See A. Jeyaratnam Wilson, "The Candidates," in Electoral Politics in an Emergent State: The Ceylon General Election of May 1970, op. cit.

17. See J. R. Jayawardene, The UNP in Opposition, 1970 (confidential, mimeographed).

18. See Taketsugu Tsurutani, The Politics of National Development: Political Leadership in Transitional Societies (New York: Chandler Publishing Company, 1973), pp. 96-99.

19. As told to the writer by one of Dudley Senanayake's most intimate friends.

20. See for example the section entitled "Mrs. Bandaranaike's Objectives," in V. Karalasingham, Politics of Coalition, op. cit., pp. 28-30.

21. Perera was a student of Harold Laski and Herman Finer. He obtained his Ph.D. for a thesis on the Weimar Constitution (in the 1930s) and his senior doctorate (D.Sc. in the early 1940s) for an exhaustive comparative examination of parliamentary procedure in Britain, France, Weimar Germany, and the United States.

22. For further details see A. Jeyaratnam Wilson, "Oppositional Politics in Ceylon (1947-1968)," Government and Opposition 4, no. 1 (Winter 1969): 54-69.

23. See Bandavanike's press release in Ceylon Daily News, July 16, 1951.

24. Extracts of this document were published in Ceylon Daily News, January 9, 1971, and The Times Weekender, January 11, 1971. (Note: Philip Gunawardene died in 1972.)

25. See N. M. Perera, "35 Years After," in Ceylon Daily News, December 22, 1970.

26. See interview given by Colvin R. de Silva to Ceylon Observer, Magazine Edition, December 20, 1970.

27. See Leslie Goonewardene, "New Outlook of the LSSP," in Ceylon Daily News, December 21, 1970. Also V. Karalasingham, "An LSSP Viewpoint: What Should Be Today's Slogans," in Ceylon Daily News, September 2, 1971.

28. Workers' Vanguard, no. 45 (May 24, 1974).

29. See A. Jeyaratnam Wilson, Politics in Sri Lanka, 1947-1973, op. cit., chap. 3, "Economic and Social Progress," pp. 61-86.

30. As mentioned by N. M. Perera in his 1974 budget speech. See Ceylon Daily News, November 7, 1974.

31. For a complete account of the 1956 general election see I. D. S. Weerawardena, Ceylon General Election 1956 (Colombo: Gunasena and Company, 1960).

32. See report of interview given by Prime Minister S. W. R. D. Bandaranaike to U.S. News and World Report, April 20, 1956, p. 61.

33. As reported in Ceylon Observer, May 10, 1964.

34. For further details see Ceylon Daily News, December 14, 1969.

35. See V. Karalasiagham, "An LSSP Viewpoint: What Should Be Today's Slogans," op. cit.

36. See statement issued by Ms. Bandaranaike in Sun, May 3, 1970.

37. See N. M. Perera, Budget Speech 1970-71 (Colombo: Government of Ceylon, 1970), p. 35.

38. For a detailed account of the 1972 Constitution see A. Jeya-ratnam Wilson, Politics in Sri Lanka 1947-1973, op. cit., pp. 234-65.

39. Ceylon received adverse press coverage in India despite the efforts of Ms. Bandaranaike to refute charges that Pakistani troop planes en route to Bangladesh stopped at Bandaranaike International Airport to refuel. See the Prime Minister's remarks on the subject in the House of Representatives in Ceylon Daily News report of December 1, 1971. Also her statement tabled in the National State Assembly on June 23, 1972. (Note: Sri Lanka's relations with India are not on a sure footing because of its Tamil minority. Further, the Tamil Federal Party with its separatist politics has ties with the DMK [Dravidian Progressive Front] in Tamil Nadu [Madras state].

40. Tissa Fernando, "Elite Politics in the New States: The Case of Post-Independence Sri Lanka," Pacific Affairs, Fall 1973, pp. 361-83.

41. Ibid.

42. Ibid.

43. See N. M. Perera, "35 Years After," in Ceylon Daily News, December 22, 1970.

44. See De Silva's interview to the Ceylon Observer, Magazine Edition, December 20, 1970, on "35 Years of the LSSP: Overthrowing Capitalism Our New Challenge."

In December 1971 Zulfikar Ali Bhutto assumed the presidency
of a tattered Pakistan—its population halved by the emergence of
Bangladesh, its legitimacy as the Muslim homeland on the subconti-
nent shaken, its political institutions in disrepute. Bhutto was a
unique leader in Pakistan political history, not only because of the
gravity of the situation, which he both helped to cause and inherited,
or because of his charisma but also because he claimed election as a
Socialist. Bhutto's party, the Pakistan People's Party, had been the
overwhelming winner in what was then West Pakistan in the December
1970 election, campaigning on a strongly socialist program. After a
prolonged period in which government and private enterprise had cooperated to accomplish rapid economic development at the cost of
growing economic disparities—between classes, between regions, and
between urban and rural areas—socialism, so it seemed, had come
into its own in Pakistan.

"STRANGER IN THE PROMISED LAND":
SOCIALISM AND THE ISLAMIC STATE

Pakistan came into being as a result of the increasing democratization and Indianization of the government of India in face of the peculiar geographic distribution of the Muslim population, its cohesive-
ness, and its fear of Hindu domination.[1] To support the demand for
a Muslim-dominated state, the Muslims developed a theory that argued that India was comprised of not one but two nations—one Hindu,
one Muslim. Pakistan had become necessary so that Indian Muslims
could survive as Muslims. Not surprisingly, the years that followed
independence in 1947 were filled with debate over the essential char-

acter of a Muslim-dominated state.[2] Islamic government, Islamic
state, and Islamic constitution became slogans that permeated political debate in the new state. Everyone sensed their importance; no
one was quite sure what they meant. The intensity of this debate left
little room for political ideologies, and, more important, forced
Pakistanis to be principally concerned with ideologies in terms of
their compatibility with Islam. This was especially the case insofar
as socialism was concerned.

The debate as to whether socialism could exist in an Islamic
state has never really ended, nor has the more general debate on the
character of the Islamic state. On the one hand, socialism has always
been accorded a certain degree of legitimacy in the political culture in
terms of its articulation of the goal of economic egalitarianism—a
goal echoed in Islamic tradition and, more recently, in the nebulously
defined ideology of Third Worldism. Iqbal, the poet-philosopher of
Pakistan, had early in the century condemned Western capitalism and
praised Lenin in a famous poem, "Lenin's Petition to God."[3] Other
writings argued that wealth cannot become the property of a few and
that indifference to such accumulation and to the deprivation of the
masses was un-Islamic.[4] The two principal leaders of Pakistan,
Mohammad Ali Jinnah and Liaqat Ali Khan, both spoke of "Islamic
Socialism," a phrase used by Ayub Khan as well as by Bhutto and his
People's Party.

On the other hand, Iqbal was equally critical of the materialistic
philosophy of communism, and ultimately repudiated it decisively.
He thought that communism had planted an excellent egalitarian economic system (identical with or close to Islam) in the barren soil of
materialism.[5] The materialism and atheism of socialism, in other
words, remained suspect. In 1966, after Ayub (in his initial discussion of the third Five-Year Plan) had proclaimed Islamic Socialism
to be the goal of the state, so much reaction was engendered that the
term was dropped when the plan was actually published. And, despite
the concerted campaign for socialism conducted by the Pakistan People's Party during the 1970 elections, the Constitution of Pakistan—
authored by Bhutto and the PPP leadership and endorsed by a National
Assembly in which the People's Party held over a two-third's majority—omits the term completely, even in its more acceptable lower-
case guise, "Islamic socialism." Socialism, in sum, has a highly
amorphous intellectual position in the Pakistani political culture.
Such amorphousness is also characteristic of the Pakistani Left organi-
zationally.

Unlike their counterparts in India or, to a lesser extent, in
Bangladesh, leftist organizations in what is now Pakistan have had
little continuity in terms of their existence. The effort to develop a
Pakistan Socialist Party was short-lived, and the party, stillborn,

was hampered by its secularism, by the earlier connections of its
leaders to the Congress and Indian Socialist parties, and by the Hindu
complexion of the party in East Pakistan.[6] The Pakistan Communist
Party was not really much more successful. The Communists, in
keeping with the Stalinist line on the nationality question, did support
the Pakistan movement, and a number of Communists and Socialists
did organize a "Progressive Group" within the Muslim League. However, such coexistence with the Muslim League was not long-lived.
Communists began to break with the league upon independence when
they organized the Pakistan Communist Party. Between 1947 and 1952
the Pakistan Communist Party followed the Zhdanov line of the International Communist movement and attempted to foment revolutionary
armed uprisings in several parts of East Pakistan.[7] As a result,
while the PCP was a legal political entity after independence, it was
carefully watched by the government of Pakistan. In March 1951 the
Prime Minister, Liaqat Ali Khan, accused the PCP of having con-
spired with certain military officers to overthrow the government.
Several leading Communist figures were tried and convicted along
with Major General Akbar Khan, the Army Chief of Staff, for their
complicity in the so-called "Rawalpindi Plot" in January 1953. A
year and a half later the party itself was banned throughout Pakistan.

Despite the disappearance of the traditional leftist parties in
West Pakistan, Socialist and Communist influence persisted, focused
around particular leaders, small groups of intellectuals, peasant organizers, and trade unionists—all the remnants of earlier organizational spurts. In Karachi, for example, vestiges of M. N. Roy's Indian Federation of Labour persisted as the West Pakistan Federation
of the Labour.[8] Communists and Socialists controlled various other
union bodies—none very large or effective—as well. Among peasants,
both Communist and Socialist influence existed, less through explicit
organization than through efforts of particular leaders to mobilize
tenants on antilandlord protests.[9] Insofar as intellectual groups were
concerned, the Progressive Writers' Movement remained by far the
most important. Organized on an all-India basis in 1932 by Sajjad
Zaheer, a Communist activist, it remained an embryo of the organized
left until it collapsed under government pressure in the late 1950s.[10]

There were other leftist "fragments" as well. In Punjab, Mian
Iftikharuddin, a millionaire long sympathetic to leftist causes within
both the Congress and the Muslim League, continued to be a focus of
such activity. In the late 1940s he had organized a newspaper publishing company that had served the Progressive Writers' Movement's
principal platform. In the early 1950s he joined with members of the
former "Progressive Group" of the Muslim League to form the Azad
Pakistan Party. In the other provinces of West Pakistan, socialism
persisted as an undercurrent of the strong regional sentiments that

characterized politics in those areas. Men such as G. M. Syed in
Sind, Khan Abdul Ghaffar Khan in the Northwest Frontier, and Abdus
Samad Achakzai in Baluchistan were all leftists as well as leaders of
parties and groups campaigning for a maximum degree of political
autonomy from the central government for their provinces.

These elites gradually coalesced in an effort to expand their influence. In 1954 the Azad Pakistan Party merged with the other groups
to form the National Party.[11] In 1957, this conglomerate of leftist-
cum-regional factions merged with the newly organized National
Awami Party, a leftist East Pakistani movement organized by Maulana
Abdul Hamid Khan Bhasani, a former Assam Muslim League leader
and active peasant organizer.[12] In NAP, Pakistan regained an avowedly
leftist, national political organization. The party not only became the
principal proponent of the "downtrodden" of Pakistani society (its declared objective)—it also led a continual legislative campaign against
Pakistan's increasingly pro-Western foreign policy.

Yet, for all the organizational rejuvenation that the emergence
of the National Awami Party gave to the Left, it also added to the ambiguous legitimacy of socialism in Pakistan. The Frontier and Baluchistan party leaders had been active in the Congress movement prior
to independence and had opposed the formation of Pakistan. Their
continuing demand for provincial autonomy was perceived by many as
a continuation of this opposition. Although Bhasani had been a leader
of the Muslim League movement, his adoption of many East Pakistani
provincial demands made him equally suspect. Socialism and region-
alism, at times, seemed to intertwine as challenges to the whole notion of Pakistan. Largely because of this, the National Awami Party
declined as an instrument of Socialist opposition to the regime of
President Ayub Khan that followed the coup d'etat of 1958. The party
itself split in 1967 in East Pakistan over issues involving both peraon-
ality and ideology (the Bhasani faction was typified as "pro-Chinese";
the other (Muzzafar) faction, "pro-Moscow"). In West Pakistan the
bulk of the party, now led by Wali Khan, the son of Ghaffar Abdul
Khan, was linked with the "pro-Moscow" group. The split merely
accentuated the regional character of the party, however, and outside
of Baluchistan and the Northwest Frontier, NAP members simply
drifted away.

The NAP "episode" overlaid yet another veneer of Socialist,
Communist, and generally leftist cadres and groups on top of those
already in existence. If socialism remained somewhat suspect to
many, it was also no longer so foreign to many. If leftist political
organization remained weak and fragmented, it was also at least
present in a minimal way. Both the ideology and the organizations
provided much of the resources for the Pakistan People's Party and
its leader, Zulfikar Ali Bhutto.

THE PAKISTAN PEOPLE'S PARTY:
SOCIALISM AS PROTEST

The election of a leftist party as the majority party in West Pakistan in 1970 can only be explained in part by reference to the PPP's organization and ideology. In large part that victory was the offshoot of escalating protest against a government that had become too onerous, too unfair, and too inefficient to bear. Although the government of Ayub Khan had initially drawn widespread support after Ayub's coup d'etat of 1958, the increasingly centralized, authoritarian character of the regime and the growing economic disparities that were the result of its policies fanned widespread resentment toward the regime. There was substantial and vigorous opposition to Ayub and his style of government in the controlled presidential elections of 1964-65.[13] This opposition accelerated in the three years that followed.[14] In the fall of 1968, police firings on student protests and arrests of leading politicians in both wings of Pakistan generated a mass movement—chaotic and not organized in any real sense—throughout Pakistan. The movement gradually intensified until it forced Ayub's abdication in March 1969 in favor of the army commander-in-chief, General Agha Mohammad Yahya Khan.[15]

Zulfikar Ali Bhutto and his People's Party were both the manufacturers and the products of this upsurge. At first glance, Bhutto's success as a leader of the opposition seems surprising. The product of a wealthy, landowning, aristocratic family in Sind, educated in the United States and England, Bhutto was preeminently a product of the Ayub regime. At the age of 30 he was appointed to the first martial law Cabinet, and as foreign minister he quickly became one of the most visible men in the government. In 1965, however, following the negotiations that ended the 1965 Indo-Pakistani War, Bhutto broke with the Ayub government over what he considered on Ayub's part to convert battlefield success into diplomatic success. The break, for a belief widely shared by the West Pakistan public, catapulted him to a high pinnacle of popularity.

Bhutto only gradually moved toward developing his own political party—a hesitation encouraged, no doubt, by Ayub's threats of legal harassment should he do so. Bhutto's tenure as foreign minister had been characterized by a strongly leftist, "anti-imperialist" orientation (he had been the architect of Pakistan cultivation of China and was a strong admirer, in particular, of Sukarno of Indonesia), and he almost immediately adopted a socialist position in his attacks on the government, an ideological move assisted by several intellectual Marxists such as J. A. Rahim (later secretary-general of the PPP and a member of Bhutto's Cabinet), who were close friends and served as informal advisers. At the same time, Bhutto seemed also keenly aware of the essential "strangeness" of socialism in Pakistan, particularly in stridently Muslim West Pakistan, and included Islam as an integral part of his emerging ideology. In November 1967 the Pakistan People's Party was launched. In a sense, the PPP was a synthesis of a man looking for a party and of a yet unformed party of diverse leftist groups looking for a leader. The party, as a result, was extremely heterogeneous. The organizing conference was attended by not only leftist organizers and "intellectual Marxists" but also aristocratic, often conservative personal followers of Bhutto.

The new party's ideological and programmatic positions were set forth in a series of papers issued under the collective title, Foundation and Policy. Pakistan, the party argued, had encouraged growth by encouraging a massive plundering of the economy by private entrepreneurs. Capitalists had financed their ventures with public funds, taking advantage of liberal foreign exchange allocations, low taxes, a permissive attitude on the part of government of fraud, government suppression of unions, and the like.[16] The result, said the documents, was a deceptive progress; the national economy remains weak, lacking in heavy industry and in the development of advanced technology. Worse, the progress that had occurred had so increased inequality in Pakistani society as to cause a general decline in the quality of Pakistani life: corruption was widespread, and there was growing disenchantment with the original goals of Pakistan.[17]

The papers asserted that socialism and only socialism could cure Pakistan.[18] At minimum, a socialist state required nationalization of all means of production basic to industrial development—banking and insurance, iron and steel, heavy engineering and construction, chemicals and petrochemicals, mining, shipping, public transport, and utilities.[19] Competent and genuinely cooperative private enterprise would be allowed to function; however, the existence of a private sector was not to detract from the establishment of the classless society that was the party's principal goal. Labor reforms were promised, as were free health care, reorganization of education, and the elimination of "feudalism" and "landlordism."

A socialist state, the PPP argued, need not be antithetical to Pakistan'a cultural and religious values. The road to socialism is not the same for all, notes the papers; and socialism can be accommodated to Pakistan's culture. Major socialist values, egalitarianism and the prohibition of exploitation, were Islamic values as well. The phrase, "Islamic socialism," was not used in Foundation and Policy, but the papers repeatedly emphasized the congruency between Islam and socialism. As Bhutto noted in a later speech,

> Islam and the principles of socialism are not mutually repugnant. Islam preaches equality and so-

> cialism is the modern technique of attaining it. . . .
> Pakistan cannot last without the supremacy of Islam.
> A socialist form of government does not rival that
> supremacy. On the contrary, socialism will make
> the whole population the custodian of Islamic values.[20]

Although Bhutto's increasingly open confrontation with the Ayub regime, especially in the fall of 1968, played a catalytic role in the protests that ultimately brought about Ayub's resignation, the protests were neither PPP-led nor, particularly at the beginning, socialist in orientation. All of the opposition parties, both right and left, supported the protests, which were focused primarily on removing Ayub and redressing economic grievances held by the participants in the protests. As the protests continued, however, they assumed an increasingly radical character. By mid-February 1969 demands had shifted from particular grievances to a call for widespread reforms, a call frequently summarized as a demand for a socialist state. This shift became particularly visible after labor unions joined the protests. Rallies organized in Lahore demanded abolition of capitalism and land-lordism, nationalization of agriculture, and the right of workers to strike.[21] Labor leaders were critical of the established opposition parties for their "preoccupation" with constitutional reform. The president of the strong Railway Workers Union argued that the people's salvation lay not in the 1956 or 1962 constitution, but in socialism and in the formation of a united front of workers, farmers, students, and the middle class to change the existing economic system.[22]

The emergence of socialism as an "ideology of protest" had dramatic consequences. In the first place, there are indications that the widening of the protests from specific demands to a demand for a change in the system as a whole played a significant role in impelling Ayub Khan's resignation. Already doubtful of his support within the military and the bureaucracy, Ayub now saw the entire constitutional edifice he had constructed in danger of being dismantled. As one commentator noted, Ayub probably felt that his retirement announcement would buy some time for him to select a "suitable" successor and perhaps "institutionalize" some of the developments he had initiated.[23]

Second (and, in the end, more important), the radicalization of the protests really served to alter the political culture by transforming the vocabulary of Pakistani politics. The rhetoric of socialism gained an immediacy and reality that the ideology had previously lacked. The People's Party, in particular, benefited from this. The increasingly radical character of the protests telescoped with the socialist rhetoric of the PPP and gave the party a visibility and legitimacy it had previously lacked.

Ayub's resignation could not save the system he had built. Although the military junta that assumed control sought to accommodate the protests by a series of economic and administrative reforms, it was impelled eventually to announce plans for returning Pakistan to civilian rule. In September 1969 General Yahya announced that political activity would again be legal January 1, 1970 and that elections would be held in the fall of 1970 to be followed by a convocation of the newly elected National Assembly to write a new constitution.

In retrospect, it is surprising that most spectators both inside and outside of Pakistan were startled by the PPP victory in the elections. To be sure, the PPP was disorganized. Provincial party structures were generally more fiction than fact. What local party structures the PPP did have were poorly coordinated. Candidate selection was extremely chaotic. Bhutto had some success in persuading a number of friends and political colleagues to contest on the PPP ticket, particularly in Sind Province and in western and southwestern Punjab (Multan and Sargodha districts). Elsewhere, however, the self-appointed PPP officials selected candidates who were generally lacking in local status. The provincial PPP leadership was able only partly to guide candidate selection.

On the other hand, the protests had altered the political climate completely, and the campaign appeals of all the parties indicated the general leftward turn of Pakistani politics. All parties stood for liquidating interregional and class disparities, calling for major reforms to benefit workers and agriculturalists. All suggested programs for insuring a more equitable distribution of wealth—a ceiling on landholdings, distribution of excess land to landless peasants, exempting small cultivators from revenue payments, and giving industrial workers a share of industry profits. Most also called for placing heavy industry in the public sector and for nationalizing banks and insurance companies.

In this context the PPP appeal was especially persuasive. In the West it quickly emerged as the least moderate party. The PPP was the most vehement advocate of socialism; coupled with Bhutto's truculent hostility toward India and his reputation as a nationalist, it was also seen as the most stridently nationalist and antiregionalist party. Bhutto claimed credit for exposing the "bankruptcy" of the Tashkent Declaration and for leading the 1967 protests against Ayub. While emphasizing socialism and nationalism, Bhutto sought to dispel the traditional fear of socialism by interpreting his "Islamic socialism" in terms of Islamic masawat (egalitarianism), and by dangling before Muslims the prospect of celebrating Shaukat-i-Islam (victory of Islam) day in Delhi and Srinigar (the capital of Indian Kashmir).[24] In the end, Bhutto and the PPP overwhelmed their opponents in the two largest provinces of West Pakistan and, through that dominance,

in West Pakistan as a whole. The PPP won control of the Punjab and
Sind provincial legislatures and 81 out of 138 National Assembly seats
in West Pakistan.[25] As the ideology of opposition, socialism had established itself in Pakistan. What remained in question, however,
was its role as a state ideology.

SOCIALISM AS ANTI-IDEOLOGY: THE
EMERGENCE OF THE POLITICS OF CONTROL

There can be no dispute that Bhutto moved Pakistan in a "socialist direction" upon his assumption of power in December 1971.
Immediately after taking office, Bhutto initiated a wide range of economic reforms, including the nationalization of a variety of industries.
Yet the persisting militancy of a population mobilized by the anti-Ayub
protests of 1968-69 and buffeted by the loss of East Pakistan in 1971,
together with the organizational weakness of the PPP and Bhutto's
limited control over the government, impelled him to emphasize rule
rather than reform. To an increasing degree, the regime has assumed
an "antimobilist" character, and socialism has become anti-ideology,
a set of slogans that explain little in the way of regime policy and that
cloak a limited regime's increasing preoccupation with increasing its
control over the political system.

Despite his emergence as the preeminent political figure in Pakistan, Bhutto assumed the presidency of Pakistan as a ruler very
much limited by his political environment. His party controlled only
two of the four major provinces that now comprised Pakistan—Baluchistan and the Northwest Frontier having rejected the PPP for a NAP-
Jamiat-ul-Ulema-i-Islam (JUI) coalition. Opposition parties, particularly the religio-political Islam-pasand (literally, "Islam loving")
parties, presented a considerable obstacle, especially in terms of
their pressure for Islamic provisions within the constitution yet to be
written. The army, despite its defeat in East Pakistan, remained a
potential opponent. The PPP had gained sizable support among both
in-service and retired officers, largely in response to Bhutto's reputation for nationalism.[26] However, a substantial section of the military, particularly at the most senior levels, remained less than en-
thusiastic about the transfer of power to civilian hands. The bureaucracy remained a potent force. While Bhutto could use the civil and
police services as subordinate government agencies because the new
configuration of power compelled obedience to his political authority,
they were only subordinate agencies and not allies. Trade unionists
and peasants remain politicized and active. Strikes, agitations, and
limited episodes of violence remained common occurrences.

The PPP did not provide Bhutto with an organizational means of resolving these problems. It was, in fact, a constraint on Bhutto in its own right. As indicated earlier, the party had developed quickly and in a tumultous period. It was in consequence less party than movement. During the 1970 election campaign a variety of enthusiasts—leftists, personal devotees of Bhutto, men convinced of the PPP's success—opened party offices with or without specific authorization of the party's "high command." In Punjab especially a kind of organizational free-for-all ensued aslocal party groups made competing claims for representing the same or at least overlapping constituencies. Such organizational chaos was exacerbated by the fact that many party elites, such as men personally linked to Bhutto, had their own factional supporters and competed for control over the local party groups. Although many of the factional rivals were leftists, there were ideological divisions. Bhutto had relied not only on ideological appeals and his personal ties to leftists to build the PPP but on his ties to old allies in the Convention Muslim League as well. In Punjab, Bhutto attracted a number of middle-level and large landowners to the PPP, some because of his previous connections with them, others because by the middle of 1970 the PPP's popularity in Punjab had become undisputable and many "fence-sitters" had begun to join. In Sind, the PPP was a landlord party. The PPP's real growth there came when Makhdoom Mohammad Zaman Khan, one of the two principal pirs (spiritual leaders) and landlords, joined the PPP. He was followed by many politically influential aristocratic, landlord families, including the Sind's former ruling family, the Talpurs. All of these had previously supported Ayub Khan and were essentially conservative in ideology. Other rightists had joined the party when Bhutto had sought to expand his support among Islam pasands by recruiting Maulana Kausar Niazi (long linked to rightist ulema) as Propaganda Secretary for the PPP. The party organization essential to manage this menage was poor at best. Efforts to formulate a central organization and to organize effectively provincial, district, and local party groups and to rationalize communications between levels were begun only after the elections and were quickly lost in the preoccupation with the growing crisis in East Pakistan.

The reforms that the new government initialed reflected both the socialist direction of the PPP during the campaign and the political constraints on Bhutto after he assumed power. After a political campaign that had stressed the unjust monopolization of wealth in Pakistan by a small number of families (commonly referred to as "the twenty-two families"), it is not surprising that the government's first target for reform would be those sectors of the economy associated with such monopolization. The attack on the 22 families had both its theatrical and real elements.[27] The former is visible in

Bhutto's seizure of passports belonging to the families and sealing of the border to all except religious pilgrims so as to prevent flight of capital from Pakistan. More real was the January 3, 1972 Economic Reforms Order in which the government nationalized 20 firms owned by the families, all in the area of "heavy industry"—iron and steel, basic metal industries, heavy engineering, heavy electrical machinery, automobile manufacturing, tractor manufacturing, chemical and petrochemical industries, cement manufacturing, and public utilities. The government also abolished the managing agency system. Under this system, the management of a company was given over by its directors to a managing agent, a separate corporate entity, which had a relatively free hand in running the company and which provided the directors wide opportunities for siphoning off profits and for expanding economic control with relatively little investment.

Life insurance companies and the banking industry (again both largely the private preserves of these economically powerful families) were also reformed. The former was almost immediately nationalized. The latter was placed under a series of government controls designed to limit the power of the banks and to secure a more equitable distribution of credit. The banks were put on notice that a failure to alter past practices would lead to nationalization—an event that did, in fact, occur less than two years later.

Economic reforms were extended beyond this emphasis on the 22 families as well. The government nationalized the rice and cotton export industries and the manufacture of vegetable ghee (cooking oil), an essential commodity in all Pakistani homes. It also instituted labor reforms. Grievance procedures were established and the real income of workers was enhanced through compulsory bonuses, a broadened profit-sharing program, pension plans, and educational allowances for workers' children.

On March 11, 1972, Bhutto used his power as Chief Martial Law Administrator to promulgate land reforms. Briefly, the land reforms cut the limit on holdings per individual from 500 to 150 irrigated acres and from 1,000 to 300 unirrigated acres.[28] Lands above the ceiling were taken without compensation, and it was announced that they would be given free to peasants. Arbitrary ejection of tenants from the land was prohibited. Civilian officials were required to surrender all lands in excess of 100 acres acquired during their tenure of service—this provision a response to the widely held belief that civil servants had massively profited from previous land acts.

Yet as significant as these reforms may have been, they were not as far-reaching as the casual observer might be led to expect. The constraints existing in the political system were simply too strong for any leader to ignore. The "assault" on the 22 families left much, if not most, of their economic power untouched. The "heavy" indus-

tries nationalized were not the only sources of economic power for
these families and represented only a relatively minor part of Pakistan's industrial capacity. The nationalization of life insurance brought
some assets to the government, but nationalization was as much impelled by the impending collapse of several of the largest companies
after their losses of assets in East Pakistan as by more "ideological"
considerations. The government feared that such collapses would
further undermine an economy already damaged by lack of confidence
in its survival. The other minor nationalization efforts possessed a
similarly involuntary character. Nationalization of the ghee industry
came only after a prolonged refusal of owners to increase production,
for example. Nationalization of the banks was delayed for so long that
its immediate impact was limited.

The labor reforms, while substantial, fell far short of those advocated by the labor movement. Nor were the agrarian reforms massive in impact. There were too many landlords in the PPP. The
land ceiling was placed so high that it did not affect a significantly
large proportion of cultivated land. Although newspaper reports initially said that 3 million acres were being redistributed, later reports
listed only 724,000 acres as having been affected. Nearly 2 million
peasants remained landless.

The relatively limited economic reforms can only in part be attributed to the government's limited power. Bhutto's own highly pragmatic political views played a role as well. The Prime Minister was
never really an ideologically oriented political actor; his socialism
was more a result of his calculation that political success in post-
Ayub Pakistan required mass support rather than of ideological commitment. Perhaps more important than this, however, was a shift
in the emphasis in Bhutto's governing strategy. Despite the reform
emphasis of the election campaign and the initial reform moves,
Bhutto was becoming increasingly concerned with the constraints on
his ability to rule and with enhancing his maneuverability in and control over a restrictive political environment. Again it should be
noted that ideology was not a significant motivating factor here. Bhutto
objected to the constraints that were reflected in the limited reforms
not so much because they hampered reform as because they hampered
his exercise of power.

Bhutto's efforts to widen and to insure his control over the political system has had both organizational and ideological dimensions.
Because the former has had considerable implications for the latter,
it is useful to survey briefly some of those changes first. As the
Bhutto government has evolved, it has, to an increasing degree, relied on patrimonialism as a means of establishing control over the
government and other political institutions, and on a deemphasis of
political mobilization as a means of controlling the mobilized sectors

of the population. Patrimonialism, which refers to the attempt of a
political leader to establish control over an institution through the
placement of officials (usually lacking a power base of their own)
in strategic positions within that institution, has long been a characteristic of Pakistani politics. Its use has increased substantially
since Bhutto assumed power. Bhutto has replaced both senior military and civil service personnel largely with his own nominees, with
relatively little regard for existing retirement and promotional procedures. He also used patrimonialism to expand his control to the
two provinces whose governments had been organized by NAP-JUI coalitions. Although the events leading up to the dismissal of the NAP-
JUI government in Baluchistan and the resignation of its counterpart
in the NWFP are too lengthy and complex to be related here, it is apparent that Bhutto found intolerable the bargaining process in which
his government and the two provincial governments were engaged.
Following a variety of center-provincial conflicts and a general deterioration of law and order in both provinces (in part engendered by the
PPP and its allies in those provinces), Bhutto replaced the coalition-
backed governors (chosen by previous agreement between the PPP,
JUI, and NAP) with his own nominees. It might be noted that even in
the "PPP-loyalist" provinces of Punjab and Sind Bhutto's patrimonial
ties to the leaders figured heavily. In Sind, Bhutto's control was
maintained through his cousin and chief minister of the province,
Mumtaz Ali Bhutto. In Punjab, Ghulam Mustafa Khar, a close personal associate, served as governor and as Ghutto's surrogate.

Nowhere did patrimonialism become more pervasive than within
the People's Party itself. Although his efforts to stimulate more effective control over provincial and local party organizations proceeded
slowly, inroads were made. Even before the elections provincial
committees were shunted aside by centrally selected provincial parliamentary boards that were formally assigned the task of supervising
selection of candidates for the PPP ticket. After assuming power,
new provincial committees were named, and it was decided that "pending party elections" each level of party organization would be responsible for selecting the officers of the levels below it. At each level,
men with personal ties to Bhutto or to his closest followers were
selected. The party was gradually reconstructed around a series of
personal networks emanating downward from Bhutto.

Related to the growing use of patrimonialism by Bhutto was the
general deemphasis of mobilization by the regime. Again, control
appears to have been the motivating factor here. Fearful of alternative bases of powers within the PPP, Bhutto fairly consistently guided
the party away from the hands of those most active in popular mobilization and political organization. In the party's 1970 convention,
Bhutto separated himself completely with the most militant and mass-

oriented faction of the party (which rejected any cooperation with the
military government then in power) by deciding that the PPP would
contest the elections. Since that time the number of mass organizers
in the party has declined rapidly. Mukhtar Rana, a militant Socialist
and labor leader in Punjab who had become increasingly vocal in his
charges of "fascism" in the party, lost his National Assembly seat in
April 1972 after being imprisoned under martial law regulations for
inciting violence. Meraj Mohammad Khan, once a student leader in
Karachi with extensive labor influence, left Bhutto's Cabinet primarily
because of his ideological disenchantment with Bhutto. In Punjab,
Bhutto's support of Mustafa Khar against the initial PPP President,
Sheikh Rashid, an influential peasant organizer, undercut much of the
latter's influence in the party. And, despite an official party rule that
elected officials should not serve as party office holders—a rule designed to stimulate the development of a mass political organization—
Bhutto has, because of his appointment of his patrimonial nominees
to government positions and because of their retention of party roles,
shaped the PPP into a relatively limited, minister-focused party.
At the national and provincial levels, the national and provincial cabinets are, in effect, the relevant PPP organizations.

The deemphasis on participation and mobilization has also manifested itself in the use of government coercion. The central and provincial governments, like their nonelected predecessors, continued
to rely heavily on a variety of legal statutes that allow suppression
of public political behavior. Bhutto also kept martial law in effect
for more than a year after assuming power, thereby allowing himself
extraordinary powers as Chief Martial Law Administrator. To some
extent, even the reforms were directed at curtailing the continued
high level of mobilization sustained by various groups. With regard
to the trade unions, for example, Bhutto argued that even the limited
reforms warranted an end to militant union activity:

> Since the 20th of December, Martial Law notwith-
> standing, "gheraos and jalaos" seems to have become
> the order of the day. This unruly and rowdy prac-
> tice, negative in its purpose, anarchist in its ap-
> proach, nihilistic in its results has been endured
> regrettably by the Government and the people for
> over seven weeks. . . . It is a self-destructive
> procedure. The majority of the people have shown
> their disgust over these demonstrations of hooligan-
> ism. . . . National leaders have spoken against it.
> . . . [This] intolerable form of threat and thunder
> must stop.[29]

The extensive use of government coercion by Bhutto's followers in office has also proved to be a formidable discouragement to political participation. Buttressed by Bhutto's personal support, those in office were seldom reluctant to harass not only members of opposition parties but their opponents within the PPP as well. Arbitrary jailing, bogus criminal charges, and physical harassment by the police all became common; and since Bhutto frequently ousted one official in favor of another, the initial instigators of these acts were often the targets of such acts later. Bhutto has been only partly successful in his efforts to restrain this factional violence. His requirements of political control seem to necessitate frequent personnel changes in government so as to prevent any individual developing an independent power base. The numerous changes only perpetuated the violence. Attacks on opposition politicians have been particularly severe. In 1972 Usman Kennedy, a Sindhi opposition leader, was severely beaten and two opposition leaders assassinated; in 1973, four unsuccessful assassination attempts were made on Abdul Wali Khan, the leader of the opposition in the National Assembly; in 1974, the deputy speaker of the Baluchistan Assembly, also an opposition leader, was assassinated. While numerous attacks were made on Bhutto's supporters as well, it was and is largely believed that most of the violence was officially inspired. Whether or not such impressions are correct, the aura of intimidation that pervades Pakistani politics has sharply curtailed participation.

Patrimonialism and discouragement of participation have also had consequences ideologically, in terms of both the ideological coloration of the PPP and the ideology itself. As to ideological coloration, while it does not appear that Bhutto's own ideological views were major motivating factors in his various organizational and antimobizational maneuvers, such maneuvers have shifted the party ideologically rightward. For the most part Bhutto's principal nominees to office have not been leftists. Since many of the initial provincial and local PPP officials were leftists and since the officials appointed later have not been and have tended to try to consolidate themselves by eliminating the influence of the old officials, the net result of party reorganization has meant a significant diminution of active socialist influence in the party. This development was accelerated by the departure of many of the "mass organizers" originally linked to the party.

Framed against this background, the state's socialist ideology has assumed a new function. It no longer guides action, it simply justifies it. As indicated earlier, the PPP's initial ideological statements were fairly specific in terms of the party's proposed goals and programs. This was particularly the case in the Election Manifesto that appeared in early 1970. The manifesto not only called for a so-

cialist state, it made specific policy commitments—80 percent of the
economy (excluding agriculture) was to be nationalized; specific agrarian reforms were promised as were day care centers, old age pensions, revision of the school curriculum, labor reforms, local self-
government, and so forth. After Bhutto assumed power, however, the
government's particular version of socialism gradually lost its programmatic quality. To be sure, the government continued to make
reference to the programs promised in its manifesto and to move in
the direction of implementing some of those programs. However, to
an increasing degree neither government spokesmen nor Bhutto himself have been willing to elaborate further on movement toward a "socialist society." The people and the party are called upon to fight
"exploitation" and to support the goal of "scientific socialism," but
such terms remain largely undefined. Just exactly how certain policies will further the accomplishment of a socialist state is unex-
plained. Socialism, or rather the slogans associated with the ideology,
is used to legitimize any government action. Both intervention and
nonintervention in the economy, for example, have been explained in
terms of "socialism."

To an increasing degree, the socialism propounded by the government has become an "anti-ideology," that is, an amalgam of slogans, vague prescriptions, and bromides proclaiming the virtues of
socialism, which offers no indication of policy direction to be taken
by a regime. Its function is no longer to direct political action but to
free its articulator—the state—to act as it pleases; and the growing
vagueness of the ideology accomplishes just that. In the area of property rights, for example, the right to private property is both currently
supported and denied in theory. That is, on the one hand the regime
continues to emphasize that it has no intention to nationalize all property, and private property is accorded some constitutional protection.
The presence of such property rights, it is argued, is not antithetical
to socialism because Pakistani socialism has its own path to follow.
On the other hand, the right to property seems to fade in face of the
regime's insistence that it can compulsorily take possession of property for "a public purpose." The contradiction is purposely left unresolved. So long as the contradiction can be obfuscated and the belief
promoted that the right to private property is compatible with government control, the government is given maximum freedom to do as it
wishes in this area. It can nationalize and has nationalized private
property. At the same time, it is under no obligation to do so and
can leave whole sectors of the economy untouched by government. In
other words, socialist ideology has ceased being a programmatic
guide for political action to be taken by the state and has been transformed, instead, into means of maximizing the government's range of
policy choices much as Bhutto's use of patrimonialism and of antimo-

bilist tactics were designed to enhance his political maneuverability.
In Pakistan, socialism has become just another means whereby political control can be consolidated.

CONCLUSION

> I am a believer in socialism; that is why, leaving my
> class and government, I have come back to workers,
> peasants, students, and poor people. What can I get
> from my deprived people except love? I am the fol-
> lower of socialism because I know that only in this
> economic system lies the salvation, progress, and
> well-being of the people. No power on earth can
> prevent the establishment of this system of truth and
> justice, equality and human dignity in Pakistan.
> —Zulfikar Ali Bhutto[30]

There is a tendency among students of politics in Pakistan to
view politics in that state largely in terms of personalities. In this
perspective, political developments are explained wholly in terms of
the particular personalities of the political elites involved. There is
much truth in this view. Certainly, as we have suggested, recent developments in Pakistan cannot be understood separate from the personality of Zulfikar Ali Bhutto. Yet reality is more complex than
this. The emergence of a government organized by a party committed
to socialism can only partly be explained by Bhutto's "charisma." As
we have seen, the legitimation of socialism was the culmination of a
prolonged dialogue between Pakistani Socialists and the Pakistani political culture, of repeated efforts to develop socialist organization.
The sporadic dialogue laid the basis for the radicalization of the anti-
Ayub movement in 1969. Even after achieving power, the new socialist vocabulary of politics has had its imperatives. The government
had to move toward reforms to preserve its legitimacy. And, despite
the changes socialism in Pakistan has undergone in becoming a doctrine of rule, it does impel action; some effort must be made by the
government to eliminate a number of the most visible social and economic disparities; some effort must be made to bring Pakistan's foreign policy more closely in alignment with the still nebulous "international socialism" of the Third World.

The role of ideology as a determinant of political reality in Pakistan, however, diminishes in face of that state's political fragmentation, a situation characterized not only by regional and communal divisions but by government disorganization as well. Such fragmentation has always been part of Pakistani politics. It was a principal
motive for Ayub's coup in 1958—and, if anything, became more mas-

sive in the aftermath of the chaos of 1968-71. Such fragmentation impels political leaders to become preoccupied with political order and with insuring their own political survival. That preoccupation has become the principal function of ideology in underdeveloped states in general. Such is particularly, the fate—Bhutto's protestations notwithstanding—of socialism in Pakistan.

NOTES

1. For an excellent study of the Pakistan movement, see Khalid Bin Sayeed, Pakistan: The Formative Phase, 1857-1948 (London: Oxford University Press, 1968).

2. The various aspects of this debate are surveyed in Richard S. Wheeler, The Politics of Pakistan: A Constitutional Quest (Ithaca, N.Y.: Cornell University Press, 1970).

3. Fazlur Rahman, "Islam and the New Constitution of Pakistan," Journal of Asian and African Studies 8, nos. 3 and 4 (1974): 191.

4. Aziz Ahmad and G. E. von Grunebaum, Muslim Self-Statement in India and Pakistan (Wiesbaden: O. Harassowitz, 1970), pp. 151-52.

5. Rahman, op. cit., p. 191.

6. The problems of the Pakistan Socialist Party are briefly discussed in Saul Rose, Socialism in Southern Asia (London: Oxford University Press, 1959), pp. 59-69.

7. Marcus F. Franda, "Communism and Regional Politics in East Pakistan," Asian Survey 9, no. 7 (1970): 589.

8. M. N. Roy was the founder of the Communist Party of India. In 1929 he was expelled from the Comintern as part of Stalin's attack on the Bukharin group in Communist movement. He later developed his own Communist group in India and achieved considerable (and long-lasting) influence in the trade union movement. See John P. Haithcox, Communism and Nationalism in India: M. N. Roy and Comintern Policy, 1920-1939 (Princeton, N.J.: Princeton University Press, 1971).

9. Interview with Sheikh Mohammad Rashid, Minister for Food, Pakistan, Lahore, February 1974. Sheikh Rashid had been active in the peasant movement in the 1950s and 1960s.

10. On this very influential organization, see Hafeez Malik, "The Marxist Literary Movement in India and Pakistan," Journal of Asian Studies 26, no. 4 (1967): 649-64.

11. This brief chronology of the coalescence of leftist groups is based upon interviews held by the author with political elites in Pakistan in 1973-74. The smallness of the parties, their brief lifespans, and their personalistic character made firm dates of formation, merger, and the like impossible.

12. Bhasani remains one of the most important yet understudied figures in South Asian politics. For a study of the more recent period of NAP's existence, see M. Rashiduzzaman, "The National Awami Party of Pakistan: Leftist Politics in Crisis," Pacific Affairs 43, no. 3 (1970): 394-409.

13. See, for example, Louis Dupres, "Pakistan, 1964-66, Part I: The Government and Opposition," American Universities Field Staff South Asia Series 4, no. 5.

14. The protest movement is chronicled in detail in Munir Ahmad, "The November Mass Movement in Pakistan," in Munir Ahmad, Aspects of Pakistan's Politics and Administration (Lahore: University of the Punjab South Asia Institute, 1974).

15. Ayub's resignation is discussed in Robert LaPorte, Jr., "Succession in Pakistan: Continuity and Change in a Garrison State," Asian Survey 9, no. 11 (1969): 842-61.

16. Pakistan People's Party, Foundation and Policy (Lahore: PPP, 1967), p. 29.

17. Ibid., pp. 30-31.

18. "Foundation Document No. 4."

19. Ibid., pp. 35-36.

20. Zulfikar Ali Bhutto, Political Situation in Pakistan, Pakistan Peoples Party's Political Series, no. 1 (Lahore: Haneef Ramay, "Al-Bayan," 1968), pp. 14-15.

21. Ahmad, op. cit., pp. 44-45.

22. Ibid., p. 45.

23. LaPorte, op. cit., p. 856.

24. Sharifal Mujahid, "Pakistan: The First General Election," Asian Survey 11, no. 2 (1971): 168.

25. The elections are surveyed and analyzed in Craig Baxter, "Pakistan Votes—1970," Asian Survey 11, no. 3 (1971): 197-218.

26. A number of retired officers ran on the PPP ticket in 1970. The PPP's popularity among the serving officers can be judged from the fact that a political novice deflated a former chief of the air force by a 2 to 1 margin in Rawalpindi, headquarters of the Pakistan military.

27. A first effort to distinguish the real from the theatrical is made in W. Eric Gustafson, "Economic Reforms Under the Bhutto Regime," Journal of Asian and African Studies 8, nos. 3 and 4 (1973): 241-57.

28. Ibid., p. 247.

29. Pakistan Times, February 11, 1972, p. 7.

30. Zulfikar Ali Bhutto, "Address to the Hyderabad Convention, September 21, 1968," in Let My People Judge (Lahore: Pakistan People's Party, 1968).

313

316

ABOUT THE EDITORS AND CONTRIBUTORS

HELEN DESFOSSES is a Research Fellow at the Russian Research Center, Harvard University, and a Member of the Population Studies Center, School of Public Health, Harvard University. She received her M.A. in Soviet Studies from Harvard University and her Ph.D. in Political Science from the African Studies Center, Boston University. She is the author of Soviet Policy Toward Black Africa: The Focus on National Integration, and a contributor to Chinese and Soviet Aid to Africa and The Superpowers in the Seventies. Her articles have appeared in Survey, Problems of Communism, Osteuropa, Studies in Comparative Communism, and Soviet Studies. She has delivered papers at national and international conferences, Department of State seminars, and the Council on Foreign Relations. She has done research in Africa, the Soviet Union, and Eastern Europe, supported by grants from the Coretta Scott King Fund of the American Association of University Women, the Ford Foundation, the Population Council, and the National Academy of Sciences.

JACQUES LEVESQUE is Professor of Political Science at Universite du Quebec a Montreal. He received his Doctorat en Etudes Politiques from the University of Paris. He is the author of a forthcoming study of the USSR and the Cuban Revolution, Le Conflit Sino-Sovietique et l'Europe de l'Est, and Le Conflit Sino-Sovietique. He is a contributor to Federalisme et Nations, and L'Historie des Civilisations. He has published articles in Etudes Internationales and Socialisme. He has been a Senior Fellow at the Research Institute on Communist Affairs, Columbia University, and a Research Fellow at the Russian Research Center, Harvard University. He has done research in Cuba, the People's Republic of China, and the Soviet Union.

VALERIE PLAVE BENNETT is a Lecturer in History at Metropolitan College, Boston University. She is a contributor to Politicians and Soldiers in Ghana and Chinese and Soviet Aid to Africa. Her articles have appeared in the Western Political Quarterly, Africa Report, West Africa, the Journal of Modern African Studies, and the Quarterly Journal of Administration.

JORGE DOMINGUEZ is currently a Fellow at Yale University, on leave from the Department of Government, Harvard University. He has published articles in the Latin American Research Review, International Organization, Comparative Political Studies, and Worldview. He is a Fellow of the Council on Foreign Relations.

W. RAYMON DUNCAN is Associate Professor of Political Science, State University of New York at Brockport. He received his M.A., M.A.L.D., and Ph.D. from the Fletcher School of Law and Diplomacy, Tufts University. He has written for Orbis, the Journal of Developing Areas, and World Affairs. He eidted Soviet Policy in Developing Countries, and coedited The Quest for Change in Latin America.

GERALD HEEGER is Associate Professor, Department of Political Science, Adelphi University. He has done research in India, and spent 1973-74 in Pakistan on a Fulbright-Hayes Faculty Research Grant. He is the author of The Politics of Underdevelopment, and has published articles in Asian Survey, Journal of Asian Studies, World Politics, and Studies on the Soviet Union. Dr. Heeger received his Ph.D. from the University of Chicago in 1971.

FRANCES HILL is Assistant Professor of Political Science at the University of Washington. She received her Ph.D. from Harvard University in 1973, and is the author of a forthcoming study of Tanzanian socialism. Her articles have appeared in the American Behavioral Scientist, Comparative Studies in Society and History, and Worldview.

TAREQ Y. ISMAEL is Professor of Political Science, University of Calgary. He is the author of Governments and Politics of the Contemporary Middle East, The U.A.R. in Africa: Egypt's Policy Under Nasser, and The Middle East in World Politics. He is also co-editor of Canada and the Third World. His articles have appeared in The Middle East Journal, Current History, Arabic Studies, and The Middle East Forum, which he eidted from 1971 to 1973.

JON KRAUS teaches Political Science at the State University College of New York at Fredonia. He received his Ph.D. from the Johns Hopkins School of Advanced International Studies. He is co-author of Arms and Politics in Ghana and Ghana 1969. His articles have appeared in the Journal of Modern African Studies and Problems of Communism.

JEAN LECA is a professor at the Institut d'Etudes Politiques in Grenoble. He is the author of many articles in Annuaire de l'Afrique du Nord, coauthor of Les Nationalismes Maghrebins, and of L'Algerie Politique: Institutions et Regimes.

GEORGE LENCZOWSKI teaches Middle East Politics at the University of California at Berkeley. He is the author of The Middle East in World Affairs, Oil and State in the Middle East, Russia and the West in Iran 1918-1948, and United States Interests in the Middle East.

J. DIRCK STRYKER received his Ph.D. from Yale University. He is currently Associate Professor of International Economic Relations, Fletcher School of Law and Diplomacy, Tufts University. He is a consultant to the Agency for International Development and the World Bank. His most recent work on Mali appeared in the Journal of Modern African Studies.

A. JEYARATNAM WILSON received his Ph.D. from the London School of Economics and Political Science. He taught at the University of Sri Lanka from 1952 to 1972; since 1972 he has been Professor and Chairman of the Department of Political Science, University of New Brunswick. He is the author of Politics in Sri Lanka 1967-1973, and Electoral Politics in an Emergent State: The Ceylon General Election of May 1970. He serves on the editorial boards of The Round Table, The Journal of Commonwealth and Comparative Politics, and The Ceylon Journal of Historical and Social Studies.

CHINA'S AFRICAN POLICY: A Study of Tanzania
George T. Yu

CHINESE AND SOVIET AID TO AFRICA
edited by Warren Weinstein

PATTERNS OF POVERTY IN THE THIRD WORLD:
A Study of Social and Economic Stratification*
Charles Elliott, assisted by
Francoise de Morsier

SOVIET AND CHINESE INFLUENCE IN THE THIRD
WORLD
edited by Alvin Z. Rubinstein

SOVIET POLICY TOWARD BLACK AFRICA*
edited by Helen Desfosses
and Jacques Levesque

SOVIET POLICY TOWARD THE MIDDLE EAST SINCE
1970
Robert O. Freedman

*Also available in paperback as a PSS Student Edition.